D1116793

The Optimum Quantity of Money
and Other Essays

The

Optimum Quantity
of Money

and Other Essays

Milton Friedman

University of Chicago

P. Tung

May 1970

Aldine Publishing Company
Chicago

First published 1969 by Aldine Publishing Company
529 South Wabash, Chicago, Illinois 60605

Library of Congress Catalog Card Number 68–8148

Designed by Chestnut House

Second printing, 1970

PRINTED IN THE UNITED STATES OF AMERICA

Preface

EXCEPT FOR THE TITLE ESSAY, which is published here for the first time, the essays in this book have previously been published. I have nonetheless thought it worthwhile to bring them together under one cover for two reasons: first, and less important, many are not readily accessible; second, and more important, the essays, though written over the course of two decades, embody a single view of monetary theory and, as a result, reinforce one another.

Monetary theory is like a Japanese garden. It has esthetic unity born of variety; an apparent simplicity that conceals a sophisticated reality; a surface view that dissolves in ever deeper perspectives. Both can be fully appreciated only if examined from many different angles, only if studied leisurely but in depth. Both have elements that can be enjoyed independently of the whole, yet attain their full realization only as part of the whole.

The title essay fits this image particularly well. It professes to be about a very special problem; it is on a highly abstract and simplified level. Yet I believe that it provides a fairly comprehensive summary of the most important propositions of monetary theory—the garden viewed as a whole and from a distance.

Only Chapters 2 and 13 of the remaining essays are on a comparable abstract and purely theoretical level, and Chapter 2 was an introduction to a book of empirical studies. The rest mix analysis and empirical evidence freely, though in varying proportions. Most are in the realm of "positive" economics—concerned with what is—but several, especially Chapter 5 (my 1967 Presidential address to the American Economic Association), deal either mainly or incidentally with monetary policy.

Many of the essays are by-products of the monetary research in which I have been engaging for nearly two decades under the auspices of the National Bureau of Economic Research in collaboration with Anna J. Schwartz. The major products of that research are a series of monographs—*A Monetary History of the United States, 1867–1960*, published in 1963 (Princeton, N.J.: Princeton University Press for the National Bureau of Economic Research), and three on *Monetary Statistics of the United States*, *Monetary Trends*, and *Monetary Cycles* still in preparation. Preliminary findings from these studies are summarized in Chapters 9 through 12 of this book. I am indebted to Mrs. Schwartz for her willingness to let me reprint here Chapter 10, which we wrote jointly.

Some of my earlier papers on monetary theory and policy are contained in my *Essays in Positive Economics* (Chicago: University of Chicago Press, 1956). Though these would have added to the comprehensiveness and unity of this book, they are so readily accessible that it did not seem desirable to reprint them. Other papers on monetary theory and policy, written mainly for the public at large rather than for fellow economists, are reprinted in my *Dollars and Deficits* (New York: Prentice-Hall, 1968).

At the time that many of the essays in this book appeared, they were highly unorthodox. They will seem much less so to those who read them here for the first time. In the interim, there has been a major shift in professional opinion. The quantity theory of money, once relegated to courses on the history of thought as an outmoded doctrine, has re-emerged as a part of the living body of economic theory. Monetary policy, once relegated to the trivial task of pegging some unimportant interest rates and facilitating routine financial transactions, has re-emerged as a major component of economic policy. As I point out in Chapter 5, the pendulum may even have swung too far.

I am indebted for permission to reprint these essays to the University of Chicago Press, the Comptroller of the Currency, the *Journal of Law and Economics*, the *American Economic Review*, the *Journal of Political Economy*, the *Review of Economics and Statistics*, the National Bureau of Economic Research, and the University of North Carolina Press.

But my main indebtedness is to my wife, Rose Director Friedman—proximately, for undertaking the task of selecting the essays for this book, and organizing and arranging the contents, but, fundamentally, for creating a home that enabled the essays to be written.

Contents

Chapter 1

The Optimum Quantity of Money

IT IS A COMMONPLACE of monetary theory that nothing is so unimportant as the quantity of money expressed in terms of the nominal monetary unit—dollars, or pounds, or pesos. Let the unit of account be changed from dollars to cents; that will multiply the quantity of money by 100, but have no other effect. Similarly, let the number of dollars in existence be multiplied by 100; that, too, will have no other essential effect, provided that all other nominal magnitudes (prices of goods and services, and quantities of other assets and liabilities that are expressed in nominal terms) are also multiplied by 100.

The situation is very different with respect to the real quantity of money—the quantity of goods and services that the nominal quantity of money can purchase, or the number of weeks' income to which the nominal quantity of money is equal. This real quantity of money has important effects on the efficiency of operation of the economic mechanism, on how wealthy people regard themselves as being and, indeed, on how wealthy they actually are. Yet

During the roughly two decades that I have puzzled over the problems covered in this paper, I have benefited from discussions with many friends, from the reactions of students to the presentation of some of this material in class (at the University of Chicago, Columbia University, and the University of California at Los Angeles), and from the reactions of audiences at several seminars at which I have presented the central ideas (at Stanford University and Princeton University). I owe a special debt to Kenneth Arrow, who saved me from several crucial errors, and to Alvin Marty and the late D. H. Robertson, who shared my interest and helped sharpen my understanding of the problem. I am indebted for helpful comments on the first draft of this paper to Martin Bronfenbrenner, Phillip Cagan, Elaine Goldstein, Franklin D. Mills, Anna J. Schwartz, and Lester Telser.

only recently has much thought been given to what the optimum quantity of money is, and, more important, to how the community can be induced to hold that quantity of money.

When this question is examined, it turns out to be intimately related to a number of topics that have received widespread attention over a long period of time, notably (1) the optimum behavior of the price level; (2) the optimum rate of interest; (3) the optimum stock of capital; and (4) the optimum structure of capital.

The optimum behavior of the price level, in particular, has been discussed for at least a century, though no definite and demonstrable answer has been reached. Interestingly enough, it turns out that when the question is tackled indirectly, via the optimum quantity of money, a definite answer can be given. The difference is that while the conventional discussion stresses short-period adjustments, this paper stresses long-run efficiency.

In examining the optimum quantity of money, I shall start in a rather roundabout way—as befits a topic that belongs in capital theory at least as much as in monetary theory. I shall begin by examining a highly simplified hypothetical world in which the elementary but central principles of monetary theory stand out in sharp relief. Though this introduction covers familiar ground I urge the reader to be patient, since it will serve as a bridge to some unfamiliar propositions.

I. HYPOTHETICAL SIMPLE SOCIETY

Let us start with a stationary society in which there are (1) a constant population with (2) given tastes, (3) a fixed volume of physical resources, and (4) a given state of the arts. It will be simplest to regard the members of this society as being immortal and unchangeable.[1] (5) The society, though stationary, is not static. Aggregates are constant, but individuals are subject to uncertainty and change. Even the aggregates may change in a stochastic way, provided the mean values do not. (6) Competition reigns.

To this fairly common specification, let us add a number of special provisions: (7) Any capital goods which exist are infinitely durable, cannot be reproduced or used up, and require no maintenance (like Ricardo's original, indestructible powers of the soil). More important, (8) these capital goods though owned by individuals in the sense that the rents they yield go to their owners, cannot be bought and sold. (They are like human capital in our society.)

(9) Lending or borrowing is prohibited and the prohibition is effectively enforced.

(10) The only exchange is of services for money, or money for services, or

---

1. This is equivalent to regarding the community as having a constant distribution of persons by age, sex, etc. Each of our infinitely long-lived individuals stands, as it were, for a family line in the alternative population of changing individuals but unchanging aggregates.

services for services. Items (7) and (8) in effect rule out all exchange of commodities.

(11) Prices in terms of money are free to change, in the sense that there are no legal obstacles to buyers' and sellers' trading at any price they wish. There may be institutional frictions of various kinds that keep prices from adjusting instantaneously and fully to any change. In that sense there need not be "perfect flexibility" whatever that much overused term may be taken to mean.

(12) All money consists of strict fiat money, i.e., pieces of paper, each labelled "This is one dollar."

(13) To begin with, there are a fixed number of pieces of paper, say, 1,000.

The purpose of conditions (7), (8) and (9) is, of course, to rule out the existence of a market interest rate. We shall relax these conditions later.

II. INITIAL EQUILIBRIUM POSITION

Let us suppose that these conditions have been in existence long enough for the society to have reached a state of equilibrium. Relative prices are determined by the solution of a system of Walrasian equations. Absolute prices are determined by the level of cash balances desired relative to income.

Why, in this simple, hypothetical society, should people want to hold money? The basic reason is to serve as a medium of circulation, or temporary abode of purchasing power, in order to avoid the need for the famous "double coincidence" of barter. In the absence of money, an individual wanting to exchange A for B must find someone who wants to exchange precisely B for A. In a money economy, he can sell A for money, or generalized purchasing power, to anyone who wants A and has the purchasing power. The seller of A can then buy B for money from anyone who has B for sale, regardless of what the seller of B in turn wishes to purchase. This separation of the act of sale from the act of purchase is the fundamental productive function of money. It gives rise to the "transactions" motive stressed in the literature.

A second reason for holding money is as a reserve for future emergencies. In the actual world, money is but one of many assets that can serve this function. In our hypothetical world, it is the only such asset. This reason corresponds to the "asset" motive for holding money.

It is worth noting that both reasons depend critically on characteristic (5) of our economy, the existence of individual uncertainty. In a world that is purely static and individually repetitive, clearing arrangements could be made once and for all that would eliminate the first reason, and there would be no unforeseen emergencies to justify holding money for the second reason.

How much money would people want to hold for these reasons? Clearly, this question must be answered not in terms of nominal units but in terms of real quantities, i.e., the volume of goods and services over which people wish to have command in the form of money. I see no way to give any meaningful answer to this question on an abstract level. The amount will depend on the details of the institutional payment arrangements that characterize the equilibrium position reached, which in turn will depend on the state of the arts, on tastes and preferences, and on the attitudes of the public toward uncertainty.

It is easier to say something about the amount of money people would want to hold on the basis of empirical evidence. If we identify the money in our hypothetical society with currency in the real world, then the quantity of currency the public chooses to hold is equal in value to about one-tenth of a year's income, or about 5.2 weeks' income.[2] That is, desired velocity is about ten per year.

If we identify money in our hypothetical society with all non-human wealth in the real world, then the relevant order of magnitude is about three to five years' income.[3] That is, desired velocity is about .2 to .3 per year.

Since we are only provisionally treating our money as the equivalent of all wealth, I shall use the first comparison, and assume, therefore, that the equilibrium position is defined by an absolute level of prices which makes nominal national income equal to $10,000 per year, so that the $1,000 available to be held amounts to one-tenth of a year's income. This is an average. Particular individuals may hold cash equal to more or less than 5.2 weeks' income, depending on their individual transactions requirements and asset preferences. As always, nominal national income has several faces: the value of final services consumed, the value of productive services rendered, and the sum of the net value added by the enterprises in the community. In our hypothetical society all of the difficult problems of national income accounting are by-passed, so we need not distinguish between different concepts of national income.

III. EFFECT OF A ONCE-AND-FOR-ALL CHANGE IN THE NOMINAL QUANTITY OF MONEY

Let us suppose now that one day a helicopter flies over this community and drops an additional $1,000 in bills from the sky, which is, of course, hastily

2. For the U.S., currency was a little over four weeks' income (personal disposable income) in the 1890's and is currently slightly under four weeks' income. It has ranged in that period from 2.1 weeks in 1917 to 8.2 weeks in 1948. In Israel, it is about the same as in the U.S. In Japan, it is about five weeks' income, in Yugoslavia, about six weeks. In a study of 27 countries, Morris Perlman found the highest figure to be fourteen weeks' (Belgium) and the lowest, two weeks' (Chile).

3. In 1958, the total national wealth of the United States was roughly four times net national product, and about 5.3 times personal disposable income. Since the wealth figure includes all government wealth, the first figure seems more relevant. Currency in the preceding footnote excluded for the U.S., and I believe also for the other countries, currency held by the Treasury and Federal Reserve. See Raymond Goldsmith, *The National Wealth of the United States in the Postwar Period* (Princeton, N.J.: Princeton University Press, 1962), p. 112.

collected by members of the community. Let us suppose further that everyone is convinced that this is a unique event which will never be repeated.

To begin with, suppose further that each individual happens to pick up an amount of money equal to the amount he held before, so that each individual finds himself with twice the cash balances he had before.

If every individual simply decided to hold on to the extra cash, nothing else would happen. Prices would remain what they were before, and income would remain at $10,000 per year. The community's cash balances would simply be 10.4 weeks' income instead of 5.2.

But this is not the way people would behave. Nothing has occurred to make the holding of cash more attractive than it was before, given our assumption that everyone is convinced the helicopter miracle will not be repeated. (In the absence of that assumption, the appearance of the helicopter might increase the degree of uncertainty anticipated by members of the community, which, in turn, might change the demand for real cash balances.)

Consider the "representative" individual who formerly held 5.2 weeks' income in cash and now holds 10.4 weeks' income. He could have held 10.4 weeks' income before if he had wanted to—by spending less than he received for a sufficiently long period. When he held 5.2 weeks' income in cash, he did not regard the gain from having $1 extra in cash balances as worth the sacrifice of consuming at the rate of $1 per year less for one year, or at the rate of ten cents less per year for ten years. Why should he now, when he holds 10.4 weeks' income in cash? The assumption that he was in a stable equilibrium position before means that he will now want to raise his consumption and reduce his cash balances until they are back at the former level. Only at that level is the sacrifice of consuming at a lower rate just balanced by the gain from holding correspondingly higher cash balances.

Note that there are two different questions for the individual:

(1) To what level will he want ultimately to reduce his cash balances? Since the appearance of the helicopter did not change his real income or any other basic condition, we can answer this unambiguously: to their former level.

(2) How rapidly will he want to return to the former level? To this question, we have no answer. The answer depends on characteristics of his preferences that are not reflected in the stationary equilibrium position.

We know only that each individual will seek to reduce his cash balances at some rate. He will do so by trying to spend more than he receives. But one man's expenditure is another man's receipt. The members of the community as a whole cannot spend more than the community as a whole receives—this is precisely the accounting identity underlying the multiple faces of national income. It is also a reflection of the capital identity: the sum of individual cash balances is equal to the amount of cash available to be held. Individuals as a whole cannot "spend" balances; they can only transfer them. One man can spend more than he receives only by inducing another to receive more than he spends.

It is easy to see what the final position will be. People's attempts to spend more than they receive will be frustrated, but in the process these attempts will bid up the nominal value of services. The additional pieces of paper do not alter the basic conditions of the community. They make no additional productive capacity available. They alter no tastes. They alter neither the apparent nor actual rates of substitution. Hence the final equilibrium must be a nominal income of $20,000 instead of $10,000, with precisely the same flow of real services as before.

It is much harder to say anything about the transition. To begin with, some producers may be slow to adjust their prices and may let themselves be induced to produce more for the market at the expense of non-market uses of resources. Others may try to make spending exceed receipts by taking a vacation from production for the market. Hence, measured income at initial nominal prices may either rise or fall during the transition. Similarly, some prices may adjust more rapidly than others, so relative prices and quantities may be affected. There might be overshooting and, as a result, a cyclical adjustment pattern. In short, without a much more detailed specification of reaction patterns than we have made, we can predict little about the transition. It might vary all the way from an instantaneous adjustment, with all prices doubling overnight, to a long drawn out adjustment, with many ups and downs in prices and output for the market.

We can now drop the assumption that each individual happened to pick up an amount of cash equal to the amount he had to begin with. Let the amount each individual picks up be purely a chance matter. This will introduce initial distribution effects. During the transition, some men will have net gains in consumption, others net losses in consumption. But the ultimate position will be the same, *not only for the aggregate, but for each individual separately.* After picking up the cash, each individual is in a position that he could have attained earlier, if he had wished to. But he preferred the position he had attained prior to the arrival of the helicopter. Nothing has occurred to change the ultimate alternatives open to him. Hence he will eventually return to his former position. The distributional effects vanish when equilibrium is re-attained.[4]

The existence of initial distributional effects has, however, one substantive implication: the transition can no longer, even as a conceptual possibility, be instantaneous, since it involves more than a mere bidding up of prices. Let prices

4. This conclusion depends on the assumption of infinitely lived people, but not on any assumption about the extent or quality of their foresight. The basic point, to put it in other terms, is that their permanent income or wealth is unchanged. Their having picked up more or less than their pro-rata share of cash is a transitory event that has purely transitory effects.

See G. C. Archibald and R. G. Lipsey, "Monetary and Value Theory: A Critique of Lange and Patinkin," *Review of Economic Studies*, vol. 26 (1958), pp. 1–22; R. W. Clower and M. L. Burstein, "On the Invariance of Demand for Cash and Other Assets," *ibid.*, vol. 28 (1960), pp. 32–36; Nissan Liviatan, "On the Long-Run Theory of Consumption and Real Balances," *Oxford Economic Papers* (July, 1965), pp. 205–18; Don Patinkin, *Money, Interest, and Prices*, 2nd edition, New York: Harper and Row (1965), pp. 50–59.

double overnight. The result will still be a disequilibrium position. Those individuals who have picked up more than their pro-rata share of cash will now have larger real balances than they want to maintain. They will want to "spend' the excess but over a period of time, not immediately. (Indeed, given continuous flows and only services to purchase, they can spend a finite extra amount immediately only by spending at an infinite rate for an infinitesimal time unit.)

On the other hand, those individuals who have picked up less than their pro-rata share have lower real balances than they want to maintain. But they cannot restore their cash balances instantaneously, since their stream of receipts flows at a finite time rate. They will have some desired rate at which they wish to build up their balances. Hence, even if all prices adjusted instantaneously and everyone had perfect foresight, there would still be an equilibrium path of adjustment to the initial differential disturbance of real balances. This path defines the rate at which the relative gainers transfer their excess balances to the relative losers. The relative gainers will have a higher than equilibrium level of consumption and a lower level of production during the period of adjustment. The relative losers will have a lower than equilibrium level of consumption, and a higher level of production.

This analysis carries over immediately from a change in the nominal quantity of cash to a once-and-for-all change in preferences with respect to cash. Let individuals on the average decide to hold half as much cash, and the ultimate result will be a doubling of the price level, a nominal income of $20,000 a year with the initial $1,000 of cash.

IV. BASIC PRINCIPLES ILLUSTRATED

Our simple example embodies most of the basic principles of monetary theory:

(1) The central role of the distinction between the *nominal* and the *real* quantity of money.

(2) The equally crucial role of the distinction between the alternatives open to the individual and to the community as a whole.

These two distinctions are the core of all monetary theory.

(2a) An alternative way to express (2) is the importance of accounting identities: the *flow* identity that the sum of expenditures equals the sum of receipts (or, the value of final services acquired equals the value of productive services rendered) and the *stock* identity that the sum of cash balances equals the total stock of money in existence.

(3) The importance of attempts, summarized in the famous distinction between *ex ante* and *ex post*. At the moment when the additional cash has been picked up, desired spending exceeds anticipated receipts (*ex ante*, spending exceeds receipts). *Ex post*, the two must be equal. But the *attempt* of individuals

to spend more than they receive, even though doomed to be frustrated, has the effect of raising total nominal expenditures (and receipts).

(4) The distinction between the final position and the transition to the final position: between long-run statics and short-run dynamics.

(5) The meaning of the "real balance" effect and its role in producing a transition from one stationary equilibrium position to another.

Our example also embodies two essential empirical generalizations of long-run monetary theory:

(1) The nominal amount of money is determined primarily by conditions of supply.

(2) The real amount of money is determined primarily by conditions of demand—by the functional relation between the real amount of money demanded and other variables in the system.

V. EFFECT OF A CONTINUOUS INCREASE IN QUANTITY OF MONEY

Let us now complicate our example by supposing that the dropping of money, instead of being a unique, miraculous event, becomes a continuous process, which, perhaps after a lag, becomes fully anticipated by everyone. Money rains down from heaven at a rate which produces a steady increase in the quantity of money, let us say, of 10 per cent per year. The path of the quantity of money is shown in Figure 1, M_0 being the initial quantity of money ($1,000 in our ex-

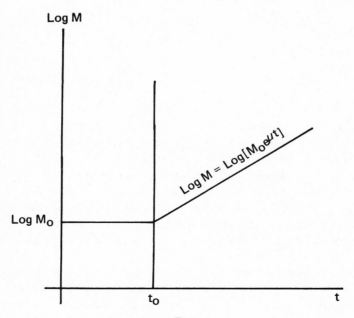

FIG. I

ample), t_0 the date at which the money starts to rain from heaven, and μ the rate of growth of the quantity of money (10 per cent per year in our example). Mathematically,

$$M(t) = M_0 c^{\mu t} \tag{1}$$

The distribution of the additional nominal balances among individuals does not matter for our purposes, provided that an individual is not able to affect the amount of additional cash he receives by altering the amount of cash balances he holds. The simplest assumption is that each individual gets a share of the new nominal balances equal to the percentage of nominal balances he initially held, and that this share, once determined, remains constant, whatever his future behavior. The reason for this assumption will become clear. Even with this assumption, there may be distributional effects, by contrast with the once-and-for-all case, if final equilibrium cash balances are distributed differently than initial balances. For the moment, however, we shall neglect any distributional effects.

Individuals could respond to this steady monetary downpour as they did to the once-and-for-all doubling of the quantity of money, namely, by keeping real balances unchanged. If they did so, and responded instantaneously and without friction, all real magnitudes could remain unchanged. Prices would behave in precisely the same manner as the nominal money stock. They would rise from their initial level at the rate of 10 per cent per year, as shown in Figure 2. Nominal income, defined as the value of services and excluding the bonanza

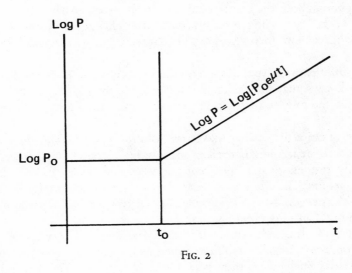

FIG. 2

from the sky, would behave in the same way; its time path could be represented by the same line. The bonanza, if included, would raise nominal income from

$$Y_1(t) = Y_0 e^{\mu t} \tag{2}$$

to

$$Y_2(t) = Y_0 e^{\mu t} + \mu M(t)$$
$$= (Y_0 + \mu M_0) e^{\mu t}, \tag{3}$$

or, in terms of our example, from a value of \$10,000 to a value of \$10,100 at $t = t_0$, the additional \$100 representing the annual rate at which the quantity of money is initially being increased, i.e., at $t = t_0$.

However, given instantaneous adjustment and unchanged real balances, individuals would not regard any of this additional \$100 as available for purchasing services. All of it would have to be added to nominal cash balances in order to keep them at the initial one-tenth of a year's income. So no real magnitude would be affected.

If individuals did not respond instantaneously, or if there were frictions, the situation would be different during a transitory period. The state of affairs just described would emerge finally when individuals succeeded in restoring and maintaining initial real balances.

One natural question to ask about this final situation is, "What raises the price level, if at all points markets are cleared and real magnitudes are stable?" The answer is, "Because everyone confidently anticipates that prices will rise." There is an old saying that difference of opinion makes a horse race. And so it is in any market involving the trading of existing assets. If there are wide differences of opinion about the course of prices on the stock market, for example, there will be heavy trading, possibly with little change in prices. If there is widespread agreement, then prices can be marked up or down with little actual trading.

In our example, prices rise, though markets are continuously cleared, because everybody knows that they will. All demand and supply curves in nominal terms rise at the rate of 10 per cent per year, and so do the market-clearing prices.

A related question is, "What makes the solution stable?" The answer is the potential effect of departures. Let prices (and nominal income) for whatever reason momentarily rise less than 10 per cent per year. Cash balances will then rise relative to income. The attempts to restore them to their former level will raise prices as in the once-and-for-all example. The converse is true if prices momentarily rise more than 10 per cent per year.

While individuals could respond to the steady monetary downpour as they did to the once-and-for-all doubling of the quantity of money, by keeping all real magnitudes unchanged, they will not in fact do so. To each individual separately, it looks as if he can do better. It looks to him as if, by reducing his cash balances, he can use for consumption some of the money he gets from the helicopter instead of simply adding all of it to his nominal cash holdings. It looks to him as if, for each dollar by which he reduces his cash balances, he can get ten cents extra a year to spend on consumption.[5]

Put differently, the individual will regard as available for spending on consumption, and for adding to nominal cash balances, the nominal amount he receives for his productive services plus the amount of cash he gets from the helicopter. When he got nothing from the helicopter and cash balances amounted to 5.2 weeks' income (for the representative individual), he added nothing to his nominal cash balances, yet they remained constant in real as well as nominal terms because prices were stable. Storage costs and depreciation costs were zero, as it were. He did not try to add to his balances because he regarded the sacrifice involved in consuming at the rate of $1 (or one cent) less for a year as just (over) balancing the satisfaction from having $1 (or one cent) more in the form of cash balances. Had half his cash balances suddenly been destroyed (as in the opposite of the once-and-for-all increase), he would have tried to add to them because, while the sacrifice from consuming at a lower rate presumably would not be affected, the satisfaction from having an extra $1 (or one cent) in cash balances would be higher when he had only half the real quantity of balances.[6] He would have continued trying to save at some rate until his cash balances were restored to 5.2 weeks' income, at which point he would again have been in equilibrium.

When the representative individual is getting cash from the helicopter, he can keep his *real* cash balances at 5.2 weeks' income from the sale of services only by adding all the extra cash to his *nominal* balances to offset rising prices. But now, if he is willing to lower his cash balances by $1 initially (and by $1 \cdot e^{.1t}$ at each point in time), he can consume at the initial extra rate of $1.10 per year (and at the rate of $1 + .10e^{.1t}$ per year at each point in time).[7] Since he was just on the margin when the extra consumption was at the rate of $1 per year, he will now be over the margin and will try to raise his consumption. Storage and depreciation costs are now ten cents per dollar per year, instead of zero, so he will try to hold a smaller real quantity of money. Let us suppose, to be specific, that when prices are rising at 10 per cent a year, he desires to hold $\frac{1}{12}$ instead of $\frac{1}{10}$ of a year's proceeds from the sale of services in cash balances, ie., $4\frac{1}{3}$ instead of 5.2 weeks' income.

We are now back to our earlier problem. While to each individual separately

5. This makes clear why it is necessary to assume that the amount of extra cash the individual receives is not related to his cash balance behavior. If it were—for example, if the amount he received were not only proportional to the initial level of his balances, as assumed above, but also altered through time in such a way as to be proportional to his cash balances at each point in time—then he would get a return from his balances that would just offset the cost. The once-and-for-all solution outlined (unchanging real balances) would be the correct solution.

6. It is enough, of course, to suppose only that the satisfaction from having extra cash balances rises relative to the sacrifice from consuming at a lower rate.

7. I am indebted to Don Roper for correcting an error in this parenthesis in my initial draft.

it looks as if he can consume more by reducing cash balances, the community as a whole cannot. Once again, the helicopter has changed no real magnitude, added no real resources to the community, changed none of the physical opportunities available. The attempt of individuals to reduce cash balances will simply mean a further bidding up of prices and income, so as to make the nominal stock of money equal to $\frac{1}{12}$ instead of $\frac{1}{10}$ of a year's nominal income. The equilibrium path of prices (and of the nominal value of services rendered) will be like the dotted line in Figure 3, parallel to the solid line but higher by an amount

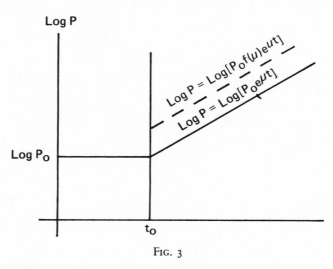

Fig. 3

depending on the size of μ. In our illustrative example, the level of prices would be 20 per cent higher than that shown by the solid line, since an increase of nominal income by 20 per cent would reduce cash balances from 5.2 to $4\frac{1}{3}$ week's income $(5.2 \div 1.2 = 4\frac{1}{3})$.

Once the community is on this path, it can stay there. Since both prices and nominal income are rising at 10 per cent a year, real income is constant. Since the nominal quantity of money is also rising at 10 per cent a year, it stays in a constant ratio to income—equal to $4\frac{1}{3}$ weeks' of income from the sale of services.

Attaining this path requires two kinds of price increase: (1) a once-and-for-all rise of 20 per cent, to reduce real balances to the level desired when it costs ten cents per dollar per year to hold cash; (2) an indefinitely continued rise in prices at the rate of 10 per cent per year to keep real balances constant at the new level.

Something definite can be said about the transition process this time. During the transition, the average rate of price rise must exceed 10 per cent. Hence, the rate of price rise must overshoot its long-term equilibrium level. It must display a cyclical reaction pattern. In Figure 4, the horizontal solid line is the ultimate equilibrium path of the rate of price change. The three broken curves illustrate

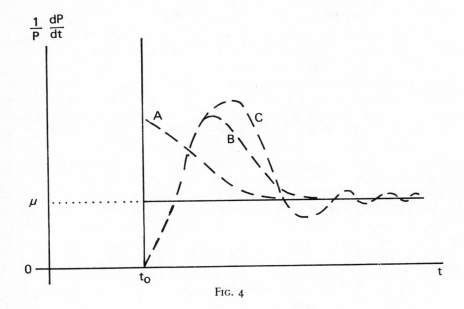

FIG. 4

alternative possible transitional paths: curve A shows a single overshooting and then gradual return to the permanent position, curves B and C show an initial undershooting, then overshooting followed by either a gradual return (curve B) or a damped cyclical adjustment (curve C).

This necessity for overshooting in the rate of price change and in the rate of income change (though not necessarily in the level of either prices or income) is in my opinion the key element in monetary theories of cyclical fluctuations. In practice, the need to overshoot is reinforced by an initial undershooting (as in curves B and C of Figure 4). When the helicopter starts dropping money in a steady stream—or, more generally, when the quantity of money starts unexpectedly to rise more rapidly—it takes time for people to catch on to what is happening. Initially, they let actual balances exceed long-run desired balances. They do so partly because they delay the adjustment of actual to desired balances; partly because they may take initial price rises as a harbinger of subsequent price declines, an anticipation which raises desired balances; and partly because the initial impact of increased money balances may be on output rather than prices, which further raises desired balances. As people catch on, prices must for a time rise even more rapidly, to undo an initial increase in real balances as well as to produce a long-run decline.

While this one feature of the transition is clear, little can be said about the details without much more precise specification of the reaction patterns of the members of the community and of the process by which they form their anticipations of price movements.

We can now refine somewhat our description of the final equilibrium path. We have implicitly been treating the real flow of services as if it were the same on the final equilibrium path as it was initially. This is wrong for two reasons.

First, and less important for our purposes, there may be permanent distributional effects. On the final path, some individuals may be receiving more cash from the helicopter than they require to keep their real cash balances constant, given their share in the downpour and their tastes. Others may be receiving less than they require. The first group is enriched relative to the second and will play a larger role in determining the structure of production. Distributional effects will be absent if, on the final path, the new money happens to be distributed among individuals in proportion to their desired holdings of cash balances.[8]

Second, and more important, real cash balances are at least in part a factor of production. To take a trivial example, a retailer can economize on his average cash balances by hiring an errand boy to go to the bank on the corner to get change for large bills tendered by customers. When it costs ten cents per dollar per year to hold an extra dollar of cash, there will be a greater incentive to hire the errand boy, that is, to substitute other productive resources for cash. This will mean both a reduction in the real flow of services from the given productive resources and a change in the structure of production, since different productive activities may differ in cash-intensity, just as they differ in labor- or land-intensity.

VI. WELFARE EFFECTS

To each individual separately, the money from the sky seems like a bonanza, a true windfall gain. Yet, when the community has adjusted to it, each individual separately is worse off—if we abstract from the distributional effects noted in the second preceding paragraph. He is worse off in two respects. (1) He is poorer because the representative individual now has a reserve for emergency equal to $4\frac{1}{3}$ weeks' income (which is also his usual consumption) rather than 5.2 weeks'. (2) He has a lower real income because productive resources have been substituted for cash balances, raising the price of consumption services relative to the price of productive services.

The loss on wealth account is the counterpart to non-pecuniary consumption returns from cash balances—it reflects the role of wealth as an argument in the utility function. The loss on income account is the counterpart to the productive services rendered by cash balances—it reflects the role of cash balances as an argument in the production function.

We can get a rough measure of the magnitude of the loss along usual consumer surplus grounds. In doing so, however, we must take into account two

8. Note that desired holdings of cash balances on the final path need not be proportional to initial holdings. Hence this condition need not be the same as the condition assumed in the second paragraph of this section.

components of the loss. An individual who holds a dollar in cash balances pays two prices: (1) the annual cost imposed by the rate of price inflation; (2) the once-and-for-all cost of refraining from $1 of consumption to accumulate the dollar of cash balances, or, equivalently, of abstaining from the dollar of consumption he could enjoy at any time by reducing his balances by a dollar.

Before the continuous downpour started, the first price was zero; but the second was still present. At his initial position, therefore, he must have valued the utility of the services he received by holding an extra dollar as much as the utility he would have gotten from raising his consumption by $1 per year for a year. In the new equilibrium position, this second price is the same, but, in addition, he must pay ten cents per year indefinitely per dollar of real balances that he holds. Accordingly, he must regard a dollar of his now lower cash balances as worth this extra price. The *average* value he attaches to a dollar of the real cash balances that have disappeared is therefore one dollar's worth of consumption (the same before and after) plus approximately five cents a year indefinitely (the average of zero and ten cents). In our numerical example, cash balances decline from 5.2 to 4.33 weeks' consumption, or by $\frac{13}{15}$ of a week's consumption. Therefore, the continuous downpour has cost the community the equivalent of $\frac{13}{15}$ of a week's consumption plus $\frac{1}{20} \cdot \frac{13}{15} = \frac{13}{300}$ of a week's consumption per year indefinitely. (Expressed in the equivalent United States magnitudes, this is about $10 billion plus $500 million a year indefinitely.) Since we have not yet introduced an interest rate, we have as yet no way of combining these two components of cost.

The reason for the loss in welfare is clear: the existence of external effects, or a difference between cost to an individual and cost to all individuals affected. Consider the initial position of constant prices. For an individual to add one dollar to his cash balances he would have to consume $1 less—at the rate, say, of $2 a year less for six months, or $1 a year less for a year, or fifty cents a year less for two years. But were any individual to do so, he would make the price level slightly lower than it would otherwise be. This would have the external effect of yielding capital gains to all other holders of money, trivial to each but enabling them in the aggregate to consume precisely $1 more while keeping their real balances constant. Total consumption would not change. The individual who adds to cash balances confers a benefit on his fellows for which he cannot collect compensation. The rate at which he can substitute cash balances for consumption thus differs from the rate at which it is technically possible to do so.

The situation is the same with the other component of cost, the ten cents a year required to hold a dollar of real balances when prices are rising at the rate of 10 per cent a year. This component too is an apparent cost to the individual, but is balanced by uncompensated gains to others, so that the cost to all together is zero per year, not ten cents per year.[9]

9. In our example, this can be seen most easily by considering a representative individual who gets just enough money from the helicopter so that, when he adds it to his cash balances, he can just maintain the real balances he desires. His consumption is equal to his income from

VII. EFFECT OF A CONTINUOUS
DECREASE IN THE QUANTITY OF MONEY

When prices are stable, one component of the cost is zero—namely, the annual cost—but the other component is not—namely, the cost of abstinence. This suggests that, perhaps, just as inflation produces a welfare loss, deflation may produce a welfare gain.

Suppose therefore that we substitute a furnace for the helicopter. Let us introduce a government which imposes a tax on all individuals and burns up the proceeds, engaging in no other functions. Let the tax be altered continuously to yield an amount that will produce a steady decline in the quantity of money at the rate of, say, 10 per cent a year. It does not matter for our purposes what the tax is, as long as an individual cannot affect his tax by altering his cash balances.

By precisely the same reasoning as before, the final equilibrium path will be the dotted line in Figure 5—prices decline at a rate of 10 per cent a year, but at a

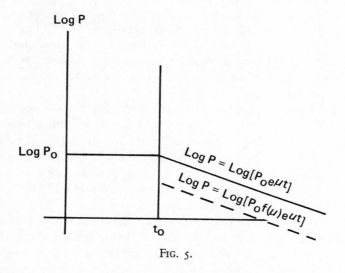

FIG. 5.

services. Suppose he now were to add an extra (real) dollar to his balances. The process of adding this (real) dollar lowers prices a trifle and enables the rest of the community to consume one (real) dollar more—this is the external effect described in the preceding paragraph of the text. But, in addition, the individual thereafter will have to consume ten (real) cents less than his income from services to maintain intact the higher level of real balances. The rest of the community will find that, at the slightly lower price level, they are receiving cash from the helicopter at a rate of ten (real) cents per year more than they need to keep their real balances intact. They therefore can, and will, spend ten (real) cents more per year on consumption than they receive from services—thereby providing the extra cash to the individual who was assumed to have added to his balances. His cost is precisely counterbalanced by their gain.

lower level than the solid line linked to the initial price level. When prices are declining, a dollar of cash balances yields a positive return. The real services that a dollar of balances will command grow at a rate of 10 per cent per year. This makes cash balances more attractive and thus raises the quantity individuals want to hold. Prices must decline not only in proportion to the quantity of money (which follows a path like the solid line in Figure 5) but by enough more to raise real balances (or the ratio of money to income) to the desired level—say, to 6.24 weeks' income. Figure 6 shows the demand curve for real balances implicit in this and the earlier examples.

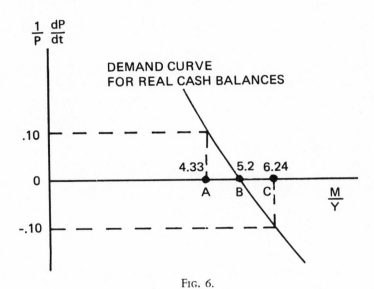

FIG. 6.

At the new equilibrium, with cash balances equal to 6.24 weeks' income, every individual is richer (if we neglect distributional effects) than he was before—he has a larger reserve for emergencies. The other real resources available to the community are the same as before. It looks, therefore, as if everyone is better off than before, and as if the higher the rate of price decline, the greater the welfare gain.

But the appearance is misleading, as we can see by considering what happens if we increase the rate of decline of prices. Beyond some point, it pays individuals to hold extra balances to benefit from their increasing purchasing power even if it costs something to do so. The retailer dispenses with an errand boy to economize on cash balances, which is a gain, but, at some point, he must hire guards to protect his cash hoard. It pays him to do so because of their rising real value. The extra real balances not only do not save productive resources, they absorb them. Similarly, on the asset side, cash will be held beyond the point at which additional cash brings non-pecuniary returns in security and satisfaction from being wealthy. The amount held will, at the margin, reduce utility—because of concern about the safety of the cash, perhaps, or because of pecuniary costs of storing and guarding the cash.

For a sufficiently small rate of decline in prices, it seems clear that there will be a net benefit; for a sufficiently large rate of decline, a net loss. What is the optimum rate of decline?

The real returns or costs to an individual from holding cash balances can be classified under four items:

(1) The rise or decline in the purchasing power of a dollar. What matters is not the actual rise or decline but the anticipated rise or decline. This item we can represent by

$$ -\left(\frac{1}{P}\frac{dP}{dt}\right)^*, \tag{4} $$

where the asterisk indicates anticipated value. If a decline in prices is anticipated, this is positive and represents a return; if a rise in price is anticipated, this is negative and represents a cost. For any individual, the anticipated rate of price decline does not depend on his own holdings of cash balances, so average and marginal return or cost are equal.

(2) The productive services rendered per year by a dollar of cash balances as a factor of production. The value of these services does depend on the amount of cash balances the individual holds, so one must distinguish between average and marginal return. The relevant magnitude is the marginal return, which we may designate

$$ MPM, \tag{5} $$

or marginal product of money. Since this is product per dollar per year, it, like (4), has the dimensions of the reciprocal of time, that is, of an interest rate. Like (4) also, it can be positive, and thus a return, or negative, and thus a cost. It is natural to assume diminishing marginal returns throughout.

(3) The non-pecuniary consumption services to the holder of cash balances. Let us suppose that we can express the marginal value of these services in a money equivalent, as cents per year per dollar of balances. Designate this marginal return

$$ MNPS, \tag{6} $$

or marginal non-pecuniary services. Again it may be positive or negative. And, again, it is natural to assume diminishing marginal returns.

(4) The cost of abstaining from a dollar of consumption. This depends on the individual's time preference or internal rate of discount of the future. Let us suppose that, at some level of real cash balances, he values the sum of the preceding three items as ten cents per year per dollar of cash balances. By consuming one dollar more (say, by consuming at the rate of one dollar per year more for a year), he would subtract a dollar from his cash balances and thereby sacrifice a

permanent consumption stream in the form of these three items of ten cents per year indefinitely. Conversely, by lowering his consumption by a total of a dollar, he could acquire an additional permanent consumption stream of 10 cents per year indefinitely. If, under those circumstances, he chooses to add to his consumption by depleting his real cash balances, his internal rate of discount is more than 10 per cent. If he chooses to keep real cash balances constant, his internal rate of discount equals 10 per cent. If he chooses to add to his real cash balances, his internal rate of discount is less than 10 per cent. Designate this internal rate of discount

$$IRD. \tag{7}$$

It, too, is marginal and has the dimensions of a percentage.

Note that the preceding paragraph defines the internal rate of discount only at the point of a constant flow of consumption. The value of the internal rate of discount at that point does not determine at how *rapid* a pace the individual will add to or subtract from his cash balances (will save or dissave), only whether he will. How much he will save or dissave depends on what happens to the IRD as he alters his rate of saving or dissaving, i.e., as he alters his prospective time pattern of consumption. The more he cuts down present consumption to raise his future consumption stream (in the form of the first three items), the more reluctant he will be to cut it down further, i.e., the higher will be IRD (this is Böhm-Bawerk's first reason for time preference). His rate of saving or dissaving at any moment will be determined by the point at which IRD rises enough to equal the sum of items (4), (5), and (6), which sum itself may change with the rate of saving or dissaving.[10] Where relevant, we shall distinguish the IRD when saving is zero from its generalized value by designating it $IRD(0)$.

For the sub-set of time patterns of consumption that consists of constant levels of consumption, it is not at all clear whether the IRD is best considered a constant for each individual or whether it should be regarded as a function of other variables, particularly (a) the level of consumption, and (b) the ratio of wealth to income. I can see no way to say how it depends on (a), i.e., whether it can be expected to rise or fall as the level of consumption rises. I shall therefore assume it to be unaffected by (a).

Variable (b) raises a much more difficult problem. It is not clear that IRD should be affected by (b) at all. Whatever the wealth-income ratio, the exchange involved is a temporary reduction in consumption in return for a permanently higher consumption stream. If IRD is affected by (b), stability considerations

10. Item (4) will not be affected by the particular individual's rate of saving or dissaving. Whether item (5) is affected depends on whether his saving or dissaving affects the supply of productive services competitive with or complementary to cash balances. Whether item (6) is affected depends on whether the non-pecuniary utility from cash balances is affected by the level of consumption. These inter-relations enter in because the level of real cash balances at any moment of time is not affected by the *rate* of saving or dissaving. In general, it is simplest to neglect these inter-relations and treat the second and third items, like the first, as unaffected by the rate of saving or dissaving, and determined only by the level of real balances.

call for *IRD* to be higher, the higher is the ratio of wealth to income. The rationalization is that the higher this ratio is, the more provision has already been made for the future, and the less willing the individual will be to sacrifice the present for the future. The difficulty with this rationalization is that it confounds the decline in *MNPS* as wealth rises relative to income with a rise in *IRD*. It is not clear that there is any way to distinguish the two. We shall return to this puzzling and sophisticated question later.

The *IRD* enables us to translate a stock into a flow. It is the device needed to combine the two components of cost in Section VI above.

The individual will be in a position of long-run equilibrium with respect to his cash balances when

$$-\left(\frac{1}{P}\frac{dP}{dt}\right)^* + MPM + MNPS = IRD(0). \tag{8}$$

If we assume for the moment that $IRD(0)$ is a positive and constant number, we can see how this equation summarizes our earlier analysis. Let prices be rising and anticipated to rise. Then the first term is negative. Cash balances must be small enough to yield a positive marginal return in productive services and non-pecuniary services, not only to offset the first term but also to balance the right-hand side. Reduce the anticipated rate of price rise and the left side will exceed the right. An increase in cash balances will now bring down $MPM + MNPS$, and thereby produce a new balance. Let prices be anticipated to fall, and the first term becomes positive. If it is larger than $IRD(0)$, then cash balances will have to be sufficiently large to make $MPM + MNPS$ negative.

Of the four terms in equation (8), *MPM* and *MNPS* are gains to the individual that involve no external effects on others. The individual gets all the benefits. As we have seen, the rate of price rise or fall is a cost or return to the individual of altering his cash balance that confers or imposes a precisely compensating return or cost on others. Similarly, the $IRD(0)$ is a cost to the individual of altering his cash balances that confers a precisely compensating benefit on others. In our simple society, if he reduces his consumption, all others will be able to consume a bit more. If all individuals simultaneously seek to reduce consumption to add to cash balances, they will lower prices, raising real cash balances without reducing total consumption.

Note that this conclusion does not hold for a commodity money (say, gold) which is produced under conditions of constant cost. The attempt by an individual to hold cash balances would initially tend to lower prices, but this would in turn divert resources to gold production and leave prices unchanged. In effect, the individual consumes a dollar less and the resources so released are diverted to producing an additional dollar's worth of gold. There are no external benefits conferred. However, if the commodity money is fixed in quantity and incapable of being produced, then the same conclusion would hold for it as for our fiat money.

It follows that cash balances of the fiat money will be at their optimum level in real terms when

$$-\left(\frac{1}{P}\frac{dP}{dt}\right)^{*} = IRD(0),\qquad(9)$$

so that

$$MPM + MNPS = 0.\qquad(10)$$

In words, under our assumptions, it costs nothing to provide an extra dollar of real balances. All that is required is a slightly lower price level. Hence cash balances will be at their optimum when they are held to satiety, so that the real return from an extra dollar held is zero.

This solution is for an individual. What of the community? If $IRD(0)$ were a constant for each individual separately, and also the same constant for all individuals, this solution would carry over to the community as well: the optimum quantity of money would be attained by a rate of price decline that would be equal to the common value of $IRD(0)$.

This conclusion raises three problems. First, why should different individuals have the same $IRD(0)$? Second, how could one know whether they had the same $IRD(0)$, and what its value would be, from observable market phenomena? Or, alternatively, how could one know whether equation (9) was satisfied? Third, if they do not all have the same $IRD(0)$, or if this is not a constant but a function of other variables, what then is the policy that yields the optimum quantity of money?

VIII. INTERNAL RATES OF DISCOUNT FOR DIFFERENT INDIVIDUALS

One possible theoretical justification for regarding $IRD(0)$ as both a constant and the same for all individuals is that, under the conditions assumed in our simple society, the "rational" individual will have an $IRD(0) = 0$, i.e., he will not discount the future.

The more obvious reasons for discounting the future relative to the present are absent. (1) One reason is anticipation of a higher future than present consumption. If marginal utility of consumption declines with the level of consumption at each point of time,[11] then, even if present consumption and future consumption are valued alike for a stable consumption stream, future consumption will be valued less than present consumption when the consumption stream is expected to rise. However, we have defined $IRD(0)$ for a stable consumption stream.

11. Or, more generally, the rate at which individuals are willing to substitute future for present consumption rises as the ratio of future consumption to present consumption rises.

(2) A second reason is limited life. This will produce a discount on future consumption if the individual attaches less importance to his heirs' utility from consumption than to his own. In that case, he will attach a lower value to consumption beyond his own lifetime than to consumption during his lifetime.

(3) Uncertainty of length of life will cause him to extend this discount on future consumption to periods less than his "expected" (i.e., average) length of life.

Our assumptions rule out both (2) and (3) by treating the individuals as immortal and unchangeable.

Are there any other "rational" reasons for discounting the future? As I interpret the literature, it answers in the negative—that is why the term "underestimation" of the future is so often used as a synonym for a positive internal rate of discount.

The appeal of this conclusion can be seen very clearly in our simple economy. By reducing his consumption temporarily—say, by $1 a year for a year—one of our immortal individuals can acquire an asset (a dollar of cash balances) that will yield him services that he regards as worth, say, ten cents a year indefinitely. By a temporary sacrifice, he can permanently raise his level of consumption. Suppose at time t_0 he does not do so. At some later time t will he not reproach himself for not having done so? He will say to himself: "Had I been sensible enough to make a temporary sacrifice years ago, it would be long past by now, but I would be enjoying today, and *forever after*, a higher level of consumption. I was a fool not to have made the sacrifice then." And this retrospective judgment does not involve any knowledge the individual did not have available at time t_0. His failure to make the temporary sacrifice then therefore conflicts with one characteristic it is natural to assign to "rational" behavior: behaving in a way that one does not later regret on the basis of data initially available.[12]

Even if the individual reasons in this way, it does not mean that there is no limit to the amount he will save at time t_0, only that he will save something. As he saves, he brings into play reason (1) for discounting future consumption. The "rational" man, on this logic, will regard a unit of present *utility* as equal to a unit of future *utility*. He will not necessarily regard a unit of present consumption as equal to a unit of future consumption.

This conception of rational behavior underlies conclusions such as that reached by Maurice Allais,[13] that the optimum real interest rate is zero and the optimum stock of capital in a stationary state is that at which the marginal productivity of capital is zero. It underlies in a more sophisticated way also the more recent work

12. The need to specify the same data is clear. Consider an individual offered a $2 to $1 wager that a coin he then and later regards as fair will come up heads. He takes the wager, betting that it will come up tails. Suppose that it happens to come up heads, so that he loses the $1. Ex post, he will regret having lost, but not having made the wager, because, on the basis of the data he could have had when he made the wager, it was an advantageous wager.

13. *Economie et Intérêt*, Paris: Librarie des Publications Officielle (1947).

on "golden growth paths" which regard the highest possible level of consumption per capita as an optimum.[14]

If one accepts this line of reasoning and supposes that the individuals in our hypothetical society behave rationally, the solution to our problem is immediate. The optimum situation is reached with a constant quantity of money and an ultimately stable price level. Equation (9) is then satisfied and, hence, so is equation (10). Individuals separately will try to accumulate cash balances up to the point at which the marginal yield of cash is zero. Their attempts will produce a price level that makes real cash balances sufficiently large to have a zero marginal yield.

However, I find it hard to accept this conclusion. Generalized to a world in which other forms of capital assets exist, it implies that a stationary equilibrium is possible only with capital satiety, i.e., a zero marginal yield of real capital. (The existence of such a situation would answer the second question raised above—the observable market phenomenon that would give the common value of $IRD(0)$.) A positive marginal yield of capital, however small, would be a sufficient condition for growth. This seems to me inconsistent with experience. Much, if not most, of human experience has consisted of a roughly stationary state—Europe in part of the middle ages, for example, and surely Japan for centuries prior to the nineteenth. Was the marginal yield on capital zero in those communities?

If it was positive, the present analysis would have to explain the lack of growth by either a lesser regard for one's heirs than for oneself, or by irrational behavior—by selfishness or short-sightedness. Neither appeals to me strongly as a satisfactory explanation. Yet I must confess that I have found no other.[15]

Nonetheless, it seems worth examining the effects of an $IRD(0)$ not equal to zero for every individual, but positive at least for some, leaving open whether such a situation is to be explained by selfishness, short-sightedness, or some still undiscovered reason for discounting the future.

In order to examine these effects, we must complicate our simple society. In that society, corresponding to any steady rate of growth or decline of the quantity of money, there will be an equilibrium position in which each individual adjusts his cash balances to satisfy equation (8). This is a stable position whether IRD is the same or different for different individuals, and market phenomena give no evidence of what the value of IRD is for any one individual. All we know is that, for all alike, given their levels of cash balances,

$$IRD(0) - MPM - MNPS = -\left(\frac{1}{P}\frac{dP}{dt}\right)^{*}. \tag{11}$$

14. Edmund S. Phelps, *Golden Rules of Economic Growth: Studies of Efficiency and Optimal Investment*, New York: W. W. Norton (1966).

15. For a while, I thought I had a rational explanation for an $IRD(0) > 0$ in a somewhat different model of individual behavior than the usual one. But Kenneth Arrow has persuaded me that, while this model (summarized in Appendix A) may be richer and more appealing than the usual one, it yields the same conclusion about rational behavior.

We need additional information to evaluate the individual terms on the left-hand side of the equation. We can get such additional information by relaxing some of our intital conditions.

IX. INTRODUCTION OF LENDING AND BORROWING

As a first step, let us relax condition (9), on page 2 above, to permit lending and borrowing, while retaining all other conditions. These other conditions mean that borrowing will be of only two kinds, (a) to finance extra consumption, or (b) to finance the holding of cash balances as a productive resource.

To simplify matters, let us suppose that there is only a single kind of debt instrument, namely, a promise to pay $1 a year indefinitely, a perpetuity or "consol."[16] Let us suppose also that productive enterprises are like corporations in our world—separate entities distinguishable from the individuals who are the ultimate wealth-owners, consumers, and sellers of productive resources. The only permanent asset enterprises have title to, under our assumptions, is cash, and they acquire this cash by borrowing from individuals. In this way, total cash balances can be divided into two parts:

$$M_e = \text{cash balances of enterprises}$$
$$M_w = \text{cash balances of ultimate wealth-holders.}$$

The counterparts of M_e in the portfolios of ultimate wealth-holders are then the debt instruments issued by the business enterprises.

We shall suppose also that all debt instruments are homogeneous, whether issued by enterprises or individuals, are regarded as default-free, and are traded in a free market like that in which services trade.

Let us call the individual debt instrument a "bond," and let B be the number of debt instruments, i.e., the number of perpetuities each promising to pay $1 a year. Let P_B be the price of a debt instrument, and r_B the reciprocal of P_B, or $1/P_B$, which is an interest rate.

If P_B is anticipated to remain constant on the average, though subject to variations, then r_B is the anticipated pecuniary return to a lender per dollar loaned and the anticipated pecuniary cost to a borrower per dollar borrowed.[17] However, just as the holding of money balances yields non-pecuniary returns in the form of a feeling of security and pride of possession, so also the possession of a bond may yield similar non-pecuniary returns and the issuance of a bond

16. This involves no essential loss of generality—if we consider only positive long-term interest rates and if the transactions costs of buying and selling perpetuities can be neglected since a short-term loan can always be broken into a purchase and subsequent sale of a perpetuity.

17. Treating the return to the lender and the cost to the borrower as equal assumes that both have the same anticipations and also that transactions costs of borrowing and lending can be neglected.

may involve non-pecuniary costs. The marginal non-pecuniary services yielded by a dollar's worth of bonds presumably depends on the stocks of both money and bonds held by the individual, and so does the marginal non-pecuniary services yielded by money balances. What matters is not the nominal value of the two stocks, but their real value, which we may represent by expressing the value of the stocks of both money and bonds as a ratio to income available for purchasing consumption goods (i.e., after debt service or inclusive of interest yield, but before savings or dissavings).

Let

$$m_i = \frac{M_i}{Y_i},$$

$$v_i = \frac{B_i P_B}{Y_i}$$

(12)

represent these ratios for money and bonds respectively for individual i, where M_i and B_i are the nominal amount of money and the number of bonds, respectively, held by individual i, and Y_i is his nominal income per unit time. Let

$$MNPS_M(m_i, v_i),$$

$$MNPS_B(m_i, v_i)$$

(13)

be the marginal value of non-pecuniary services, measured in cents per unit time per dollar of capital value, yielded by money and bonds to individual i when his holdings of them are m_i and v_i. Note that v_i may be positive or negative and that $(m_i + v_i)$ may be negative.

Intuitively, money seems to be a more efficient carrier of non-pecuniary services of the kind under consideration than bonds (this is the central idea imbedded in Keynesian liquidity preference). To represent this feature, we shall assume

$$MNPS_M(m_i, v_i) \text{ and } MNPS_B(m_i, v_i) \text{ have the same sign,} \qquad (14a)$$

and

$$| MNPS_M(m_i, v_i) | \geqslant | MNPS_B(m_i, v_i) | \qquad (14b)$$

for all values of m_i and v_i, the equality sign holding only when $MNPS_M$ is zero. In words, if money yields positive marginal non-pecuniary services, so do bonds; if money yields negative marginal non-pecuniary services, so do bonds. When both yield positive services, an individual who is compensated for any loss of pecuniary return will always prefer a portfolio which has $1 more of money and $1 less of bonds. If he is sated with one, he is sated with both, and therefore indifferent to bonds and money. When both yield negative returns, he will prefer the bonds to the money.[18] That is, money dominates bonds in the provi-

18. This seems a reasonable translation of our intuition when $MNPS_M$ is positive—the only region with which we have much experience. If money is superior because it gives greater security or more ready availability of resources for emergencies, this advantage should

sion of non-pecuniary services. This condition looks innocuous, yet it turns out to be critical.

A. Quantity of Money Constant

Let us revert to the first case considered, with neither helicopter nor furnace, in which the quantity of money is constant. Also, let us neglect M_e for a time by assuming that $MPM = 0$ for all values of M_e, so that M_e is also 0 (i.e., cash balances do not enter the production function).

Suppose lending and borrowing are introduced into our earlier society when it is in an equilibrium position with different individuals having different values of $IRD(0)$. Consider two individuals, Mr. Swinger, or S for short, who is willing to give up 20 cents a year indefinitely to raise his rate of consumption by \$1 a year for one year [$IRD(0) = .20$], and Mr. Rational, or R for short, who would not be willing to reduce his permanent consumption stream at all in order to get a temporary increase in consumption of \$1 a year for a year [$IRD(0) = 0$].

At the initial position,

$$\text{For } S: MNPS_M(m_S, 0) = IRD(0) = .20 \qquad (15)$$
$$\text{For } R: MNPS_M(m_R, 0) = IRD(0) = .00.$$

Each can now acquire or issue bonds by saving or dissaving. Let s_i equal the amount individual i saves expressed as a fraction of income available for consumption (the base of m_i and v_i). Then both initially and at every later moment, if all individuals act as if P_B will remain constant on the average,[19] each will save up to the point at which

$$MNPS_M(m_i, v_i) = IRD(s_i) = r_B + MNPS_B(m_i, v_i), \qquad (16)$$

or, subtracting $MNPS_B$ from all terms, at which

$$MNPS_M(m_i, v_i) - MNPS_B(m_i, v_i) = IRD(s_i) - MNPS_B(m_i, v_i) = r_B. \qquad (17)$$

---

decline as $MNPS_M$ approaches zero. When it is zero, the individual is sated with liquidity, hence would be indifferent, if compensated for any difference in pecuniary returns, between money and bonds.

The specified condition is more conjectural when $MNPS_M$ is negative. Presumably such negative non-pecuniary services reflect costs of safeguarding money, or worry over being robbed, etc. It seems plausible that bonds would be less worrisome, easier to safeguard, etc. which is the reason for the absolute value relation making bonds preferable under such circumstances.

However, if this is so, it raises a question about the positive side because then there will be some range for which this advantage of bonds will more than compensate for the higher liquidity of money, so the break-even point need not be zero but may be higher. Since only the positive side is particularly relevant for what follows, I have suppressed my misgivings about this point.

19. It is, of course, the uncertainty about P_B which makes cash more "liquid" than bonds and largely explains, under our assumptions, the inequalities (14b).

Equations (16) and (17) are simplified versions of equation (8), simplified because they assume

$$\left(\frac{1}{P}\frac{dP}{dt}\right)^* = MPM = 0,$$

amplified because they include bonds and admit the possibility of non-zero saving.

At the initial point, when $v_i = 0$, and $s_i = 0$ for both, we know from (14) and (15) that the first two expressions of (17) [$MNPS_M - MNPS_B$ and $IRD - MNPS_B$] are positive for S and zero for R. Hence there will be some range of positive rates of interest at which it will be mutually advantageous for S to borrow from R. How much S will want to borrow and R to lend will depend on the precise interest rate and on their tastes. When borrowing takes place, each shifts from a constant consumption stream to a changing one—declining for S, because current consumption is raised by his borrowing to a higher level than he can expect to maintain, rising for R, because current consumption is reduced by his loan to a lower level than he plans to maintain, which will lower the IRD for S and raise it for R. Since, on our assumptions, $MNPS_M$ and $MNPS_B$ depend only on m_i and v_i and not their rate of change, and since, for a given r_B, m_i and v_i are fixed at a given moment of time (except possibly for an initial reshuffling considered below), the change in IRD is what limits the amount that lenders are willing to lend and borrowers are willing to borrow at each interest rate.

If bonds yielded no non-pecuniary services, the size of $IRD(0)$ would determine which individuals would be savers and which dissavers, as it does in the example of S and R because the $IRD(0)$ of $R = 0$. Individuals with a high internal rate of discount would borrow from those with a low internal rate of discount, and borrowing and lending would be at a level at which all $IRD(s_i)$'s were equal. This is no longer necessarily true when bonds yield non-pecuniary returns. An individual who values such non-pecuniary returns highly relative to the non-pecuniary returns from money may save even though his $IRD(0)$ is relatively high. But, at each interest rate, some will be borrowers, some lenders. At lower and lower interest rates, more will be borrowers and each of these will be willing to borrow more, while fewer will be lenders and each will be willing to lend less. Hence there will be some interest rate, at each point in time, at which equation (17) will be satisfied for each individual, and at which the quantity of bonds demanded is equal to the quantity supplied. But at that interest rate, the $IRD(s_i)$'s need not be equal.

What initial effect, if any, will the introduction of borrowing and lending have on the demand for cash balances? For Mr. Swinger, his IRD is now lower, hence he will want to hold larger cash balances. Indeed, he may want to borrow precisely to accumulate cash balances. For Mr. Rational, his IRD is now higher, hence he will want to hold lower cash balances. Indeed, he may finance his lending by drawing down cash balances.

Insofar as people want to borrow to hold higher cash balances or lend to hold lower cash balances, this can occur at an instant of time by a reshuffling of cash and securities, a transfer of stocks of cash for stocks of securities. Insofar as they want to borrow to raise the current level of consumption of currently produced services or lend to reduce the current level of consumption and raise the future level, this is a transfer of flows for flows and must occur over time.

Let there be an instantaneous reshuffling of cash and securities. Will the real amount of cash demanded remain the same, rise, or fall? I see no way of knowing. That depends on the precise structure of tastes for cash balances on the part of those with high $IRD(0)$'s and those with low $IRD(0)$'s. If the real amount of cash demanded is higher, that will require and produce a reduction in prices; if lower, a rise in prices. For simplicity, let us assume that the real amount of cash demanded is unchanged and hence that there is no change in prices.[20]

As the borrowing and lending process proceeds, some members of the community accumulate bonds, others accumulate an obligation to pay interest on the bonds. What will be the final stationary equilibrium position?

That position is defined by the satisfaction of equation (17) for all individuals at a value of $s_i = 0$. Three sets of forces put in motion by the process of borrowing and lending may contribute to the attainment of such an equilibrium.

(1). *Changing distribution of wealth.* As the process proceeds, the lenders accumulate wealth and hence have higher and higher incomes available for consumption (if Y_i^0 is the original income of lender i from the sale of services, his income becomes $Y_i^0 + B_i$, and B_i is positive), while borrowers decumulate and hence have lower and lower incomes available for consumption. Suppose that for each individual all terms in (17) remained unchanged in the process. Then at each interest rate s_i would be unchanged. But positive s_i's would be applied to larger and larger bases, and negative s_i's to smaller and smaller bases. The absolute demand for bonds would shift to the right and the absolute supply of bonds to the left, forcing down r_B, which would increase the number of borrowers and decrease the number of lenders. The asymptotic limit would be that at which only those individuals who had the lowest common value of $IRD(0) - MNPS_B(m_i, v_i)$ would have funds left from which to save. The value of r_B would be equal to that lowest value and there would be no net saving or dissaving.[21]

20. Note that the total consolidated transferable wealth of the community remains throughout equal to M, since the positive value of bonds to their holders is precisely offset by the negative value to their issuers. The question therefore is whether there is any reason to expect the average desired wealth–income ratio to be higher or lower after the introduction of lending and borrowing than before its introduction.

21. This analysis continues to assume that each individual expects P_B to be constant on the average, which is an unsatisfactory assumption given the declining values of r_B. Similarly we continue to assume

$$\left(\frac{1}{P}\frac{dP}{dt}\right)^* = 0,$$

which may also be unsatisfactory.

(2). *Changing values of non-pecuniary services.* As the process proceeds, the ratio of wealth to income available for consumption ($m_i + v_i$) is likely to grow for the savers and decline for the dissavers.[22] For the savers, this will tend to lower both $MNPS_B$ and $MNPS_M$, and so, for a given interest rate, require a reduction in $IRD(s_i)$ for equilibrium.[23] This will be produced by a reduction in the fraction of income saved. For borrowers, the effect will be to raise both $MNPS_B$ and $MNPS_M$ and so to require a higher $IRD(s_i)$ for equilibrium. This will be produced by a reduction in the fraction of income dissaved. Both the supply of bonds and the demand for bonds will decline on this account. There is no way of saying what, on this score alone, will happen to the interest rate; we can only

22. This ratio, call it w, is equal to

$$w = \frac{M_i + V_i}{Y_i + B_i} = \frac{M_i + V_i}{Y_i + r_B V_i}, \qquad (a)$$

where $V_i = B_i P_B$.
Differentiate with respect to V, dropping subscripts for simplicity. This gives

$$\frac{dw}{dV} = \left[Y - rM + (Y + rV) \frac{dM}{dV} \right] / (Y + rV)^2. \qquad (b)$$

so $\frac{dw}{dV} > 0$ if

$$\frac{dM}{dV} \geqslant \frac{rM - Y}{Y + rV} = \frac{r(M + V)}{Y + rV} - 1. \qquad (c)$$

In general $(dM/dV) > 0$, i.e., as wealth and income increase, so will desired money holdings but by less than the increase in wealth. Hence (c) will be satisfied if

$$\frac{r(M + V)}{Y + rV} \leqslant 1 \qquad (d)$$

or

$$\frac{Y + rV}{M + V} \geqslant r, \qquad (e)$$

i.e., the ratio of total income (including income from human services) to total wealth is greater than the rate of interest, which seems a condition very likely to be satisfied.

If income were defined inclusive of that component of non-pecuniary services of money that can be measured, namely, its excess over the non-pecuniary services of bonds, or r_B, the wealth–income ratio would necessarily move in the direction indicated. For then the wealth–income ratio (call it w') would be:

$$w' = \frac{M_i + V_i}{Y_i + r_B(M_i + V_i)} = \frac{W}{Y_i + rW}.$$

On our assumptions, for the individual, as W grows, so do M_i and V_i. But

$$\frac{dw'}{dW} = \frac{Y_i}{(Y_i + rW)^2} > 0.$$

23. As implied in the preceding footnote, after the initial reshuffling of cash and securities, borrowers may be expected to be reducing their cash balances—financing their extra consumption by both borrowing and drawing down cash balances—and lenders to be adding to their cash balances—using their savings to add to both their bond holdings and their cash. Borrowers are getting poorer in wealth and having lower incomes available for consumption. The reverse is true for lenders. The initial reshuffling simply corrects an initial stock disequilibrium produced by the prior forcible suppression of lending and borrowing.

say that the volume of lending and borrowing will be reduced. If this factor alone were at work, equilibrium would be attained by changes in the $MNPS_M$ and $MNPS_B$ that would bring (17) into equality for each individual at $s_i = 0$, with $IRD(0) - MNPS_B(m_i, v_i)$ equal for all individuals.

(3). *Changing internal rates of discount.*   A third possible equilibrating factor is changes in $IRD(0)$, the internal rate of discount when saving is zero. It is sometimes argued that this rate should depend on the level of consumption. The savers, when they reach equilibrium, will have a higher level of consumption than initially, while the dissavers will have a lower level. The usual relation supposed is that the lower the level of consumption, the higher the internal rate of discount ("The poor are more short-sighted than the rich"). However, this would produce a disequilibrating movement as the process went on, because it would increase the gap between $IRD(0)$ and $MNPS_B$ for dissavers to close by dissaving. Moreover, it is hard to see on theoretical grounds any reason why the internal rate of discount should be systematically related to the level of consumption, when the level of consumption is constant over time. If current consumption is low, so is future consumption; hence, if current needs are regarded as urgent, future needs will be also. I am inclined therefore to rule out this possibility.

A more appealing possibility, though one that for reasons already suggested raises difficulties as well, is that $IRD(0)$ depends on the wealth–income ratio, rising as the wealth–income ratio rises and falling as the wealth–income ratio falls. Since the wealth–income ratio is likely to rise for savers and decline for dissavers, this will produce an equilibrating movement, tending to bring the values of $IRD(0) - MNPS_B$ together for savers and dissavers.

(4). *Final stationary equilibrium position.*   Whether brought about by one or a combination of these three forces, the final stationary equilibrium will equate

$$MNPS_M - MNPS_B = IRD(0) - MNPS_B = r_B \qquad (18)$$

for all individuals. Moreover, because of our assumption that M, the nominal stock of money, is fixed, the price level will be stationary when (18) is satisfied, so

$$\left(\frac{1}{P}\frac{dP}{dt}\right) = \left(\frac{1}{P}\frac{dP}{dt}\right)^* = 0. \qquad (19)$$

The final equilibrium price level need not of course be the same as the price level immediately after the introduction of borrowing and lending. General considerations suggest that it should be higher, i.e., that real balances should be lower as a fraction of income. There is now an additional means of providing for emergencies, so the utility of cash balances for this purpose should be less. Of the three forces listed as tending toward stationary equilibrium, the first (the changing distribution of wealth) clearly works in this direction, since the individuals who initially are led to hold lower money balances come to play a more and more dominant role in the final position. Neither of the other forces has a similarly unambiguous effect on desired cash balances.

We can readily reintroduce money as a productive resource and drop the assumption that $M_e = MPM = 0$. At every moment, businesses will acquire that stock of cash balances for which $MPM = r_B$, provided that they anticipate P_B will be constant on the average. No non-pecuniary elements enter in, so this is an easy problem.

The final equilibrium will then be characterized by

$$MPM = MNPS_M - MNPS_B = IRD(0) - MNPS_B = r_B \qquad (20)$$

for every business enterprise and every individual separately. (I.e., MPM stands for a set of MPM's, one for each business enterprise. Similarly, the next two expressions each stand for a set, one for each individual, so that, if written out in full, (20) would contain $n_e + 2n_w + 1$ expressions linked by equality signs, where n_e is the number of enterprises and n_w the number of ultimate wealth-holders.) The variables that enable this solution to be attained are: the division of the fixed nominal money stock among enterprises and individuals, the price level, which permits the real money stock to be whatever is desired, the rate of interest, and the volume of bonds issued and held by different individuals.

Equation (20) takes us one step in the direction of separating out the terms on the left-hand side of (11)—when prices are constant we can evaluate MPM as equal to r_B. But we still cannot separate out $IRD(0)$ from the non-pecuniary services of bonds, and hence cannot determine separately the non-pecuniary services of money. Let us see what happens when we reintroduce changes in the quantity of money.

B. Quantity of Money Changes at a Steady Rate

Let us now substitute for $M = M_0$ a steady exponential rate of change: $M(t) = M_0 e^{\mu t}$, where μ can be positive or negative.

In the final position of stationary state equilibrium, by reasoning precisely the same as we used before we introduced bonds,

$$\frac{1}{P}\frac{dP}{dt} = \left(\frac{1}{P}\frac{dP}{dt}\right)^* = \mu. \qquad (21)$$

Equation (20) must now be changed to include the effect of changing prices. Consider first for both enterprises and individuals the alternatives of issuing a fraction of a bond to hold an extra dollar of cash, or acquiring a fraction of a bond with $1 of cash. In this case, the effect of $\mu \neq 0$ cancels out. If prices are rising, the asset depreciates in value but so does the liability. Hence it must still be true that

$$MPM = MNPS_M - MNPS_B = r_B. \qquad (22)$$

This is the condition for portfolio balance, i.e., stock equilibrium.

However, for the individual, the acquisition of money or bonds by saving now involves a different set of costs or returns. Let him save an additional dollar to acquire a dollar of cash balances or a dollar's worth of the bond. The anticipated gain to him from the extra dollar of cash balance is

$$MNPS_M - \left(\frac{1}{P}\frac{dP}{dt}\right)^*,$$

and from the extra dollar of bond

$$MNPS_B + r_B - \left(\frac{1}{P}\frac{dP}{dt}\right)^*,$$

since

$$\left(\frac{1}{P}\frac{dP}{dt}\right)^*$$

is the loss he experiences in the purchasing power of his cash or bond. In either case the cost is $IRD(0)$. So we have

$$MNPS_M - \left(\frac{1}{P}\frac{dP}{dt}\right)^* = MNPS_B + r_B - \left(\frac{1}{P}\frac{dP}{dt}\right)^* = IRD(0). \qquad (23)$$

Subtract

$$MNPS_B - \left(\frac{1}{P}\frac{dP}{dt}\right)^*$$

from all terms and we have, with the order rearranged,

$$MNPS_M - MNPS_B = IRD(0) - MNPS_B + \left(\frac{1}{P}\frac{dP}{dt}\right)^* = r_B. \qquad (24)$$

This is the condition for zero savings, i.e., for flow equilibrium.

Combining (22) and (24), the conditions for full equilibrium are

$$MPM = MNPS_M - MNPS_B = IRD(0) - MNPS_B + \left(\frac{1}{P}\frac{dP}{dt}\right)^* = r_B, \qquad (25)$$

which reduces to (20) when

$$\left(\frac{1}{P}\frac{dP}{dt}\right)^* = 0.$$

Suppose now that we start with a position in which (20) is satisfied for $\mu = 0$ and introduce a positive μ. How will this affect the final equilibrium, i.e., when

$$\left(\frac{1}{P}\frac{dP}{dt}\right)^* = \mu?$$

To begin with, at the same r_B, equations (22) remain satisfied, i.e., there is no effect on portfolio balance. However, equations (24) are now out of equilibrium: the middle expression is now higher than the others: the cost of acquiring either bonds or money by saving now exceeds the gain therefrom. Hence, there will be attempted dissaving, an attempted reduction in the volume of real cash balances, an attempted reduction in the amount of bonds held, and an attempted increase in the amount of bonds issued. As before, these attempts cannot succeed, but they will produce a higher price level (over and above the rise from the increasing quantity of money), which lowers the real quantity of money to be held, and also a higher rate of interest, which lessens the desire both to reduce bond holdings and to issue more bonds. It is not clear what will happen to the aggregate value of bonds outstanding. The higher rate of interest will have lowered the value of the bonds initially outstanding, but will have offset both the initial desire to reduce the amount of bonds held and the initial desire to issue more bonds. It is clear that bonds decline less in attractiveness than cash because of the rise in interest rates. Total wealth held in the final equilibrium position must decline, since this is, after consolidating accounts, equal simply to real cash balances. However, the volume of bonds outstanding will tend to be larger relative to the amount of cash balances, and conceivably could be larger in absolute real amount.

As in our simpler example, there is clearly a welfare loss from inflation: with r_B higher, MPM is higher because a smaller real volume of cash is being held for productive purposes. Thus there is a lower real flow of consumer services and total wealth is lower, so the community has lost some non-pecuniary services from wealth.

Let μ be negative and the reverse effects follow: the price level will fall (beyond that required by the change in the quantity of money) and r_B will also fall. For small rates of price decline there will clearly be a welfare gain. So long as $r_B > 0$, so is MPM, and additional business cash balances will add to the flow of consumer services. Similarly, so long as $r_B > 0$, so is $MNPS_M$, hence the additional wealth adds to the welfare of ultimate wealth-holders. Let us now try higher and higher rates of price decline until we reach a rate at which, in equilibrium, $r_B = 0$.

At this equilibrium, we know from equation (22) that

$$MNPS_M - MNPS_B = 0. \tag{26}$$

How can that be? From equations (14), only if $MNPS_M = MNPS_B = 0$. But, this means that, from equations (25),

$$IRD(0) + \left(\frac{1}{P}\frac{dP}{dt}\right)^* = 0 \tag{27}$$

or

$$IRD(0) = -\mu. \tag{28}$$

We finally have a market measure of the internal rate of discount—that rate of steady price decline that makes the nominal interest rate equal to zero. Moreover, this situation is clearly an optimum: further increases in the rate of price decline would induce wealth-holders to hold so large a stock of wealth that it would yield negative marginal non-pecuniary returns, and so lower welfare.

The forces contributing to the attainment of this equilibrium position are the three that were described above as tending toward long-run stationary equilibrium when the quantity of money was held constant. However, the second of those three—the changing values of non-pecuniary services—can no longer by itself be sufficient, since the present solution specifies that these are zero at equilibrium. Hence, differences among individuals in the values they attach to non-pecuniary services cannot compensate for other differences among them. The equilibrium will have to be achieved by an elimination of any initial differences in $IRD(0)$, either through changes in the distribution of wealth which concentrate all wealth and consumption in the hands of that set of individuals with the lowest single value of $IRD(0)$, or by changes in $IRD(0)$ for each individual brought about by alterations in the wealth-income ratio.

Our *final rule for the optimum quantity of money is that it will be attained by a rate of price deflation that makes the nominal rate of interest equal to zero.* The yield on cash balances from their appreciation in value will then just balance, for each individual, the cost of abstaining from consumption and, for each enterprise that borrows to hold cash balances, the cost imposed by a rising real value of debt. Hence each individual and each enterprise will be induced to hold that volume of cash balances which yields zero marginal yield, in utility to the one and in productive services to the other. Since it costs all together no physical resources to add to real cash balances, returns to all together just balance costs.

X. INTRODUCTION OF REPRODUCIBLE CAPITAL

We can now readily relax some of our other initial conditions, in particular conditions (7) and (8)—infinitely durable, non-reproducible, non-marketable capital goods.

Let capital goods be of varying durabilities, reproducible, and marketable. Perhaps the simplest way to introduce such capital goods, with minimum alteration in the framework of the analysis, is to assume that only business enterprises hold these capital goods, and that they finance them by issuing equities held by ultimate wealth-holders. Let the typical equity be, like our bond, a perpetuity, but one that offers to pay one real dollar rather than one nominal dollar per year, i.e., in dollars of year 0, one that promises to pay $P(t)/P(0)$ dollars per year, where $P(t)$ is the price index of final consumer services in year t. Let $P_E(t)$ be the price of such an equity in year (t), then

$$r_E(t) = \frac{P(t)}{P(0)} \bigg/ P_E(t) \qquad (29)$$

will be the yield per dollar of equity in year t, if P_E is constant. The transition to a final stationary equilibrium is complicated, even more so than that dealt with briefly for borrowing and lending. But the conditions for final equilibrium are straightforward. For productive enterprises, the cost of producing a unit of capital capable of yielding one real dollar a year in productive services must be equal to the price for which such an equity can be sold. Or, equivalently

$$MRY = r_E, \tag{30}$$

where MRY is marginal real yield in cents per dollar per year. In nominal terms, if prices are changing, the rate of rise in prices must be added to both sides. If the enterprise is to be indifferent between borrowing by bonds and by equities,

$$r_B - \left(\frac{1}{P}\frac{dP}{dt}\right)^* = r_E, \tag{31}$$

since the real cost of borrowing a real dollar through a bond is reduced, when prices are rising, by the decline in the real value of the obligation incurred.[24]

For the wealth-holder, the analysis is complicated by the existence of non-pecuniary returns from bonds and equities. Let $MNPS_E$ be the marginal non-pecuniary services per unit time derived from a dollar of equities. For the wealth-holder to be in equilibrium with respect to the holding of bonds and equities, it must be that

$$r_B - \left(\frac{1}{P}\frac{dP}{dt}\right)^* + MNPS_B = r_E + MNPS_E. \tag{32}$$

However, (31) and (32) can be valid simultaneously only if

$$MNPS_B = MNPS_E. \tag{33}$$

Hence, the individual will always hold a portfolio for which this is true. We can therefore use $MNPS_B$ to refer to both kinds of securities. Adding these equations to those in (25), our final conditions of equilibrium are

$$MRY + \left(\frac{1}{P}\frac{dP}{dt}\right)^* = MPM = MNPS_M - MNPS_B$$

$$= IRD(0) - MNPS_B + \left(\frac{1}{P}\frac{dP}{dt}\right)^*$$

$$= r_E + \left(\frac{1}{P}\frac{dP}{dt}\right)^* = r_B. \tag{33}$$

24. Note that satisfaction of (31) assures that the cost of capital to a firm is independent of the debt–equity ratio. This is a very special case of the much more general proposition to this effect asserted by Franco Modigliani and Merton Miller. Our result reflects the assumption that both bonds and equities are default-free, the only difference being whether the return is nominal or real. By this assumption, we essentially rule out any effect of variability of the income stream from an enterprise on the "quality" of bonds and equities as the debt–equity ratio changes, or, for a given debt–equity ratio, as the variability of the income stream changes. These are at the heart of the Modigliani–Miller analysis. See Franco Modigliani and Merton Miller, "The Cost of Capital, Corporation Finance, and the Theory of Investment," *American Economic Review*, vol. 48 (June 1958), pp. 261–97.

The optimum position will be the same as before, when $\left(\dfrac{1}{P}\dfrac{dP}{dt}\right)^*$ is a sufficiently large negative number so that $r_B = 0$. At that point,

$$MRY = IRD\,(0) = r_E = -\left(\frac{1}{P}\frac{dP}{dt}\right)^*,$$

$$MPM = MNPS_M = MNPS_B = r_B = 0.$$

(34)

The reason that this is an optimum is that, while external effects offset the cost to an individual or to an enterprise of holding an extra dollar of cash balances, they do not offset the cost of adding a real dollar's worth of physical productive capital. It uses up a dollar's worth of productive resources to produce a dollar's worth of physical productive capital, so someone or other must consume one dollar's worth less in order to make those real resources available.

This is reflected in the first line of equations (34). At the optimum, all these terms are positive. MRY is the permanent income stream gained by adding a real dollar's worth of productive capital. $IRD\,(0)$ is the real cost to an individual of abstaining from a dollar's worth of consumption, expressed also as the permanent income stream that he would regard as compensating him for that abstention. r_E is a market cost mediating between the other two terms. It is the real cost, as it appears to the enterprise, of acquiring the capital from the market via equities to finance the production of the extra real dollar of productive capital, and it is the real gain as it appears to the wealth-holder of providing the capital. The final term in the first line, $-\left(\dfrac{1}{P}\dfrac{dP}{dt}\right)^*$, is also a market cost mediating between the other two terms. It is the real cost to the enterprise of financing the additional capital by holding a dollar less of cash balances or by borrowing in the form of bonds (given that $r_B = 0$); it is the real gain as it appears to the wealth-holder of providing the capital by purchasing bonds rather than equity (given that $r_B = 0$). The final two terms can also be regarded as assuring portfolio balance for the individual, since r_E is the return from equities, and $-\left(\dfrac{1}{P}\dfrac{dP}{dt}\right)^*$ is the return from either bonds or cash balances (given the equalities in the second line).

Thus the first line assures the optimization of the quantity of physical productive capital, given the tastes of individuals as expressed in their internal rates of discount, and, in conjunction with the second line, assures equilibrium between holdings of nominal and real assets.

The second line, in turn, assures the optimization of the real quantity of nominal assets, given that the real marginal cost of providing an additional real quantity of nominal assets is zero. The first three terms represent the yield to business enterprises and wealth-holders of holding an additional real dollar in cash (the first two terms) or bonds (the third term). The last two terms represent the net cost of acquiring a real dollar to hold in these forms. For a business, the real cost of acquiring a real dollar by issuing bonds is r_B plus the rising real value of its obligation $\left[-\left(\frac{1}{P}\frac{dP}{dt}\right)^* \right]$, but this additional cost is precisely offset by the rising real value of the cash balances acquired. For individuals, the gain from acquiring bonds is r_B plus the rising real value of the assets, but this additional return is precisely offset by the real cost of abstention from consumption.

To express the final result in more general terms, it is technically feasible to produce certain services rendered by capital assets at zero real cost—namely, the transactions services of cash and the feelings of security, pride of possession, and the like from owning wealth. Other services rendered by capital assets cannot be produced at zero real cost—namely, the productive services of physical assets. It is desirable in each case that the services be provided up to the point where their marginal return equals their properly calculated marginal cost. In a world of stable prices, the cost to the individual of the first category of services appears to be greater than it actually is, if all costs and all returns are accounted for. By having prices decline at the appropriate rate, it is possible to provide the individual with a return that appears greater to him than it actually is if all costs and returns are accounted for. The apparent return just offsets the apparent cost and leads him to behave precisely as he would if, in the first instance, he bore all the costs and received all the returns.

XI. OTHER INITIAL CONDITIONS

We have now relaxed in effect all the special conditions added to the usual stationary state specification, except (11)—that prices are free to change—and (12)—that all money consists of strict fiat money.

Condition (11) is not intended to be restrictive, since we admitted the possibility of institutional frictions. About all it rules out is widespread governmental price control.

Condition (12) has in effect been relaxed already by introducing bonds and equities. Money in the form of demand deposits adds no special complexity. Provided banks assess service charges to cover the cost of services rendered, they would be willing to pay interest on demand deposits at some rate less than r_B, when r_B is positive, the difference depending on their average non-interest bearing reserves. As the rate of price decline increased, this difference would disappear and the rate they paid would approach r_B; both would approach zero as the rate of price decline approached the optimum rate. As already noted, the use of commodity money changes the situation drastically.

We can relax the usual stationary state restrictions without altering the basic conclusion. Substitution of individuals with finite lives for immortal individuals gives a possible reason to expect a positive internal rate of discount. Growth in population, capital, and technology means we must consider a moving dynamic equilibrium instead of a stationary one. It, too, gives a reason for a positive internal rate of discount. But it remains true throughout that it is costless to provide individuals with the satiety volume of real cash balances. And it remains true that one way to achieve this result is to have prices decline at a rate that will make the equivalent of r_B equal to zero. Of course, in such a world, the term "prices" has no unique meaning. Different classes of prices may well behave differently, so that the optimum numerical rate of price decline will depend on the index number chosen to measure prices. This optimum rate need not be constant over time. But none of these complications raises any essential difficulty in principle. The relevant price index is whatever index buyers and sellers of securities use in comparing yields on bonds and equities. A monetary policy that kept the equivalent of r_B equal to zero would automatically produce the optimum rate of decline in the relevant price index.

A more serious problem is the existence of many different securities and interest rates, so that it is not obvious what the "equivalent of r_B" is.

One qualification required for the actual world is that it is not literally costless to provide additional real balances. There are transfer costs of raising taxes in a stationary society to reduce the quantity of money in order to produce a steady rate of decline in prices. There is an initial real capital cost of providing the money in the form of notes and coins or deposit accounts. There are operating costs in replacing worn out notes and keeping deposit accounts. The existence of these costs means that the optimum is not $r_B = 0$, but r_B positive and above zero by enough to match the marginal costs of keeping real balances higher by one real dollar.

Hence, while our key conclusion can be derived for a highly simplified world, it remains valid for the actual world with only slight modification. But it is valid, it should be emphasized, as a proposition about the long-run optimum. I shall return to this point later.

XII. ALTERNATIVE WAY TO ACHIEVE THE OPTIMUM

Instead of having prices decline, an alternative way to offset the apparent cost to the individual of holding additional cash balances is to pay interest on money. Instead of burning up the proceeds of taxes to produce a decline in the quantity of money, as assumed so far, these proceeds could be used to pay interest to individuals on their cash balances and the nominal quantity of money kept constant. Indeed, the declining prices of our earlier solution can be viewed as about the only administratively feasible way of paying interest on currency.

An alternative would be to permit free entry into banking, and to allow banks to issue both currency and deposits and to pay interest on both. In order to set a limit on the total nominal quantity of money, let there be a fiat issue bearing no interest that the banks are required to hold as reserves, the reserve requirement being the same for currency and deposits. The level of the reserve requirement would be set with the aim of making the net cost of holding cash balances (the excess of r_B over r_M, the rate paid by banks on money) equal to the real costs of managing and administering the system.

If the quantity of the fiat currency remained fixed, under stationary state conditions, the equilibrium price level would be constant. Competition among banks would force them to pay interest on deposits at a rate falling short of r_B by the costs of running the banks, including loss of interest on assets required to be held as non-interest bearing fiat money. Competition would force banks also to pay interest on currency at a rate below the rate paid on deposits by the extra costs of administering the payment of interest on currency. They would, of course, have an incentive to devise an economical way to pay such interest.

For a progressive society, the equilibrium price level of products would decline. So long as the price decline did not go beyond the optimum rate, everything would be essentially the same. But if the society were growing rapidly, the price decline might go too far. To avoid that result, secular growth could be introduced into the nominal amount of the fiat money available for use as reserves.

This may all seem highly fanciful, yet it corresponds to many tendencies currently at work in the financial community. The development of commercial banks has been spurred mostly, of course, by their role in facilitating trans-actions and improving the capital market by mediating between borrower and lender. But the need to have such banks commit themselves to redeem their liabilities in either a basic commodity money (such as gold) or fiat currency arises from the absence of any physical limit on the volume of something that can be produced at zero cost. Their growth has also been stimulated by the gap between the return on cash balances and the cost of producing them. This gap has played an even larger role in the attempts by banks to issue currency, to reduce prudential reserves, and to pay interest on deposits. These attempts have produced welfare gains to the community by the payment of interest on at least some cash balances. They have also produced losses to the community because of other phenomena that have accompanied fractional reserve banking, notably instability in the total quantity of money.

XIII. THE SIZE OF THE POSSIBLE WELFARE GAIN

It may give some perspective to the analysis, and summarize some parts of it, to make some rough estimates of the gain in welfare in the U.S. that could currently (1968) be achieved by a policy leading to the optimum quantity of money.

To make such estimates we need to specify (1) "the" current internal rate of discount of a "representative" individual, and the rate of discount that would prevail with the optimum quantity of money;[25] (2) the anticipated rate of change

25. In principle, no such estimate is needed to conduct a monetary policy to achieve the optimum quantity of money. It is necessary only to have an interest rate that is the equivalent of r_B, and to force a sufficient rate of price decline to bring that rate close to zero. The rate of price decline will then be a measure of the internal rate of discount.

of prices; (3) the monetary total that is to be regarded as the counterpart of the money of our analysis; and (4) the difference between the optimum and the current quantity of that monetary total.

A. Internal Rate of Return

If there were some asset which was known to yield zero net non-pecuniary services to all holders, the nominal pecuniary yield on such an asset, less the anticipated rate of price change, would, by equation (23) generalized by replacing $IRD(0)$ by $IRD(s_i)$, provide an estimate of the internal rate of discount. However, a key point of our analysis is that, so long as $r_B \neq 0$, there need be no such asset. Every form of holding wealth may yield non-pecuniary returns in the form of security, pride of possession, and so on, as long as there is no way that is costless at the margin of acquiring and holding additional wealth. Of course, some particular way of holding wealth may have negative features that just counterbalances such returns. So there may exist some asset that yields zero net non-pecuniary returns. But even if there is such an asset, there is no way of identifying it by market prices or yields. These permit at most measurement of the differences between the services yielded by different assets.

For example, equities have yielded on the average, over long periods, something like 9 or 10 per cent per year; high-grade bonds, something like 3 to 5 per cent during periods when prices were roughly stable. Are these yields to be interpreted as reflecting non-pecuniary services of zero from equities and of between 4 and 7 per cent per year from bonds? Or non-pecuniary services of zero from bonds and non-pecuniary costs (disservices) from equities of between 4 and 7 per cent per year? There is no way on this evidence to choose between these interpretations, or any others involving the same differential between non-pecuniary services rendered.

To take another example, many persons apparently simultaneously have funds in saving accounts bearing interest at rates of from 3 to 5 per cent per year and purchase goods on installment contracts involving interest rates up to and beyond 35 per cent per year. Are we to interpret this as meaning that the internal rate of discount is 35 per cent per year and that savings accounts yield non-pecuniary services valued at about 30 per cent per year? Or that the internal rate of discount is 5 per cent per year and 30 of the 35 per cent paid as interest on the installment contract is counterbalanced by non-pecuniary services from being in debt (e.g., being forced to save)? Along this line, there is again no way of extracting a satisfactory answer.

In another context, I have used a wholly different approach to estimate the internal rate of discount, namely, attempting to explain consumption behavior. That approach yields an estimate of an internal rate of discount of about $\frac{1}{3}$.[26]

26. See Milton Friedman, "Windfalls, the 'Horizon,' and Related Concepts in the Permanent-Income Hypothesis" in K. Arrow, *et al.* (eds.), *Measurement in Economics: Studies*

This rate would be consistent with the first of the two interpretations of the preceding paragraph.

Let us take this rate of .33 as something of an upper estimate of the internal rate of discount. For a lower estimate, let us take .05, which assumes that high-grade government or corporate bonds, or savings accounts, yield trivial net non-pecuniary returns.

These are estimates of current internal rates of discount. We also need estimates of the internal rate of discount when there is an optimum quantity of money. Since a policy producing the optimum quantity of money would raise the wealth–income ratio, it would bring actual wealth closer to desired wealth. This could be expected to lower the desired savings ratio, which would, as we argued earlier, unambiguously tends to mean a lower internal rate of discount (see Sections VIII and IX A above). The higher wealth–income ratio might produce an offsetting rise in the internal rate of discount, but this is uncertain (section IX A).

As a rough way of allowing for possible changes in internal rates of discount, let us assume that the lower limit, 5 per cent, is unchanged, since that requires only a small change in the wealth–income ratio to reach the optimum quantity of money, but that the upper limit, .33, is cut in half to .17.

B. Anticipated Rate of Change of Prices

We need an estimate of the anticipated rate of change of prices to add to the estimated initial internal rate of discount if we are to find the initial marginal non-pecuniary services of money [equation (23) generalized to non-zero saving ratios]. We need it also to get the initial cost of holding money balances.

Prices are currently rising at the rate of about 4 per cent per year. However, we know that it takes a long time for people fully to adjust their anticipations to experience. Hence an estimate of $\left(\frac{1}{P}\frac{dP}{dt}\right)^{*}$ of about 2 per cent per year seems reasonable.

C. Monetary Total

The direct counterpart to the money of our analysis is "high-powered" money —total currency, both in the hands of the public and in the vaults of banks, plus deposits at Federal Reserve Banks other than those of the U.S. Treasury. This total is non-interest-bearing and, in effect, currently all fiat, although some of it originated as warehouse receipts for gold and silver.

High-powered money was about six weeks' personal disposable income in

in Mathematical Economics and Econometrics in Memory of Yehuda Grunfeld (Stanford, Calif.: Stanford University Press, 1963).

early 1968. We may take this as a minimum estimate of the quantity of "money."

If the legal prohibition of interest payments on demand deposits were fully effective, with the costs of all transactions services rendered by banks being covered by explicit service charges, then demand deposits also would be non-interest-bearing assets of individuals and enterprises capable of being expanded with little real cost. However, this is a big *if*. There is abundant evidence that competition forces banks to find indirect ways to pay interest on deposits and that they have been successful in doing so.[27] As an arbitrary compromise, let us treat half of demand deposits as the maximum fraction that is equivalent to non-interest-bearing money. This gives a maximum estimate of the quantity of "money" of about ten weeks' personal disposable income.

D. *The Optimum Quantity of Money*

The optimum quantity of money depends on the shape of the demand curve for real balances (Figure 6) and the change in the cost of holding money balances required to attain the optimum quantity.

Demand studies all show that the quantity of money demanded is rather inelastic with respect to changes in the rate of interest. These may underestimate the elasticity relevant for our purposes, since they are for monetary totals part of which pay interest (demand deposits or time deposits), so that a change in market interest rates is partly offset by a change in the rate of interest paid on money. To allow for this, let us take a cost elasticity rather on the high side, of about $-.5$ when the interest rate is about 5 per cent. This would mean that a one percentage point change in the interest rate (or, by transference, in the rate of change of prices) would change real balances in the opposite direction by 10 per cent.

At an internal rate of discount of 5 per cent, the optimum quantity of money would be attained with a rate of price decline of 5 per cent per year, or, given the assumption that prices are currently anticipated to rise at 2 per cent per year, with a 7 percentage point decline in the cost of holding non-interest-bearing balances. Given the assumption of the preceding paragraph, this implies that money balances would a bit more than double.[28]

27. Benjamin Klein, in a Ph.D. thesis nearing completion as this is written, tests the hypothesis that the prohibition of the payment of interest is almost wholly ineffective. His results suggest that that hypothesis explains observable phenomena better than the hypothesis that the prohibition is fully effective.

28. Treat the 10 per cent of the preceding paragraph as the change in the natural logarithm of money balances. I.e., assume that the demand function for money is

$$\log M = a - 10 \left(\frac{1}{P} \frac{dP}{dt} \right)^*.$$

Then a decline of 7 percentage points means a change in $[(1/P)(dP/dt)]^*$ by $-.07$, or in $\log M$ by $+.7$, the antilog of which is about 2.

At an ultimate internal discount rate of 17 per cent, the optimum quantity of money would be attained with a rate of price decline of 17 per cent per year, or a shift of 19 percentage points in the cost of holding non-interest-bearing balances.[29] This implies that money balances would rise to over six-and-a-half times their initial level.

E. Combining the Items

The table on page 44, which combines the various assumptions into estimates of the potential welfare gain, is mostly self-explanatory.[30] Our assumptions give us four cases: the two alternative sets of internal rates of discount, and the two alternative concepts of money. Lines A to F summarize our assumptions. The calculation in line G assumes (a) that the initial marginal non-pecuniary return on money is equal to the internal rate of discount plus the anticipated rate of change in prices, (b) that the terminal marginal non-pecuniary return is zero, and, most important, (c) that we can approximate the *average* non-pecuniary returns by the average of the initial and terminal values.[31] Line

29. Given rates comparable to r_B in the neighborhood of 5 per cent, it may seem impossible that anything like a rate of price decline of 17 per cent per year would be required to reduce the rate to near zero. This is correct so far as allowance for the rate of price decline alone is concerned. That would tend to reduce r_B percentage point for percentage point. However, the assumption that the internal rate of discount is high means that a large part of the yield from bonds is non-pecuniary. As cash expanded, the non-pecuniary yield from bonds would decline, to compensate for which r_B would have to fall by less than the change in the rate of decline of prices. This would make it less attractive for issuers to issue bonds, thereby producing the decline in the volume of bonds required by the change in the desired portfolios of wealth-holders.

At the optimum point, as equations (34) show, an internal rate of discount of 17 per cent requires, with our simplified assumptions, a real yield on capital of 17 per cent and hence a cost of capital of 17 per cent. Since non-pecuniary services of capital would be provided by money holdings, these costs and yields will all be monetary.

If we complicate our assumptions by introducing additional classes of securities with different degrees of risk or other characteristics, there may still remain non-pecuniary returns not completely substituted for by those from money, which would permit yields different from 17 per cent.

30. To reconcile this calculation with the hypothetical one in section VI above, note that the internal rate of discount does not enter there, but is replaced by the once-and-for-all component ($10 billion in the numerical example). This sum multiplied by the internal rate of discount is the flow counterpart to the capital sum, and is automatically included in the present calculation in the estimate of the non-pecuniary returns from money.

31. For the demand curve used to calculate the initial and terminal balances, assumption. (c) makes for a slight overestimate. For cases I and II, for which the internal rate of discount is assumed not to change, this is clear; the correct calculation involves integrating under the semi-log demand curve of footnote 29 above, replacing

$$\left(\frac{1}{P}\frac{dP}{dt}\right)^* \quad \text{by} \quad \left[.05 + \left(\frac{1}{P}\frac{dP}{dt}\right)\right]^*.$$

The result of doing so with the relevant numerical values is to make the correct multiple of F .03 rather than the .035 used in the table.

H converts the potential gains from number of weeks' personal disposable income to billions of early 1968 dollars.

Alternative Estimates of Potential Welfare Gain from
Policy Leading to Optimum Quantity of Money

	CASE			
	I	*II*	*III*	*IV*
Internal rate of discount (per cent per year)				
A. Initial	.05	.05	.33	.33
B. Terminal	.05	.05	.17	.17
C. Anticipated rate of rise of prices (per cent per year)	.02	.02	.02	.02
Quantity of money (in weeks of personal disposable income)				
D. Initial	6	10	6	10
E. Optimum	12	20	39	65
F. Increment in money $(E - D)$	6	10	33	55
Welfare gain as a flow				
G. (In weeks of personal disposable income) $\frac{1}{2}(A + C) \cdot F$	.21	.35	5.8	9.6
H. In billions of dollars per year	$2.3	$3.8	$64	$105
Welfare gain as a capital sum (billions of dollars)				
I. Capitalized at initial internal rate of discount	$46	$76	$192	$315
J. Capitalized at terminal rate			$384	$630

NOTE: All dollar figures for first quarter, 1968.

The results are clearly extremely sensitive to the assumption about the internal rate of discount. If the internal rate is as low as 5 per cent, then the potential gain, while not negligible, is minor—$2 billion to $4 billion a year—the equivalent, at this discount rate, of, say, the discovery of hitherto unknown mineral resources with a capital value of $46 to $76 billion, or an addition to national wealth of about one year's net private capital formation. On the other hand, if the internal rate of discount is as high as 33 per cent, then even though it is cut in half in the process, the potential gain is from $60 to $100 billion *per year*, equivalent, even at these high discount rates, to capital windfalls of $200 to $600 billion.

For cases III and IV, it is not possible to make the corresponding adjustment without further assumptions, because what needs to be added to $[(1/P)(dP/dt)]$* is not a constant amount but a variable one, starting at .33 at the initial quantity of money and ending at .17 at the optimum. The correct multiple depends on how this increment varies with the quantity of money.

Further evidence on the appropriate internal rate of discount is clearly essential to determine whether the potential gains are modest or mammoth.

XIV. SOME PRACTICAL CONSIDERATIONS AND CONCLUSIONS FOR POLICY

The desirable behavior of the price level has attracted the attention of economists for decades. The early literature stressed equity between debtor and creditor and frictions in adjusting to changing prices. Almost all writers favored stable prices, but some favored stable prices of final products, which meant rising prices of factor services (especially wages) in a progressive economy. Others favored stable prices of factor services, which meant declining prices of final products in a progressive economy. The first group tended to stress frictions, the second equity.

More recent literature has emphasized supposed "trade-offs" between inflation and the level of employment or growth. A considerable part of that literature compares the welfare costs of inflation and of unemployment, and seeks the point of optimum trade-off. Some writers have favored a policy of mild inflation, in the belief that this would give a higher average level of employment.

This paper has had little or no overlap with the earlier literature, but it yields, as that literature does not, a specific and potentially objective criterion for an optimum behavior of the price level.

Why this difference? The main reason is that the earlier discussion was almost entirely about *unanticipated* inflations or deflations, while this paper is mostly about *anticipated* inflations or deflations. Anticipated inflations or deflations produce no transfers from debtors to creditors which raise questions of equity; the interest rate on claims valued in nominal terms adjusts to allow for the anticipated rate of inflation. Anticipated inflations or deflations need involve no frictions in adjusting to changing prices. Every individual can take the anticipated change in the price level into account in setting prices for future trades. Finally, anticipated inflations or deflations involve no trade-offs between inflation and employment.[32] Hence these considerations do not enter the analysis.

Before the analysis can serve as a guide to practical policy, however, these considerations must be taken into account. We now operate in a world in which it is generally anticipated that prices of final products will, if anything, rise and that prices of factor services will certainly rise, and in which interest rates incorporate these expectations. Transition to a new policy would take time. Many prices are slow to adjust. Any decided change in the trend of prices would involve significant frictional distortion in employment and production.

One practical consideration, which I have so far neglected completely, but

32. See "The Role of Monetary Policy," Chapter 5 in this volume, for a fuller discussion of this issue.

which is given considerable emphasis in the earlier literature, is the literal transactions cost involved in adjusting to a changing price level. The marking up or down of all prices, whether through explicit escalator clauses or otherwise involves real costs. To some extent, these costs cannot be avoided in a progressive society in which product prices and factor prices have different trends. But the costs can be more or less.

Another extremely important practical consideration is that the optimum rate of price decline will change from time to time. It will be more difficult to judge from objective evidence when the actual rate of price decline exceeds the optimum than when it falls short of it. The reason for the asymmetry is the phenomenon underlying the Keynesian liquidity trap.[33]

These practical considerations, I believe, make it unwise to recommend as a policy objective a policy of deflation of final-product prices sufficient to yield a full optimum in the sense of this paper. The rough estimates of the preceding section indicate that that would require for the U.S. a decline in prices at the rate of at least 5 per cent per year, and perhaps decidedly more. The rapid transition to such a state, in a world in which there is a positive internal rate of discount, would, I conjecture, be inordinately costly; and once there, the chance of occasionally or often overshooting would be serious.

A policy fairly close to the optimum would probably be to hold the absolute quantity of money constant—a policy that has recommended itself on other grounds to many writers on monetary policy, notably Henry Simons. Given a growth in output at the rate of about 3 to 4 per cent a year, that policy would produce a decline in prices of about 4 to 5 per cent a year, if the real demand for money continues to rise with real income as it has on the average of the past century. According to some of the most widely used growth models, this policy would correspond to a full optimum in the capital–labor ratio as well as in the quantity of money.[34]

However, this policy, too, seems to me too drastic to be desirable in the near future although it might very well serve as a long-term objective. A more limited policy objective might be to stabilize the price of factor services. If the real demand for cash balances had a unitary income elasticity, this would require for the U.S. a rise in the quantity of money of about 1 per cent per year, to match the growth in population and labor force. If the elasticity exceeds unity as much as it has during the past century, this would require a rise in the quantity of money at the rate of about 2 per cent per year.

33. To put it in other terms, as the actual rate of price decrease exceeds the optimum, r_B will tend to be negative. However, it seems likely that the costs of holding cash ($-MNPS_M$), while they will increase with the real quantity of money, will increase only very slowly—that there will be a very high elasticity of demand for real cash balances in this range. In that case, r_B will be only a very small negative number and will not vary much with wide variations in the rate of price decline. Hence, it will be difficult to determine when r_B is approximately equal to zero.

34. See Harry G. Johnson, *Essays in Monetary Economics*, London: Allen and Unwin 1967), p. 170.

This compromise is especially appealing because the major costs of price change and the major price rigidities are for factor services. The decline in the price of products relative to factor services reflects largely technological change which alters the form and character of products and so requires changes in individual prices, whatever may be happening to the price level as a whole.

While there would be some transitional problems in moving to such a policy, they would not, I believe, be serious, though that judgment will require change if the recent trends of U.S. policy continue much longer. From 1956 to 1966 as a whole, for example, we were probably reasonably close to a stable final product price on the average, if allowance is made for the bias in the consumer price index because of inadequate inclusion of quality changes. To go from such a policy to a decline in final product prices at the rate of about 2 per cent per year would not seem to involve major frictional costs. However, we seem headed for an upward price trend in final products at a rate of 3 per cent to 5 per cent a year in the relatively near future. To go from such a trend to the suggested declining price level would involve far more serious transitional costs.

Finally, the analysis has implications for aspects of financial policy other than the rate of growth in the quantity of money. The analysis in this paper strongly argues against the present prohibition on the payment of interest by commercial banks on demand deposits and in favor of payment of interest by the Federal Reserve System on bank reserves held in the form of deposits at Federal Reserve Banks—measures that I have long favored for the reasons advanced in this paper.[35] If feasible, it would be desirable to extend the payment of interest to vault cash held by commercial banks. These measures, by enabling holders of money to receive interest on the greater part of their holdings, would go far to remove the discrepancy between the apparent cost to the individual of holding money balances and the real cost to all together of doing so.

The analysis supports also the desirability of minimizing restriction of entry into banking. Free entry would promote competition and thereby bring the interest paid on deposits closer to the nominal yield on physical capital.

XV. A FINAL SCHIZOPHRENIC NOTE

The reader who knows something about my earlier work will recognize that the policy with respect to the quantity of money outlined in the preceding section is different from the policy I have long advocated. I have favored increasing the quantity of money at a steady rate designed to keep final product prices constant, a rate that I have estimated to be something like 4 to 5 per cent per year for the U.S. for a monetary total defined to include currency outside of banks and all deposits of commercial banks, demand and time.

I do not want to gloss over the real contradiction between these two policies,

35. See Milton Friedman, *A Program for Monetary Stability*, New York: Fordham University Press (1959).

between what for simplicity I shall call the 5 per cent and the 2 per cent rules, There are two reasons for this contradiction. One is that the 5 per cent rule was constructed with an eye primarily to short-run considerations, whereas the 2 per cent rule puts more emphasis on long-run considerations. The more basic reason is that I had not worked out in full the analysis presented in this paper when I came out for the 5 per cent rule. I simply took it for granted, in line with a long tradition and a near-consensus in the profession, that a stable level of prices of final products was a desirable policy objective. Had I been fully aware then of the analysis of this paper, I suspect that I would have come out for the 2 per cent rule.

One extenuating circumstance is that, in presenting the 5 per cent rule, I have always emphasized that a *steady* and known rate of increase in the quantity of money is more important than the precise numerical value of the rate of increase. The work I have done since, both theoretical and empirical, has reinforced that belief. Either a 5 per cent rule or a 2 per cent rule would be far superior to the monetary policy we have actually followed. The gain from shifting to the 5 per cent rule would, I believe, dwarf the further gain from going to the 2 per cent rule, even though that gain may well be substantial enough to be worth pursuing. Hence I shall continue to support the 5 per cent rule as an intermediate objective greatly superior to present practice.

APPENDIX

A MODEL OF TIME PREFERENCE

For the model that follows, we treat the individual as simultaneously supplier of resource services, organizer of production, consumer, and ultimate wealth-holder. That is, there are no enterprises, and no financial assets such as bonds or equities, though there is money.

We shall consider an individual as owning four kinds of capital assets:

1. Physical productive capital
2. Human productive capital
3. Physical consumption capital
4. Human consumption capital

The first three are self-explanatory. Only the fourth requires further elaboration. Just as an individual can invest in his capacity to produce goods and services (i.e., in human productive capital), so he can invest in his capacity to derive utility. For example, that is what he does when he takes piano lessons, or lessons in musical appreciation: he is building up his future capacity to derive utility,

The idea of the present model is to generalize this notion. Thus I shall assume that the individual's flow of utility at any time depends solely on the *stocks* at that time of items (3) and (4). What is ordinarily regarded as consumption, we shall regard as either maintenance of human consumption capital or addition to such capital. For example, expenditure on going to the movie is regarded as expenditure for the maintenance or building up of capital in the form of a stock of memories of movies seen. The stock may depreciate very rapidly, in which case, for example, for some individuals, it may require going to one movie a week to keep the stock constant, but the utility derived from the stock is regarded as not concentrated at the moment of paying for the movie ticket, or even during the time of seeing the movie, but as derived at a steady rate so long as the stock is maintained.

This way of looking at the matter has by now become conventional with item (3), physical consumption capital. We do not regard utility as derived from the *purchase* of an automobile but from the flow of services from the stock owned.

Extending this notion to the consumption of what we usually regard as services (e.g., viewing a movie) seems not only "natural" on a theoretical level, but also has intuitive appeal. The "travel now, pay later" ads do correspond to a real human condition: the vacation we take now will yield its returns later. Indeed, it may yield disutilities when taken, suffered for the utility derived later from reviewing memories, viewing slides, and boring friends. The child's music lesson is a clear case in point.

On this view, the individual gets an income from items (1) and (2), all of which is used either to maintain the four stocks or to increase them.

There exist production functions describing the transformation possibilities: between (a) the stock of productive capital and (b) the stocks of (1), (2), (3). and (4) that can be maintained and the rates at which they can be increased. Let C_1, C_2, C_3, C_4 stand for the stock of capital of each kind. Then there exists some transformation function of the form:

$$\left(C_1,\ C_2,\ C_3,\ C_4,\ \frac{1}{C_1}\frac{C_1}{dt},\ \frac{1}{C_2}\frac{dC_2}{dt},\ \frac{1}{C_3}\frac{dC_3}{dt},\ \frac{1}{C_4}\frac{dC_4}{dt}\right)=0.$$

There exists a utility function describing the current utility yield from C_3 and C_4:

$$U(t)=U[C_3(t),\ C_4(t)],$$

and also some function relating future utilities to present.

Let there be no time preference among utilities, i.e., the individual seeks to maximize $\int_T U(t)\ dt$. This is the usual assumption about "rationality" discussed above.

When I initially elaborated this model, I thought it gave a reason for observed time preference even when C_1, C_2, C_3, and C_4 were stationary, with physical capital having a positive yield. Kenneth Arrow pointed out my mistake and persuaded me that the model only gives a reason for time preference, so long as capital is productive, along a growth path.

It may help to bring out the implications of the model if I give my initial interpretation and then Arrow's rectification of it.

Consider, I said, stocks of C_1, C_2, C_3, and C_4 such that the yield from C_1 and C_2 is just sufficient to enable the consumer to maintain C_3 and C_4 constant. At this point, suppose that he contemplates cutting down "consumption" to add, say, to C_1. Then, I said, the increased yield from C_1 will enable him to have higher consumption later, but to get it he must cut down on either C_3 or C_4, which will involve lower consumption later. For example, perhaps he gives up a music lesson worth a dollar which will enable him to increase his productive capital so that it yields him an extra income of 5 cents a year indefinitely. If, however, giving up the music lesson reduces his future utility by an amount he values at 5 cents a year indefinitely, he has gained nothing. He has only changed the form of consumption. Thus, I argued, there is a reason for what appears to be time preference even though the individual does not discount future utilities. It is a requirement for balance of different capital stocks.

If the individual is in the position described, and *if* reductions in C_3 and C_4 are ruled out, the argument just made is entirely valid. But, as Arrow pointed out, these are big if's. So long as (a) C_1 and C_2 are productive in the sense that increments yield more than enough to maintain the increments, (b) C_3 and C_4 can be added to, and (c) they are not at satiety levels, the "rational" individual will never be in the position described or if, by mistake, he were, he would move away from it by reducing C_3 and C_4.

By assumption, if he stays at the position described he cannot increase C_3 and C_4. But if he reduces them, he can add to C_1 and C_2, which will enable him later to achieve and then surpass the initial C_3 and C_4. He will therefore only temporarily reduce his stock of consumption capital. Since he does not discount utilities, it will pay him to run down his stock of consumption capital for the future gain.

In short, in this model as in the more usual one, there can be equilibrium only with a balanced growth path in which apparent time preference, imposed by the rising level of consumption, sets a limit to the rate of growth.

Chapter 2

The Quantity Theory of Money:
A Restatement

THE QUANTITY THEORY of money is a term evocative of a general approach
rather than a label for a well-defined theory. The exact content of the approach
varies from a truism defining the term "velocity" to an allegedly rigid and
unchanging ratio between the quantity of money—defined in one way or
another—and the price level—also defined in one way or another. Whatever
its precise meaning, it is clear that the general approach fell into disrepute after
the crash of 1929 and the subsequent Great Depression and only recently has
been slowly re-emerging into professional respectability.

The present volume [*Studies in the Quantity Theory of Money*] is partly a
symptom of this re-emergence and partly a continuance of an aberrant tradition.
Chicago was one of the few academic centers at which the quantity theory
continued to be a central and vigorous part of the oral tradition throughout the
1930's and 1940's, where students continued to study monetary theory and to
write theses on monetary problems. The quantity theory that retained this role
differed sharply from the atrophied and rigid caricature that is so frequently
described by the proponents of the new income-expenditure approach—and
with some justice, to judge by much of the literature on policy that was
spawned by quantity theorists. At Chicago, Henry Simons and Lloyd Mints

Reprinted from Milton Friedman (Ed.), *Studies in the Quantity Theory of Money*, Chicago:
University of Chicago Press (1956).

directly, Frank Knight and Jacob Viner at one remove, taught and developed a more subtle and relevant version, one in which the quantity theory was connected and integrated with general price theory and became a flexible and sensitive tool for interpreting movements in aggregate economic activity and for developing relevant policy prescriptions.

To the best of my knowledge, no systematic statement of this theory as developed at Chicago exists, though much can be read between the lines of Simons' and Mints's writings. And this is as it should be, for the Chicago tradition was not a rigid system, an unchangeable orthodoxy, but a way of looking at things. It was a theoretical approach that insisted that money does matter—that any interpretation of short-term movements in economic activity is likely to be seriously at fault if it neglects monetary changes and repercussions and if it leaves unexplained why people are willing to hold the particular nominal quantity of money in existence.

The purpose of this introduction is not to enshrine—or, should I say, inter— a definitive version of the Chicago tradition. To suppose that one could do so would be inconsistent with that tradition itself. The purpose is rather to set down a particular "model" of a quantity theory in an attempt to convey the flavor of the oral tradition which nurtured the remaining essays in this volume [*Studies in the Quantity Theory of Money*]. In consonance with this purpose, I shall not attempt to be exhaustive or to give a full justification for every assertion.

1. The quantity theory is in the first instance a theory of the *demand* for money. It is not a theory of output, or of money income, or of the price level. Any statement about these variables requires combining the quantity theory with some specifications about the conditions of supply of money and perhaps about other variables as well.

2. To the ultimate wealth-owning units in the economy, money is one kind of asset, one way of holding wealth. To the productive enterprise, money is a capital good, a source of productive services that are combined with other productive services to yield the products that the enterprise sells. Thus the theory of the demand for money is a special topic in the theory of capital; as such, it has the rather unusual feature of combining a piece from each side of the capital market, the supply of capital (points 3 through 8 that follow), and the demand for capital (points 9 through 12).

3. The analysis of the demand for money on the part of the ultimate wealth-owning units in the society can be made formally identical with that of the demand for a consumption service. As in the usual theory of consumer choice, the demand for money (or any other particular asset) depends on three major sets of factors: (*a*) the total wealth to be held in various forms—the analogue of the budget restraint; (*b*) the price of and return on this form of wealth and alternative forms; and (*c*) the tastes and preferences of the wealth-owning units. The substantive differences from the analysis of the demand for a consumption service are the necessity of taking account of intertemporal rates of substitution in (*b*) and (*c*) and of casting the budget restraint in terms of wealth.

4. From the broadest and most general point of view, total wealth includes all sources of "income" or consumable services. One such source is the productive capacity of human beings, and accordingly this is one form in which wealth can be held. From this point of view, "the" rate of interest expresses the relation between the stock which is wealth and the flow which is income, so if Y be the total flow of income, and r, "the" interest rate, total wealth is

$$W = \frac{Y}{r}. \tag{1}$$

Income in this broadest sense should not be identified with income as it is ordinarily measured. The latter is generally a "gross" stream with respect to human beings, since no deduction is made for the expense of maintaining human productive capacity intact; in addition, it is affected by transitory elements that make it depart more or less widely from the theoretical concept of the stable level of consumption of services that could be maintained indefinitely.

5. Wealth can be held in numerous forms, and the ultimate wealth-owning unit is to be regarded as dividing his wealth among them (point [a] of 3), so as to maximize "utility" (point [c] of 3), subject to whatever restrictions affect the possibility of converting one form of wealth into another (point [b] of 3). As usual, this implies that he will seek an apportionment of his wealth such that the rate at which he *can* substitute one form of wealth for another is equal to the rate at which he is just willing to do so. But this general proposition has some special features in the present instance because of the necessity of considering flows as well as stocks. We can suppose all wealth (except wealth in the form of the productive capacity of human beings) to be expressed in terms of monetary units at the prices at the point of time in question. The rate at which one form can be substituted for another is then simply $1 worth for $1 worth, regardless of the forms involved. But this is clearly not a complete description, because the holding of one form of wealth instead of another involves a difference in the composition of the income stream, and it is essentially these differences that are fundamental to the "utility" of a particular structure of wealth. In consequence, to describe fully the alternative combinations of forms of wealth that are available to an individual, we must take account not only of their market prices—which except for human wealth can be done simply by expressing them in units worth $1—but also of the form and size of the income streams they yield.

It will suffice to bring out the major issues that these considerations raise to consider five different forms in which wealth can be held: (i) money (M), interpreted as claims or commodity units that are generally accepted in payment of debts at a fixed nominal value; (ii) bonds (B), interpreted as claims to time streams of payments that are fixed in nominal units; (iii) equities (E), interpreted as claims to stated pro-rata shares of the returns of enterprises; (iv) physical non-human goods (G); and (v) human capital (H). Consider now the yield of each.

(i) Money may yield a return in the form of money, for example, interest on demand deposits. It will simplify matters, however, and entail no essential loss of generality, to suppose that money yields its return solely in kind, in the usual form of convenience, security, etc. The magnitude of this return in "real" terms per nominal unit of money clearly depends on the volume of goods that unit corresponds to, or on the general price level, which we may designate by P. Since we have decided to take \$1 worth as the unit for each form of wealth, this will be equally true for other forms of wealth as well, so P is a variable affecting the "real" yield of each.

(ii) If we take the "standard" bond to be a claim to a perpetual income stream of constant nominal amount, then the return to a holder of the bond can take two forms: one, the annual sum he receives—the "coupon"; the other, any change in the price of the bond over time, a return which may of course be positive or negative. If the price is expected to remain constant, then \$1 worth of a bond yields r_b per year, where r_b is simply the "coupon" sum divided by the market price of the bond, so $1/r_b$ is the price of a bond promising to pay \$1 per year. We shall call r_b the market bond interest rate. If the price is expected to change, then the yield cannot be calculated so simply, since it must take account of the return in the form of expected appreciation or depreciation of the bond, and it cannot, like r_b, be calculated directly from market prices (so long, at least, as the "standard" bond is the only one traded in).

The nominal income stream purchased for \$1 at time zero then consists of

$$r_b(0) + r_b(0)\frac{d[1/r_b(t)]}{dt} = r_b(0) - \frac{r_b(0)}{r_b^2(t)} \cdot \frac{dr_b(t)}{dt}, \tag{2}$$

where t stands for time. For simplicity, we can approximate this functional by its value at time zero, which is

$$r_b - \frac{1}{r_b}\frac{dr_b}{dt}. \tag{3}$$

This sum, together with P already introduced, defines the real return from holding \$1 of wealth in the form of bonds.

(iii) Analogously to our treatment of bonds, we may take the "standard" unit of equity to be a claim to a perpetual income stream of constant "real" amount; that is, to be a standard bond with a purchasing-power escalator clause, so that it promises a perpetual income stream equal in nominal units to a constant number times a price index, which we may, for convenience, take to be the same price index P introduced in (i).[1] The nominal return to the holder of the equity can then be regarded as taking three forms: the constant nominal amount he would receive per year in the absence of any change in P; the increment or decrement to this nominal amount to adjust for changes in P; and any change in the nominal price of the equity over time, which may of course arise from changes either in interest rates or in price levels. Let r_e be the market interest rate

1. This is an oversimplification, because it neglects "leverage" and therefore supposes that any monetary liabilities of an enterprise are balanced by monetary assets.

on equities defined analogously to r_b, namely, as the ratio of the "coupon" sum at any time (the first two items above) to the price of the equity, so $1/r_e$ is the price of an equity promising to pay \$1 per year if the price level does not change or to pay

$$\frac{P(t)}{P(0)} \cdot 1$$

if the price level varies according to $P(t)$. If $r_e(t)$ is defined analogously, the price of the bond selling for $1/r_e(0)$ at time 0 will be

$$\frac{P(t)}{P(0)\,r_e(t)}$$

at time t, where the ratio of prices is required to adjust for any change in the price level. The nominal stream purchased for \$1 at time zero then consists of

$$r_e(0) \cdot \frac{P(t)}{P(0)} + \frac{r_e(0)}{P(0)} \cdot \frac{d[P(t)/r_e(t)]}{dt} = r_e(0) \cdot \frac{P(t)}{P(0)}$$
$$+ \frac{r_e(0)}{r_e(t)} \cdot \frac{1}{P(0)} \cdot \frac{dP(t)}{dt} - \frac{P(t)}{P(0)} \cdot \frac{r_e(0)}{r_e^2(t)} \cdot \frac{dr_e(t)}{dt}. \tag{4}$$

Once again we can approximate this functional by its value at time zero, which is

$$r_e + \frac{1}{P}\frac{dP}{dt} - \frac{1}{r_e}\frac{dr_e}{dt}. \tag{5}$$

This sum, together with P already introduced, defines the "real" return from holding \$1 of wealth in the form of equities.

(iv) Physical goods held by ultimate wealth-owning units are similar to equities except that the annual stream they yield is in kind rather than in money. In terms of nominal units, this return, like that from equities, depends on the behavior of prices. In addition, like equities, physical goods must be regarded as yielding a nominal return in the form of appreciation or depreciation in money value. If we suppose the price level P, introduced earlier, to apply equally to the value of these physical goods, then, at time zero,

$$\frac{1}{P}\frac{dP}{dt} \tag{6}$$

is the size of this nominal return per \$1 of physical goods.[2] Together with P, it defines the "real" return from holding \$1 in the form of physical goods.

2. In principle, it might be better to let P refer solely to the value of the services of physical goods, which is essentially what it refers to in the preceding cases, and to allow for the fact that the prices of the capital goods themselves must vary also with the rate of capitalization, so that the prices of services and their sources vary at the same rate only if the relevant interest rate is constant. I have neglected this refinement for simplicity; the neglect can perhaps be justified by the rapid depreciation of many of the physical goods held by final wealth-owning units.

(v) Since there is only a limited market in human capital, at least in modern non-slave societies, we cannot very well define in market prices the terms of substitution of human capital for other forms of capital and so cannot define at any time the physical unit of capital corresponding to $1 of human capital. There are some possibilities of substituting non-human capital for human capital in an individual's wealth holdings, as, for example, when he enters into a contract to render personal services for a specified period in return for a definitely specified number of periodic payments, the number not depending on his being physically capable of rendering the services. But, in the main, shifts between human capital and other forms must take place through direct investment and disinvestment in the human agent, and we may as well treat this as if it were the only way. With respect to this form of capital, therefore, the restriction or obstacles affecting the alternative compositions of wealth available to the individual cannot be expressed in terms of market prices or rates of return. At any one point in time there is some division between human and non-human wealth in his portfolio of assets; he may be able to change this over time, but we shall treat it as given at a point in time. Let w be the ratio of non-human to human wealth or, equivalently, of income from non-human wealth to income from human wealth, which means that it is closely allied to what is usually defined as the ratio of wealth to income. This is, then, the variable that needs to be taken into account so far as human wealth is concerned.

6. The tastes and preferences of wealth-owning units for the service streams arising from different forms of wealth must in general simply be taken for granted as determining the form of the demand function. In order to give the theory empirical content, it will generally have to be supposed that tastes are constant over significant stretches of space and time. However, explicit allowance can be made for some changes in tastes in so far as such changes are linked with objective circumstances. For example, it seems reasonable that, other things being the same, individuals want to hold a larger fraction of their wealth in the form of money when they are moving around geographically or are subject to unusual uncertainty than otherwise. This is probably one of the major factors explaining a frequent tendency for money holdings to rise relative to income during wartime. But the extent of geographic movement, and perhaps of other kinds of uncertainty, can be represented by objective indexes, such as indexes of migration, miles of railroad travel, and the like. Let u stand for any such variables that can be expected to affect tastes and preferences (for "utility" determining variables).

7. Combining 4, 5, and 6 along the lines suggested by 3 yields the following demand function for money:

$$M = f\left(P, r_b - \frac{1}{r_b}\frac{dr_b}{dt}, r_e + \frac{1}{P}\frac{dP}{dt} - \frac{1}{r_e}\frac{dr_e}{dt}, \frac{1}{P}\frac{dP}{dt}; w; \frac{Y}{r}; u\right). \tag{7}$$

A number of observations are in order about this function.

(i) Even if we suppose prices and rates of interest to be unchanged, the function contains three rates of interest: two for specific types of assets, r_b and r_e, and one intended to apply to all types of assets, r. This general rate, r, is to be interpreted as something of a weighted average of the two special rates plus the rates applicable to human wealth and to physical goods. Since the last two cannot be observed directly, it is perhaps best to regard them as varying in some systematic way with r_b and r_e. On this assumption, we can drop r as an additional explicit variable, treating its influence as fully taken into account by the inclusion of r_b and r_e.

(ii) If there were no differences of opinion about price movements and interest-rate movements, and bonds and equities were equivalent except that the former are expressed in nominal units, arbitrage would of course make

$$r_b - \frac{1}{r_b}\frac{dr_b}{dt} = r_e + \frac{1}{P}\frac{dP}{dt} - \frac{1}{r_e}\frac{dr_e}{dt}, \tag{8}$$

or, if we suppose rates of interest to be either stable or changing at the same percentage rate,

$$r_b = r_e + \frac{1}{P}\frac{dP}{dt}, \tag{9}$$

that is, the "money" interest rate equal to the "real" rate plus the percentage rate of change of prices. In application the rate of change of prices must be interpreted as an "expected" rate of change and differences of opinion cannot be neglected, so we cannot suppose (9) to hold; indeed, one of the most consistent features of inflation seems to be that it does not.[3]

(iii) If the range of assets were to be widened to include promises to pay specified sums for a finite number of time units—"short-term" securities as well as "consols"—the rates of change of r_b and r_e would be reflected in the difference between long and short rates of interest. Since at some stage it will doubtless be desirable to introduce securities of different time duration (see point 23 below), we may simplify the present exposition by restricting it to the case in which r_b and r_e are taken to be stable over time. Since the rate of change in prices is required separately in any event, this means that we can replace the cumbrous variables introduced to designate the nominal return on bonds and equities simply by r_b and r_e.

(iv) Y can be interpreted as including the return to all forms of wealth, including money and physical capital goods owned and held directly by ultimate wealth-owning units, and so Y/r can be interpreted as an estimate of total wealth, only if Y is regarded as including some imputed income from the stock of money and directly owned physical capital goods. For monetary analysis the simplest procedure is perhaps to regard Y as referring to the return to all forms of wealth other than the money held directly by ultimate wealth-owning units, and so to regard Y/r as referring to total remaining wealth.

3. See Reuben Kessel, "Inflation: Theory of Wealth Distribution ,and Application in Private Investment Policy" (unpublished doctoral dissertation, University of Chicago).

8. A more fundamental point is that, as in all demand analyses resting on maximization of a utility function defined in terms of "real" magnitudes, this demand equation must be considered independent in any essential way of the nominal units used to measure money variables. If the unit in which prices and money income are expressed is changed, the amount of money demanded should change proportionately. More technically, equation (7) must be regarded as homogeneous of the first degree in P and Y, so that

$$f\left(\lambda P, r_b, r_e, \frac{1}{P}\frac{dP}{dt}; w; \lambda Y; u\right) = \lambda f\left(P, r_b, r_e, \frac{1}{P}\frac{dP}{dt}; w; Y; u\right). \tag{10}$$

where the variables within the parentheses have been rewritten in simpler form in accordance with comments 7 (i) and 7 (iii).

This characteristic of the function enables us to rewrite it in two alternative and more familiar ways.

(i) Let $\lambda = 1/P$. Equation (7) can then be written

$$\frac{M}{P} = f\left(r_b, r_e, \frac{1}{P}\frac{dP}{dt}; w; \frac{Y}{P}; u\right) \tag{11}$$

In this form the equation expresses the demand for real balances as a function of "real" variables independent of nominal monetary values.

(ii) Let $\lambda = 1/Y$. Equation (7) can then be written

$$\frac{M}{Y} = f\left(r_b, r_e, \frac{1}{P}\frac{dP}{dt}, w, \frac{P}{Y}, u\right) = 1 \Big/ v\left(r_b, r_e, \frac{1}{P}\frac{dP}{dt}, w, \frac{Y}{P}, u\right) \tag{12}$$

or

$$Y = v\left(r_b, r_e, \frac{1}{P}\frac{dP}{dt}, w, \frac{Y}{P}, u\right)M. \tag{13}$$

In this form the equation is in the usual quantity theory form, where v is income velocity.

9. These equations are, to this point, solely for money held directly by ultimate wealth-owning units. As noted, money is also held by business enterprises as a productive resource. The counterpart to this business asset in the balance sheet of an ultimate wealth-owning unit is a claim other than money. For example, an individual may buy bonds from a corporation, and the corporation use the proceeds to finance the money holdings which it needs for its operations. Of course, the usual difficulties of separating the accounts of the business and its owner arise with unincorporated enterprises.

10. The amount of money that it pays business enterprises to hold depends, as for any other source of productive services, on the cost of the productive services, the cost of substitute productive services, and the value product yielded by the productive service. Per dollar of money held, the cost depends on how the corresponding capital is raised—whether by raising additional capital in the form of bonds or equities, by substituting cash for real capital goods, etc. These

ways of financing money holdings are much the same as the alternative forms in which the ultimate wealth-owning unit can hold its non-human wealth, so that the variables r_b, r_e, P, and $(1/P)(dP/dt)$ introduced into (7) can be taken to represent the cost to the business enterprise of holding money. For some purposes, however, it may be desirable to distinguish between the rate of return received by the lender and the rate paid by the borrower, in which case it would be necessary to introduce an additional set of variables.

Substitutes for money as a productive service are numerous and varied, including all ways of economizing on money holdings by using other resources to synchronize more closely payments and receipts, reduce payment periods, extend use of book credit, establish clearing arrangements, and so on in infinite variety. There seem no particularly close substitutes whose prices deserve to be singled out for inclusion in the business demand for money.

The value product yielded by the productive services of money per unit of output depends on production conditions: the production function. It is likely to be especially dependent on features of production conditions affecting the smoothness and regularity of operations as well as on those determining the size and scope of enterprises, degree of vertical integration, etc. Again there seem no variables that deserve to be singled out on the present level of abstraction for special attention; these factors can be taken into account by interpreting u as including variables affecting not only the tastes of wealth-owners but also the relevant technological conditions of production. Given the amount of money demanded per unit of output, the total amount demanded is proportional to total output, which can be represented by Y.

11. One variable that has traditionally been singled out in considering the demand for money on the part of business enterprises is the volume of trans-actions, or of transactions per dollar of final products; and, of course, emphasis on transactions has been carried over to the ultimate wealth-owning unit as well as to the business enterprise. The idea that renders this approach attractive is that there is a mechanical link between a dollar of payments per unit time and the average stock of money required to effect it—a fixed technical coefficient of production, as it were. It is clear that this mechanical approach is very different in spirit from the one we have been following. On our approach, the average amount of money held per dollar of transactions is itself to be regarded as a resultant of an economic equilibrating process, not as a physical datum. If, for whatever reason, it becomes more expensive to hold money, then it is worth devoting resources to effecting money transactions in less expensive ways or to reducing the volume of transactions per dollar of final output. In consequence, our ultimate demand function for money in its most general form does not contain as a variable the volume of transactions or of transactions per dollar of final output; it contains rather those more basic technical and cost conditions that affect the costs of conserving money, be it by changing the average amount of money held per dollar of transactions per unit time or by changing the num-ber of dollars of transactions per dollar of final output. This does not, of course,

exclude the possibility that, for a particular problem, it may be useful to regard the transactions variables as given and not to dig beneath them and so to include the volume of transactions per dollar of final output as an explicit variable in a special variant of the demand function.

Similar remarks are relevant to various features of payment conditions, frequently described as "institutional conditions," affecting the velocity of circulation of money and taken as somehow mechanically determined—such items as whether workers are paid by the day, or week, or month; the use of book credit; and so on. On our approach these, too, are to be regarded as resultants of an economic equilibrating process, not as physical data. Lengthening the pay period, for example, may save book-keeping and other costs to the employer, who is therefore willing to pay somewhat more than in proportion for a longer than a shorter pay period; on the other hand, it imposes on employees the cost of holding larger cash balances or providing substitutes for cash, and they therefore want to be paid more than in proportion for a longer pay period. Where these will balance depends on how costs vary with length of pay period. The cost to the employee depends in considerable part on the factors entering into his demand curve for money for a fixed pay period. If he would in any event be holding relatively large average balances, the additional costs imposed by a lengthened pay period tend to be less than if he were holding relatively small average balances, and so it will take less of an inducement to get him to accept a longer pay period. For given cost savings to the employer, therefore, the pay period can be expected to be longer in the first case than in the second. Surely, the increase in the average cash balance that has occurred for other reasons over the past century in this country has been a factor producing a lengthening of pay periods and not the other way around. Or, again, experience in hyperinflations shows how rapidly payment practices change under the impact of drastic changes in the cost of holding money.[3a]

12. The upshot of these considerations is that the demand for money on the part of business enterprises can be regarded as expressed by a function of the same kind as equation (7), with the same variables on the right-hand side. And, like (7), since the analysis is based on informed maximization of returns by enterprises, only "real" quantities matter, so it must be homogeneous of the first degree in Y and P. In consequence, we can interpret (7) and its variants (11) and (13) as describing the demand for money on the part of a business enterprise as well as on the part of an ultimate wealth-owning unit, provided only that we broaden our interpretation of u.

13. Strictly speaking, the equations (7), (11), and (13) are for an individual wealth-owning unit or business enterprise. If we aggregate (7) for all wealth-owning units and business enterprises in the society, the result, in principle,

3a. Hans Neisser has expressed the view to me since this article was first published that this sentence overstates the rapidity with which payment practices change. In the German hyperinflation after World War I, he points out, payment practices did change drastically, but only near the end of the hyperinflation, i.e., after several years of very rapid inflation.

depends on the distribution of the units by the several variables. This raises no serious problem about P, r_b and r_e, for these can be taken as the same for all, or about u, for this is an unspecified portmanteau variable to be filled in as the occasion demands. We have been interpreting $(1/P)(dP/dt)$ as the expected rate of price rise, so there is no reason why this variable should be the same for all, and w and Y clearly differ substantially among units. An approximation is to neglect these difficulties and take (7) and the associated (11) and (13) as applying to the aggregate demand for money, with $(1/P)(dP/dt)$ interpreted as some kind of an average expected rate of change of prices, w as the ratio of total income from non-human wealth to income from human wealth, and Y as aggregate income. This is the procedure that has generally been followed, and it seems the right one until serious departures between this linear approximation and experience make it necessary to introduce measures of dispersion with respect to one or more of the variables.

14. It is perhaps worth noting explicitly that the model does not use the distinction between "active balances" and "idle balances" or the closely allied distinction between "transaction balances" and "speculative balances" that is so widely used in the literature. The distinction between money holdings of ultimate wealth-owners and of business enterprises is related to this distinction but only distantly so. Each of these categories of money-holders can be said to demand money partly from "transaction" motives, partly from "speculative" or "asset" motives, but dollars of money are not distinguished according as they are said to be held for one or the other purpose. Rather, each dollar is, as it were, regarded as rendering a variety of services, and the holder of money as altering his money holdings until the value to him of the addition to the total flow of services produced by adding a dollar to his money stock is equal to the reduction in the flow of services produced by subtracting a dollar from each of the other forms in which he holds assets.

15. Nothing has been said above about "banks" or producers of money. This is because their main role is in connection with the supply of money rather than the demand for it. Their introduction does, however, blur some of the points in the above analysis: the existence of banks enables productive enterprises to acquire money balances without raising capital from ultimate wealth-owners. Instead of selling claims (bonds or equities) to them, it can sell its claims to banks, getting "money" in exchange: in the phrase that was once so common in textbooks on money, the bank coins specific liabilities into generally acceptable liabilities. But this possibility does not alter the preceding analysis in any essential way.

16. Suppose the supply of money in nominal units is regarded as fixed or more generally autonomously determined. Equation (13) then defines the conditions under which this nominal stock of money will be the amount demanded. Even under these conditions, equation (13) alone is not sufficient to determine money income. In order to have a complete model for the determination of money income, it would be necessary to specify the determinants of the structure

of interest rates, of real income, and of the path of adjustment in the price level. Even if we suppose interest rates determined independently—by productivity, thrift, and the like—and real income as also given by other forces, equation (13) only determines a unique equilibrium level of money income if we mean by this the level at which prices are stable. More generally, it determines a time path of money income for given initial values of money income.

In order to convert equation (13) into a "complete" model of income determination, therefore, it is necessary to suppose either that the demand for money is highly inelastic with respect to the variables in v or that all these variables are to be taken as rigid and fixed.

17. Even under the most favorable conditions, for example, that the demand for money is quite inelastic with respect to the variables in v, equation (13) gives at most a theory of money income: it then says that changes in money income mirror changes in the nominal quantity of money. But it tells nothing about how much of any change in Y is reflected in real output and how much in prices. To infer this requires bringing in outside information, as, for example, that real output is at its feasible maximum, in which case any increase in money would produce the same or a larger percentage increase in prices; and so on.

18. In light of the preceding exposition, the question arises what it means to say that someone is or is not a "quantity theorist". Almost every economist will accept the general lines of the preceding analysis on a purely formal and abstract level, although each would doubtless choose to express it differently in detail. Yet there clearly are deep and fundamental differences about the importance of this analysis for the understanding of short- and long-term movements in general economic activity. This difference of opinion arises with respect to three different issues: (i) the stability and importance of the demand function for money; (ii) the independence of the factors affecting demand and supply; and (iii) the form of the demand function or related functions.

(i) The quantity theorist accepts the empirical hypothesis that the demand for money is highly stable—more stable than functions such as the consumption function that are offered as alternative key relations. This hypothesis needs to be hedged on both sides. On the one side, the quantity theorist need not, and generally does not, mean that the real quantity of money demanded per unit of output, or the velocity of circulation of money, is to be regarded as numerically constant over time; he does not, for example, regard it as a contradiction to the stability of the demand for money that the velocity of circulation of money rises drastically during hyperinflations. For the stability he expects is in the functional relation between the quantity of money demanded and the variables that determine it, and the sharp rise in the velocity of circulation of money during hyperinflations is entirely consistent with a stable functional relation, as Cagan so clearly demonstrates in his essay.[4] On the other side, the quantity theorist must sharply limit, and be prepared to specify explicitly, the variables that it is

4. Phillip Cagan, "The Monetary Dynamics of Hyperinflation," in Friedman (Ed.), *Studies in the Quantity Theory of Money*, pp. 25–117.

empirically important to include in the function. For to expand the number of variables regarded as significant is to empty the hypothesis of its empirical content; there is indeed little if any difference between asserting that the demand for money is highly unstable and asserting that it is a perfectly stable function of an indefinitely large number of variables.

The quantity theorist not only regards the demand function for money as stable; he also regards it as playing a vital role in determining variables that he considers of great importance for the analysis of the economy as a whole, such as the level of money income or of prices. It is this that leads him to put greater emphasis on the demand for money than on, let us say, the demand for pins, even though the latter might be as stable as the former. It is not easy to state this point precisely, and I cannot pretend to have done so. (See item [iii] below for an example of an argument against the quantity theorist along these lines.)

The reaction against the quantity theory in the 1930's came largely, I believe, under this head. The demand for money, it was asserted, is a will-o'-the-wisp, shifting erratically and unpredictably with every rumor and expectation; one cannot, it was asserted, reliably specify a limited number of variables on which it depends. However, although the reaction came under this head, it was largely rationalized under the two succeeding heads.

(ii) The quantity theorist also holds that there are important factors affecting the supply of money that do not affect the demand for money. Under some circumstances these are technical conditions affecting the supply of specie; under others, political or psychological conditions determining the policies of monetary authorities and the banking system. A stable demand function is useful precisely in order to trace out the effects of changes in supply, which means that it is useful only if supply is affected by at least some factors other than those regarded as affecting demand.

The classical version of the objection under this head to the quantity theory is the so-called real-bills doctrine: that changes in the demand for money call forth corresponding changes in supply and that supply cannot change otherwise, or at least cannot do so under specified institutional arrangements. The forms which this argument takes are legion and are still widespread. Another version is the argument that the "quantity theory" cannot "explain" large price rises, because the price rise produced both the increase in demand for nominal money holdings and the increase in supply of money to meet it; that is, implicitly that the same forces affect both the demand for and the supply of money, and in the same way.

(iii) The attack on the quantity theory associated with the Keynesian underemployment analysis is based primarily on an assertion about the form of (7) or (11). The demand for money, it is said, is infinitely elastic at a "small" positive interest rate. At this interest rate, which can be expected to prevail under underemployment conditions, changes in the real supply of money, whether produced by changes in prices or in the nominal stock of money, have no effect on anything. This is the famous "liquidity trap." A rather more complex version involves the shape of other functions as well: the magnitudes in (7) other than "the" interest rate, it is argued, enter into other relations in the economic system and can be regarded as determined there; the interest rate does not enter into these other functions; it can therefore be regarded as determined by this equation. So the only role of the stock of money and the demand for money is to determine the interest rate.

19. The proof of this pudding is in the eating; and the essays in this book [Studies in the Quantity Theory of Money] contain much relevant food, of which I may perhaps mention three particularly juicy items.

One cannot read Lerner's description of the effects of monetary reform in the Confederacy in 1864 without recognizing that at least on occasion the supply of money can be a largely autonomous factor and the demand for money highly stable even under extraordinarily unstable circumstances.[5] After three years of war, after widespread destruction and military reverses, in the face of impending defeat, a monetary reform that succeeded in reducing the stock of money halted and reversed for some months a rise in prices that had been going on at the rate of 10 per cent a month most of the war! It would be hard to construct a better controlled experiment to demonstrate the critical importance of the supply of money.

On the other hand, Klein's examination of German experience in World War II is much less favorable to the stability and importance of the demand for money.[6] Though he shows that defects in the figures account for a sizable part of the crude discrepancy between changes in the recorded stock of money and in recorded prices, correction of these defects still leaves a puzzlingly large discrepancy that it does not seem possible to account for in terms of the variables introduced into the above exposition of the theory. Klein examined German experience precisely because it seemed the most deviant on a casual examination. Both it and other wartime experience will clearly repay further examination.

Cagan's examination of hyperinflations is another important piece of evidence on the stability of the demand for money under highly unstable conditions. It is also an interesting example of the difference between a numerically stable velocity and a stable functional relation: the numerical value of the velocity varied enormously during the hyperinflations, but this was a predictable response to the changes in the expected rate of changes of prices.

20. Though the essays in this book [Studies in the Quantity Theory of Money] contain evidence relevant to the issues discussed in point 18, this is a by-product rather than their main purpose, which is rather to add to our tested knowledge about the characteristics of the demand function for money. In the process of doing so, they also raise some questions about the theoretical formulation and suggest some modifications it might be desirable to introduce. I shall comment on a few of those without attempting to summarize at all fully the essays themselves.

5. Eugene M. Lerner, "Inflation in the Confederacy, 1861–65," ibid., pp. 163–75.

6. John J. Klein, "German Money and Prices, 1932–44," ibid., pp. 121–59.

21. Selden's material covers the longest period of time and the most "normal" conditions.[7] This is at once a virtue and a vice—a virtue, because it means that his results may be applicable most directly to ordinary peacetime experience; a vice, because "normality" is likely to spell little variation in the fundamental variables and hence a small base from which to judge their effect. The one variable that covers a rather broad range is real income, thanks to the length of the period. The secular rise in real income has been accompanied by a rise in real cash balances per unit of output—a decline in velocity—from which Selden concludes that the income elasticity of the demand for real balances is greater than unity—cash balances are a "luxury" in the terminology generally adopted. This entirely plausible result seems to be confirmed by evidence for other countries as well.

22. Selden finds that for cyclical periods velocity rises during expansions and falls during contractions, a result that at first glance seems to contradict the secular result just cited. However, there is an alternative explanation entirely consistent with the secular result. It will be recalled that Y was introduced into equation (7) as an index of wealth. This has important implications for the measure or concept of income that is relevant. What is required by the theoretical analysis is not usual measured income—which in the main corresponds to current receipts corrected for double counting—but a longer term concept, "expected income," or what I have elsewhere called "permanent income."[8] Now suppose that the variables in the v function of (13) are unchanged for a period. The ratio of Y to M would then be unchanged, provided Y is *permanent* income. Velocity as Selden computes it is the ratio of *measured* income to the stock of money and would not be unchanged. When measured income was above permanent income, measured velocity would be relatively high, and conversely. Now measured income is presumably above permanent income at cyclical peaks and below permanent income at cyclical troughs. The observed positive conformity of measured velocity to cyclical changes of income may therefore reflect simply the difference between measured income and the concept relevant to equation (13).

23. Another point that is raised by Selden's work is the appropriate division of wealth into forms of assets. The division suggested above is, of course, only suggestive. Selden finds more useful the distinction between "short-term" and "long-term" bonds; he treats the former as "substitutes for money" and calls the return on the latter "the cost of holding money." He finds both to be significantly related to the quantity of money demanded. It was suggested above that this is also a way to take into account expectations about changes in interest rates.

Similarly, there is no hard-and-fast line between "money" and other assets, and for some purposes it may be desirable to distinguish between different forms

7. Richard T. Selden, "Monetary Velocity in the United States," *ibid.*, pp. 195–262.

8. See Milton Friedman, *A Theory of the Consumption Function*, Princeton, N.J.: Princeton University Press for the National Bureau of Economic Research (1957).

of "money" (e.g., between currency and deposits). Some of these forms of money may pay interest or may involve service charges, in which case the positive or negative return will be a relevant variable in determining the division of money holdings among various forms.

24. By concentrating on hyperinflations, Cagan was able to bring into sharp relief a variable whose effect is generally hard to evaluate, namely, the rate of change of prices. The other side of this coin is the necessity of neglecting practically all the remaining variables. His device for estimating expected rates of change of prices from actual rates of change, which works so well for his data, can be carried over to other variables as well and so is likely to be important in fields other than money. I have already used it to estimate "expected income" as a determinant of consumption,[9] and Gary Becker has experimented with using this "expected income" series in a demand function for money along the lines suggested above (in point 22).

Cagan's results make it clear that changes in the rate of change of prices, or in the return to an alternative form of holding wealth, have the expected effect on the quantity of money demanded: the higher the rate of change of prices, and thus the more attractive the alternative, the less the quantity of money demanded. This result is important not only directly but also because it is indirectly relevant to the effect of changes in the returns to other alternatives, such as rates of interest on various kinds of bonds. Our evidence on these is in some way less satisfactory because they have varied over so much smaller a range; tentative findings that the effect of changes in them is in the expected direction are greatly strengthened by Cagan's results.

One point which is suggested by the inapplicability of Cagan's relations to the final stages of the hyperinflations he studies is that it may at times be undesirable to replace the whole expected pattern of price movements by the rate of change expected at the moment, as Cagan does and as is done in point 5 above. For example, a given rate of price rise, expected to continue, say, for only a day, and to be followed by price stability, will clearly mean a higher (real) demand for money than the same rate of price rise expected to continue indefinitely; it will be worth incurring greater costs to avoid paying the latter than the former price. This is the same complication that occurs in demand analysis for a consumer good when it is necessary to include not only the present price but also past prices or future expected prices. This point may help explain not only Cagan's findings for the terminal stages but also Selden's findings that the inclusion of the rate of change of prices as part of the cost of holding money worsened rather than improved his estimated relations, though it may be that this result arises from a different source, namely, that it takes substantial actual rates of price change to produce firm enough and uniform enough expectations about price behavior for this variable to play a crucial role.

Similar comments are clearly relevant for expected changes in interest rates.

9. See *ibid.*

25. One of the chief reproaches directed at economics as an allegedly empirical science is that it can offer so few numerical "constants," that it has isolated so few fundamental regularities. The field of money is the chief example one can offer in rebuttal: there is perhaps no other empirical relation in economics that has been observed to recur so uniformly under so wide a variety of circumstances as the relation between substantial changes over short periods in the stock of money and in prices; the one is invariably linked with the other and is in the same direction; this uniformity is, I suspect, of the same order as many of the uniformities that form the basis of the physical sciences. And the uniformity is in more than direction. There is an extraordinary empirical stability and regularity to such magnitudes as income velocity that cannot help impressing anyone who works extensively with monetary data. This very stability and regularity contributed to the downfall of the quantity theory, for it was overstated and expressed in unduly simple form; the numerical value of the velocity itself, whether income or transactions, was treated as a natural "constant." Now this it is not; and its failure to be so, first during and after World War I and then, to a lesser extent, after the crash of 1929, helped greatly to foster the reaction against the quantity theory. The studies in this volume [*Studies in the Quantity Theory of Money*] are premised on a stability and regularity in monetary relations of a more sophisticated form than a numerically constant velocity. And they make, I believe, an important contribution toward extracting this stability and regularity, toward isolating the numerical "constants" of monetary behavior. It is by this criterion at any rate that I, and I believe also their authors, would wish them to be judged.

I began this Introduction by referring to the tradition in the field of money at Chicago and to the role of faculty members in promoting it. I think it is fitting to end the Introduction by emphasizing the part which students have played in keeping that tradition alive and vigorous. The essays that follow are one manifestation. Unpublished doctoral dissertations on money are another. In addition, I wish especially to express my own personal appreciation to the students who have participated with me in the Workshop in Money and Banking, of which this volume is the first published fruit. I owe a special debt to David I. Fand, Phillip Cagan, Gary Becker, David Meiselman, and Raymond Zelder, who have at various times helped me to conduct it.

We all of us are indebted also to the Rockefeller Foundation for financial assistance to the Workshop in Money and Banking. This assistance helped to finance some of the research reported in this book and has made possible its publication.

Chapter 3

Post-War Trends in
Monetary Theory and Policy

THE POST-WAR PERIOD has seen a dramatic change in the views of academic students of economics about monetary theory and of governmental officials about monetary policy. At the end of the war most professional economists and most governmental officials concerned with economic policy took it for granted that money did not matter, that it was a subject of minor importance. Since then there has been something of a counter-revolution in both theory and policy.

In theory, the direction of change has been toward the earlier attitudes associated with the quantity theory of money, but with a different emphasis, derived from the Keynesian analysis, on the role of money as an asset rather than as a medium of exchange. In the field of policy, the direction of change has been away from what we might call "credit policy," i.e., policy which emphasizes rates of interest and availability of credit, and toward monetary policy, i.e., policy which is concerned with the quantity of money. The emphasis has been away from qualitative controls and toward quantitative controls. And, finally, in the field of policy there has been renewed attention to the problem of relating internal stability to external stability. In examining these changes I shall outline

Reprinted from *National Banking Review*, vol. 2, no. 1 (September, 1964). This paper is adapted from a talk given in Athens in January 1963, under the auspices of the Center for Economic Research.

briefly what the situation was at the end of the war; I shall then discuss in more detail the changes in theory that I have just sketched, and finally analyze the changes in policy.

I. THE POST-WAR SITUATION

Economic thought at the end of the war was greatly affected by the Keynesian revolution which occurred in the 1930's. Keynes himself was much less extreme in rejecting the importance of money than were some of his later disciples. Keynes stressed the particular problem of under-employment equilibrium. He argued that under such circumstances one might run into something he called absolute liquidity preference. His analysis concentrated on the relation between money, on the one hand, and bonds or other fixed interest securities, on the other. He argued that bonds were the closest substitute for money, and that in the first instance one could regard people as choosing between holding their wealth in the form of money or holding it in the form of bonds. The cost of holding wealth in the form of money was the interest that could otherwise be received on bonds. The higher the rate of interest, the less money people would want to hold and vice versa. But, Keynes said, there exists some rate of interest so low that if the rate were forced still lower nobody would hold any bonds.

At that interest rate, liquidity preference is absolute. At that rate of interest, if more money were introduced into the economy people would try to get rid of the money by buying bonds. This, however, would tend to lower the rate of interest. But even the slightest decline in the rate of interest would lead people to hold money instead. So, said Keynes, under such circumstances, with the interest rate so low that people were indifferent whether they held money or bonds, no matter what quantity of the one they held or what quantity of the other, changes in the stock of money would have no effect on anything. If the quantity of money were increased by buying bonds, for example, the only effect would be that people would substitute money for bonds. If the quantity of money was decreased by selling bonds, then the opposite effect would occur.

Keynes did not of course deny the validity of the famous quantity equation, $MV = PT$. That is an identity which is a question of arithmetic, not of theory. What he said, in effect, was that, in conditions of under-employment, V (velocity) is a very unstable, passive magnitude. If M (quantity of money) increases, V will go down and the product will not change. If M decreases, V will go up and the product will not change. I emphasize this point in order to make clear that the question at issue is an empirical question and not a theoretical question. There was never any dispute on a purely theoretical level in this respect between Keynes and the quantity theorists.

Keynes himself felt that such a position of unstable velocity would occur only under conditions of under-employment equilibrium. He said that under conditions of inflation the quantity theory comes into its own. But some of his disciples went much farther. They argued that even under conditions less extreme than those of absolute liquidity preference, changes in the stock of money would not have any significant effect. It is true, they said, that under such circumstances changes in the stock of money would lead to changes in interest rates. But, changes in interest rates, they argued, would have little effect on real flows of spending: the amount of money people want to invest in projects is determined by considerations other than the rate of interest they have to pay; in technical language, the demand for investment is highly inelastic with respect to the interest rate. Consequently, they argued that, even under conditions of full employment or of inflation, changes in the quantity of money are of minor importance. An increase in M would tend to lower the interest rate a little, but this in turn would have very slight effect in expanding investment. And hence, they argued, one would find again that V of the MV equation fluctuated widely, tending to offset changes in M.

The general presumption among most economists at the end of the war was that the post-war problem was going to be depression and unemployment. The problem was going to be to stimulate sufficient investment and sufficient consumption to prevent substantial unemployment. The appropriate monetary policy in their view was very simple. The monetary authorities should keep money plentiful so as to keep interest rates low. Of course, interest rates according to this view did not make much difference, but insofar as they had any effect it would be in the direction of expanding investment slightly and hence contributing to the investment that would be urgently needed to offset deficiencies of demand. Nearly two decades have elapsed since then, and it is hard now to remember how widespread these views were and how strongly they were held by people in responsible positions, as well as by economists in general. For example, in 1945, E. A. Goldenweiser, who at the time was the Director of Research of the Federal Reserve Board's Division of Research and Statistics, wrote:

This country will have to adjust itself to a $2\frac{1}{2}$ per cent interest rate as the return on safe, long-time money, because the time has come when returns on pioneering capital can no longer be unlimited as they were in the past.[1]

This whole approach was shattered by the brute evidence of experience. In the first place, and most important, the problem of the post-war world turned out to be inflation and not deflation. Country after country that adopted an easy money policy because of the views I just described discovered that it was faced with rising prices. Equally important, no country succeeded in stopping inflation without taking measures which had the effect of controlling the quantity of money. Italy stopped inflation in 1947. How? By measures designed to hold down the quantity of money. The experience was repeated in Germany after the monetary reform in 1948; in the U.S., after the Federal Reserve-Treasury Accord in 1951; in Britain, when it restored orthodox monetary policy

1. "Postwar Problems and Policies," *Federal Reserve Bulletin*, February, 1945, p. 117.

in 1951 to keep prices down; in Greece; and in France, a recent (1960) addition to the list. Those countries that continued to follow low interest rate policies, or continued to increase the quantity of money rapidly, continued to suffer inflation, whatever other measures they took.

Though this experience was in many ways the most important single factor that produced a radical change in attitudes toward money, it was reinforced by several other factors. One was the developments which were proceeding in the world of economic theory in the analysis and re-examination of the body of doctrine which had emerged out of the Keynesian revolution. The most important element here was the emphasis on the role of real cash balances in affecting flows of expenditures, first pointed out by Haberler and then by Pigou in several articles which received more attention. An essential element of the Keynesian approach has been the view that only substitution between money and bonds is important, that real goods or real expenditures are not an important substitute for cash balances, and that, when cash balances are larger than people desire to hold, they alter solely their desired holdings of other securities. The intellectual importance of the forces brought to the fore by Haberler and Pigou was the emphasis they placed on the possibility of substitution between cash on the one hand and real flows of expenditures on the other. This contributed to a re-emphasis on the role of money.

Another development that had the same effect, in a negative way, was the disillusionment with fiscal policy. The counterpart of the Keynesian disregard for money was the emphasis placed on fiscal policy as the key element in controlling the level of aggregate demand. In the U.S. in particular, governmental expenditures have proved to be the most unstable element in the economy in the post-war years, and they have been unstable in a way that has tended to increase fluctuations rather than to decrease them. It has proved to be extremely hard to change expenditures and receipts in advance in such a way as to offset other forces making for fluctuations. This led to re-emphasis on monetary policy as a more flexible instrument which could be used in a sensitive way.

II. DEVELOPMENTS IN MONETARY THEORY

Let me turn now to the developments in monetary theory that have followed this post-war experience and the re-emphasis on money as an important economic magnitude. One development has been that many economists who continue to use the Keynesian apparatus have revised their empirical presumptions. These economists now say that liquidity preference is seldom absolute, that there is some elasticity in the demand for cash balances, and that if there are changes in the stock of money there will be changes in interest rates. They say also that investment is not completely insensitive to interest rates, that when borrowing becomes more expensive, the amount spent on investment is reduced, and conversely. This view goes along with the attitude that, while money is more important than these economists used to think it was, monetary policy still can influence income only indirectly. A change in the stock of money may affect the interest rate, the interest rate may affect investment, the change in investment may affect income, but it is only by this indirect route, the argument runs, that monetary changes have an effect on economic change.

This is purely a semantic question of how one wants to describe the channels of influence. The crucial issue is the empirical one of whether in fact the links between money and income are more stable and more regular than the links between investment and income. And it is on this empirical issue that the post-war evidence spoke very strongly and led to a re-examination of the role of money.

A more fundamental and more basic development in monetary theory has been the reformulation of the quantity theory of money in a way much influenced by the Keynesian liquidity analysis. That reformulation emphasizes money as an asset that can be compared with other assets; its emphasis is on what is called "portfolio analysis," analysis of the structure of peoples' balance sheets, of the kinds of assets they want to hold. This emphasis looks at monetary theory as part of capital theory, or the theory of wealth. This is a rather different emphasis than that derived from earlier approaches, particularly that of Irving Fisher, which put major emphasis on transactions and on money as a mechanical medium of exchange somehow connected with the transactions process.

The emphasis on money as an asset has gone in two different directions. On the one hand, it has led to emphasis on *near moneys*, as an alternative source of liquidity. One example is the work of Gurley and Shaw and their analysis of financial intermediaries as providing money substitutes. Another example, in its most extreme form, is in the Radcliffe Committee report which attempts to widen the concept of money to make it synonymous with the concept of liquidity, itself an undefined term which covers the universe. My own view is that this particular trail toward widening the range of reference of the concept of money is a false trail. It will peter out and will not in fact be followed. The reaction which the Radcliffe Committee analysis has received among academic economists and others seems to suggest that my opinion is widely shared.

The other direction in which the emphasis on money as an asset has led is toward the development of a theory of the demand for money along the same lines as the theory of the demand for other assets and for commodities and services. In such a theory, one asks what determines the amount of cash balances that people want to hold. Here it is essential to distinguish between cash balances in two senses: nominal cash balances, the nominal quantity of money as defined in terms of monetary units such as drachmas, dollars, and so forth; and real cash balances, the real stock of money as defined in terms of command over goods and services.

The essential feature of the quantity theory of money in both its older versions and its more recent and modern version is the assertion that what really matters to people is not the number of things called drachmas or dollars they hold but the real stock of money they have, the command which those pieces of paper give them over goods and services. In talking about the demand for money, one must ask what determines the command over goods and services that people want to keep in the form of money. For example, take a very simple definition of money as consisting only of currency, of the pieces of paper we carry in our pockets. We must then ask what determines whether the amount that people hold is on the average equal to a little over six weeks' income, as it is in Greece, or a little over four weeks' income, as it is in the U.S., or five weeks' income, as it is in Turkey. Thus, when we talk about the demand for money, we must be talking about the demand for real balances in the sense of command over goods and services and not about nominal balances.

In the theory of demand as it has been developed, the key variables include *first,* wealth or some counterpart of wealth, for example, income or, preferably, something like permanent income, which is a better index of wealth than measured income. Because the problem is one of a balance sheet, the first restriction is that there is a certain total amount of wealth which must be held in the form of money, or bonds, or other securities, or houses, or automobiles, or other physical goods, or in the form of human earning capacity. Hence, income or wealth acts as a restraint in determining the demand for money in exactly the same way that the total income people have operates to determine their demand for shoes or hats or coats by setting a limit to aggregate expenditures. The *second* important set of variables is the rates of return on substitute forms of holding money. Here, the most important thing that has happened has been a tendency to move away from the division of assets into money and bonds that Keynes emphasized, into a more pluralistic division of wealth, not only into bonds but also into equities and real assets. The relevant variables therefore are the expected rate of return on bonds, the expected rate of return on equities and the expected rate of return on real property; each of these may of course be multiplied by considering different specific assets of each type. A major component of the expected rate of return on real property is the rate of change in prices. It is of primary importance when there is extensive inflation or deflation.

I should like to stress the significance of the emphasis on money as one among many assets, not only for the kinds of variables that people consider as affecting the demand for money, but also for the process of adjustment. According to the earlier view of money as primarily a medium of exchange, as something which is used to facilitate transactions between people, it was fairly natural to think of a short link between changes in the stock of money and changes in expenditure and to think of the effects of changes in the stock of money as occurring very promptly. On the other hand, according to the more recent emphasis, money is something more basic than a medium of transactions; it is something which enables people to separate the act of purchase from the act of sale. From this point of view, the role of money is to serve as a temporary abode of purchasing power. It is this view that is fostered by considering money as an asset or as part of wealth.

Looked at in this way, it is plausible that there will be a more indirect and complicated process of adjustment to a change in the stock of money than looked at the other way. Moreover, it seems plausible that it will take a much longer time for the adjustment to be completed. Suppose there is a change in the stock of money. This is a change in the balance sheet. It takes time for people to readjust their balance sheets. The first thing people will do is to try to purchase other assets. As they make these purchases, they change the prices of those assets. As they change the prices of those assets, there is a tendency for the effect to spread further. The ripples spread out as they do on a lake. But as prices of assets change, the *relative* price of assets, on the one hand, and flows, on the other hand, also change. And now people may adjust their portfolios not only by exchanging assets but by using current income to add to, or current expenditures to subtract from, certain of their assets and liabilities. In consequence, I think that this reformulation of monetary theory with its emphasis on monetary theory as a branch of the theory of wealth has very important implications for the process of adjustment and for the problem of time lags.

III. DEVELOPMENTS IN MONETARY POLICY

Policy does not always have a close relation to theory. The world of the academic halls and the world of policy makers often seem to move on two wholly different levels with little contact between them. The developments in post-war monetary policy have not been the same throughout the world. However, the makers of monetary policy in different countries have been in closer and more systematic touch with one another than the monetary theorists. As a result, I think one can speak to some extent of general trends in policy without necessarily referring to the country.

As I indicated earlier, I think two features dominate and characterize the trends in post-war monetary policy. The first is the shift of emphasis away from credit policy and toward monetary policy. I think this is a distinction of first rate importance, and yet one which is much neglected. Therefore let me say a word about the meaning of this distinction. When I refer to credit policy, I mean the effect of the actions of monetary authorities on rates of interest, terms of lending, the ease with which people can borrow, and conditions in the credit markets. When I refer to monetary policy, I mean the effect of the actions of monetary authorities on the stock of money—on the number of pieces of paper in people's pockets, or the quantity of deposits on the books of banks.

Policy makers, and central bankers in particular, have for centuries concentrated on credit policy and paid little attention to monetary policy. The Keynesian analysis, emphasizing interest rates as opposed to the stock of money, is only the latest rationalization of that concentration. The most important earlier rationalization was the so-called real bills doctrine. The belief is still common among central bankers today that, if credit were somehow issued in relation to productive business activities, then the quantity of money could be left to itself. This notion of the real bills doctrine goes back hundreds of years; it is endemic to central bankers today. It understandably derives from their close connection with commercial banking, but it is basically fallacious.

The emphasis on credit policy was closely linked with the emphasis at the end of the war on qualitative controls. If what matters is who borrows and at what rate, then it is quite natural to be concerned with controlling the specific use of credit and the specific application of it. In the U.S., for example, emphasis on credit policy was linked with emphasis on margin controls on the stock market, and with controls over real estate credit and installment credit. In Britain, it was linked with controls over hire-purchase credit. In each of these cases, there was a qualitative policy concerned with credit conditions. The failure of the easy money policy and of these techniques of qualitative control promoted a shift both toward less emphasis on controlling specific rates of return and toward more emphasis on controlling the total quantity of money.

The distinction that I am making between credit and monetary policy may seem like a purely academic one of no great practical importance. Nothing could be farther from the truth. Let me cite the most striking example that I know; namely, U.S. experience in the great depression from 1929 to 1933. Throughout that period the Federal Reserve System was never concerned with the quantity of money. It did not in fact publish monthly figures of the quantity of money until the 1940's. Indeed, the first mention in Federal Reserve literature of the quantity of money as a criterion of policy was in the 1950's. Prior to that time there was much emphasis upon easy or tight money, by which was meant low or high interest rates. There was much emphasis on the availability of loans, but there was no emphasis and no concern with the quantity of money.

If there had been concern with the quantity of money *as such*, we could not have had the great depression of 1929–33 in the form in which we had it. If the Federal Reserve System had been concerned with monetary policy in the sense in which I have just defined it, it literally would have been impossible for the System to have allowed the quantity of money in the U.S. to decline from 1929 to 1933 by a third, the largest decline in the history of the U.S. in that length of time. In reading many of the internal papers of the Federal Reserve Board during that period, the communications between the various governors of the Federal Reserve Banks and the Board of Governors, and so forth, I have been struck with the lack of any quantitative criterion of policy. There are vague expressions about letting the market forces operate. There are comments about "easy" money or "tight" money but no indication of precisely how a determination is to be made whether money is "easy" or "tight." This distinction between emphasis on credit policy and emphasis on monetary policy is a distinction of great importance in the monetary history of the U.S., and I think also in the monetary history of other countries.

The failure of the easy money policy was reinforced by another factor which promoted a shift in policy away from qualitative measures involving control of particular forms of credit, and toward quantitative measures involving concern with changes in the stock of money. This other factor was a reduction of exchange controls and quantitative restrictions on international trade, as in the post-war period one country after another began to improve its international position. There was a move toward convertibility in international payments. This shift toward convertibility led to a reduction of emphasis on qualitative direct controls and toward increased emphasis on general measures that would affect the course of events through altering the conditions under which people engaged in trade. In turn, this led to a final development in monetary policy— the renewed concern about the relation between internal monetary policy and external policy, the problem of the balance of payments. In this area we have had, most surprisingly of all, I think, a return to an earlier era of something approximating a gold standard.

In the immediate post-war period, concern with the balance of payments tended to be centered in the countries of Western Europe that were having a so-called dollar shortage. Those countries were at that time facing the problem of recurrent drains of their international reserves. They were in the position of having somehow to restrain their residents from converting their local currencies into foreign currencies. Those were also the countries that emerged from the war with fairly extensive exchange controls and direct restrictions on trade. And thus in the first years after the war the solution to this problem took the form of direct control rather than of monetary policy.

At that time the U.S. was in a very different position. It was gaining gold and it was able to take the position that it could conduct its monetary policy entirely in terms of internal conditions and need pay no attention to the effects that its policies had abroad. Of course, that was not what happened. There is little doubt that during the immediate post-war period the ease in the U.S. gold position contributed toward a greater readiness to accept inflation than would otherwise have prevailed, so that the ease in the international balance produced a relatively easier monetary policy than we otherwise would have had. But once the U.S. started selling gold on net instead of buying gold on net, to use a more accurate term than the term "losing gold," the situation changed drastically and the U.S. itself became much more concerned with the effect of monetary policy and much more driven toward a pre-World War I gold standard approach.

In recent years, the concern with the international balance of payments has given rise to greater co-operation among central banks. They have tried to develop techniques which will assure that any temporary drains on the reserves of one country will be matched by offsetting movements by central banks in the other countries. Despite the immense amount of good will and of human ingenuity that has gone into this effort to avoid payments difficulties through central bank co-operation, I must confess that I regard the tendency as an exceedingly dangerous one. The danger is that the arrangements developed will provide an effective system for smoothing minor difficulties but only at the cost of permitting them to develop into major ones.

I am much struck by the analogy between what is now happening in this respect and what happened in the U.S. between 1919 and 1939. The U.S. in that earlier period developed a monetary system which turned out to be an effective device for smoothing minor difficulties. The system was highly successful in helping to make the years from 1922 to 1929 relatively stable. But this stability was purchased at the cost of major difficulties from 1920 to 1921, from 1929 to 1933, and again from 1937 to 1938. I very much fear that the same results may emerge from present trends toward international co-operation among central banks, because these measures do not go to the root of the problem of inter-national adjustment.

In international financial arrangements, as in personal finances, the problem of having enough liquid assets to meet temporary drains must be sharply distin-guished from the adjustment to changed circumstances. The central bank arrangements look only to providing liquidity for temporary drains. More fundamental adjustment to changed circumstances can come only through: (1) domestic monetary and fiscal policy directed toward holding down or reducing domestic prices relative to foreign prices when the country is experiencing a deficit, or toward permitting domestic prices to rise relative to foreign prices when the country is experiencing a surplus; or (2) changes in exchange rates to achieve a similar alteration in the relative level of domestic and foreign prices when expressed in the same currency; or (3) direct measures designed to alter the flows of receipts or expenditures, such as changes in tariffs, subsidies, and quotas, direct or indirect control of capital movements, restrictions on foreign aid or other governmental expenditures, extending ultimately to that full panoply of foreign exchange controls that strangled Western Europe after the war and remains today one of our most unfortunate gifts to many under-developed countries.

The great danger is that central bank co-operation and other means to enlarge liquidity, by providing palliatives that can at best smooth over temporary imbalances, will encourage countries to postpone undertaking such fundamental adjustments to changed circumstances. The consequence will be to allow minor imbalances to accumulate into major ones; to convert situations that could have been corrected by gradual and minor monetary tightness or ease, or by small movements in exchange rates, into situations that would require major changes in monetary policy or exchange rates. The consequence is likely to be not only international financial crises, but also the encouragement of the use of the third method of adjustment, direct controls. Paradoxically, most economists and most policy makers would agree that it is the worst of the three; yet it is the one that has most regularly been resorted to in the post-war period.

These developments in monetary policy are much more difficult to pin down precisely than the developments in monetary theory, as may be expected from the fact that monetary policy is and must be much more a matter of oppor-tunism, of day-to-day adjustment, of meeting the particular problems of the time. The theorist can sit in his ivory tower and make sure that his structure is coherent and consistent. This is, I must say, an advantage of the theorist and a great disadvantage of the policy maker, and not the other way around. But I think it is clear that we are likely to see in the future still further developments in monetary policy.

There is almost invariably a long cultural lag before developments in theory manifest themselves in policy. If you were to look at what is being proposed today in domestic policy in the U.S., you would say that my analysis of changes in the field of monetary theory must be a figment of my imagination. The policy proposals that are being made in the U.S. today are all reflections of the ideas of the late 1930's, or at the latest of the early 1940's. That is natural and widespread. The people who make the policy, who are involved in policy formation, are inevitably people who got their training and their education and their attitudes some 20 or more years earlier. This is a special case of a much more general phenomenon. I am sure all are aware of that famous book by A. V. Dicey on *Law and Public Opinion in the 19th Century*, the main thesis of which is precisely that trends in ideas take about 20 years before they are effective in the world of action. What is happening in the U.S. today is a dramatic illustration of his thesis. And so I expect that monetary policy will in the course of the next 20 years show some radical changes as a result of the changes I have described in monetary theory.

Chapter 4

The Monetary Theory and
Policy of Henry Simons

IT IS A GREAT HONOR for me to give the Henry Simons Lecture. He was my
teacher and my friend—and above all, a shaper of my ideas. No man can say
precisely whence his beliefs and his values come—but there is no doubt that
mine would be very different than they are if I had not had the good fortune
to be exposed to Henry Simons. If, in this lecture, I express much disagreement
with him, that, too, bespeaks his influence. He taught us that an objective,
critical examination of a man's ideas is a truer tribute than slavish repetition of
his formulas.

I am especially pleased to be giving this lecture under the auspices of the Law
School. One of the unique advantages of the University of Chicago for
economists has always been the close co-operation and interchange between
economists and lawyers. Henry Simons was for many years on the Law School
faculty, and Aaron Director and Ronald Coase have continued that fine tradition.
The Journal of Law and Economics has set the seal on a happy affair.

On re-reading Henry Simons' work in preparation for this lecture, I was
struck by the contrast between my reaction to his discussion of monetary theory,
on the one hand, and to his proposals for monetary reform, on the other. The
monetary theory impressed me as sophisticated and correct; the proposals for

The third Henry Simons Lecture, delivered at the Law School, University of Chicago, May
5, 1967. Reprinted from *The Journal of Law and Economics*, vol. 10, October, 1967.

reform as largely irrelevant and wrong. This contrast and how it can be explained are the themes of this lecture.

Though Simons nowhere set forth a consistent and comprehensive statement of his monetary theory, his views are implicit in his discussion of policy proposals, and explicit in many parenthetical remarks in his often lengthy and always penetrating footnotes.[1] I find myself, not only in full agreement with the views so revealed, but more important, enlightened by them and impressed by their sophistication.

Simons wrote on money mostly during the dozen years from 1933 to 1945. That was a period when, thanks to the Keynesian Revolution, the economics profession came to regard money—in the sense of currency, deposits, banking, and allied issues—as an unimportant and uninteresting subject. The fraction of the profession's attention devoted to this area probably reached an all time low from the late 'thirties to the early 'fifties. Since then there has been a tremendous revival of interest in this area, so that monetary theory is at the moment a dramatic growth industry. Recent developments have deepened and widened our understanding, but they have cast no doubt on Simons' basic analysis of how money enters into the economic system or of the influence it exerts. Quite the contrary. These developments have produced a return to Simons' view that the quantity of money and its behavior play a central role in affecting the course of prices and of economic activity; that monetary stability is an essential prerequisite for economic stability.

Simons' policy proposals are a very different matter. They consist of two separable elements: (1) proposals for reforming the banking and financial structure—as he put it "transition to a less preposterous structure of private money contracts" (p. 170), (2) proposals for "establishment of a simple, mechanical rule of monetary policy" (p. 170). In his role as a monetary theorist, he clearly found the second much more intriguing and interesting. Yet he regarded it as the less important. The urgent and immediate task, the essential pre-condition for the satisfactory operation of any monetary rule, was, he believed, financial reform.

In Simons' view, the "financial good society" (p. 239) required "financial reform . . . aiming at sharp differentiation between money and private obligations" (p. 79). He viewed his well-known proposal for 100 per cent reserve banking "only as the proper first step toward reconstruction of our whole financial organization. Standing by itself, as an isolated measure, it would promise little but evasion . . . and would deserve classification as merely another

1. One partial exception to the statement that Simons nowhere set forth a consistent statement of his theory is an *Appendix on Banking and Business Cycles* in an unpublished and unsigned memorandum dated November, 1933, *Banking and Currency Reform*. In a footnote, Simons describes this memorandum as having been "prepared and circulated by several Chicago economists" but, according to Aaron Director, one of the group, it was written primarily by Simons. See Henry Simons, *Economic Policy for a Free Society*, Chicago, Ill.: University of Chicago Press (1948), p. 326, note 2. All subsequent page references in the text are to this book.

crank scheme" (p. 331, n. 17).[2] In addition to 100 per cent reserve banking, "Narrow limitation of the formal borrowing powers of other corporations would obviously be necessary. . . . Further limitations might also be necessary with respect to financing via the open account (book credit) and instalment sales" (p. 171). For government, the debt structure should be drastically simplified, with all government obligations taking the form either of non-interest bearing money or very long-term securities, ideally perpetuities (consols).

On monetary policy, Simons vacillated between favoring a rule expressed in terms of the quantity of money—for example, that the quantity of money be kept constant—and a rule expressed in terms of a price index—for example, that the authorities be instructed to keep the wholesale price index stable. His final position was, roughly, that the price-index rule was the only feasible rule pending a closer approximation to the "financial good society," but that the quantity of money rule was much preferable, when and if the "financial good society" was attained.

I would myself be inclined precisely to reverse Simons' priorities—and so, I believe, would most other modern students of money, even those of us who share most completely Simons' basic objectives of social policy. Financial reform along his lines seems not only unnecessary but in the wrong direction.[3] Why should we not have variety and diversity in the market for borrowing and lending as in other markets? Is it not desirable that borrowers tailor their obligations to the demands of lenders? Is it not a sign of the ingenuity and efficiency of the free market that financial intermediaries develop which reconcile the needs of borrowers and lenders—providing funds on terms desired by borrowers and borrowing on terms desired by lenders? This simultaneously lowers the cost of capital to borrowers and raises the effective return on capital to lenders—thereby fostering a higher level of capital formation than would otherwise occur.

I agree with Simons on the desirability of 100 per cent reserve banking—but I regard it as less important and basic than he did and favor it in some ways for almost the opposite reasons. He viewed it as a step toward simplifying the structure of financial claims, as a step toward making effective the legislative limitations he favored on the terms on which people could borrow and lend. I view it as a step toward reducing government interference with lending and borrowing in order to permit a greater degree of freedom and variety in the arrangements for borrowing and lending.

2. His proposal involved separating existing commercial banks into two sets of institutions. One would be essentially a warehouse for money. It would accept demand deposits transferable by check but be required to keep a reserve in cash (or deposits at the Federal Reserve) of 100 per cent of such deposits, and would get its income from service charges paid by depositors. The other would be an investment trust which would take over the lending activities of commercial banks, getting its capital by issuing securities to the public.

3. Emphasis on this type of reform has almost disappeared from the literature. Its only counterpart was a temporary flurry of interest in non-bank financial intermediaries a few years ago.

Even on monetary policy, where the passage of time has only strengthened my belief in the lesson he taught me—that rules are greatly to be preferred to authorities, I am inclined to reverse his emphasis. A rule in terms of the quantity of money seems to me far superior, for both the short and the long-run, than a rule in terms of price-level stabilization.

What explains this contrast? How is it that I can admire so greatly Simons' grasp of monetary theory and disagree so completely with his proposals for reform?

We have all of us in our personal lives had the experience of coming on a fact that suddenly illuminated an issue in a flash, showing us how wrong we had been and leading us to a fresh and very different opinion. It is something of an oversimplification, but only a slight one, I believe, to say that that is the explanation of the contrast I have been stressing. A few facts, which we now know and he did not, have made all the difference.

The facts have to do primarily with the Great Depression of 1929–1933. Were I to interpret that episode as Simons did, I would agree with his recommendations. Had he interpreted that episode as I do, he would not have made the policy recommendations he did. And our difference of interpretation is not simply a difference of personality or taste: It reflects—or so I would like to believe—the accumulation of evidence through scientific study.

Needless to say, Simons' interpretation was not unique to him. On the contrary, it was widely shared by his contemporaries. In particular, I have been struck that the statements I have been making about Simons apply almost verbatim to John Maynard Keynes. He, too, was led to make policy recommendations that seem wrong now—and in his case that differed drastically from his own earlier views—because he accepted the same interpretation of 1929–1933 as did Henry Simons. In his case, too, I find his monetary theory sophisticated and modern, yet his policy recommendations unacceptable. As we shall see later, though some of his policy recommendations parallel Simons', in other respects they differ drastically. But they differ not because of a difference in monetary theory or a different interpretation of 1929–1933 but because of a different basic attitude toward social policy—Keynes was a reformer, Simons, a radical.

In exploring this thesis further, I shall outline Simons' interpretation of the 1930's and similar episodes, show how his policy recommendations follow from that interpretation, and contrast his policy recommendations with Keynes'. I shall then indicate what our current interpretation of this episode is and suggest what policy views derive from that interpretation.

I. SIMONS' INTERPRETATION OF BUSINESS CYCLES IN GENERAL AND THE GREAT DEPRESSION IN PARTICULAR

"The problem of synchronous industrial . . . fluctuations," wrote Simons, "is a problem (a) of rigidities in crucial areas of the price structure . . . and (b) of perverse flexibility in the total turnover (quantity and velocity) of effective money" (p. 165).

The perverse flexibility in "total turnover"—Keynes' aggregate demand—was reinforced, Simons thought, but not essentially produced, by changes in the quantity of money. It reflected rather changes in "the speculative temper of the community."[4] Such changes, he argued, produce changes in velocity that can develop into "catastrophic disturbances as soon as short-term borrowing develops on a large scale. . . . Short-term obligations provide abundant money substitutes during booms, thus releasing money from cash reserves [that is, raising velocity]; and they precipitate hopeless efforts at liquidation during depressions [that is, lowering velocity]" (p. 166).

These "cumulative maladjustments are likely to be peculiarly severe" "in an economy where most of the effective money is provided by private banks" because "the quantity of effective money, as well as its velocity, responds promptly and markedly to changes in business earnings."[5]

Widespread borrowing on short-term in order to finance long-term obligations is the key to instability because, in Simons' view, it makes the economy vulnerable to changes in confidence and hence in the desire for liquidity. Each individual separately may be in a position to convert his assets into cash but the economy as a whole is not. There is "shiftability" but not "liquidity." The commercial banking system makes this problem more serious not primarily as a creator of money, but because it fosters more widespread and extensive borrowing on demand and lending on time.

This vision undoubtedly was derived largely from the 1929–33 crash. Hence, Simons put special emphasis on the potentialities in such a system for deflation. ". . . [W]e evolved a fantastic financial structure and collections of enterprises for money-bootlegging, whose sanctimonious respectability and marble solidity only concealed a mass of current obligations and a shoestring of equity that would have been scandalous in any other type of business. . . . [W]e evaded long term deflation by continuously courting deflation catastrophe" (pp. 198–99).

Or again, "once a crisis has developed, and once earnings have begun to decline, the process is even more chaotic. Each bank seeks to contract its loans; but none augments its reserves unless it contracts more rapidly than the rest. Every reduction in bank loans means reduction in the community's effective money; and this in turn means lower prices, smaller volume of business, and still lower earnings. . . .

"It is more than an incidental aggravation that practically all the banks of necessity become insolvent in the process, and that large numbers are actually forced to close."[6]

---

4. Appendix to *Banking and Currency Reform*, p. 2 (see note 1 above).

5. See *ibid.*, p. 3.

6. See *ibid.*, p. 5.

For our purposes, the key feature of this interpretation is that the channel of influence runs from changes in business confidence to changes in velocity to changes in the quantity of money. For the depression, it is the collapse of confidence (Keynes' collapse of the marginal efficiency of investment) that sets off a demand for liquidity. This demand cannot be met but the attempt to meet it forces widespread liquidation, including the liquidation of bank loans with a resultant decline in the quantity of money and runs on banks.

Simons implicitly regarded the Great Depression as occurring despite, not because of, governmental monetary policy. Though he made no explicit statement to this effect, Simons' quite clearly accepted the official apologia of the Federal Reserve System—it had done its best, but was powerless to stop the collapse, once private confidence was sapped, as it was by the stock-market crash. "Reflect casually," says Simons, "on what the thirties might have been if only we had not permitted the stock-market crash to initiate a long and precipitous deflation in the United States. . . ." (p. 272).

II. SIMONS' THEORY OF CYCLES AND HIS POLICY PROPOSALS

It is clear how Simons' policy proposals derive from his interpretation of the Great Depression. It is the rigidity of prices that converts fluctuations in aggregate demand into fluctuations in output and employment. Hence, greater flexibility of prices is highly desirable, whatever else is done. This is the link between Simons' views on money, on the one hand, and on monopoly in industry and labor and government price-fixing, on the other. The way to make prices less rigid was by measures that are desirable in any event in order to make the economy more competitive. Hence, in his monetary writings, he only stated the objective of price flexibility, without a bill of particulars.

Since the inherent instability of the financial structure is the source of cumulative maladjustments, the *sine qua non* of stability in a free market economy is an improved financial structure. The "approximately ideal condition" would be one in which "there were no fixed money contracts at all—if all property were held in a residual-equity or common-stock form. With such a financial structure, no one would be in a position either to create effective money substitutes (whether for circulation or for hoarding) or to force enterprises into wholesale efforts at liquidation. Hoarding and dishoarding (changes in velocity) would, to be sure, still occur; but the dangers of cumulative maladjustment would be minimized" (p. 165).

In the absence of such financial reform, "The obvious weakness of fixed quantity [of money], as a sole rule of monetary policy, lies in the danger of sharp changes on the velocity side. . . . The fixing of the quantity of circulating media might merely serve to increase the perverse variability in the amounts of 'near moneys' and in the degree of their general acceptability. . . ." (p. 164).

Hence, pending such financial reform, the theoretically attractive quantity of money criterion had to be relegated to the "more distant future" (p. 183) despite its unique advantage of providing an objective rule and minimizing the role of discretion by monetary authorities. "For the present, we obviously must rely on a large measure of discretionary money management. . . ." (p. 170). But this discretion should be guided by some definite policy objective, not be ". . . merely the composite of the uncertain daily actions of an indefinite number of agencies, governmental and private" (p. 174). Simons was led by this route to endorse reluctantly the stabilization of a price index as the only feasible means of ". . . bringing the totality of monetary measures under the discipline of some rule. . . ." (pp. 174–75). "If price-level stabilization is a poor system," he wrote, "it is still, from a liberal viewpoint, infinitely better than no system at all. And it seems now highly questionable whether any better system is feasible or possible at all within the significant future" (p. 174).

Finally, if, in the existing financial structure, the fluctuations in aggregate demand originate in the private sector and in turn affect the commercial banking system, and if a major problem is the ease with which non-banks can create and destroy near-moneys, then the banking authorities, strictly interpreted, operate on too narrow a base to be able to control the price level. "Banking," Simons said, "is a pervasive phenomenon, not something to be dealt with merely by legislation directed at what we call banks" (p. 172). Hence, "The task [of stabilizing the price level] is certainly not one to be intrusted to banking authorities, with their limited powers and restricted techniques, as should be abundantly evident from recent experience. Ultimate control over the value of money lies in fiscal practices—in the spending, taxing, and borrowing operations of the central government" (p. 175).

III. SIMONS AND KEYNES

There is clearly great similarity between the views expressed by Simons and by Keynes—as to the causes of the Great Depression, the impotence of monetary policy, and the need to rely extensively on fiscal policy. Both men placed great emphasis on the state of business expectations and assigned a critical role to the desire for liquidity. Indeed, in many ways, the key novelty of Keynes' *General Theory* was the role he assigned to "absolute" liquidity preference under conditions of deep depression. It was this, in his view, that made it impossible for the monetary authorities to influence interest rates. It was this that meant that changes in the quantity of money produced by the monetary authorities would simply be reflected in opposite movements in velocity and have no effect on income or employment.

Keynes had earlier been a strong champion of relying primarily on orthodox monetary policy to promote economic stability. He abandoned this position when he concluded that liquidity preference could frustrate central bank attempts to alter long-term interest rates. Like Simons, he turned instead to fiscal policy

—changes in government expenditures and taxes—as his primary reliance.[7]

Despite the similarity between the views held by Simons and Keynes, Simons, as best I can determine, arrived at his views independently. My earlier quotation from Simons that "ultimate control over the value of money lies in fiscal practices" comes from an article published in February, 1936, or at roughly the same time as Keynes' *General Theory*. (The preface is dated December, 1935, and the book bears the publication date of 1936.) More important yet, Simons' basic ideas on both theory and policy are all contained in an unpublished mimeographed memorandum dated November, 1933. Already in that memorandum, Simons had written "at the present time, increase of expenditures or reduction of taxes would be far more immediately effective toward raising prices than conversion of the federal debt into the non-interest bearing form."[8] Indeed, I have always thought that it was because such ideas as these, and the earlier ones I have summarized, were in the air at the University of Chicago in the early and mid-1930's that the Chicago students were so much less susceptible to the Keynesian virus than their contemporaries in London, England, and Cambridge, Massachusetts, who were taught that the Great Depression was a necessary and ultimately healthy purgative.

The major differences between Keynes and Simons on policy reflected their difference in temperament. To both, the financial structure threatened instability. To Keynes the reformer, with his emphasis on short-run problems—it was he, after all, who said, "in the long-run we are all dead," with his confidence in civil servants to control and regulate—he was himself, after all, in and out of the civil service, with his belief that we had seen "the end of laissez-faire," as he entitled a famous article, the solution was to substitute government intervention

---

7. In a letter commenting on this lecture, Friedrich A. Hayek writes: "I believe you are wrong in suggesting that the common element in the doctrines of Simons and Keynes was the influence of the Great Depression. We all held similar ideas in the 1920's. They had been most fully elaborated by R. G. Hawtrey who was all the time talking about the 'inherent instability of credit' but he was by no means the only one. . . . It seems to me that all the elements of the theories which were applied to the Great Depression had been developed during that great enthusiasm for 'business cycle theory' which preceded it."

No doubt the elements of the theories were all present and Hayek may be right that the Great Depression did not have the effect on Keynes' views that I attributed to it. However, the Great Depression surely produced a different emphasis. More important, my impression is that the Great Depression also produced an important difference in substance. Hawtrey and others emphasized the inherent instability of banking credit proper; their stress was on the forces that Simons described as explaining why these "cumulative maladjustments are likely to be peculiarly severe" "in an economy where most of the effective money is provided by private banks," not on the earlier effects to which Simons attributed the cumulative maladjustments themselves. The Great Depression led, I believe, Keynes and Simons to emphasize the inherent instability of the financial structure more generally—the effect of near-moneys rather than of money itself. Unfortunately, I have not had the opportunity to investigate this point at all fully, so this reaction to Hayek's comment is a tentative impression, not a documented conclusion.

8. Appendix to *Banking and Currency Reform*, p. 13.

for market adjustment, to replace where necessary private investment by government spending. To Simons the radical, who always took the long view, who had the Midwesterner's suspicion of the bureaucrats in Washington, who regarded a large measure of laissez-faire as an essential requisite for the preservation of political liberty, the solution was to go to the root of the problem by reforming drastically the financial structure.

IV. THE KEY FACTS AS WE NOW KNOW THEM

The keystone of Simons' interpretation of 1929–1933 was that the trouble originated with business earnings and the shock to business confidence, documented or perhaps initiated by the stock-market crash. The subsequent widespread pressure for liquidation, on his interpretation, left the monetary authorities, narrowly defined, largely powerless. Once the scramble for liquidity was on, there was no way they could prevent a decline in the value of private claims and debts, which in turn rendered banks insolvent, and induced their depositors to try to withdraw deposits.

We now know that the critical relations ran precisely the other way. Beginning in mid-1928, the Federal Reserve System, concerned about stock-market speculation, adopted a monetary policy of nearly continuous restraint, despite its desire to foster business expansion. The result was a policy that was ". . . not restrictive enough to halt the bull market yet too restrictive to foster vigorous business expansion."[9] The stock of money failed to rise and even fell slightly during most of the cyclical expansion from November, 1927 to August, 1929—a phenomenon not matched in any prior or subsequent cyclical expansion.

Cyclical contraction began in August, 1929, well before the stock-market crash in October, 1929. That crash no doubt did shake business confidence and may well have produced a rise in liquidity preference (that is, a decline in velocity). But there is no sign that it produced any panicky pressure for liquidation, any tendency for bankers to call loans, any concern about the safety of banks, or any widespread deterioration in the value of bank assets—on the contrary, the prices of the kinds of bonds banks held initially went up rather than down.

The downward pressure on velocity produced by the reaction to the stock-market crash was strongly reinforced by the behavior of the quantity of money, which fell by 2.6 per cent from August, 1929, to October, 1930. This may seem like a small decline—and it is, compared to the total decline of over 30 per cent that occurred before the depression was over. But the decline should be interpreted in the light of prior and subsequent experience. Because of the long-term growth in the quantity of money, there are only four earlier cyclical contractions

9. M. Friedman and A. Schwartz, *A Monetary History of the United States, 1867–1960*, Princeton, N.J.: Princeton University Press for the National Bureau of Economic Research (1963), p. 298.

and no later ones in which the quantity of money declined as much—and all of these earlier exceptions were also unusually severe contractions.

For our purposes, the source of the decline in the quantity of money is even more important than its magnitude. It was produced entirely by a decline in Federal Reserve credit outstanding. No part whatever was played by weakness in the banking structure, attempted liquidation of loans by banks, or an attempt by depositors to convert deposits to currency. On the contrary, the banks' willingness to reduce reserves and the public's willingness to hold more deposits relative to currency offset half of the decline in Federal Reserve credit. The monetary authorities, not the private economy, were the major source of deflationary pressure.

The character of the contraction changed drastically in December, 1930, when a series of scattered bank failures culminated in the dramatic failure of the Bank of the United States in New York—the largest single bank failure in the United States up to that time. For the first time, there was widespread distrust of banks and runs on banks. But again the sequence was the opposite of that which Simons postulated. The runs on banks produced pressure on banks to liquidate. This did lower the market value of their assets and so gave substance to the initially unfounded fears about the safety of the banks. But their position was not weakened by declines in the value of their assets originating in the rest of the financial structure.

A major objective in establishing the Federal Reserve System in 1913 was to meet precisely this kind of situation—to serve as a "lender of last resort" in order to enable banks to meet the demands of depositors without having to dump assets. In the immediate month of December, 1930, the Reserve System behaved to some extent as initially intended. But no sooner was the immediate crisis over than it retreated back to its earlier position and renewed its deflationary pressure on the money supply.

When a second banking crisis began in March, 1931, the Reserve System did not even temporarily step in to ease the situation. The only relief came from gold imports. The Reserve System renounced its heritage and treated the banking crisis as something outside its sphere of competence.

But worse was yet to come. When Britain left gold in September, 1931, the Reserve System embarked on an active deflationary policy—taking the most extreme deflationary measures in its history before or since. The result was to turn a crisis into a catastrophe. The quantity of money had fallen at an annual rate of 13 per cent from March, 1931, to August, 1931. It fell at the incredible annual rate of 31 per cent in the five months from August, 1931, to January, 1932.

One fact during this episode highlights the error in Simons' interpretation. The chief problem confronting banks was not the collectibility of their commercial loans but the decline in the prices of the bonds they held in their portfolios. Among the prices that declined was the price of U.S. government bonds, which fell by 10 per cent. This price decline clearly did not reflect a scramble for liquidity on the part of the community at large or the decline in earnings of business enterprises or a fear about the safety of the bonds. Like the accompanying decline of 20 per cent in the price of high grade corporate bonds, it reflected the inevitable effect of the dumping of bonds by banks which was enforced by the failure of the Federal Reserve System to provide sufficient liquidity to enable banks to meet the demands of their customers.

In our *Monetary History*, Anna Schwartz and I summarized the role of the Reserve System in the great contraction from 1929–1933 as follows:

"The System pleaded impotence, arguing explicitly that the non-monetary forces making for contraction were so strong and violent that it was powerless to stem the tide, and implicitly that the depth of the decline in the money stock was due to the depth of the decline in business activity, rather than . . . the reverse. Many others, recognizing the good intentions of the monetary authorities and the ability of many individuals in the System, while independently holding a wide variety of views about the role of money in economic affairs, accepted the System's plea"—as we have seen, Simons and Keynes were of this company.

Evaluating the claim of impotence, we concluded that "At all times throughout the 1929–33 contraction, alternative policies were available to the System by which it could have kept the stock of money from falling, and indeed could have increased it at almost any desired rate. These policies did not involve radical innovations. They involved measures of a kind the System had taken in earlier years, of a kind explicitly contemplated by the founders of the System to meet precisely the kind of banking crisis that developed in late 1930 and persisted thereafter. They involved measures that were actually proposed and very likely would have been adopted under a slightly different bureaucratic structure or distribution of power, or even if the men in power had had somewhat different personalities. Until late 1931—and we believe not even then—the alternative policies involved no conflict with the maintenance of the gold standard. Until September, 1931, the problem that recurrently troubled the System was how to keep the gold inflows under control, not the reverse."[10]

I have stressed the Great Depression because this climactic episode clearly played a key role in leading Simons—and also Keynes—to believe that the orthodox powers of the monetary authorities were too weak to cope with disorders arising in the private financial markets. In fact, as I have emphasized, the private financial markets displayed extraordinary resilience and stability—but not enough to cope with the disorders arising from the actions—and inaction—of the monetary authorities.

Since Simons wrote, an enormous amount of evidence has accumulated that bears not only on these few years but also on a far wider range of economic history. This evidence, too, contradicts Simons' interpretation of the source of instability. It turns out that the rate of growth of the quantity of money has systematically tapered off well before the economy in general slows down, and

10. Ibid., pp. 691, 693.

has speeded up well before the economy speeds up. The movements in velocity —which Simons took as an independent source of instability—come later than the movements in the quantity of money and are mild when the movements in the quantity of money are mild. They have been sharp only when there have been sharp movements in the quantity of money. There is no evidence to support Simons' fear that a fixed quantity of money might involve "the danger of sharp changes on the velocity side." On the contrary, the evidence is precisely the reverse—that it would lessen the danger of sharp changes in velocity.

V. POLICY IMPLICATIONS

Had Simons known the facts as we now know them, he would, I believe, have been confirmed in "his earlier persuasion as to the merits of the rule of a fixed quantity of money. . . ." (p. 170)[11] rather than have accepted, albeit with great reluctance, stabilization of a price level as at least a temporary objective pending the establishment of the "financial good society." He would not have felt constrained to denigrate monetary powers narrowly conceived and to elevate fiscal powers to the forefront as the major weapon of monetary policy.

In short, as it happens, a correct view of the facts would have strengthened his basic intuitions, would have reinforced his confidence in policies fully consistent with his central belief in laissez-faire for the private economy and the rule of law for governmental bodies.

Instead, because of a misconception of the facts, he was led to compromise for the short run and to propose radical reform for the long-run.

Is it just a happy accident that a fuller study of the facts would have led Henry Simons to compromise less with his basic intuitions, would have supported the conclusions to which he was drawn by his economic theorizing? I believe not. Those intuitions, those conclusions were derived from a sophisticated body of economic theory that had developed over centuries. Such a body of theory has implicit in it a set of empirical judgments about the character of the world. It

---

11. To avoid misunderstanding, I should note explicitly that Simons' rule is not identical with the rule I have come to favor. Simons proposed that the quantity of money be held constant in amount. I propose that it grow at a fixed rate year after year, the rate of growth being designed to produce roughly stable final product prices.

Simons explicitly rejected the rule of a constant rate of growth. He recognized that his rule of a constant money supply involved a secular decline in final product prices. His basic reason for favoring it nonetheless was that the sticky and inflexible prices were factor prices, especially wages, and that a constant quantity of money would (aside from growth of population, which he thought would decline and might disappear, and aside from secular changes in velocity, which he ignored) mean stability in these prices and hence would minimize the necessity for changes in the sticky prices. Supplementary reasons were the greater ease of public understanding of a constant quantity of money than of a necessarily arbitrary rate of growth and the greater pressure for fiscal discipline it would impose on legislators.

survives if and only if those implicit judgments are vindicated by experience. It may go into temporary eclipse when casual empiricism seems to run counter to it. That is what happened during the 'thirties. But the sign that it is a good theory is that it will revive and be restored to grace as emerging evidence vindicates it. That is what has been happening in the past decade. That is why Simons' keen theoretical understanding has proved more permanent than his empirical compromises.

Chapter 5

The Role of Monetary Policy

THERE IS WIDE AGREEMENT about the major goals of economic policy: high employment, stable prices, and rapid growth. There is less agreement that these goals are mutually compatible or, among those who regard them as incompatible, about the terms at which they can and should be substituted for one another. There is least agreement about the role that various instruments of policy can and should play in achieving the several goals.

My topic for tonight is the role of one such instrument—monetary policy. What can it contribute? And how should it be conducted to contribute the most? Opinion on these questions has fluctuated widely. In the first flush of enthusiasm about the newly created Federal Reserve System, many observers attributed the relative stability of the 1920s to the System's capacity for fine tuning—to apply an apt modern term. It came to be widely believed that a new era had arrived in which business cycles had been rendered obsolete by advances in monetary technology. This opinion was shared by economist and layman alike, though, of course, there were some dissonant voices. The Great Contraction destroyed this naive attitude. Opinion swung to the other extreme. Monetary policy was a string. You could pull on it to stop inflation but you could not

Presidential address delivered at the Eightieth Annual Meeting of the American Economic Association, Washington, D.C., December 29, 1967. Reprinted from *The American Economic Review*, vol. 58, no. 1, March, 1968. I am indebted for helpful criticisms of earlier drafts from Armen Alchian, Gary Becker, Martin Bronfenbrenner, Arthur F. Burns, Phillip Cagan, David D. Friedman, Lawrence Harris, Harry G. Johnson, Homer Jones, Jerry Jordan, David Meiselman, Allan H. Meltzer, Theodore W. Schultz, Anna J. Schwartz, Herbert Stein, George J. Stigler, and James Tobin.

push on it to halt recession. You could lead a horse to water but you could not make him drink. Such theory by aphorism was soon replaced by Keynes' rigorous and sophisticated analysis.

Keynes offered simultaneously an explanation for the presumed impotence of monetary policy to stem the depression, a nonmonetary interpretation of the depression, and an alternative to monetary policy for meeting the depression. His offering was avidly accepted. If liquidity preference is absolute or nearly so —as Keynes believed likely in times of heavy unemployment—interest rates cannot be lowered by monetary measures. If investment and consumption are little affected by interest rates—as Hansen and many of Keynes' other American disciples came to believe—lower interest rates, even if they could be achieved, would do little good. Monetary policy was twice damned. The contraction, set in train on this view by a collapse of investment or by a shortage of investment opportunities or by stubborn thriftiness, could not, it was argued, have been stopped by monetary measures. But there was available an alternative—fiscal policy. Government spending could make up for insufficient private investment. Tax reductions could undermine stubborn thriftiness.

The wide acceptance of these views in the economics profession meant that for some two decades monetary policy was believed by all but a few reactionary souls to have been rendered obsolete by new economic knowledge. Money did not matter. Its only role was the minor one of keeping interest rates low, in order to hold down interest payments in the government budget, contribute to the "euthanasia of the rentier," and, maybe, stimulate investment a bit to assist government spending in maintaining a high level of aggregate demand.

These views produced a widespread adoption of cheap money policies after the war. And they received a rude shock when these policies failed in country after country, when central bank after central bank was forced to give up the pretense that it could indefinitely keep "the" rate of interest at a low level. In this country, the public denouement came with the Federal Reserve-Treasury Accord in 1951, although the policy of pegging government bond prices was not formally abandoned until 1953. Inflation, stimulated by cheap money policies, not the widely heralded postwar depression, turned out to be the order of the day. The result was the beginning of a revival of belief in the potency of monetary policy.

This revival was strongly fostered among economists by the theoretical developments, initiated by Haberler but named for Pigou, that pointed out a channel—namely, changes in wealth—whereby changes in the real quantity of money can affect aggregate demand even if they do not alter interest rates. These theoretical developments did not undermine Keynes' argument against the potency of orthodox monetary measures when liquidity preference is absolute, since under such circumstances the usual monetary operations involve simply substituting money for other assets without changing total wealth. But they did show how changes in the quantity of money produced in other ways could affect total spending even under such circumstances. And, more fundamentally, they did undermine Keynes' key theoretical proposition, namely, that even in a world of flexible prices, a position of equilibrium at full employment might not exist. Henceforth, unemployment had again to be explained by rigidities or imperfections, not as the natural outcome of a fully operative market process.

The revival of belief in the potency of monetary policy was fostered also by a re-evaluation of the role money played from 1929 to 1933. Keynes and most other economists of the time believed that the Great Contraction in the United States occurred despite aggressive expansionary policies by the monetary authorities—that they did their best but their best was not good enough.[1] Recent studies have demonstrated that the facts are precisely the reverse: the U.S. monetary authorities followed highly deflationary policies. The quantity of money in the United States fell by one-third in the course of the contraction. And it fell not because there were no willing borrowers—not because the horse would not drink. It fell because the Federal Reserve System forced or permitted a sharp reduction in the monetary base, because it failed to exercise the responsibilities assigned to it in the Federal Reserve Act to provide liquidity to the banking system. The Great Contraction is tragic testimony to the power of monetary policy—not, as Keynes and so many of his contemporaries believed, evidence of its impotence.

In the United States the revival of belief in the potency of monetary policy was strengthened also by increasing disillusionment with fiscal policy, not so much with its potential to affect aggregate demand as with the practical and political feasibility of so using it. Expenditures turned out to respond sluggishly and with long lags to attempts to adjust them to the course of economic activity, so emphasis shifted to taxes. But here political factors entered with a vengeance to prevent prompt adjustment to presumed need, as has been so graphically illustrated in the months since I wrote the first draft of this talk. "Fine tuning" is a marvelously evocative phrase in this electronic age, but it has little resemblance to what is possible in practice—not, I might add, an unmixed evil.

It is hard to realize how radical has been the change in professional opinion on the role of money. Hardly an economist today accepts views that were the common coin some two decades ago. Let me cite a few examples.

In a talk published in 1945, E. A. Goldenweiser, then Director of the Research Division of the Federal Reserve Board, described the primary objective of monetary policy as being to "maintain the value of Government bonds. . . . This country" he wrote, "will have to adjust to a $2\frac{1}{2}$ per cent interest rate as the return on safe, long-time money, because the time has come when returns on pioneering capital can no longer be unlimited as they were in the past".[2]

1. In "The Monetary Theory and Policy of Henry Simons," Chapter 4 above, I have argued that Henry Simons shared this view with Keynes, and that it accounts for the policy changes that he recommended.

2. E. A. Goldenweiser, "Postwar Problems and Policies," *Federal Reserve Bulletin*, February, 1945, pp. 112–21.

In a book on *Financing American Prosperity*, edited by Paul Homan and Fritz Machlup and published in 1945, Alvin Hansen devotes nine pages of text to the "savings-investment problem" without finding any need to use the words "interest rate" or any close facsimile thereto.[3] In his contribution to this volume, Fritz Machlup wrote, "Questions regarding the rate of interest, in particular regarding its variation or its stability, may not be among the most vital problems of the postwar economy, but they are certainly among the perplexing ones".[4] In his contribution, John H. Williams—not only a professor at Harvard but also a long-time adviser to the New York Federal Reserve Bank—wrote, "I can see no prospect of revival of a general monetary control in the postwar period".[5]

Another of the volumes dealing with postwar policy that appeared at this time, *Planning and Paying for Full Employment*, was edited by Abba P. Lerner and Frank D. Graham[6] and had contributors of all shades of professional opinion—from Henry Simons and Frank Graham to Abba Lerner and Hans Neisser. Yet Albert Halasi, in his excellent summary of the papers, was able to say, "Our contributors do not discuss the question of money supply. . . . The contributors make no special mention of credit policy to remedy actual depressions. . . . Inflation . . . might be fought more effectively by raising interest rates. . . . But . . . other anti-inflationary measures . . . are preferable'.[7] *A Survey of Contemporary Economics*, edited by Howard Ellis and published in 1948, was an "official" attempt to codify the state of economic thought of the time. In his contribution, Arthur Smithies wrote ,"In the field of compensatory action, I believe fiscal policy must shoulder most of the load. Its chief rival, monetary policy, seems to be disqualified on institutional grounds. This country appears to be committed to something like the present low level of interest rates on a long-term basis".[8]

These quotations suggest the flavor of professional thought some two decades ago. If you wish to go further in this humbling inquiry, I recommend that you compare the sections on money—when you can find them—in the "Principles" texts of the early postwar years with the lengthy sections in the current crop even, or especially, when the early and recent "Principles" are different editions of the same work.

The pendulum has swung far since then, if not all the way to the position of the late 1920s, at least much closer to that position than to the position of 1945.

3. Paul T. Homan and Fritz Machlup (Eds.), *Financing American Prosperity*, New York: Twentieth Century Fund (1945), pp. 218–27.

4. *Ibid.*, p. 446.

5. *Ibid.*, p. 383.

6. A. P. Lerner and Frank D. Graham (Eds.), *Planning and Paying for Full Employment*, Princeton, N.J.: Princeton University Press (1946).

7. *Ibid.*, pp. 23–24.

8. Howard S. Ellis (Ed.), *A Survey of Contemporary Economics*, Homewood, Ill.: Richard D. Irwin (1948), p. 208.

There are of course many differences between then and now, less in the potency attributed to monetary policy than in the roles assigned to it and the criteria by which the profession believes monetary policy should be guided. Then, the chief roles assigned monetary policy were to promote price stability and to preserve the gold standard; the chief criteria of monetary policy were the state of the "money market," the extent of "speculation," and the movement of gold. Today, primacy is assigned to the promotion of full employment, with the prevention of inflation a continuing but definitely secondary objective. And there is major disagreement about criteria of policy, varying from emphasis on money market conditions, interest rates, and the quantity of money to the belief that the state of employment itself should be the proximate criterion of policy.

I stress nonetheless the similarity between the views that prevailed in the late 'twenties and those that prevail today because I fear that, now as then, the pendulum may well have swung too far, that, now as then, we are in danger of assigning to monetary policy a larger role than it can perform, in danger of asking it to accomplish tasks that it cannot achieve, and, as a result, in danger of preventing it from making the contribution that it is capable of making.

Unaccustomed as I am to denigrating the importance of money, I therefore shall, as my first task, stress what monetary policy cannot do. I shall then try to outline what it can do and how it can best make its contribution, in the present state of our knowledge—or ignorance.

I. WHAT MONETARY POLICY CANNOT DO

From the infinite world of negation, I have selected two limitations of monetary policy to discuss: (1) It cannot peg interest rates for more than very limited periods; (2) It cannot peg the rate of unemployment for more than very limited periods. I select these because the contrary has been or is widely believed, because they correspond to the two main unattainable tasks that are at all likely to be assigned to monetary policy, and because essentially the same theoretical analysis covers both.

A. Pegging of Interest Rates

History has already persuaded many of you about the first limitation. As noted earlier, the failure of cheap money policies was a major source of the reaction against simple-minded Keynesianism. In the United States, this reaction involved widespread recognition that the wartime and postwar pegging of bond prices was a mistake, that the abandonment of this policy was a desirable and inevitable step, and that it had none of the disturbing and disastrous consequences that were so freely predicted at the time.

The limitation derives from a much misunderstood feature of the relation between money and interest rates. Let the Fed set out to keep interest rates down. How will it try to do so? By buying securities. This raises their prices and lowers their yields. In the process, it also increases the quantity of reserves available to banks, hence the amount of bank credit, and, ultimately the total quantity of money. That is why central bankers in particular, and the financial community more broadly, generally believe that an increase in the quantity of money tends to lower interest rates. Academic economists accept the same conclusion, but for different reasons. They see, in their mind's eye, a negatively sloping liquidity preference schedule. How can people be induced to hold a larger quantity of money? Only by bidding down interest rates.

Both are right, up to a point. The *initial* impact of increasing the quantity of money at a faster rate than it has been increasing is to make interest rates lower for a time than they would otherwise have been. But this is only the beginning of the process, not the end. The more rapid rate of monetary growth will stimulate spending, both through the impact on investment of lower market interest rates and through the impact on other spending and thereby relative prices of higher cash balances than are desired. But one man's spending is another man's income. Rising income will raise the liquidity preference schedule and the demand for loans; it may also raise prices, which would reduce the real quantity of money. These three effects will reverse the initial downward pressure on interest rates fairly promptly, say, in something less than a year. Together they will tend, after a somewhat longer interval, say, a year or two, to return interest rates to the level they would otherwise have had. Indeed, given the tendency for the economy to overreact, they are highly likely to raise interest rates temporarily beyond that level, setting in motion a cyclical adjustment process.

A fourth effect, when and if it becomes operative, will go even farther, and definitely mean that a higher rate of monetary expansion will correspond to a higher, not lower, level of interest rates than would otherwise have prevailed. Let the higher rate of monetary growth produce rising prices, and let the public come to expect that prices will continue to rise. Borrowers will then be willing to pay and lenders will then demand higher interest rates—as Irving Fisher pointed out decades ago. This price expectation effect is slow to develop and also slow to disappear. Fisher estimated that it took several decades for a full adjustment and more recent work is consistent with his estimates.

These subsequent effects explain why every attempt to keep interest rates at a low level has forced the monetary authority to engage in successively larger and larger open market purchases. They explain why, historically, high and rising nominal interest rates have been associated with rapid growth in the quantity of money, as in Brazil or Chile or in the United States in recent years, and why low and falling interest rates have been associated with slow growth in the quantity of money, as in Switzerland now or in the United States from 1929 to 1933. As an empirical matter, low interest rates are a sign that monetary policy *has been* tight—in the sense that the quantity of money has grown slowly; high interest rates are a sign that monetary policy *has been* easy—in the sense that the quantity of money has grown rapidly. The broadest facts of experience run in precisely the opposite direction from that which the financial community and academic economists have all generally taken for granted.

Paradoxically, the monetary authority could assure low nominal rates of interest—but to do so it would have to start out in what seems like the opposite direction, by engaging in a deflationary monetary policy. Similarly, it could assure high nominal interest rates by engaging in an inflationary policy and accepting a temporary movement in interest rates in the opposite direction.

These considerations not only explain why monetary policy cannot peg interest rates; they also explain why interest rates are such a misleading indicator of whether monetary policy is "tight" or "easy." For that, it is far better to look at the rate of change of the quantity of money.[9]

B. Employment as a Criterion of Policy

The second limitation I wish to discuss goes more against the grain of current thinking. Monetary growth, it is widely held, will tend to stimulate employment; monetary contraction, to retard employment. Why, then, cannot the monetary authority adopt a target for employment or unemployment—say, 3 per cent unemployment; be tight when unemployment is less than the target; be easy when unemployment is higher than the target; and in this way peg unemployment at, say, 3 per cent? The reason it cannot is precisely the same as for interest rates—the difference between the immediate and the delayed consequences of such a policy.

Thanks to Wicksell, we are all acquainted with the concept of a "natural" rate of interest and the possibility of a discrepancy between the "natural" and the "market" rate. The preceding analysis of interest rates can be translated fairly directly into Wicksellian terms. The monetary authority can make the market rate less than the natural rate only by inflation. It can make the market rate higher than the natural rate only by deflation. We have added only one wrinkle to Wicksell—the Irving Fisher distinction between the nominal and the real rate of interest. Let the monetary authority keep the nominal market rate for a time below the natural rate by inflation. That in turn will raise the nominal natural rate itself, once anticipations of inflation become widespread, thus requiring still more rapid inflation to hold down the market rate. Similarly, because of the Fisher effect, it will require not merely deflation but more and more rapid deflation to hold the market rate above the initial natural rate.

9. This is partly an empirical, not a theoretical, judgment. In principle, "tightness" or "ease" depends on the rate of change of the quantity of money supplied compared to the rate of change of the quantity demanded excluding effects on demand from monetary policy itself. However, empirically, demand is highly stable, if we exclude the effect of monetary policy, so it is generally sufficient to look at supply alone.

This analysis has its close counterpart in the employment market. At any moment of time, there is some level of unemployment which has the property that it is consistent with equilibrium in the structure of *real* wage rates. At that level of unemployment, real wage rates are tending on the average to rise at a "normal" secular rate, i.e., at a rate that can be indefinitely maintained so long as capital formation, technological improvements, etc., remain on their long-run trends. A lower level of unemployment is an indication that there is an excess demand for labor that will produce upward pressure on real wage rates. A higher level of unemployment is an indication that there is an excess supply of labor that will produce downward pressure on real wage rates. The "natural rate of unemployment," in other words, is the level that would be ground out by the Walrasian system of general equilibrium equations, provided there is imbedded in them the actual structural characteristics of the labor and commodity markets, including market imperfections, stochastic variability in demands and supplies, the cost of gathering information about job vacancies and labor availabilities, the costs of mobility, and so on.[10]

You will recognize the close similarity between this statement and the celebrated Phillips Curve. The similarity is not coincidental. Phillips' analysis of the relation between unemployment and wage change is deservedly celebrated as an important and original contribution. But, unfortunately, it contains a basic defect—the failure to distinguish between *nominal* wages and *real* wages—just as Wicksell's analysis failed to distinguish between *nominal* interest rates and *real* interest rates. Implicitly, Phillips wrote his article for a world in which everyone anticipated that nominal prices would be stable and in which that anticipation remained unshaken and immutable whatever happened to actual prices and wages. Suppose, by contrast, that everyone anticipates that prices will rise at a rate of more than 75 per cent a year—as, for example, Brazilians did a few years ago. Then wages must rise at that rate simply to keep real wages unchanged. An excess supply of labor will be reflected in a less rapid rise in nominal wages than in anticipated prices,[11] not in an absolute decline in wages. When Brazil embarked on a policy to bring down the rate of price rise, and succeeded in bringing the price rise down to about 45 per cent a year, there was a sharp initial rise in unemployment because, under the influence of earlier anticipations, wages kept rising at a pace that was higher than the new rate of price rise, though lower than earlier. This is the result experienced, and to be expected, of all attempts to reduce the rate of inflation below that widely anticipated.[12]

10. It is perhaps worth noting that this "natural" rate need not correspond to equality between the number unemployed and the number of job vacancies. For any given structure of the labor market, there will be some equilibrium relation between these two magnitudes, but there is no reason why it should be one of equality.

11. Strictly speaking, the rise in nominal wages will be less rapid than the rise in anticipated nominal wages to make allowance for any secular changes in real wages.

12. Stated in terms of the rate of change of nominal wages, the Phillips Curve can be expected to be reasonably stable and well defined for any period for which the *average* rate

To avoid misunderstanding, let me emphasize that by using the term "natural" rate of unemployment, I do not mean to suggest that it is immutable and unchangeable. On the contrary, many of the market characteristics that determine its level are man-made and policy-made. In the United States, for example, legal minimum wage rates, the Walsh-Healy and Davis-Bacon Acts, and the strength of labor unions all make the natural rate of unemployment higher than it would otherwise be. Improvements in employment exchanges, in availability of information about job vacancies and labor supply, and so on, would tend to lower the natural rate of unemployment. I use the term "natural" for the same reason Wicksell did—to try to separate the real forces from monetary forces.

Let us assume that the monetary authority tries to peg the "market" rate of unemployment at a level below the "natural" rate. For definiteness, suppose that it takes 3 per cent as the target rate and that the "natural" rate is higher than 3 per cent. Suppose also that we start out at a time when prices have been stable and when unemployment is higher than 3 per cent. Accordingly, the authority increases the rate of monetary growth. This will be expansionary. By making nominal cash balances higher than people desire, it will tend initially to lower interest rates and in this and other ways to stimulate spending. Income and spending will start to rise.

To begin with, much or most of the rise in income will take the form of an increase in output and employment rather than in prices. People have been expecting prices to be stable, and prices and wages have been set for some time in the future on that basis. It takes time for people to adjust to a new state of demand. Producers will tend to react to the initial expansion in aggregate demand by increasing output, employees by working longer hours, and the unemployed, by taking jobs now offered at former nominal wages. This much is pretty standard doctrine.

But it describes only the initial effects. Because selling prices of products typically respond to an unanticipated rise in nominal demand faster than prices of factors of production, real wages received have gone down—though real wages anticipated by employees went up, since employees implicitly evaluated the wages offered at the earlier price level. Indeed, the simultaneous fall *ex post* in real wages to employers and rise *ex ante* in real wages to employees is what

---

of change of prices, and hence the anticipated rate, has been relatively stable. For such periods, nominal wages and "real" wages move together. Curves computed for different periods or different countries for each of which this condition has been satisfied will differ in level, the level of the curve depending on what the average rate of price change was. The higher the average rate of price change, the higher will tend to be the level of the curve. For periods or countries for which the rate of change of prices varies considerably, the Phillips Curve will not be well defined. My impression is that these statements accord reasonably well with the experience of the economists who have explored empirical Phillips Curves.

Restate Phillips' analysis in terms of the rate of change of real wages—and even more precisely, anticipated real wages—and it all falls into place. That is why students of empirical Phillips Curves have found that it helps to include the rate of change of the price level as an independent variable.

enabled employment to increase. But the decline *ex post* in real wages will soon come to affect anticipations. Employees will start to reckon on rising prices of the things they buy and to demand higher nominal wages for the future. "Market" unemployment is below the "natural" level. There is an excess demand for labor so real wages will tend to rise toward their initial level.

Even though the higher rate of monetary growth continues, the rise in real wages will reverse the decline in unemployment, and then lead to a rise, which will tend to return unemployment to its former level. In order to keep unemployment at its target level of 3 per cent, the monetary authority would have to raise monetary growth still more. As in the interest rate case, the "market" rate can be kept below the "natural" rate only by inflation. And, as in the interest rate case, too, only by accelerating inflation. Conversely, let the monetary authority choose a target rate of unemployment that is above the natural rate, and they will be led to produce a deflation, and an accelerating deflation at that.

What if the monetary authority chose the "natural" rate—either of interest or unemployment—as its target? One problem is that it cannot know what the "natural" rate is. Unfortunately, we have as yet devised no method to estimate accurately and readily the natural rate of either interest or unemployment. And the natural rate will itself change from time to time. But the basic problem is that even if the monetary authority knew the natural rate, and attempted to peg the market rate at that level, it would not be led to a determinate policy. The "market" rate will vary from the natural rate for all sorts of reasons other than monetary policy. If the monetary authority responds to these variations, it will set in train longer term effects that will make any monetary growth path it follows ultimately consistent with the rule of policy. The actual course of monetary growth will be analogous to a random walk, buffeted this way and that by the forces that produce temporary departures of the market rate from the natural rate.

To state this conclusion differently, there is always a temporary trade-off between inflation and unemployment; there is no permanent trade-off. The temporary trade-off comes not from inflation per se, but from unanticipated inflation, which generally means, from a rising rate of inflation. The widespread belief that there is a permanent trade-off is a sophisticated version of the confusion between "high" and "rising" that we all recognize in simpler forms. A rising rate of inflation may reduce unemployment, a high rate will not.

But how long, you will say, is "temporary"? For interest rates, we have some systematic evidence on how long each of the several effects takes to work itself out. For unemployment, we do not. I can at most venture a personal judgment, based on some examination of the historical evidence, that the initial effects of a higher and unanticipated rate of inflation last for something like two to five years; that this initial effect then begins to be reversed; and that a full adjustment to the new rate of inflation takes about as long for employment as for interest rates, say, a couple of decades. For both interest rates and employment, let me add a qualification. These estimates are for changes in the rate of inflation of the order of magnitude that has been experienced in the United States. For much more sizable changes, such as those experienced in South American countries, the whole adjustment process is greatly speeded up.

To state the general conclusion still differently, the monetary authority controls nominal quantities—directly, the quantity of its own liabilities. In principle, it can use this control to peg a nominal quantity—an exchange rate, the price level, the nominal level of national income, the quantity of money by one or another definition— or to peg the rate of change in a nominal quantity— the rate of inflation or deflation, the rate of growth or decline in nominal national income, the rate of growth of the quantity of money. It cannot use its control over nominal quantities to peg a real quantity—the real rate of interest, the rate of unemployment, the level of real national income, the real quantity of money, the rate of growth of real national income, or the rate of growth of the real quantity of money.

II. WHAT MONETARY POLICY CAN DO

Monetary policy cannot peg these real magnitudes at predetermined levels. But monetary policy can and does have important effects on these real magnitudes. The one is in no way inconsistent with the other.

My own studies of monetary hisory have made me extremely sympathetic to the oft-quoted, much reviled, and as widely misunderstood, comment by John Stuart Mill. "There cannot . . . ," he wrote, "be intrinsically a more insignificant thing, in the economy of society, than money; except in the character of a contrivance for sparing time and labour. It is a machine for doing quickly and commodiously, what would be done, though less quickly and commodiously, without it: and like many other kinds of machinery, it only exerts a distinct and independent influence of its own when it gets out of order".[13]

True, money is only a machine, but it is an extraordinarily efficient machine. Without it, we could not have begun to attain the astounding growth in output and level of living we have experienced in the past two centuries—any more than we could have done so without those other marvelous machines that dot our countryside and enable us, for the most part, simply to do more efficiently what could be done without them at much greater cost in labor.

But money has one feature that these other machines do not share. Because it is so pervasive, when it gets out of order, it throws a monkey wrench into the operation of all the other machines. The Great Contraction is the most dramatic example but not the only one. Every other major contraction in this country

13. J. S. Mill, *Principles of Political Economy* (1848), Ashley (Ed.), London: Longmans Green (1929), p. 488.

has been either produced by monetary disorder or greatly exacerbated by monetary disorder. Every major inflation has been produced by monetary expansion—mostly to meet the overriding demands of war which have forced the creation of money to supplement explicit taxation.

The first and most important lesson that history teaches about what monetary policy can do—and it is a lesson of the most profound importance—is that monetary policy can prevent money itself from being a major source of economic disturbance. This sounds like a negative proposition: avoid major mistakes. In part it is. The Great Contraction might not have occurred at all, and if it had, it would have been far less severe, if the monetary authority had avoided mistakes, or if the monetary arrangements had been those of an earlier time when there was no central authority with the power to make the kinds of mistakes that the Federal Reserve System made. The past few years, to come closer to home, would have been steadier and more productive of economic well-being if the Federal Reserve had avoided drastic and erratic changes of direction, first expanding the money supply at an unduly rapid pace, then, in early 1966, stepping on the brake too hard, then, at the end of 1966, reversing itself and resuming expansion until at least November, 1967, at a more rapid pace than can long be maintained without appreciable inflation.

Even if the proposition that monetary policy can prevent money itself from being a major source of economic disturbance were a wholly negative proposition, it would be none the less important for that. As it happens, however, it is not a wholly negative proposition. The monetary machine has gotten out of order even when there has been no central authority with anything like the power now possessed by the Fed. In the United States, the 1907 episode and earlier banking panics are examples of how the monetary machine can get out of order largely on its own. There is therefore a positive and important task for the monetary authority—to suggest improvements in the machine that will reduce the chances that it will get out of order, and to use its own powers so as to keep the machine in good working order.

A second thing monetary policy can do is provide a stable background for the economy—keep the machine well oiled, to continue Mill's analogy. Accomplishing the first task will contribute to this objective, but there is more to it than that. Our economic system will work best when producers and consumers, employers and employees, can proceed with full confidence that the average level of prices will behave in a known way in the future—preferably that it will be highly stable. Under any conceivable institutional arrangements, and certainly under those that now prevail in the United States, there is only a limited amount of flexibility in prices and wages. We need to conserve this flexibility to achieve changes in relative prices and wages that are required to adjust to dynamic changes in tastes and technology. We should not dissipate it simply to achieve changes in the absolute level of prices that serve no economic function.

In an earlier era, the gold standard was relied on to provide confidence in future monetary stability. In its heyday it served that function reasonably well. It clearly no longer does, since there is scarce a country in the world that is prepared to let the gold standard reign unchecked—and there are persuasive reasons why countries should not do so. The monetary authority could operate as a surrogate for the gold standard, if it pegged exchange rates and did so exclusively by altering the quantity of money in response to balance of payment flows without "sterilizing" surpluses or deficits and without resorting to open or concealed exchange control or to changes in tariffs and quotas. But again, though many central bankers talk this way, few are in fact willing to follow this course—and again there are persuasive reasons why they should not do so. Such a policy would submit each country to the vagaries not of an impersonal and automatic gold standard but of the policies—deliberate or accidental—of other monetary authorities.

In today's world, if monetary policy is to provide a stable background for the economy it must do so by deliberately employing its powers to that end. I shall come later to how it can do so.

Finally, monetary policy can contribute to offsetting major disturbances in the economic system arising from other sources. If there is an independent secular exhilaration—as the postwar expansion was described by the proponents of secular stagnation—monetary policy can in principle help to hold it in check by a slower rate of monetary growth than would otherwise be desirable. If, as now, an explosive federal budget threatens unprecedented deficits, monetary policy can hold any inflationary dangers in check by a slower rate of monetary growth than would otherwise be desirable. This will temporarily mean higher interest rates than would otherwise prevail—to enable the government to borrow the sums needed to finance the deficit—but by preventing the speeding up of inflation, it may well mean both lower prices and lower nominal interest rates for the long pull. If the end of a substantial war offers the country an opportunity to shift resources from wartime to peacetime production, monetary policy can ease the transition by a higher rate of monetary growth than would otherwise be desirable—though experience is not very encouraging that it can do so without going too far.

I have put this point last, and stated it in qualified terms—as referring to major disturbances—because I believe that the potentiality of monetary policy in offsetting other forces making for instability is far more limited than is commonly believed. We simply do not know enough to be able to recognize minor disturbances when they occur or to be able to predict either what their effects will be with any precision or what monetary policy is required to offset their effects. We do not know enough to be able to achieve stated objectives by delicate, or even fairly coarse, changes in the mix of monetary and fiscal policy. In this area particularly the best is likely to be the enemy of the good. Experience suggests that the path of wisdom is to use monetary policy explicitly to offset other disturbances only when they offer a "clear and present danger."

III. HOW SHOULD MONETARY POLICY BE CONDUCTED?

How should monetary policy be conducted to make the contribution to our goals that it is capable of making? This is clearly not the occasion for presenting a detailed "Program for Monetary Stability"—to use the title of a book in which I tried to do so.[14] I shall restrict myself here to two major requirements for monetary policy that follow fairly directly from the preceding discussion.

The first requirement is that the monetary authority should guide itself by magnitudes that it can control, not by ones that it cannot control. If, as the authority has often done, it takes interest rates or the current unemployment percentage as the immediate criterion of policy, it will be like a space vehicle that has taken a fix on the wrong star. No matter how sensitive and sophisticated its guiding apparatus, the space vehicle will go astray. And so will the monetary authority. Of the various alternative magnitudes that it can control, the most appealing guides for policy are exchange rates, the price level as defined by some index, and the quantity of a monetary total—currency plus adjusted demand deposits, or this total plus commercial bank time deposits, or a still broader total.

For the United States in particular, exchange rates are an undesirable guide. It might be worth requiring the bulk of the economy to adjust to the tiny percentage consisting of foreign trade if that would guarantee freedom from monetary irresponsibility—as it might under a real gold standard. But it is hardly worth doing so simply to adapt to the average of whatever policies monetary authorities in the rest of the world adopt. Far better to let the market, through floating exchange rates, adjust to world conditions the 5 per cent or so of our resources devoted to international trade while reserving monetary policy to promote the effective use of the 95 per cent.

Of the three guides listed, the price level is clearly the most important in its own right. Other things the same, it would be much the best of the alternatives —as so many distinguished economists have urged in the past. But other things are not the same. The link between the policy actions of the monetary authority and the price level, while unquestionably present, is more indirect than the link between the policy actions of the authority and any of the several monetary totals. Moreover, monetary action takes a longer time to affect the price level than to affect the monetary totals, and both the time lag and the magnitude of effect vary with circumstances. As a result, we cannot predict at all accurately just what effect a particular monetary action will have on the price level and, equally important, just when it will have that effect. Attempting to control directly the price level is therefore likely to make monetary policy itself a source of economic disturbance because of false stops and starts. Perhaps, as our under-

14. Milton Friedman, *A Program for Monetary Stability*, New York: Fordham University Press (1959).

standing of monetary phenomena advances, the situation will change. But at the present stage of our understanding, the long way around seems the surer way to our objective. Accordingly, I believe that a monetary total is the best currently available immediate guide or criterion for monetary policy—and I believe that it matters much less which particular total is chosen than that one be chosen.

A second requirement for monetary policy is that the monetary authority avoid sharp swings in policy. In the past, monetary authorities have on occasion moved in the wrong direction—as in the episode of the Great Contraction that I have stressed. More frequently, they have moved in the right direction, albeit often too late, but have erred by moving too far. Too late and too much has been the general practice. For example, in early 1966, it was the right policy for the Federal Reserve to move in a less expansionary direction—though it should have done so at least a year earlier. But when it moved, it went too far, producing the sharpest change in the rate of monetary growth of the post-war era. Again, having gone too far, it was the right policy for the Fed to reverse course at the end of 1966. But again it went too far, not only restoring but exceeding the earlier excessive rate of monetary growth. And this episode is no exception. Time and again this has been the course followed—as in 1919 and 1920, in 1937 and 1938, in 1953 and 1954, in 1959 and 1960.

The reason for the propensity to overreact seems clear: the failure of monetary authorities to allow for the delay between their actions and the subsequent effects on the economy. They tend to determine their actions by today's conditions—but their actions will affect the economy only six or nine or twelve or fifteen months later. Hence they feel impelled to step on the brake, or the accelerator, as the case may be, too hard.

My own prescription is still that the monetary authority go all the way in avoiding such swings by adopting publicly the policy of achieving a steady rate of growth in a specified monetary total. The precise rate of growth, like the precise monetary total, is less important than the adoption of some stated and known rate. I myself have argued for a rate that would on the average achieve rough stability in the level of prices of final products, which I have estimated would call for something like a 3 to 5 per cent per year rate of growth in currency plus all commercial bank deposits or a slightly lower rate of growth in currency plus demand deposits only.[15] But it would be better to have a fixed rate that would on the average produce moderate inflation or moderate deflation, provided it was steady, than to suffer the wide and erratic perturbations we have experienced.

Short of the adoption of such a publicly stated policy of a steady rate of monetary growth, it would constitute a major improvement if the monetary authority followed the self-denying ordinance of avoiding wide swings. It is a

15. In Chapter 1 of this book, "The Optimum Quantity of Money," I conclude that a still lower rate, something like 2 per cent for the broader definition, might be better yet, in order to eliminate or reduce the difference between private and total costs of adding to real balances.

matter of record that periods of relative stability in the rate of monetary growth have also been periods of relative stability in economic activity, both in the United States and other countries. Periods of wide swings in the rate of monetary growth have also been periods of wide swings in economic activity.

By setting itself a steady course and keeping to it, the monetary authority could make a major contribution to promoting economic stability. By making that course one of steady but moderate growth in the quantity of money, it would make a major contribution to avoidance of either inflation or deflation of prices. Other forces would still affect the economy, require change and adjustment, and disturb the even tenor of our ways. But steady monetary growth would provide a monetary climate favorable to the effective operation of those basic forces of enterprise, ingenuity, invention, hard work, and thrift that are the true springs of economic growth. That is the most that we can ask from monetary policy at our present stage of knowledge. But that much—and it is a great deal—is clearly within our reach.

Chapter 6

The Demand for Money:
Some Theoretical and
Empirical Results

IN COUNTRIES EXPERIENCING a secular rise in real income per capita, the
stock of money generally rises over long periods at a decidedly higher rate than
does money income. Income velocity—the ratio of money income to the stock
of money—therefore declines secularly as real income rises. During cycles, to
judge from the United States, the only country for which a detailed analysis has
been made, the stock of money generally rises during expansions at a lower rate
than money income and either continues to rise during contractions or falls at a
decidedly lower rate than money income. Income velocity therefore rises during
cyclical expansions as real income rises and falls during cyclical contractions as

Reprinted from *The Journal of Political Economy*, vol. 67, no. 4, August 1959. This paper
reports on part of a broader study being conducted at the National Bureau of Economic
Research by Anna J. Schwartz and myself. I am indebted to Mrs. Schwartz for extensive
assistance and numerous suggestions in connection with the present paper.

   This paper was approved for publication as a report of the National Bureau of Economic
Research by the Director of Research and the Board of Directors of the National Bureau, in
accordance with the resolution of the board governing National Bureau reports (see the
Annual Report of the National Bureau of Economic Research). It was reprinted as the National
Bureau's Occasional Paper no. 68 (1959).

real income falls—precisely the reverse of the secular relation between income and velocity.

These key facts about the secular and cyclical behavior of income velocity have been documented in a number of studies,[1] For the United States, Anna Schwartz and I have been able to document them more fully than has hitherto been possible, thanks to a new series on the stock of money that we have constructed which gives estimates at annual or semi-annual dates from 1867 to 1907 and monthly thereafter. This fuller documentation does not, however, dispel the apparent contradiction between the secular and the cyclical behavior of income velocity. On the contrary, as the summary of our findings in the following section makes explicit, it reveals an additional contradiction or, rather, another aspect of the central contradiction.

Previous attempts to reconcile the secular and cyclical behavior of the velocity of circulation of money have concentrated on variables other than income, such as the rate of interest or the rate of change of prices. These attempts have been unsuccessful. While such other variables doubtless affect the quantity of money demanded and hence the velocity of circulation of money, most do not have a cyclical pattern that could explain the observed discrepancy. In any event, it seems dubious that their influence on velocity is sufficiently great to explain so large a discrepancy.

An alternative theoretical explanation of the discrepancy is suggested by the work I have done on consumption—a rather striking example of how work in one field can have important implications for work in another that has generally been regarded as only rather distantly related. This theoretical explanation, which concentrates on the meaning attached to "income" and to "prices," is presented in Sections II and III below and turns out to be susceptible of quantitative test. The quantitative evidence in Section IV is highly favorable. The result is both a fuller understanding of the observed behavior of velocity and a different emphasis in the theory of the demand for money.

One important feature of monetary behavior not accounted for by this explanation is the consistent tendency for actual cash balances, adjusted for trend, to lead at both peaks and troughs in general business. In Section V, a preliminary attempt is made to explore factors that might account for the discrepancy between desired cash balances as determined by income alone and actual cash balances. Finally, in Section VI, some broader implications of the results presented in this paper are explored.

1. See in particular Richard T. Selden, "Monetary Velocity in the United States," in Milton Friedman (Ed.), *Studies in the Quantity Theory of Money*, Chicago: University of Chicago Press (1956), pp. 179–257; and Ernest Doblin, "The Ratio of Income to Money Supply: An International Survey," *Review of Economics and Statistics*, August, 1951, p. 201.

I. A SUMMARY OF THE EMPIRICAL
EVIDENCE FOR THE UNITED STATES

A full documentation of our findings about the secular and cyclical behavior of the stock of money and its relation to income and prices is given in a series of National Bureau of Economic Research monographs by Anna J. Schwartz and myself. For present purposes, a brief summary of a few of our findings will suffice.

A. Secular Behavior

1. Secular changes in the real stock of money per capita are highly correlated with secular changes in real income per capita. In order to study this relation, we have used average values over complete reference cycles as our elementary observations. For twenty cycles, measured from trough to trough and covering the period from 1870 to 1954, the simple correlation between the logarithm of the real stock of money per capita and the logarithm of real income per capita is 0.99, and the computed elasticity is 1.8.[2]

A 1 per cent increase in real income per capita has therefore, on the average, been associated with a 1.8 per cent increase in real cash balances per capita and hence with a 0.8 per cent *decrease* in income velocity. If we interpret these results as reflecting movements along a stable demand relation, they imply that money is a "luxury" in the terminology of consumption theory. Because of the strong trend element in the two series correlated, the high correlation alone does not justify much confidence that the statistical regression is a valid estimate of a demand relation rather than the result of an accidental difference in trends. However, additional evidence from other sources leads us to believe that it can be so regarded.

We have investigated the influence of both rates of interest and rates of change of prices. In our experiments, the rate of interest had an effect in the direction to be expected from theoretical considerations but too small to be statistically significant. We have not as yet been able to isolate by correlation techniques any

2. The corresponding figures for cycles measured from peak to peak are 0.99 and 1.7. In these and later correlations, "money" is defined as including currency held by the public, adjusted demand deposits, and time deposits in commercial banks. This total is available for the period from 1867 on, whereas the total exclusive of time deposits is not available until 1914. For other reasons supporting our definition see our NBER monographs. For income, we have used Simon Kuznets' estimates of net national product adjusted for wartime periods to a concept approximating that underlying the current Department of Commerce estimates, and for prices, the deflator implicit in Kuznets' estimates of net national product in constant prices.

effect of the rate of change of prices, though a historical analysis persuades us that such an effect is present.[2a]

2. Over the nine decades that we have studied, there have been a number of long swings in money income. As a matter of arithmetic, these swings in money income can be attributed to movements in the nominal stock of money and in velocity. If this is done, it turns out that the swings in the stock of money are in the opposite direction from those in velocity and so much larger in amplitude that they dominate the movements in money income. As a result, the long swings in prices mirror faithfully the long swings in the stock of money per unit of output. These long swings are much more marked in money income and in the nominal stock of money than in real income and in the real stock of money, which is to say that the long swings are largely price swings.

B. Cyclical Behavior

1. The real stock of money, like real income, conforms positively to the cycle; that is, it tends to rise during expansions and to fall, or to rise at a less rapid rate, during contractions. However, the amplitude of the movement in the real stock of money is decidedly smaller than in real income. If we allow for secular trends, a 1 per cent change in real income during a cycle is accompanied by a change in the real stock of money in the same direction of about one-fifth of 1 per cent.

It follows that income velocity tends to rise during cyclical expansions when real income is rising and to fall during cyclical contractions when real income is falling—that is, to conform positively. So far as we can tell from data that are mostly annual, velocity reaches both its peak and its trough at roughly the same time as general economic activity does.

2. Cyclical movements in money income, like the long swings, can be attributed to movements in the nominal stock of money and in velocity. If this is done, it turns out that the movements in the stock of money and in velocity are in the same direction and of roughly equal magnitude, so that neither can be said to dominate the movements in money income.

3. Table 1 summarizes the size of the cyclical movements in the variables used in the analysis, where the size of cyclical movement is measured by the excess of the rate of change per month during cyclical expansions over that during cyclical contractions.

2a. In subsequent work since this article was first published, we have succeeded in doing so. The results will be published in one of our NBER monographs.

Table 1. *Cyclical Movements in Income, Money Stock, Income Velocity, and Prices: Difference in Monthly Rate of Change between Reference Expansion and Contraction, Annual Analysis, 1870–1954, Excluding War Cycles*

	CHANGE PER MONTH IN REFERENCE-CYCLE RELATIVES DURING REFERENCE		EXCESS OF EXPANSION OVER CONTRACTION
	Expansion (1)	*Contraction* (2)	(3)
Twelve mild depression cycles:			
Money income	.64	− .07	.71
Money stock	.55	.28	.27
Income velocity	.08	− .32	.40
Implicit price deflator	.12	− .02	.14
Real income	.52	− .05	.57
Real stock of money	.43	.30	.13
Six deep depression cycles:			
Money income	.64	− .97	1.61
Money stock	.60	− .28	.88
Income velocity	.02	− .69	.71
Implicit price deflator	.16	− .44	.60
Real income	.46	− .53	.99
Real stock of money	.42	.18	.24

The series were analyzed as described in A. F. Burns and W. C. Mitchell, *Measuring Business Cycles*, New York: National Bureau of Economic Research (1947), pp. 197–202. Deep depression cycles are 1870–78, 1891–94, 1904–8, 1919–21, 1927–32, and 1932–38. All others are mild depression cycles except for war cycles 1914–19 and 1938–46, which are excluded. The basis of classification is described in the NBER monograph on the money supply. *Money income* is net national product at current prices, preliminary estimates by Simon Kuznets, prepared for use in the NBER study of long-term trends in capital formation and financing in the United States. Variant III (from 1929 based on estimates of commodity flow and services prepared by the Department of Commerce). *Money stock* is averaged to center on June 30 from data in the money monograph just mentioned. *Income velocity* is money income divided annually by money stock. *Implicit price deflator* is money income divided by real income. *Real income* is net national product, 1929 prices, Variant III from the same source as money income. *Real stock of money* is money stock divided by the implicit price deflator.

C. The Contrast

These findings are clearly in sharp contrast. Over long periods, *real* income and velocity tend to move in opposite directions; over reference cycles, in the same direction. Over long periods, changes in the nominal stock of money dominate, at least in a statistical sense, the swings in *money* income, and the inverse movements in velocity are of minor quantitative importance; over reference cycles, changes in velocity are in the same direction as changes in the nominal stock of money and are comparable in quantitative importance in accounting for changes in money income. I turn to an attempted reconciliation.

II. A SUGGESTED EXPLANATION

It is important to note at the outset an essential difference between the determinants of the nominal stock of money, on the one hand, and the real stock of money, on the other. The nominal stock of money is determined in the first instance by the monetary authorities or institutions and cannot be altered by the non-bank holders of money. The real stock of money is determined in the first instance by the holders of money.

This distinction is sharpest and least ambiguous in a hypothetical society in which money consists exclusively of a purely fiduciary currency issued by a single money-creating authority at its discretion. The nominal number of units of money is then whatever amount this authority creates. Holders of money cannot alter this amount directly. But they can make the real amount of money anything that in the aggregate they want to. If they want to hold a relatively small real quantity of money, they will individually seek to reduce their nominal cash balances by increasing expenditures. This will not alter the nominal stock of money to be held—if some individuals succeed in reducing their nominal cash balances, it will only be by transferring them to others. But it will raise the flow of expenditures and hence money income and prices, and thereby reduce the real quantity of money to the desired level. Conversely, if they want to hold a relatively large real quantity of money, they will individually seek to increase their nominal cash balances. They cannot, in the aggregate, succeed in doing so. However, in the attempt, they will lower the nominal flow of expenditures, and hence money income and prices, and so raise the real quantity of money. Given the level of real income, the ratio of income to the stock of money, or income velocity, is uniquely determined by the real stock of money. Consequently, these comments apply also to income velocity. It, too, is determined by the holders of money, or, to put it differently, it is a reflection of their decisions about the real quantity of money that they desire to hold. We can therefore speak more or less interchangeably about decisions of holders of money to change their real stock of money or to change the ratio of the flow of income to the stock of money.

The situation is more complicated for the monetary arrangements that actually prevailed over the period which our data cover. During part of the period, when the United States was on an effective gold standard, an attempt by holders of money to reduce their cash balances relative to the flow of income raised domestic prices, thereby discouraging exports and encouraging imports, and so tended to increase the outflow of gold or reduce its inflow. In addition, the rise in domestic prices raised, among other things, the cost of producing gold and hence discouraged gold production. Both effects operated to reduce the nominal supply of money. Conversely, an attempt by holders of money to increase their cash balances relative to the flow of income tended to increase the nominal supply of money through the same channels. These effects still occur but can be, and typically are, offset by Federal Reserve action.

Throughout the period, more complicated reactions operated on the commercial banking system, sometimes in perverse fashion. For example, an attempt by holders of money to reduce cash balances relative to income tended to raise income and prices, thus promoting an expansionary atmosphere in which banks were generally willing to operate on a slenderer margin of liquidity. The result was an increase rather than a reduction in the nominal supply of money. Similarly, changes in the demand for money had effects on security prices and interest rates that affected the amount of money supplied by the banking system. And there were further effects on the actions of the Federal Reserve System for the period since 1914.

There were also indirect effects running in the opposite direction, from changes in the conditions of supply of money to the nominal quantity of money demanded. If, for whatever reason, money-creating institutions expanded the nominal quantity of money, this could have effects, at least in the first instance, on rates of interest and so on the quantity of money demanded, and perhaps also on money income and real income.

Despite these qualifications, all of which would have to be taken into account in a complete analysis, it seems useful to regard the nominal quantity of money as determined primarily by conditions of supply, and the real quantity of money and the income velocity of money as determined primarily by conditions of demand. This implies that we should examine the demand side for an initial interpretation of the observed behavior of velocity.

Along these lines, the changes in the real stock of money and in the income velocity of circulation reflect either (a) shifts along a relatively fixed demand schedule for money produced by changes in the variables entering into that schedule; (b) changes in the demand schedule itself; or (c) temporary departures from the schedule, that is, frictions that make the actual stock of money depart from the desired stock of money. The rest of this paper is an attempt to see the extent to which we can reconcile the secular and cyclical behavior of velocity in terms of a alone without bringing in the more complicated phenomena that would be involved in b and c.

One way to do so would be to regard the cyclical changes in velocity as reflecting the influence of variables other than income. In order for this explanation to be satisfactory, these other variables would have to exert an influence opposite to that of income and also be sufficiently potent to dominate the movement of velocity. Our secular results render this implausible, for we there found that income appeared to be the dominant variable affecting the demand for real cash balances. Moreover, the other variables that come first to mind are interest rates, and these display cyclical patterns that seem most unlikely to account for the sizable, highly consistent, and roughly synchronous cyclical pattern in velocity. Long-term corporate interest rates fairly regularly reached their trough in mid-expansion and their peak in mid-contraction prior to World War I. Since then, the pattern is less regular and is characterized by shorter lags. Rates on short-term commercial paper also tend to lag at peaks and troughs, though by a briefer interval, and the lag has similarly shortened since 1921. Call-money rates come closer to being synchronous with the cycle, and this is true of yields on long- and short-term government obligations for the six cycles for which they are available. Of the rates we have examined these are the only ones that have anything like the right timing pattern to account for the synchronous pattern in velocity. However, neither call-money rates nor government bond yields have been highly consistent in behavior from cycle to cycle. Even if they had been, it seems dubious that the effects of changes in these particular rates, or other unrecorded rates like them, would be sufficiently more important cyclically than secularly to offset the effects of counter-movements both in other rates and in income. Furthermore, earlier studies that have attempted to explain velocity movements in these terms have had only limited success.[3]

A very different way to reconcile the cyclical and secular behavior of velocity is to regard the statistical magnitude called "real income" as corresponding to a different theoretical construct in the cyclical than in the secular analysis. This possibility was suggested by my work on consumption. In that field, too, it will be recalled, there is an apparent conflict between empirical findings for short periods and long periods: cross-section data for individual years suggest that the average propensity to consume is lower at high-income levels than at low-income levels; yet aggregate time-series data covering a long period reveal no secular decline in the average propensity to consume with a rise in income. It turned out that this conflict could be reconciled by distinguishing between "measured" income, the figure recorded by statisticians, and "permanent" income, a longer-term concept to which individuals are regarded as adjusting their consumption.[4]

According to the permanent income hypothesis, when a consumer unit experiences a transitory increment of income, that is, when its measured income exceeds its permanent income, this transitory component is added to its assets (perhaps in the form of durable consumer goods) or used to reduce its liabilities rather than spent on consumption. Conversely, when it experiences a transitory decrement of income, it nonetheless adjusts consumption to permanent income, financing any excess over measured income by drawing down assets or increasing liabilities.

This theory of consumption behavior is directly applicable to that part of the stock of money held by consumer units rather than by business enterprises. The problem is how to interpret money holding. Much of the theoretical literature

3. E.g., see Selden, *op. cit.*, pp. 195–202.

4. See my *A Theory of the Consumption Function*, for the National Bureau of Economic Research, Princeton: Princeton University Press (1957).

on "motives" for holding money suggests interpreting money holdings as one of the balance-sheet items that act as shock absorbers for transitory components of income; as an asset item that is increased temporarily when the transitory component is positive and that is drawn down, if necessary, to finance consumption when the transitory component is negative.

This interpretation may be valid for very short time periods. However, if it were valid for periods as long as a business cycle, it would produce a cyclical behavior of velocity precisely the opposite of the observed behavior. Measured income presumably exceeds permanent income at cyclical peaks and falls short of permanent income at cyclical troughs. Hence cash balances would be drawn down abnormally at troughs and built up abnormally at peaks. In consequence, cash balances would fluctuate more widely over the cycle than income, and velocity would conform inversely to the cycle, falling during expansions and rising during contractions, whereas in fact it conforms positively.[4a]

An alternative is to interpret money as a durable consumer good held for the services it renders and yielding a flow of services proportional to the stock, which implies that the shock-absorber function is performed by other items in the balance sheet, such as the stock of durable goods, consumer credit outstanding, personal debt, and perhaps securities held. On this interpretation, the quantity of money demanded, like the quantity of consumption services in general, is adapted not to measured income but to permanent income. This interpretation is consistent with our secular results. The income figure we used in obtaining these is an average value over a cycle, which may be regarded as a closer approximation to permanent income than an annual value. In any case, the long time period covered assures that the movements in money are dominated by the movements in the permanent component of income.[5] For the cyclical analysis, permanent income need not itself be stable over a cycle. It may well rise during expansions and fall during contractions. Presumably, however, it will rise less than measured income during expansions and fall less during contractions. Hence, if money holdings were adapted to permanent income, they might rise and fall more than in proportion to permanent income, as is required by our secular results, yet less than in proportion to measured income, as is required by our cyclical results.

To put the matter differently, suppose that the demand for real cash balances were determined entirely by real permanent income according to the relation estimated in the secular analysis and that actual balances throughout equaled

4a. As David Laidler pointed out to me after this was published, this paragraph contains an error, the common one of confusing a function and its derivative. Cash balances would be built up so long as measured income exceeded permanent income, which means until mid-contraction, and would be drawn down so long as measured income fell short of permanent income, which means until mid-expansion. Hence, the cyclical behavior of velocity would not be 'precisely the opposite of the observed behavior', though it would still tend to differ from the observed behavior.

5. *Ibid.*, pp. 125–29.

desired balances. Velocity would then fall during expansions and rise (or fall at a smaller rate) during contractions, *provided* that it was computed by dividing *permanent income* by the stock of money. But the numbers we have been calling "velocity" were not computed in this way; they were computed by dividing measured income by the stock of money. Such a *measured* velocity would tend to be lower than what we may call *permanent* velocity at troughs, because measured income is then lower than permanent income, and would tend to be higher at peaks, because measured income is then higher than permanent income. Measured velocity might therefore conform positively to the cycle, even though permanent velocity conformed inversely.

These comments apply explicitly only to consumer cash balances. However, they can readily be extended to business cash balances. Businesses hold cash as a productive resource. The question is whether cash is a resource like inventories, in which case it might be expected to fluctuate more over the cycle than current production, or like fixed capital, in which case it might be expected to fluctuate less and to be adapted to the longer-term level of production at which a firm plans to operate. This latter possibility involves a concept analogous to that of permanent income. If the observed positive cyclical conformity of velocity reflects wider movements in income than in both business holdings and consumer holdings, as seems likely in view of the changing importance of these two components and the consistent behavior of velocity, the answer must be that cash balances are analogous to fixed capital rather than to inventories and that some other assets or liabilities serve as shock absorbers for business as for consumers.

The distinction between permanent and measured income can rationalize the observed cyclical behavior of income velocity in terms of a movement along a stable demand curve. It cannot by itself easily rationalize the behavior of real cash balances. Our secular analysis implies that real cash balances should conform positively to the cycle with an amplitude nearly twice that of permanent real income. Observed real cash balances do conform positively, but their amplitude, at any rate for cycles containing mild contractions, is so small that it seems implausible to regard it as larger than that in permanent real income. Put differently, it would take only very moderate changes in the index of prices, well within the margin of error in such indexes, to convert the positive conformity into inverted conformity.

The resolution is straightforward. We have not yet carried our logic far enough. If applied to both money income and real income, the distinction between measured and permanent income implies a corresponding distinction for prices. To put the matter in terms of economics rather than arithmetic, our analysis suggests that holders of cash balances determine the amount to hold in light of their longer-term income position rather than their momentary receipts —this is the justification for distinguishing measured from permanent income. By the same token, they may be expected to determine the amount of cash balances to hold in light of longer-term price movements—permanent prices, as it were—rather than current or measured prices. Suppose, for example, prices were to double permanently or, alternatively, to double for day X only and then return to their initial level and that this behavior was correctly anticipated by holders of money. Holders of money would hardly want to hold the same nominal cash balances on day X in these two cases, even though prices were the same on that day. More generally, whatever the motives for holding cash balances, they are held and are expected to be held for a sizable and indefinite period of time. Holders of money presumably judge the "real" amount of cash balances in terms of the quantity of goods and services to which the balances are equivalent, not at any given moment of time, but over a sizable and indefinite period; that is, they evaluate them in terms of "expected" or "permanent" prices, not in terms of the current price level. This consideration does not, of course, rule out some adjustment to temporary movements in prices. Such movements offer opportunities of profit from shifting wealth from cash to other forms of assets and conversely, and they may affect people's expectations about future price levels. Like "permanent income," the "permanent" price level need not be—and presumably is not—a constant over time; it departs from the current price level in having a smoother and less fluctuating pattern in time but need not go to the extreme of displaying no fluctuations.

On this view, the current price level would presumably fall short of the permanent price level at troughs and exceed it at peaks of cycles; hence measured real cash balances would tend to be larger than permanent real cash balances at troughs and smaller at peaks. It follows that measured real cash balances would show a smaller cyclical movement than permanent real cash balances and, indeed, might conform inversely to the cycle, even though permanent real cash balances conformed positively.

III. A SYMBOLIC RESTATEMENT

The distinction between permanent and measured magnitudes can thus reconcile the qualitative behavior during reference cycles of both measured velocity—its tendency to conform positively—and measured real cash balances—its tendency to show an exceedingly mild cyclical movement—with their behavior over secular periods. The crucial question remains whether it not only can reconcile the qualitative behavior but does in fact rationalize the quantitative behavior of these magnitudes. After all, an interpretation in terms of interest rates can also rationalize the qualitative results; we reject it because it appears likely to be contradicted on a more detailed quantitative level.

It will facilitate such a quantitative test to restate symbolically and more precisely the explanation just presented. Let

Y be measured aggregate income in nominal terms;
P be measured price level;

M be aggregate stock of money in nominal terms, measured and permanent being taken throughout as identical;

N be population, measured and permanent being taken as identical;

Y_p, P_p be permanent nominal aggregate income and permanent price level, respectively;

$y = \dfrac{Y}{P}$ be measured aggregate income in real terms;

$y_p = \dfrac{Y_p}{P_p}$ be permanent aggregate income in real terms;

$m = \dfrac{M}{P}$ be measured aggregate stock of money in real terms;

$m_p = \dfrac{M}{P_p}$ be permanent aggregate stock of money in real terms;

$V = \dfrac{Y}{M} = \dfrac{y}{m}$ be measured velocity;

$V_p = \dfrac{Y_p}{M} = \dfrac{y_p}{m_p}$ be permanent velocity.

In these symbols, the demand equation fitted to the secular data can be written thus:

$$\frac{M}{NP_p} = \gamma \left(\frac{Y_p}{NP_p}\right)^{\delta}, \tag{1}$$

which expresses permanent real balances per capita as a function of permanent real income per capita, or in the equivalent form,

$$m_p = \gamma N \left(\frac{y_p}{N}\right)^{\delta} = \gamma N^{1-\delta} y_p^{\delta}, \tag{2}$$

which expresses aggregate permanent real balances as a function of aggregate permanent real income and population, where γ and δ are parameters and δ was estimated to be approximately $1.8.$[6]

By definition,

$$m = \frac{M}{P} = \frac{M}{P_p}\frac{P_p}{P} = \frac{P_p}{P} m_p, \tag{3}$$

so that still a third form of the demand equation is

$$m = \frac{P_p}{P} \gamma N^{1-\delta} y_p^{\delta}, \tag{4}$$

6. The basic analysis holds, of course, whatever the precise form of the demand equation for money. I use this particular form for simplicity and because it gave a satisfactory fit to the available evidence. The whole analysis could, however, be restated in terms of a generalized demand function whose form was unspecified.

which expresses aggregate measured real balances as a function of aggregate permanent real income, population, and permanent and measured prices.

This relation can also be expressed in terms of velocity. By definition, $V_p = y_p/m_p$. Divide y_p successively by the two sides of equation (2). This gives

$$V_p = \frac{y_p}{m_p} = \frac{1}{\gamma} N^{\delta-1} y_p^{1-\delta} = \frac{1}{\gamma} \left(\frac{y_p}{N}\right)^{1-\delta}. \tag{5}$$

By definition,

$$V = \frac{Y}{M} = \frac{Y}{Y_p} \frac{Y_p}{M} = \frac{Y}{Y_p} V_p, \tag{6}$$

so that

$$V = \frac{Y}{Y_p} \frac{1}{\gamma} \left(\frac{y_p}{N}\right)^{1-\delta}. \tag{7}$$

In interpreting equations (1), (2), (4), (5), and (7), it should be borne in mind that they will not, of course, be satisfied precisely by observed data. In consequence, at a later stage, I shall want to distinguish observed values of, for example, measured velocity and the value estimated from, say, equation (7).

IV. TESTS OF THE EXPLANATION

It has so far been sufficient to suppose only that the permanent magnitudes introduced—permanent income and permanent prices—fluctuate less over the cycle than the corresponding measured magnitudes. We can clearly go farther and ask how much less the permanent magnitudes must fluctuate in order to account for the quantitative, as well as the qualitative, average behavior of velocity and real cash balances. The answer may provide some internal evidence on the plausibility of the suggested explanation and will also provide a starting point for bringing external evidence to bear.

Consider the data for the mild depression cycles shown in Table 1 and neglect the mild cyclical movements in population, so that aggregate and per capita values can be regarded as interchangeable. If measured and permanent magnitudes were treated as identical, the income elasticity of 1.8 computed from the secular data would convert the .57 cyclical movement in real income into a movement of 1.03 in *real* cash balances demanded. The movement of .14 in the implicit price index would, in turn, convert this into a movement of 1.17 in *money* cash balances demanded. The actual movement in cash balances is .27, or 23 per cent as large. Hence, to reconcile the secular and cyclical results, the cyclical movements in permanent income and permanent prices would each have to be 23 per cent of those in measured income and measured prices—a result that seems not implausible. For deep depression cycles, the corresponding figure turns out to be 37 per cent, which is equally plausible. Moreover, it seems eminently reasonable that this figure should be larger for deep, than for mild, depression cycles, since the deep depression cycles are longer on the average than the mild depression cycles.[7]

Of course, this test of intuitive plausibility is a weak one. To get a stronger test, we must introduce some independent evidence on the relation of permanent to measured magnitudes. One source of such evidence is the work on consumption that suggested the explanation under test. In deriving a consumption function from aggregate time-series data, I concluded that an *estimate* of permanent income—which I called "expected" income to distinguish it from the theoretical concept—was given by

$$y_p(T) = \beta \int_{-\infty}^{T} e^{(\beta-\alpha)(t-T)} y(t) dt. \tag{8}$$

In words, an estimate of expected income at time T is given by a weighted average of past incomes, adjusted for secular growth at the rate of α per cent per year, the weights declining exponentially and being equal to $e^{\beta(t-T)}$, where t is the time of the observation being weighted. The numerical value of β was estimated to be .4; of α, .02.[8] It is by no means necessary that the concept of

7. Let M and $\dot{P}$ be the cyclical movements as measured in the final column of Table 1 in the nominal stock of money and in measured prices; let $\dot{m}_p$ and $\dot{P}_p$ be the cyclical movements in permanent real balances and permanent prices. Then, to a first approximation,

$$\dot{M} = \dot{m}_p + \dot{P}_p, \tag{i}$$

since the stock of money is the product of permanent real cash balances and the permanent price level. Using the demand equation (2), we get

$$\dot{m}_p = 1.8 \dot{y}_p, \tag{ii}$$

where $\dot{y}_p$ is the cyclical movement in permanent real income (recall that we are neglecting any cyclical movement in population, so $\dot{y}_p$ also equals the movement in permanent real per capita income).

Let

$$\dot{y}_p = k\dot{y}, \tag{iii}$$

$$\dot{P}_p = k'\dot{P}, \tag{iv}$$

where $\dot{y}$ is the cyclical movement in measured real income and k and k' are unspecified constants to be determined. Substituting equations (ii), (iii), and (iv) in equation (i) gives

$$\dot{M} = 1.8k\dot{y} + k'\dot{P}. \tag{v}$$

At first glance, it seems possible to derive both k and k' from one set of data by deriving a similar equation starting with an identity like (i) expressing measured velocity in terms of permanent velocity. However, the resulting equation is identical with eq. (v), thanks to the definitional relations connecting velocity, money, and income.

The calculations in the text implicitly assume that $k=k'$ in eq. (v). Separate estimates for k and k' require two sets of data. One possibility is to assume that k and k' differ but that each is the same for mild and for deep depression cycles, an assumption that seems less plausible than the one made in the text that $k=k'$. This calculation yields an estimate of .11 for k and 1.15 for k'. The value for k' contradicts the concepts of permanent and measured prices that underlie the analysis.

8. Friedman, *A Theory of the Consumption Function*, pp. 146–47.

permanent income that is relevant in determining total consumption expenditures should also be the one that is relevant in determining cash balances.[9] But it would not be at all surprising if it were. On the assumption that it is, we can get independent estimates of the percentages cited in the previous paragraph by computing estimates of permanent real income and permanent prices from the corresponding observed annual series, using the weighting pattern just described.

The results of these computations are summarized in columns 1, 2, and 3 of Table 2.[10] The agreement between the estimates in column 3 so obtained and the estimates constructed above from internal evidence alone is very good—the

Table 2. *Two Estimates of Cyclical Movements of Permanent Real Income and Prices as Percentages of Those of Measured Real Income and Prices, Reference Cycles 1870–1954, Excluding War Cycles*

	EXCESS OF CHANGE PER MONTH IN REFERENCE–CYCLE RELATIVES DURING REFERENCE EXPANSION OVER THAT DURING REFERENCE CONTRACTION		PERMANENT AS PERCENTAGE OF MEASURED	
	Permanent Magnitude (1)	*Measured Magnitude* (2)	*Permanent Estimated Separately* (3)	*Ratio Estimated from Money Equations* (4)
Twelve mild depression cycles:				
Real income	.11	.57	19	23
Prices	.02	.14	16	23
Six deep depression cycles:				
Real income	.29	.99	29	37
Prices	.18	.60	30	37

The sources for the columns are as follows (cycles grouped as in Table 1):

1. Permanent real income and permanent prices were estimated as described in the text, using Kuznets' data (see note to Table 1). These data begin in 1869. To obtain an estimate of the permanent magnitude in 1869, measured figures covering the years 1858–69 are required, the weights assigned declining exponentially. Measured figures were therefore extrapolated: for real income by assuming a constant rate of growth of 3.5 per cent per year; for implicit prices by assuming that in each of the years 1858–68 they bore the same relation to the wholesale price index as in 1869.
2. Table 1, col. 3.
3. Column 1 divided by col. 2, the figures in each case being carried to an additional place.
4. Values from Table 1, col. 3, were substituted in the expression $\dot{M}/(1.8\dot{y}+\dot{P})$, where M is money stock, y is real income, P is implicit price deflator, and the dot on top means "excess of change per month in reference-cycle relatives during reference expansion over that during reference contraction."

9. See *ibid.*, pp. 150–51.

10. These results at first seemed to me relevant also to the choice between the two alternative assumptions used above—the one in the text that $k=k'$ and the one noted in footnote 7, that $k \neq k'$ but that k is the same for mild and deep depression cycles and so is $k.'$ On this issue, the result is unambiguous. The entries in col. 3 clearly speak for the first assumption.

two differ by only 15–30 per cent, even though they are based on independent bodies of data and even though the weights used in estimating the permanent magnitudes directly were derived for another purpose and rest on still other data. Moreover, the discrepancy is consistent; the difference between deep and mild depression cycles is in the same direction and of roughly the same magnitude for both columns.

These results are sufficiently encouraging to justify going beyond this indirect test and seeing how far our interpretation is consistent not only with the size of the cyclical movement in cash balances and measured velocity but also with their entire cyclical patterns and not only on the average but also cycle by cycle.

In order to perform this test on a fully consistent basis, we first recomputed the secular demand equation, using as the independent variable the cycle averages of estimated permanent income rather than measured income. This substitution slightly raised the correlation coefficient, thus giving a minor bit of additional evidence in favor of the permanent income interpretation. It also raised slightly the estimated elasticity of demand, but not by enough to change the numerical value to the number of significant figures given above.

The resulting calculated equation for nominal cash balances is

$$M^* = (.00323)\left(\frac{y_p}{N}\right)^{1.810} NP_p, \tag{9}$$

and, for measured velocity,

$$V^* = \frac{1}{0.00323}\left(\frac{y_p}{N}\right)^{-0.810}\frac{Y}{Y_p}, \tag{10}$$

where the asterisks are used to indicate values computed from the equation rather than directly observed. These equations, it will be recalled, were estimated from average values over whole reference cycles.[11]

However, James Ford has pointed out to me that this result is largely a consequence of an assumption made in estimating permanent income and prices, namely, the use of the same value of β for both. There is no independent empirical evidence for this assumption, and hence results based on it can give no independent evidence for the essentially equivalent assumption that $k = k'$.

For the special case in which the measured magnitude is given by a sine curve, the relative amplitude of a permanent and a measured magnitude when the permanent is estimated by a weighted average of the measured is determined entirely by the value of β and the duration of the cycle. For $\beta = .4$ and a cycle 43 months in length, which is the average length of the mild depression cycles, the relative amplitude for the sine curve is .22. For $\beta = .4$ and a cycle 47.5 months in length, the average length of the deep depression cycles, the relative amplitude for the sine curve is .25. These results are fairly similar to the computed values in Table 2. They differ enough, however, to suggest that the departure from a sine curve affects the results appreciably.

I am indebted to James Ford for these calculations.

11. The numerical values given were computed from combined data for trough-to-trough and peak-to-peak averages. However, separate regressions for each set of averages are almost identical.

From these equations, one can estimate for each year separately, from the corresponding annual data, desired cash balances and the value of measured velocity that would be observed if actual cash balances equaled desired balances as so estimated. I shall call these "computed cash balances" and "computed measured velocity."[12]

The estimates of computed measured velocity are plotted in Chart I, along

CHART I

OBSERVED AND COMPUTED MEASURED VELOCITY, ANNUALLY, 1869–1957

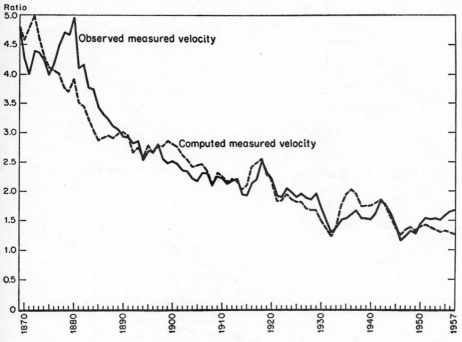

12. To make these calculations, estimates of Y, Y_p, γ_p, P_p, and N are needed. Measured money income, Y, was taken to be Kuznets' annual net national product in current prices adjusted for wartime periods; Y_p was computed by applying eq. (8) to this same series, except for a minor adjustment in level; γ_p, by applying eq. (8) to Kuznets' net national product in constant prices similarly adjusted, and again with a minor adjustment in level; P_p by applying eq. (8) to the price index implicit in computing net national product in constant prices; and N was taken as the mid-year population of the United States as estimated by the Census.

Equation (8) with $\beta = .40$ and $\alpha = .02$ implies that expected income is 1.05 times the weighted average of actual income, where the weights are the declining exponential weights inside the integral of eq. (8), adjusted to sum to unity. When permanent net national product per capita in constant prices was computed in this way, it turned out that the geometric mean of the ratios of the cycle bases of real measured net national product per capita to the cycle bases of permanent net national product in constant prices so computed was 1.057. This factor of 1.057 was used to adjust the level of the latter series rather than the 1.05 strictly called for by eq. (8) and was used also for permanent net national product in

CHART II

OBSERVED AND COMPUTED MEASURED VELOCITY, REFERENCE-CYCLE PATTERNS, 1870–1954

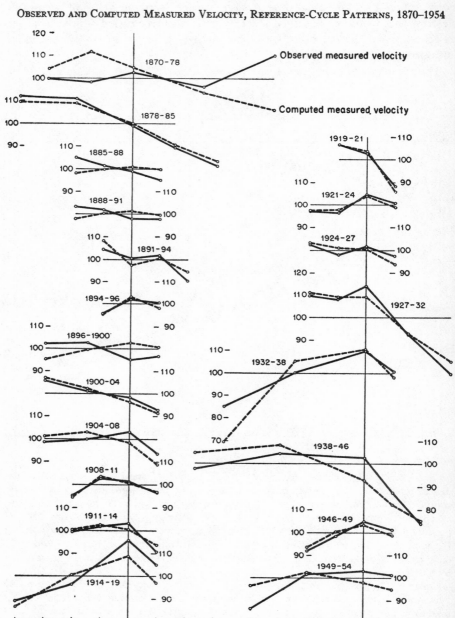

NOTE: These are reference-cycle relatives computed in the course of the cyclical analysis of the data shown in Chart I (see A. F. Burns and W. C. Mitchell, *Measuring Business Cycles* (New York: National Bureau of Economic Research [1946], pp. 197–202).

with observed measured velocity. In judging this figure, it should be borne in mind that the computed velocities were not obtained by trying to fit these observed velocities directly. They were obtained from a correlation for forty-one overlapping cycle bases—averages of groups of years varying in number from two to seven—plus a formula for estimating permanent income derived from an analysis of the relation of consumption expenditures to income plus a theoretical linkage between these two, summarized in equations (9) and (10). The high correlation between the cycle bases insures a close connection between the longer-term movements in computed and measured velocity; in this respect, Chart I is simply a repetition in a different form of the secular finding. What is added by this chart is the relation between year-to-year movements. The secular results in no way insure that these will correspond; still, if anything, the computed velocity series mirrors the year-to-year cycles in observed velocity even more faithfully than it does the longer-term changes.

In order to isolate the cyclical aspect of the analysis, we have computed reference-cycle patterns of computed measured velocity and computed cash balances, thereby eliminating entirely the part of Chart I that repeats the secular finding. Chart II gives the reference-cycle patterns of computed and observed

CHART III

OBSERVED AND COMPUTED MONEY STOCK AND MEASURED VELOCITY, AVERAGE REFERENCE-CYCLE PATTERNS, MILD AND DEEP DEPRESSION CYCLES, 1870–1954

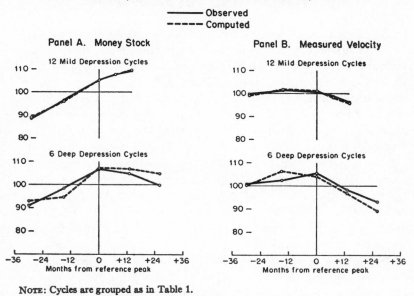

NOTE: Cycles are grouped as in Table 1.

current prices. The logical implication of employing the same multiple for net national product in constant and current prices is that α was treated as zero for prices alone. None of these adjustments is of any moment for the present analysis, since they affect only the level of the series and hence all cancel out when cycle relatives are computed.

measured velocity cycle by cycle, and Chart III gives average patterns for the mild and deep depression cycles, for both cash balances and measured velocity. It is clear from these that my interpretation accounts for the bulk of the fluctuations in observed measured velocity. The average pattern of computed measured velocity duplicates almost perfectly that for observed measured velocity for the mild depression cycles and corresponds very closely to that for the deep depression cycles. The cycle-by-cycle patterns demonstrate that this coincidence is not simply in the averages. This closeness might reflect the use of the same values of measured income in both the observed and the computed velocities, in which case it could be regarded as largely spurious. The cash-balance patterns are included in Chart III to test this possibility. They demonstrate that this purely statistical interpretation of the findings is not valid. The cash-balance patterns agree about as closely as the velocity patterns.

These results give strong support to the view that cyclical movements in velocity largely reflect movements along a stable demand curve for money and that the apparent discrepancy between the secular and the cyclical results reflects a divergence between measures of income and of prices constructed by statisticians for short periods and the magnitudes to which holders of money adjust their cash balances.

V. LIMITATIONS OF THE EXPLANATION

Important though this explanation is, it cannot be the whole of the story, since it fails to account for some of the most important of our findings about the behavior of money balances. If the desired real stock of money were determined entirely by permanent real income and if the desired stock were always equal to the actual stock, then the actual real stock (computed in terms of permanent prices) would have a cyclical pattern that duplicated the pattern of permanent real income except for amplitude. Now our evidence suggests that permanent real income conforms positively to the cycle and is either synchronous or lags at the turning points. Hence real cash balances computed at permanent prices would do likewise. Nominal cash balances equal these real cash balances times permanent prices, and our evidence suggests equally that permanent prices conform positively to the cycle either synchronously or with a lag. This train of reasoning therefore implies that, under the supposed conditions, nominal cash balances would conform positively to the cycle and would be either synchronous or lag at the turning points. Yet one of the major findings of the broader study of which the results reported in this paper are a part is that the nominal stock of money, adjusted for trend, tends to lead at both peaks and troughs. Hence there is a residual element in the cyclical behavior of velocity that requires explanation.

A satisfactory analysis of this residual element requires the use of monthly rather than annual data. Annual data are unduly crude for studying timing relationships. For example, the cyclical patterns of the observed money stock in Chart III, Panel *A*, reveal no average lead; yet our more detailed analysis of monthly money data establish such a lead, after adjustment for trend, beyond any reasonable doubt.

It may nevertheless be worth examining the residual element in the annual data as a first step. This residual element is approximated in Chart IV by the ratio of the observed measured velocity to computed measured velocity. This ratio varies very much less over the cycle than measured velocity itself, and hence the movements it measures tend to be concealed by the movements in velocity arising out of the descrepancy between measured and permanent income. Yet our analysis of the stock of money suggests that this residual element may play a critical cyclical role. Indeed, perhaps the major significance of our analysis of velocity is that it enables us to extract this residual element, to eliminate the largely spurious movements of velocity that have hitherto masked the economically significant movements.

For deep depressions, the residual element has a clearly marked cyclical pattern. During expansion, the residual element at first falls, then rises, reaching a trough in mid-expansion. During contractions, the behavior is harder to determine, because one cycle—the earliest, from 1870 to 1878—has a major influence on the pattern for all cycles and the figures for this cycle are highly dubious.[13] If this cycle is omitted, the pattern for contractions is a mild fall from peak to mid-contraction and a sharper fall thereafter.

The residual element varies much less, on the average, for mild depression cycles than for deep depression cycles. Such cyclical movement as it does show is similar to that for deep depression cycles during expansion and just the reverse of that for deep depression cycles during contraction. This residual element is the cyclical component in cash balances that cannot be explained simply by a movement along a univariate demand curve in response to a cyclical movement in permanent income. It is perhaps not surprising that this component should be so much larger for deep than for mild depression cycles. In the mild depression cycles, there is a relatively small cyclical movement in general, which presumably means that there are only relatively small movements in whatever other variables operate to produce a discrepancy between desired cash balances as judged from income alone and actual cash balances.

What are these other variables? The obvious candidates are measures of the return on other assets that could be held instead of money. One alternative to holding money is to hold securities; another, to hold physical goods. The return to the first is measured by the rate of return received on the securities. The return to the holding of physical goods is measured by the rate of change of prices minus storage costs; and either of these terms may be positive or negative

13. The problem is in the income estimates for the early period. These are characterized by an extraordinarily rapid rate of increase from 1869 to 1879. Other evidence suggests that this is at least partly a statistical artifact, reflecting the extreme paucity of reliable data for estimating income for this period.

CHART IV

RATIO OF OBSERVED TO COMPUTED MEASURED VELOCITY, COMPARED WITH OTHER ECONOMIC VARIABLES, AVERAGE REFERENCE-CYCLE PATTERNS, MILD AND DEEP DEPRESSION CYCLES, 1870–1954

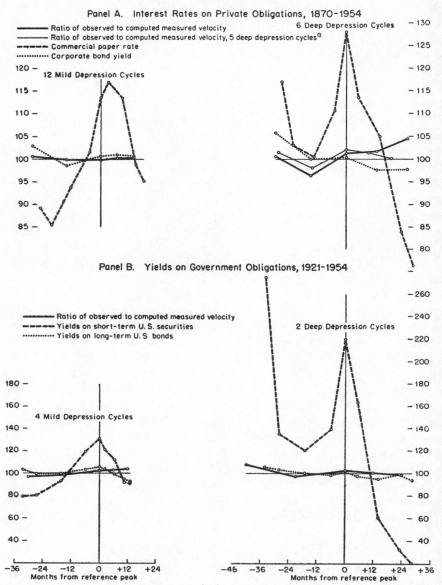

Panel A. Interest Rates on Private Obligations, 1870-1954

Panel B. Yields on Government Obligations, 1921-1954

NOTE: Vertical scales are in reference-cycle relatives, except scale for prices in Panel C, which is in rate of change of reference-cycle relatives per month. The scale of reference-cycle relatives in Panel B is one-fourth that in Panel A, and the scale in Panel C is two and a half times that in Panel A.

ᵃ Excluding 1870–78.

CHART IV—*Continued*

Panel C. Rate of Change of Wholesale Prices, 1870-1954

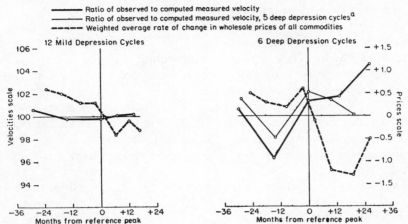

—prices may rise or fall and storage of goods may yield a convenience return in excess of costs of handling and maintenance. In either case, these returns must be compared with those on money, which may be positive, as when interest is paid on deposits, or negative, as when service charges are incurred.

In our secular analysis, we have found that the yield on corporate bonds is correlated with the real stock of money and velocity in the expected direction: a rise in the bond yield tends to reduce the real stock of money demanded for a given real income—that is, to raise velocity—and conversely. Bond yields, however, play nothing like so important and regularly consistent a role in accounting for changes in velocity as does real income. The short-term interest rate was even less highly correlated with velocity than the yield on corporate bonds.

Chart IV is designed to provide a rough test of whether these secular results carry over to cyclical movements. In addition to the ratio of observed measured velocity to computed measured velocity, which is the residual element we are seeking to explain, Chart IV also shows the average reference-cycle patterns of corporate bond yields as derived from annual data, of commercial paper rates as derived from monthly data (Panel *A*),[14] and of the yields on short- and long-

14. The corporate bond yield data through 1900 are railroad bond yields from F. R. Macaulay, *Some Theoretical Problems Suggested by the Movements of Interest Rates, Bond Yields and Stock Prices in the United States since 1856*, New York: National Bureau of Economic Research (1938), pp. A145–A152, col. 5, with .114 per cent arithmetic addition to raise them to the level of the following segment. After 1900 the data are "Basic Yields of Corporate Bonds to 50 Years Maturity," from *Historical Statistics of the United States, 1789–1945* (Bureau of the Census), p. 279; *Continuation to 1952 of Historical Statistics*, p. 36; *Statistical Abstract of the United States*, annually from 1953. Commercial paper rates in New York

term United States securities, as derived from monthly data (Panel *B*).[15] Panel *A* covers the whole period 1870–1954, excluding only war cycles; Panel B covers only the six non-war cycles after 1921, since yields on United States securities are not readily available for the earlier cycles.

Short-term rates have, of course, a much larger cyclical amplitude than long-term rates, which in turn have roughly the same amplitude as the residual element in velocity. These differences in amplitude are of no special significance for our purpose except as they reflect the consistency of the cyclical pattern, since the effect of a change in interest rates depends not only on the size of the change but also on the elasticity of the response of cash balances to a change. Volatility of rate can be offset by a small elasticity of response and vice versa. The differences in amplitude do, however, make it more difficult to read the chart and tend somewhat to obscure the similarity or divergence in pattern that is of major interest.

The most striking feature of the charts is the high degree of similarity between the pattern of interest rates and that of the residual element of velocity during the expansion phase of deep depression cycles. Long and short rates and rates on private and public obligations all show much the same pattern for this phase, and the pattern of all four is similar to the pattern in the residual element in velocity: interest rates are high at the initial stage of expansion, and so is velocity, which is an appropriate response to a high rate of return on non-cash assets; interest rates then decline to mid-expansion, and so does velocity; interest rates then rise to the peak of the cycle, and so does velocity.

There is no such unanimity of movement for the remaining phase of the deep depression cycles or for the mild depression cycles. For these phases, there is, at best, a family similarity between the movements in rates and those in the residual element in velocity. During the contraction phase of deep depression cycles, short and long rates diverge, short rates declining throughout, long rates leveling off or recovering in mid-contraction. The residual element behaves rather more like short rates, if we abstract from the unusual behavior during the 1870–78 cycle, but the similarity is not close in detail. For mild depression cycles, the cyclical movements in short and long rates are fairly similar, the main differences being a shorter lag in commercial paper rates at peaks and troughs than in the corporate bond yield. For the period as a whole (Panel *A*), the cyclical movement in the residual element, though fairly clear, is so small that no very precise comparison is justified; for the period since 1921 (Panel *B*), it is almost non-

---

City, monthly, through January, 1937, are from Macaulay, *op. cit.*, pp. A145–A161; thereafter, monthly averages of weekly figures from *Bank and Quotation Record of the Commercial and Financial Chronicle*. This series was seasonally adjusted through December, 1933. No seasonal adjustment has been necessary since.

15. Yields on short-term United States securities are from *Banking and Monetary Statistics*, p. 460, and *Federal Reserve Bulletin*, monthly issues, May, 1945, to May, 1948, and September 1950, to December, 1954. This series was seasonally adjusted, 1920–30, 1951–54. Yields on long-term United States securities are from the same sources and are unadjusted.

existent, the average reference-cycle pattern being dominated by an intracycle trend.

A number of empirical studies have demonstrated that the rate of change of prices has an important effect on the quantity of money demanded during periods of considerable instability of prices—as during hyperinflations or major and long-continued inflations.[16] These studies suggest, further, that the expected rate of change of prices, which is the variable that directly influences the demand for money, can be regarded as derived largely from past experience with the actual movement of prices and that it changes more smoothly than actual prices; it is something like the rate of change in what I earlier designated "permanent" prices. These findings imply that any changes in the expected rate of change of prices during periods of relative price stability will be small, perhaps too small to have any appreciable effect. And this is, indeed, the conclusion reached by Richard Selden in his study of the behavior of velocity.[17]

As a further check on this conclusion, we have plotted in Chart IV, Panel C, the rate of change of prices from reference stage to reference stage. This is derived from the nine-stage reference-cycle patterns of the monthly wholesale price index,[18] by dividing the difference between successive average standings by the average time interval between them. The resulting eight rates of change per month are plotted at the mid-points of the corresponding intervals. Since these are the actual rates of change, they presumably vary more than expected rates of change and, in addition, may lead the latter in time. However, one might expect enough similarity between the actual rates of change and the expected rates of change to permit the detection of any moderately close relation between expected rates of change and the residual element in velocity.

Interestingly enough, the results largely duplicate those for interest rates. For the expansion phase of the deep depression cycles, there is the same striking agreement in pattern between the rate of change of prices and the residual element in velocity as there is between interest rates and the residual element. There is only slightly less similarity in pattern for the expansion phase of mild depression cycles. There is no systematic relation for the contraction phase of either group of cycles.

The analysis, based as it is on annual velocity data and on a comparison solely of average reference-cycle patterns, is too crude to be at all decisive. Yet the results are most suggestive. If the cyclical patterns of interest rates and the rate

16. See Phillip Cagan, "The Monetary Dynamics of Hyperinflation," in Milton Friedman (Ed.), *Studies in the Quantity Theory of Money*, pp. 25–117. The same relation has been documented for other countries and episodes in a number of unpublished studies done in the Workshop on Money and Banking of the University of Chicago.

17. Selden, *op. cit.*, p. 202.

18. *Historical Statistics of the United States, 1789–1945* (Warren-Pearson series, 1870–89; B.L.S. series, 1890–1945 [Bureau of the Census]), p. 344; *Continuation to 1952 of Historical Statistics*, p. 47; thereafter, U.S. Department of Labor, Bureau of Labor Statistics, *Wholesale (Primary Market) Price Index*, monthly issues.

of change in prices are compared with the pattern of measured velocity itself (Chart III, Panel *B*), there is no clear relation—as we noted at the outset in explaining why an alternative reconciliation of the secular and cyclical behavior of velocity is required. When the comparison is made instead with the residual element of velocity—that part of the movement in measured velocity that is accounted for neither by the effect of changes in permanent income on desired cash balances nor by the discrepancy between measured and permanent income —there is a striking consistency for one phase of one set of cycles, and at least a family resemblance elsewhere, though, of course, not without considerable irregularity. These results are of the kind that might be expected if the returns on alternative ways of holding assets were the chief factor other than permanent income affecting desired cash balances. Of course, they do not demonstrate that this is so. They might, for example, reflect accidental concurrence of movement in just a few cycles. And they do not provide any estimate of the quantitative strength of the connection. But they certainly justify further research in this direction. The main requirements for such research are the use of monthly data on velocity or indicators of velocity and the examination of cycle-by-cycle relations and not simply relations between average patterns.

VI. CONCLUSION

The results summarized in this paper have implications for the theory of money, the study of business cycles, and the conduct and possibilities of monetary policy.

In the theory of money, much emphasis has been placed on different "motives" for holding money—the "transactions" motive, the "speculative" motive, and the "assets" or "precautionary" motive being the three commonly distinguished. The transactions motive is often regarded as implying something of a quasi-mechanical relation between cash balances and the flow of payments and is frequently given priority of importance as well as place. Our results cast serious doubt on the acceptability of this emphasis. In the first place, the cyclical results make it clear that changes in cash balances over short periods are adapted to magnitudes less volatile than the volume of transactions. In the second place, the secular decline in income velocity is hard to explain in terms of transactions. It is dubious that there has been any secular increase in the ratio of transactions to income large enough to explain the growth in the ratio of money balances to income that has occurred. Further, improvements in transportation and communication, let alone in financial organization, have almost surely reduced any mechanical requirement for cash balances per unit of transactions—indeed, it was on these grounds that Irving Fisher implied nearly half a century ago that velocity was likely to increase secularly and that others have since expressed similar views.[19]

Our findings equally cast doubt on the importance of the so-called speculative

19. Irving Fisher, *The Purchasing Power of Money* (rev. ed.) New York: Macmillan (1913), pp. 79–88.

motive. One would expect this motive to be subject to wide cyclical variations and hence, if it dominated the demand for money, to lead to correspondingly wide cyclical variations in desired cash balances, whereas we observe the reverse.

The assets or "precautionary" motive is in a different state. Permanent income can be regarded as a concept closely allied to wealth and indeed as an index of wealth, provided that we count both human and non-human sources of income as components of total wealth. Along these lines, our results can be interpreted in either of two ways. One is that the relevant asset motive is equivalent to a consumption or income motive. As permanent income, which is to say, total wealth, rises, consumer units expand their expenditures on some items disproportionately—we term these items "luxuries." On this interpretation, the services rendered by money can be included among these luxuries. The other interpretation is more nearly an asset motive proper. It is that the holdings of cash are linked not to total wealth but primarily to non-human wealth and that, as permanent income rises, the total value of non-human wealth rises more rapidly than permanent income, either because such a more rapid rise is a necessary condition for a rise in income or because it corresponds to the preferences of individuals as their total wealth rises. Unfortunately, the available evidence on the secular or cyclical behavior of the ratio of non-human wealth to income is inadequate to provide a test of this explanation.[20] On either interpretation, however, our results suggest that motivations and variables linked with assets are the most fruitful category to explore—that the most fruitful approach is to regard money as one of a sequence of assets, on a par with bonds, equities, houses, consumer durable goods, and the like.

Our results have a bearing on another aspect of the so-called precautionary motive, namely, the view that the amount of cash balances held is highly sensitive to "the" or "a" rate of interest, at least for some range of rates of interest. If this were so for rates of interest within the range observed during the period our data cover, it would imply that real cash balances and the ratio of income to money would be highly variable, both secularly and cyclically, since small movements in interest rates would be accompanied by large movements in desired cash balances. The highly stable secular behavior of velocity is evidence against this view. So is our inability to find any close connection between changes in velocity from cycle to cycle and any of a number of interest rates. So also is our finding that most of the cyclical movement in income velocity as ordinarily measured can be accounted for by the use of measured rather than permanent income in the numerator. The remaining movement in velocity, though characterized by a consistent cyclical pattern and though, on the basis of our tentative explorations, it may well be accounted for by movements in interest rates, is much too small to reflect any very sensitive adjustment of cash balances to interest rates.

Some of these comments about the implications of our results for the theory of

20. Raymond Goldsmith's estimates in *A Study of Savings*, Princeton, N.J.: Princeton University Press (1955) suggest that, if anything, the ratio of non-human wealth to income has declined secularly rather than risen.

money have their direct and obvious counterparts for the empirical study of business cycles. The most important additional implications are two that have to do with the interpretation of cyclical movements in velocity. The fact that velocity changes have been about as important as changes in the stock of money in accounting, in an arithmetic sense, for the movements in money income, together with the small amplitude of cyclical movements in the stock of money, has fostered the view that changes in the stock of money cannot be the prime mover, or even of major independent importance, in cyclical change. This view may of course be correct, but it needs re-examination in light of our findng that most of the velocity movement is, from one point of view, "spurious," as well as a possible consequence of this finding, discussed more fully below, that measured income may be highly sensitive to changes in the stock of money. The other important implication for the study of cycles is that the cyclical pattern of velocity changes that needs study and explanation is very different from what it has been supposed to be. Measured velocity has a cyclical pattern roughly synchronous with that in general business, tending to rise relative to its trend from reference trough to reference peak and to fall from reference peak to reference trough. But when this pattern is corrected for the deviation of measured income from permanent income, the residual movement is very different, and it is the residual movement that needs explanation.

The most interesting implication of our analysis for monetary policy is highly speculative and involves taking our findings more seriously in detail than I can fully justify. It may nonetheless be worth recording if only in the hope of stimulating further work. Suppose one accepts fully both the reasonably well-supported finding that money holdings are adapted to permanent magnitudes and also the much more questionable and tentative suggestion that the economic actors derive their estimates of permanent magnitudes from prior measured magnitudes by implicitly constructing some kind of weighted average of them.

It will then follow that, given a stable demand function for money, measured income will be highly sensitive in short periods to changes in the nominal stock of money—the short-run money multiplier will be large and decidedly higher than the long-run money multiplier.[21] To illustrate with some figures based on our tentative results: In the long run, if we take real income as given, a $1 increase in the stock of money would imply an annual level of money income higher than otherwise by $1 times the velocity of circulation, or, at current levels of velocity, about $1.50 higher—the long-run money multiplier equals the velocity of circulation. In the short run, however, an increase of $1.50 in measured income would be inadequate, since that much of a rise in measured income would raise permanent money income by decidedly less than $1.50 and hence desired cash balances by less than $1. If we take a year as our unit and accept the numerical weights we have used in estimating permanent income from measured income, measured income would have to rise by roughly

21. This point was first suggested to me by Gary S. Becker.

$4.50 for estimated permanent income to rise by $1.50, the rise required to raise desired cash balances by $1 for given real income—the short-run money multiplier is thus triple the long-run multiplier.

The story does not, of course, end here. There would be carry-over effects into future years, as estimated permanent income continued to be revised in the light of measured income. These would make the initially assumed rise in money income not sustainable without further rises in the stock of money and hence would give rise to a cyclical reaction in measured income. Further, the assumed change in money income would presumably be associated with changes in output and in prices that would affect the relation of desired cash balances to the change in measured money income. These further complications require much more study than I have given them. They do not, however, affect the main point—the sensitivity of measured income to changes in the stock of money that is implied by our results if they are accepted at face value.

It is interesting that the permanent-income hypothesis should have such contrasting implications for the sensitivity of the economy to changes in the stock of money and to changes in investment—the major other factor regarded as a prime mover in cyclical change. The permanent-income hypothesis implies that the economy is much less sensitive to changes in investment than it would be if consumption were adapted to measured rather than permanent income— the short-run investment multiplier is decidedly smaller than the long-run multiplier.[22] On the other hand, we have just seen that the economy is much more sensitive to changes in the stock of money than it would be if money balances were adapted to measured rather than permanent income.

A corollary for policy is that the effects of monetary policy may be expected to operate rather more than would otherwise be supposed through the direct effects of changes in the stock of money on spending, and rather less through indirect effects on rates of interest, thence on investment, and thence on income. Another corollary is to emphasize the potency of relatively small changes in the stock of money—a potency, needless to say, for good or evil. Relatively small changes in the stock of money, properly timed and correct in magnitude, may be adequate to offset other changes making for instability. On the other hand, relatively small changes in the stock of money, random in timing and size, may equally be an important source of instability. If the reaction mechanism I have described is in any substantial measure valid, the system may not have a large tolerance for mistakes in monetary management.

22. See *A Theory of the Consumption Function*, p. 238.

Chapter 7

Interest Rates
and the Demand for Money

ONE MAJOR STRAND of Keynesian analysis traces the implications of a particular empirical assumption about the demand for money—that its elasticity
with respect to interest rates is very high, approaching infinity (in Keynes' own
terms, liquidity preference is, if not absolute, approximately so). Such a situation
would have very far-reaching implications: it would greatly limit the effectiveness of price flexibility in correcting unemployment; it would render changes
in the quantity of money produced by open market operations impotent to
affect economic conditions; it would make the effect of government deficits on
income and employment independent of the way in which the deficits are
financed.

By now, there is wide agreement that conditions of near-absolute liquidity
preference, if they occur at all, are very rare, so that this strand of Keynesian
analysis has receded to the status of a theoretical curiosity.

More recently, a number of economists have attributed major theoretical
importance to the opposite empirical assumption about the demand for money—

Reprinted from *The Journal of Law and Economics*, vol. 9, October, 1966. I am grateful to
David Fand, David Lindsey, and George Tolley for helpful comments on an earlier draft of
this paper. I was helped also by a general discussion at the Workshop in Money and Banking at the University of Chicago, and by extensive correspondence with Harry G. Johnson
on some of the main issues.

that its elasticity with respect to interest rates is negligible. Such a situation, they assert, would have far-reaching implications for the theoretical possibility of separating monetary and real forces and for monetary policy.

Like Keynes' analysis, these assertions raise two separable issues. One issue is empirical: What is the elasticity of the demand for one or another monetary total with respect to various interest rates? How stable is the relation between the (real) quantity of money demanded and interest rates, for both different monetary totals and different interest rates? How consistent are the elasticities for different periods and countries? How important are interest rates compared with other variables in explaining changes in the quantity of money demanded? The other issue is theoretical: Would a highly inelastic demand for money with respect to interest rates have the far-reaching implications alleged?

There already is something of a consensus on the empirical issue, though the natural tendency for writers to differentiate their products tends somewhat to conceal it. (1) I know no empirical student of the demand for money who denies that interest rates affect the real quantity of money demanded—though others have misinterpreted me as so asserting.[1] (2) There is no agreement whether

---

1. This misunderstanding stems from my article, "The Demand for Money: Some Theoretical and Empirical Results," Chapter 6 above. The empirical demand function presented in that article did not include interest rates as a variable. Further, in summarizing my conclusions, I stated "our inability to find any close connection between changes in velocity and any of a number of interest rates" is evidence against "the view that the amount of cash balances held is highly sensitive to 'the' or 'a' rate of interest."

However, inability to pin down the elasticity is very different from assigning a zero value to it. Neither in that article, nor, to the best of my knowledge, elsewhere, have I ever asserted that interest rates have no effect on the quantity of money demanded or on velocity, only that (a) they appear to be less important as a determinant of quantity demanded than real per capita income and as a determinant of measured velocity than the ratio of measured to permanent income; and (b) that the interest elasticity is not very high. Both of these conclusions have on the whole been supported by subsequent research.

I stressed at a number of points in that article the potential significance of interest rates. In answer to the question what variables other than income and prices affect the quantity of money demanded, I wrote:

"The obvious candidates are measures of the return on other assets that could be held instead of money . . ., the rate of return received on . . . securities . . . [and] the rate of change of prices. . . .

"In our secular analysis, we have found that the yield on corporate bonds is correlated with the real stock of money and velocity in the expected direction. . . . Bond yields, however, play nothing like so important and regularly consistent a role in accounting for changes in velocity as does real income. The short-term interest rate was even less highly correlated with velocity than the yield on corporate bonds."

I then went on to make a "rough test whether these secular results carry over to cyclical movements," and subsequently, also, a rough test of the effect of the rate of change of prices. My conclusion was

"This analysis, based as it is on annual velocity data and on a comparison solely of average reference-cycle patterns is too crude to be at all decisive. Yet the results are most suggestive. . . . These results are of the kind that might be expected if the returns on alternative ways of holding assets were the chief factor other than permanent income affecting desired cash

short-term or long-term interest rates are more closely related to the quantity of money demanded, though it is clear that elasticities are lower (in absolute value) for short than for long rates. (3) Almost all estimates, even for long rates, show an inelastic response, i.e., elasticities less than unity in absolute value, though most estimates, including some we have obtained in our own subsequent work, are higher (in absolute value) than the estimate Anna J. Schwartz and I used in *A Monetary History* (—.15). (4) With only one exception, every study for the United States I know of finds that variations in real income or wealth are a more important source of variations in the real quantity of money demanded than are variations in interest rates.[2] (5) There is less agreement about the relative importance of different variables for velocity than for the real quantity of money demanded. Some studies find income or wealth elasticities around unity for some monetary totals, which means that the corresponding velocities are independent of income. In many of these studies, interest rates are treated as the major variable affecting velocity. Other studies find income or wealth elasticities significantly different from unity and hence find income or wealth variables as important as or more important than interest rates in explaining variations in velocity, and some find still other variables dominating velocity.[3]

Since empirical work on the demand for money is a dramatic growth industry, additional evidence on the empirical issues is accumulating rapidly and we may confidently expect a still further convergence of answers.

The promise of a consensus on the empirical issue renders it all the more important to examine the theoretical issue. Are "fundamental issues in monetary theory" associated with the precise answers reached, as one writer has stated?[4]

---

balances. Of course they do not demonstrate that this is so. . . . But they certainly justify further research in this direction."

It is baffling to me how anyone could interpret this statement as asserting that interest rates have no effect on the quantity of money demanded!

In chapter 12 of Friedman and Schwartz, *A Monetary History of the United States, 1867–1960* (1963), we used an estimate of the interest-elasticity of money of about-.15. This is lower in absolute value than the elasticity estimated by others, and indeed by ourselves in later work. But that is simply a question of different estimates of an empirical magnitude.

2. The reason for limiting this statement to the U.S. studies is because in countries that have experienced substantial or hyper-inflation, the rate of change of prices is generally a much more important source of variation than real income.

For the United States, the one exception I know of is a study of post-World-War II, U.S. quarterly data for households by M. J. Hamburger, "The Demand for Money by Households, Money Substitutes, and Monetary Policy," in *The Journal of Political Economy*, vol. 74, no. 6, December, 1966, p. 600.

3. The comment in the preceding footnote for periods of substantial inflation applies here as well. For such periods, anticipated rates of change of prices are almost always the most important single variable affecting velocity. See David Laidler, "The Rate of Interest and the Demand for Money—Some Empirical Evidence," in *The Journal of Political Economy*, vol. 74, no. 6, December, 1966, p. 593.

4. Harry G. Johnson, "A Quantity Theorist's Monetary History of the United States," *Economic Journal*, vol. 75, no. 298, June, 1965, pp. 388–96.

I believe that only a finding of near-absolute liquidity preference would raise such fundamental issues, and that any other finding would not. It is important to determine as accurately as possible the size of the elasticities in order to have a better empirical basis for understanding the course of economic events and for guiding policy. The size of the elasticities will have important effects on the quantitative magnitude of changes in certain economic variables that can be expected to be produced by changes in other economic variables. But the precise value of the elasticity will not, in my opinion, have major implications for either fundamental issues or the basic role and functioning of monetary policy. The purpose of this note is to explain and justify that conclusion.

The theoretical issue was forcibly impressed on me by two reviewers of *A Monetary History*.[5] Both reviewers criticized Mrs. Schwartz and me severely for assigning a low interest elasticity to the demand for money. Both asserted that our doing so had far-reaching implications for the conclusions in that book and for policy recommendations I have made elsewhere. However, this note is not intended primarily to reply to their criticisms, though I hope that as a by-product it will do so. After those reviews called the issue to my attention, ·I came across repeated statements of a similar kind in other connections. Hence, I believe that the issue is of more general significance.

I. THE THEORETICAL ISSUE

I can best present the issue by quoting the reviewers already referred to.

H. G. Johnson: "[1] If interest rates do not affect velocity, monetary analysis can be divorced from analysis of the real sector, since the quantity of money will affect money income in the short run and prices in the long run without interference from the real forces. If, on the other hand, interest rates do affect velocity, monetary analysis must incorporate the real sector in a general equilibrium model simultaneously explaining interest rates, velocity, real income and prices. [2] Moreover, this need for a general equilibrium model comprising the real and monetary sectors is what the Keynesian Revolution was about; hence to admit interest rates into the demand function for money is to accept the Keynesian Revolution and Keynes' attack on the quantity theory. [3] And, finally, in the absence of a velocity function independent of interest rates, the case for replacing discretionary monetary management by a fixed rule of monetary increase related to the normal growth of the economy, advocated elsewhere by Professor Friedman, loses its attractiveness, because variations in interest rates generated by the real sector would make such a policy rule automatically destabilizing."[6]

Allan Meltzer: "[4] Had the authors systematically incorporated interest rates

5. Johnson, *ibid.*; Allan Meltzer, "Monetary Theory and Monetary History," *Schweizerische Zeitschrift fur Volkswirtschaft und Statistik*, vol. 101, 1965, p. 404.

6. Johnson, *ibid.*, p. 396, numbers added.

or asset yields as a determinant of velocity or of the money supply, they would have been forced to do what they have otherwise avoided doing, develop a more extensive analysis of the real system to supplement their treatment of the monetary sector."[7]

I may add one quotation from a non-reviewer, though I should note that it was partly called forth by his discussion of my work.

Daniel Brill: "The significance for the conduct and evaluation of monetary policy of dropping the assumption that money demand is almost completely interest-inelastic deserves more careful attention than it has been given. . . .

"[5] . . . Interest-elasticity of the public's demand for money breaks the tight linkage between the stock of money and money income. It permits fluctuations in propensities to spend, given the money stock, to influence equilibrium interest rates and income; it also [6] allows fiscal policies to alter the level of aggregate expenditures for goods and services, quite apart from their influence on the stock of money.

"[7] The degree of financial restraint or stimulus imposed on the economic system, accordingly, is no longer reflected in any simple way by variations in the money stock. . . ."[8]

II. THE DIVORCE BETWEEN MONETARY AND REAL FACTORS

The comments I have numbered [1], [4], and [5] all assert (or imply) that exclusion of interest rates from the demand function for money (zero elasticity) permits (or requires?) a divorce between the monetary sector and the real sector of the economy, whereas inclusion of interest rates (non-zero elasticity) renders such a divorce impossible. As a matter of pure theory these statements seem to me either seriously incomplete or flatly wrong, depending on the precise inter-pretation of the statement "monetary analysis can be divorced from analysis of the real sector."[9]

Two different interpretations seem worth attention:

(a) That knowledge of the nominal quantity of money alone is enough in principle to permit prediction of (that is, to determine) the level of nominal

7. Meltzer, op. cit., p. 420, number added.

8. Daniel Brill, "Criteria for the Conduct of Monetary Policy: The Implications of Recent Research," paper delivered at Conference of University Professors, sponsored by American Bankers Association and Purdue University, on September 1, 1965; numbers added.

9. They are also wrong if, as some Keynesians have done, interest rates are themselves regarded as a purely monetary phenomenon, determined by liquidity performance, and having no influence on the real sector through either investment or consumption. However, the writers quoted clearly assume implicitly that interest rates depend on and influence real magnitudes and since I agree fully with them that such an assumption is more useful, I have neglected what might be called the strict Keynesian case.

income[10] and perhaps also of prices.[11] On this interpretation, the assertion is incomplete: exclusion of interest rates is a necessary but not a sufficient condition for a divorce in this sense. However, if "level of nominal income" is replaced by "changes in nominal income," exclusion of interest rates is not even a necessary condition, let alone a sufficient one.

(b) That the nominal quantity of money and changes in it have no effects on real magnitudes, including interest rates, although real magnitudes may affect the level of incomes and prices associated with a given nominal quantity of money. In this, which I believe is much the more important sense, the exclusion of interest rates is neither a necessary nor a sufficient condition. It is simply irrelevant.

As a matter of experience, the conditions necessary for a divorce of the first kind are often approximated for changes in nominal income and, less frequently, in prices. I believe that they are seldom if ever approximated for a divorce of the second kind. Indeed, the central message of our *Monetary History* is precisely that monetary changes have an extraordinarily important impact on real phenomena.

Let me turn to a more detailed examination of these two interpretations.

(a) *Does the quantity of money alone determine nominal income and prices?* If interest rates enter the demand function for money,[12] it is clearly impossible to predict the level of nominal income or of prices solely from the nominal quantity of money. Knowledge of the interest rate, which is to say, indirectly of the real forces affecting the interest rate, is necessary to get a numerical value of velocity. However, if interest rates are stable, knowledge of interest rates is not necessary to predict changes in nominal income or in prices, so exclusion of interest rates is not even a *necessary* condition for a divorce for such magnitudes.

For sufficient conditions, it is best to consider nominal income and prices separately.

For nominal income, a divorce in the sense under discussion between monetary and real factors requires not only that interest rates not enter the demand function but also that (i) no other real factors enter the function giving desired velocity, and (ii) either desired velocity is always equal to actual velocity or the adjustment between the two does not depend on real factors. If these conditions are satisfied, velocity is either a numerical constant or a function solely of the past history of the quantity of money. For changes in nominal income, it is

10. I am using "nominal income" as a synonym for what Johnson refers to as "money income" in order to avoid using "money" in two different senses.

11. To keep the analysis simple, I am interpreting "monetary analysis" as referring to analysis of the quantity of a single monetary total called money. A more general treatment would recognize a number of monetary magnitudes, such as currency, demand deposits, time deposits, etc. This would complicate the exposition without, so far as I have been able to determine, affecting any essential point.

12. I shall throughout interpret this expression as meaning "enter with an elasticity different from zero."

sufficient that any real factors that enter the demand or adjustment functions be stable.

To be more concrete, consider the demand functions for money that have generally been used in recent empirical work. These make the real quantity of money demanded a function of population and real per capita income, as well as of interest rates, rate of change of prices, and other variables. Suppose all variables except population and real income per capita are excluded, that the elasticity with respect to population is taken as unity, and that desired real money balances are assumed always equal to actual real money balances. Even then it is necessary for the elasticity of demand for real money balances per capita with respect to real per capita income to be unity in order to divorce monetary analysis from the real sector in the sense under consideration.[13] This would make velocity independent of real factors.[14]

13. Let

$$\frac{M^D}{NP} = f\left(\frac{Y}{NP}\right) \tag{1}$$

be a demand function expressing the real per capita balances desired as a function solely of real per capita income, where M^D is desired nominal balances, N is population, P price level, and Y nominal income, and assume that

$$M^D = M^S, \tag{2}$$

where M^S is nominal quantity of money supplied. If (1) is unit elastic, it becomes

$$\frac{M^D}{NP} = k \cdot \frac{Y}{NP}, \tag{1'}$$

and we can solve (1') and (2) to get

$$Y = \frac{1}{k} M^S, \tag{3}$$

so knowledge of M^S alone is enough to predict Y. If (1) is not unit elastic, then the counterpart of (3) will take the form

$$Y = g\left(\frac{Y}{NP}\right) \cdot M^S \tag{4}$$

so it is necessary to know real per capita income as well as M^S to predict Y.

Alternatively suppose that (1') holds but that (2) is replaced by an adjustment equation, such as

$$\frac{dY}{dt} = \beta(M^S - M^D) \tag{2'}$$

If β is a constant, then the time pattern of Y will depend solely on initial conditions and the time pattern of M^S. However, if β depends on real variables (including but not limited to interest rates), real factors will again enter in.

14. Two other comments seem worth making. (a) If in the comment by Johnson numbered [1] above, "real sector" means solely the effect of real factors on interest rates, then the statement is an uninteresting tautology. (b) In my own work, I have generally concluded that the elasticity of real per capita money balances with respect to real per capita income is greater than unity. The essence of my permanent income hypothesis of the demand for money is that equation (2) of the preceding footnote is incorrect if measured income is the income variable in (1), so I have always left still another avenue for real factors to enter.

For prices, I have been able to formulate no economically meaningful conditions under which their level would depend only on monetary magnitudes. Even if nominal income is divorced from the real sector in the above sense, the level of prices depends on total real output. However, *changes* in prices could be regarded as purely monetary under the conditions given for nominal income if in addition total real output can be regarded as constant.

To turn from the theoretical to the empirical, the evidence I have examined suggests that this kind of divorce is seldom if ever approximated for levels of nominal income or prices over considerable periods. On the other hand, I believe it is frequently approximated for year-to-year and similar changes in nominal income under a wide variety of conditions, and for *changes* in prices under a rather narrower set of conditions.

For the United States, for example, the correlation between year-to-year percentage changes in the nominal quantity of money (defined as currency outside banks plus all commercial bank deposits adjusted) and year-to-year percentage changes in nominal income (defined as net national product) for the ninety-four years from 1870 to 1963 is .70, and the relation seems to have displayed no secular change.[15] The correlations are decidedly lower though still statistically significant for prices: .54 for wholesale prices, and .58 for the price deflator implicit in nominal income.[16] I have seen similar correlations for nominal income for a number of other countries that vary widely in economic structure and financial institutions. The results are almost always very similar.

The closest approximation to a divorce in this sense is observed for conditions of substantial or hyper-inflation. Under such conditions, the rate of change of prices becomes the most important single variable in the demand function for

15. For example, the use of the simple regression corresponding to the above correlation gives the following results for the years from 1962–66 (only data through 1963 were used in computing the regression):

Rate of Change of Nominal Income
(*Percentage per year, continuously compounded*)

Year	Computed from Regression	Actual
1962	5.9	6.9
1963	6.6	5.2
1964	6.4	7.1
1965	7.5	7.8
1966	6.5	8.7

16. Comparisons for prices like those in the preceding footnote are

Year	WHOLESALE PRICES		IMPLICIT PRICE INDEX	
	Computed	Actual	Computed	Actual
1962	1.6	0.3	1.6	1.1
1963	2.1	−0.3	1.9	1.3
1964	1.9	0.2	1.8	1.7
1965	2.7	2.0	2.3	1.8
1966	2.0	3.2	1.8	3.0

real money balances, but the rate of change of prices can itself be "explained" by the past history of the quantity of money, so the behavior of both nominal income and prices can be predicted. Changes in real income are likely to be minor compared to changes in the quantity of money.[17]

To avoid misunderstanding, let me emphasize the desirability of improving on the approximations just described. Further scientific progress has consisted of and will consist of such improvements. Some improvements have been and will be the development of more sophisticated and accurate methods of allowing for the influence of changes in the quantity of money itself; others have been and will be more precise estimates of the influence of such variables as the real rate of yield on capital, the structure of interest rates, and so on, and the construction of more sophisticated models incorporating explicitly the interrelations between monetary and real magnitudes.

(b) *Does the quantity of money affect real magnitudes?* The second interpretation of "divorce" is related to the extensive theoretical discussion about the "neutrality" of money that has been so important a feature of the post-Keynesian developments.[18] However, the details of that discussion need not concern us, since the only question at issue here is the effect of including or excluding interest rates in the demand for money on the possibility of regarding money as "neutral."

Consider the IS-LM analysis of the kind first introduced by J. R. Hicks[19] that has become standard in the textbooks. Consider further, the flexible price, full-employment versions.[20] In these, interest rates and real per capita income are determined entirely in the real sector; these in turn determine the real quantity of money demanded, which interacts with the nominal quantity supplied to determine the price level. Or to put it another way, interest rates and real per capita income determine velocity; given velocity and real income, changes in the quantity of money can be taken, in Johnson's words, "to affect money income in the short run and prices in the long run without interference from the real forces." Changes in the quantity of money need not affect interest rates, and so redound on the real sector, if prices react rapidly enough so that there are no changes in the *real* money stock, which is the desired magnitude affected by interest rates.

17. The already classic study on this point is Cagan, "The Monetary Dynamics of Hyper-inflation" in my *Studies in the Quantity Theory of Money*, p. 25; since then, other studies by John Deaver for Chile, Adolfo C. Diz for Argentina, Allen Hynes for a number of Latin American countries and Maurice Allais for a large number of countries have confirmed and extended Cagan's results.

18. For an excellent summary, see H. G. Johnson, "Monetary Theory and Policy," *American Economic Review*, 52: 334, 343–57 (1962).

19. John R. Hicks, "Mr. Keynes and the 'Classics;' A Suggested Interpretation," *Econometrica*, 5: 147 (1937).

20. A particularly clear exposition is given by M. J. Bailey, *National Income and the Price Level*, New York: McGraw-Hill (1962), pp. 11–42.

To put the matter still more abstractly, the divorce of money from real factors in the sense under discussion requires that there be a way of expressing the equations comprising the theoretical model such that it has a subset of equations sufficient to determine the real magnitudes which do not contain as separate variables either the nominal quantity of money or the price level.[21] In that case, the system of equations simultaneously determining the real and monetary variables can be dichotomized into one set which determines the level of real income and the interest rate and a second set which together with the solution of the first set determines the level of nominal income and the price level, and this is true *regardless of whether the demand equation for money in the second set has the interest rate as one of its variables.* The "real variables" may then affect the level of nominal income and prices consistent with a given money stock, but the level of the money stock will not affect the real variables, only nominal income and the price level. One of Bailey's full employment models is a system of precisely this kind.[22]

The italicized statement flatly contradicts the comments I have numbered [1] and [4]. Its relation to comment [5] requires a little more exegesis. The first sentence of that comment seems to refer to the sense of divorce discussed in section (a), above. As to the second sentence, I assume that Brill means by "propensities to spend," saving and investing propensities. In that case, "fluctuations in propensities to spend" will influence equilibrium interest rates, contrary to his assertion, whether or not interest rates enter the demand function for money. These are real factors affecting interest rates referred to in the preceding paragraph.[23]

As to income, Brill's comment is correct for the usual versions of the IS-LM analysis. On a more sophisticated level, there are ways in which "fluctuations in spending propensities" can influence *real* income for a given money stock whether or not interest rates enter the demand function for money, though even then, if the demand for money is unit-elastic with respect to real income, zero interest elasticity will mean that fluctuations in the propensities do not affect nominal income.[24]

21. The word "separate" is included because it is entirely permissible for M/P or the real quantity of money, to be included, or for M and P to enter as deflators of other nominal magnitudes. To put the condition differently, the requirement is that the reduced form equations of the subset, expressing the real endogenous magnitudes as a function of other variables, be homogenous of degree zero in M and P.

22. *Ibid.* pp. 35–36.

23. Perhaps Brill had in mind the strict Keynesian case referred to in footnote 9 in which interest rates are assumed not to affect either investment or saving. In that case, it is true that, if interest rates do not enter the demand function for money, "fluctuations in propensities" will not influence interest rates. However, in that case, interest rates apparently enter nowhere, hence the whole problem has disappeared. In the textual discussion above, I have continued to exclude this strict Keynesian case.

24. (1) *Full-employment, flexible price version of IS-LM analysis.* In this version, real income is determined entirely by the production sector, including the supply of labor, and is a given

To avoid misunderstanding, let me emphasize that what I am asserting is that the possibility of constructing a theoretical model in which monetary changes do not impinge on the real sector in no way hinges on whether the interest elasticity of demand for money is zero. I am not asserting that such a model is the most useful, or even *a* useful model to interpret reality. On the contrary, as I should have supposed is abundantly clear from all of my work in the field of money, I am myself persuaded that it is far more useful to introduce interactions between the real and monetary sectors than to omit them in the analysis of both long-run growth and short-run cyclical fluctuations. For growth models, the

---

number, which is not affected by any monetary change, whether or not the rate of interest enters into the demand function for money. However, this version implicitly assumes that there is only a single commodity, with consumption and capital formation representing simply different uses of the same commodity. While such one-commodity models are very useful for many purposes, they are exceedingly misleading for the present purpose, which is precisely to trace the effects of shifts between consumption and capital formation. If these are different commodities, a shift in propensities means a change in the composition of income. Unless the rate of substitution between the two commodities in production is independent of relative output (in which case, they are perfect substitutes in production and hence can be regarded as a single commodity), there is an index-number problem in determining whether real output has risen or fallen. Clearly, it has been affected in a meaningful way. (I am indebted to Axel Leijonhufvud for this point.) In addition, of course, the change in the rate of accumulation will change real income in every sense in the future.

(2) *Unemployment, inflexible price version of the IS-LM analysis.* This is clearly the more important case for Brill's comment. In the usual text book analysis, the *LM* curve shows the combinations of interest rates and real income consistent with the given real demand function for money and the given nominal quantity of money (or supply schedule, if interest rates or real income are assumed to affect the nominal quantity of money). If interest rates as well as income enter the demand function, the *LM* curve has a positive slope. An upward shift in the negatively sloping *IS* curve produced by a "fluctuation in propensities to spend" will then mean higher interest rates and higher real income; a downward shift, lower interest rates and lower real income; given complete rigidity of prices, nominal income will move in the same direction as real income and by the same percentage. If interest rates do not enter the demand function, and if, as Brill assumes, the nominal quantity of money is fixed, then the *LM* curve will be vertical, so upward and downward shifts in the *IS* function affect only the interest rate and not real income or, with rigid prices, money income. This is presumably the analysis underlying Brill's comment and on these assumptions his comment is entirely valid for income though not for interest rates.

However, on a more sophisticated level, there are three channels whereby changes in propensities can influence real income, starting from a position of unemployment. (*a*) The effects via a shift in composition of output described in (1) above. (*b*) Price inflexibility need not mean complete rigidity, but rather slow adjustment. The initial unemployment situation presumably means that prices are tending to fall relative to their anticipated behavior. Changes in spending propensities can affect the rate of fall by increasing or decreasing deflationary pressure; this will in turn affect real income. (*c*) Price inflexibility means that some dynamic adjustment mechanism is at work, which permits actual and desired or temporary and full equilibrium positions to differ for prices. But then, this must be true also of the money market, so changes in the spending propensities can produce (or alter) discrepancies between actual and desired balances, requiring the introduction of an adjustment equation like equation (2′) in footnote 13.

desired capital stock or wealth, and the desired distribution between money and other wealth should, I believe, be made to depend on the rate of change of prices as well as on the real yield of capital; and the desired rate of change in wealth should be made to depend on the discrepancy between actual and desired stocks of wealth (which means that the so-called Pigou effect will operate). For cyclical fluctuations, discrepancies between desired and actual stocks of money (or between anticipated and actual rates of monetary growth) should be regarded as affecting rates of change of both real output and prices. Indeed, I believe they may well be the key element in cyclical fluctuations.

III. KEYNES AND INTEREST-ELASTICITY OF MONETARY DEMAND

Johnson's statement, "to admit interest rates into the demand function for money is to accept the Keynesian Revolution and Keynes' attack on the quantity theory," seems to me a misleading interpretation of the history of thought. Keynes' analysis of liquidity preference and of how interest rates affect the quantity of money demanded is certainly a basic contribution to monetary theory and it has stimulated important and valuable research. But this part of his analysis is in the older tradition. Indeed, it was foreshadowed by the strictly quantity theory approach of his *Tract on Monetary Reform*.[25] Certainly, Irving Fisher and other classical writers were aware of the effect of interest rates on velocity.[26] In my own theoretical essay, "The Quantity Theory of Money—A Restatement," I emphasize the role of interest rates in the demand function for money without in any way accepting either the Keynesian Revolution or Keynes' attack on the quantity theory.[27]

The specifically Keynesian innovation in this area, I believe, was the idea that absolute liquidity-preference, that is, the liquidity trap or an infinitely elastic demand for money, might be empirically relevant in deep depressions. As noted earlier, this empirical assertion does have far-reaching theoretical implications. But simply introducing interest rates in the demand function for money does not.

25. J. M. Keynes, *Tract on Monetary Reform*, 81–95 (1924).

26. For example, Pigou wrote in 1917, "Other things being equal, the variable *k* ['the *proportion* of his resources the average man chooses to keep . . . in the form of titles to legal tender'] will be larger the less attractive is the production use and the more attractive is the rival money use of resources. The chief factor upon which the attractiveness of the production use depends is the expected fruitfulness of industrial activity," i.e., the real yield on capital. Pigou, *The Value of Money*, 32 Q.J. Econ. 38, 42–46 (1917); reprinted in *Readings in Monetary Theory*, 162, 166–68 (1950).

27. Chapter 2 above.

IV. POLICY IMPLICATIONS

(a) *Fiscal policy.* Whether, as Brill asserts in the comment I have numbered [6], zero interest elasticity would prevent fiscal policy from affecting "the level of aggregate [nominal] expenditures for goods and services, quite apart from their influence on the stock of money," depends on the same considerations adduced above in discussing his comment [5]. Fiscal policy could alter interest rates and through them, the composition and level of income, and these in turn might affect velocity and so aggregate nominal expenditures.[28] Whether or not they affected aggregate nominal expenditures, they would affect prices.

(b) The degree of financial restraint, referred to by Brill in the comment I have numbered [7], is not reflected in any simple way by variations in the nominal money stock whether or not interest rates enter into the demand for money. To illustrate, a 10 per cent per year rate of growth of the quantity of money that comes after a period in which the quantity of money has been rising at the rate of 50 per cent per year implies a very different degree of financial restraint than if it comes after a period in which the monetary growth rate has been zero per cent per year. The former may produce a financial panic; the latter a "sloppy" money market, in Federal Reserve terminology.

Points (a) and (b) both illustrate what seems to me the most serious and widespread defect in current discussions of monetary theory and policy—the tendency to neglect the price level and its determination. This is the legacy of Keynes, surely unintended, that has been most productive of misunderstanding.

(c) *Discretion vs. rule.* There are a set of conditions under which interest rate effects on the demand for money would, as Johnson asserts in the comment I have numbered [3], make the rule of a steady growth in the quantity of money automatically destabilizing.[29] They are first, that total output grow at a steady rate without fluctuations, second, that real fluctuations take the form of changes in the ratio of saving and investment to full employment income mediated through interest rate changes, and third, that velocity be a function solely of interest rates. In that case, a rise in interest rates would raise velocity. Since income is growing at a steady rate, the rate of growth of the real quantity of money would have to decline to equate actual with desired balances. Since the nominal quantity of money is growing at a steady rate, a decline in the rate of growth of real balances would in turn require an increased rate of rise of prices. Conversely, whenever interest rates fell, the rate of rise of prices would slow down. Hence fluctuations in interest rates would produce fluctuations in the rate of change of prices. These could be counteracted only by changes in the rate of growth of the quantity of money sufficient to offset the changes in desired velocity.

28. See footnote 24.

29. I am indebted to Harry Johnson for spelling out the conditions he had in mind.

These conditions are highly special. Moreover, they differ in a number of crucial respects from those that I have assumed to hold in recommending the rule that the quantity of money be made to grow at a constant rate.

(i) Though stressing the importance of monetary change, I have always emphasized "the existence of other factors that affect the course of business or that account for the quasi-rhythmical character of business fluctuations."[30] For the moment, keep the assumption that velocity is independent of all variables except, possibly, interest rates but suppose that "real factors" produce fluctuations (or a tendency to fluctuations) not only in the ratio of investment to output but also in output itself, involving a tendency for interest rates and output to move in the same direction (which roughly corresponds to actual experience). In that case, if velocity were independent of interest rates as well (that is, if velocity were a numerical constant), a constant rate of monetary growth would mean that nominal income would rise at a constant rate, which in turn would mean that prices would decline relative to their trend when output rose and rise relative to trend when output fell—movements that most would regard as automatically stabilizing. Let velocity now be sensitive to interest rates. Movements in velocity would then tend to produce movements in nominal income in the same direction as in output. The amplitude of these movements and hence the direction of movement in prices depends on the amplitude of the interest rate movements and the interest-elasticity of velocity. Prices might still move counter to output, though by less than for a zero interest-elasticity, or they might be stable, or they might move in the same direction. Only in this final case, when prices and output move in the same direction, does it seem to me meaningful to speak of the result as in any sense "automatically destabilizing." In the other cases, the most one can say is that velocity movements offset to some extent the automatically stabilizing effects of the steady rate of monetary growth.

(ii) In practice, velocity does tend to move in the same direction as output, which reflects partly interest rate variations and partly other factors. Also, prices and output tend to move together. However, in practice, the quantity of money also behaves pro-cyclically and so reinforces the movements in velocity. Hence, whether or not the rule might be "destabilizing" relative to some utopian norm, it has always seemed to me likely to be stabilizing relative to actual discretionary policy.

(iii) Finally, the major argument for the rule has always seemed to me to be far less that it would moderate minor cyclical fluctuations than that it would render impossible the major mistakes in monetary policy that have from time to time had such devastating effects. This consideration has nothing to do with the interest elasticity of demand.

30. Quotation from Friedman and Schwartz, "Money and Business Cycles," *Review of Economics and Statistics*, vol. 45, no. 1, part 2: supplement (February, 1963), p. 55 (Chapter 10 in this volume). See also Friedman, "The Supply of Money and Changes in Prices and Output," Chapter 9 in this volume, and *A Program for Monetary Stability*, New York: Fordham University Press (1959), pp. 98–99.

V. CONCLUSION

It is important that we try to determine as accurately as possible the characteristics of the demand function for money, including the elasticity of demand with respect to interest rates. But in my opinion no "fundamental issues" in either monetary theory or monetary policy hinge on whether the estimated elasticity can for most purposes be approximated by zero or is better approximated by $-.1$ or $-.5$ or -2.0, provided it is seldom capable of being approximated by $-\infty$.

The important consideration for monetary theory and policy is whether the demand for money can be treated as a reasonably stable function of a fairly small number of variables and whether this function can be empirically specified with reasonable accuracy. Whether one important argument of the function is an interest rate or set of interest rates is much less important.

The significance that has been attached to the interest elasticity of demand for money reflects, I believe, sophisticated versions of the errors of confusing a movement along a demand or supply function with a shift of such a function and of confusing real with nominal magnitudes. If the interest elasticity is not zero, there will be movements along the function that it is easy to interpret as a sign of instability of the function.[31] The tendency to treat prices as if they were determined outside the monetary system, or as if they were constant, which may be illuminating for some problems, tends to lead to the neglect of factors that may affect real but not nominal magnitudes.

31. Though in practice, perhaps a more important source of confusion of this type is failure to allow for leads and lags.

Chapter 8

Price, Income,

and Monetary Changes

in Three Wartime Periods

THE WIDESPREAD TENDENCY in empirical studies of economic behavior to discard war years as "abnormal," while doubtless often justified, is, on the whole, unfortunate. The major defect of the data on which economists must rely—data generated by experience rather than deliberately contrived experiment—is the small range of variation they encompass. Experience in general proceeds smoothly and continuously. In consequence, it is difficult to disentangle systematic effects from random variation since both are of much the same order of magnitude.

From this point of view, data for wartime periods are peculiarly valuable. At such times, violent changes in major economic magnitudes occur over relatively brief periods, thereby providing precisely the kind of evidence that we would like to get by "critical" experiments if we could conduct them. Of course, the source of the changes means that the effects in which we are interested are necessarily intertwined with others that we would eliminate from a contrived

Reprinted from *The American Economic Review*, volume 42, no. 2, May, 1952. I am greatly indebted to Phillip Cagan and David Fand for able assistance in the research underlying this paper.

experiment. But this difficulty applies to all our data, not to data for wartime periods alone.

To the student of monetary phenomena, the three wartime episodes with which this paper deals—the experience of the United States in the Civil War, first World War, and second World War—offer an especially close approximation to the kind of critical experiment he would like to conduct. As we shall see, in all three cases the rise in prices was of almost precisely the same magnitude, so this critical variable is under control. Yet other crucial features varied, offering the opportunity to test alternative hypotheses designed to explain price changes.

Besides their significance for the general understanding of monetary phenomena, the wartime experiences are unfortunately of interest in their own right. The current period of mobilization raises much the same financial problems as previous wartime periods; and the unhappy possibility that the resemblance will become even closer cannot be dismissed.

I. PRICE AND INCOME CHANGES

The appended table (p. 168) summarizes the key magnitudes for the three wartime periods. In all cases, I have taken the outbreak of the war as the starting point, since this seems more nearly comparable for the different wars than the date of our active entry into the war, and the date of the war or first postwar price peak-as the terminal point. This gives a period of nearly four years for the Civil War price movement,[1] nearly six years for World War I, and nearly nine years for World War II.

The price peak came approximately at the end of the Civil War, a year and a half after the end of World War I, and three years after World War II. This successively later timing of the peak is one of the most interesting features of the three wartime periods. Measured by the available monthly indexes of wholesale prices, the magnitude of the full price rise was very nearly identical in the three wars (see line 5 of table), prices at the price peak being from 2.1 to 2.3 times their level at the outbreak of the war. This similarity of behavior is not an accident resulting from the use of wholesale prices; it would be shown equally by other broad and equally reliable index numbers. Given the difference in the length of the periods, the rate of rise was of course successively lower in the three wars (line 6).

Unfortunately, no satisfactory data are available on short period movements in national income in the Civil War. General considerations together with some scattered evidence suggest that money income rose in approximately the same or a somewhat higher ratio than prices; i.e., that real output was either unchanged or moderately higher. Money income somewhat more than doubled

---

1. All statements for Civil War are for the North ("loyal states") only.

in the first World War, and more than tripled in the second (line 7).[2] Since prices roughly doubled in both wars, real output changed little in World War I but rose about 50 per cent in World War II (line 9). Somewhat less than half of this rise in output can be attributed to the higher volume of unemployment at the outbreak of the second than at the outbreak of the first World War; the rest, which meant an increase in output of about 2.5 per cent a year, is less readily explained.

II. THE MAGNITUDE OF THE WAR EFFORT

The immediate occasion for the rise in prices and money income was of course the diversion of resources to war use. We can get a rough measure of the magnitude of diversion in each wartime period as a whole by expressing federal expenditures in each year as a fraction of national income, to render the expenditures comparable from year to year and war to war; subtracting the corresponding fraction for an immediate pre-war year, to allow for changes from war to war in the "normal" activities of government; and summing the resultant figures for all full fiscal years from the outbreak of the war to the price peak. According to this measure, slightly over one-half of one year's national income was diverted to war use during the Civil War price movement and also during the World War I movement, and about one and two-thirds years' national income during the World War II price movement (line 11). On a per-year basis, the diversion was about 14 per cent for the Civil War, 9 per cent for World War I, and 18 per cent for World War II (line 12).

Numerous qualifications attach to both the statistical and economic significance of these figures. My own judgment is that the aggregate diversion of resources to the war effort was significantly smaller in the first World War than in either of the other two wars in the sense that it raised a less serious economic problem, and probably larger in World War II than in the Civil War.[3] From the point of view of a well-designed experiment, this is a rather happy outcome, since it enables us to distinguish, as it were, the effects of secular change from other effects. If the same factors turn out to explain why the full price rise was roughly the same in the earliest and the latest war as in the first World War despite a more serious economic problem, the results are not rendered question-

2. The concept of national income here and elsewhere in this paper is not identical with that currently being used by the U.S. Department of Commerce. To obtain comparability of data for the different wars, it has seemed preferable to use the concept in Simon Kuznets, *National Product in Wartime*, New York: National Bureau of Economic Research (1945).

3. One set of numbers that brings out dramatically the problem of judging the relative magnitude of diversion is the total number of persons who died in military service in the three wars. The number is roughly 360 thousand for the North in the Civil War, 126 thousand in World War I and 400 thousand in World War II. The corresponding figures for total population at the outbreak of the wars are 22, 99, 131 million. By this index, the Civil War was far and away the costliest.

able by the possibility that would otherwise exist that they merely reflect secular change.

III. THE PROBLEM OF INTERPRETATION

How is it that despite substantial differences in the stimulus, the magnitude of the full price rise is much the same in the three wars while the rate of price rise is successively smaller? What features of policy or circumstance account for the less effective handling in the first World War than in either of the other wars of the inflationary threat raised by the wartime need to devote a significant fraction of resources to the production of goods and services not available for sale on the market?

Three factors are generally cited as explaining part or all of the better performance in the second than in the first World War: first, the larger fraction of government expenditures financed through taxes; second, the greater increase in output documented above; third, the more extensive direct controls over prices, wages, and the distribution of goods. Are these an adequate explanation? And do they also explain the better performance in the Civil than in the first World War?

A. The Importance of Taxation

Total federal tax receipts averaged about one-fifth of total expenditures during the Civil War price movement, two-fifths during World War I, and three-fifths during World War II, a dramatic and impressive improvement in the tax effort (line 13).

These differences in the level of taxation increase the difficulty of explaining the common behavior of prices in the Civil War and World War I, since not only was the war effort apparently of larger magnitude during the Civil War, but also the fraction of expenditures financed by taxes was smaller. On a per-year basis and as a percentage of the national income, expenditures one and half times as large in the Civil War as in World War I were converted by the smaller tax effort into a deficit nearly twice as large—12 per cent of national income compared with 6.5 per cent (lines 15 or 17).[4] The cumulated deficit over the four years of the Civil War period amounted to about one-half of one year's national income; over the six years of the World War I period, to two-fifths of a year's income (lines 14 and 16).

For the two world wars, on the other hand, the difference in the level of taxation helps to explain the common behavior of prices. But it does so only in part, since the higher level of taxation in World War II fell far short of offsetting fully the higher level of expenditures. Despite the larger tax effort, the deficit

4. The two lines give the same answer because the budget was approximately balanced just prior to both the Civil War and World War I.

was substantially higher: 13 per cent of national income per year compared to 6.5 per cent for the total deficit (line 15); and 8.5 per cent of national income per year, compared to 6.5 per cent for the excess deficit (the deficit as a fraction of national income minus the corresponding pre-war fraction; see line 17). The cumulated total deficit is nearly three times as large in World War II as in World War I; the cumulated excess deficit nearly twice as large.[5]

B. Changes in Real Output

There seems no reason to believe that real output behaved very differently during the Civil War than during the first World War; so this factor is largely neutral as between these two wars.

The substantial rise in real output during World War II, compared to little change during World War I, undoubtedly eased the physical and psychological problems of attaining such an impressively large war output. It is less obvious just how it affected the financial and monetary problem of avoiding inflation. For the increase in real output involved an increase in income payments to the factors of production but, since it was absorbed by government for war purposes, no increase in goods available for purchase on the market.

From the point of view of the quantity theory of money, increased output helps the problem of avoiding inflation by raising the demand for money. In consequence, the government can finance part of its expenditures by creating money without any inflationary pressure on prices. Quantitative estimates along these lines indicate that only a small part of the difference between the deficits in the two world wars can be regarded as non-inflationary because of the increase in real output—from one-tenth to one-fifth of the difference, depending on the exact estimate used and on whether the deficit prior to World War II is or is not regarded as "normal."

From the point of view of the income-expenditure theory, the increased output helps the problem of avoiding inflation because at a correspondingly higher income the amount not spent on consumption (or, more generally, not devoted to "induced expenditures") will be larger, so permitting a larger amount of income-creating or "autonomous" expenditures. Quantitative estimates based on this approach vary more widely than those based on the quantity-theory approach, primarily because there is more uncertainty just how to make them. It turns out that the final result depends critically on two factors: the

---

5. I have assumed implicitly that a balanced budget (or the balanced part of the budget) raises no inflationary problem regardless of size. According to the so-called "balanced budget theorem," however, an increase of federal expenditures and taxes by the same amount has a "multiplier" of unity, and hence a larger balanced budget is more inflationary than a smaller one. To the extent that this theorem is relevant to the present problem, it strengthens the conclusion reached above; namely, that the difference in the level of taxation cannot account for the difference in performance.

interpretation placed on the deficit prior to World War II compared with the balanced budget prior to World War I; and the numerical value used for the "multiplier." If the difference in pre-war deficits is regarded as "accidental" and hence the total deficits in the two wars regarded as comparable, this approach yields essentially the same result as the quantity-theory approach: between one-twelfth and two-thirds of the difference between the deficits in the two wars can be regarded as non-inflationary because of the increase in real output, the exact estimate depending on the multiplier that is used. This range includes the whole of the range given earlier. On the other hand, if the pre-World War II deficit is regarded as normal, i.e., as reflecting a secular shift toward "stagnation" so that a deficit of given size was less inflationary, the results are highly ambiguous: between one-half and three times the difference in the excess deficit can then be regarded as non-inflationary because of the increase in real output.

In my judgment, the balance of evidence justifies the conclusion that the large increase in output in World War II explains only in part, and probably only in minor part, why the larger per-year and accumulated deficits in that war than in World War I were associated with a price rise that was somewhat smaller in aggregate and decidedly smaller per year.

C. Direct Controls

Direct controls were completely absent in the Civil War, present to some extent in World War I and extensive in World War II. If they tend to reduce the ultimate inflationary impact of wartime expenditures, they, like the differences in tax effort, increase the difficulty of explaining the common magnitude of the price rise in the Civil War and World War I.

The major channel whereby direct controls can be regarded as reducing inflationary pressure is by inducing income recipients at a given level of prices to accumulate larger cash balances or purchase a larger amount of government securities than otherwise.[6] Figures on holdings of money and of government securities during World War II suggest that the controls may have had such effects when they were in force; but, if so, the effects were not lasting and had completely disappeared by mid-1948 when prices reached their peak. From the outbreak of the war to the subsequent price peak, cash balances as a fraction of national income fell by about the same amount in World War II as in World War I, and cash balances plus government security holdings rose by a smaller amount (lines 18 and 19). So direct controls can be rejected as a factor affecting the ultimate magnitude of the price rise.

6. I neglect the so-called "wage-price spiral" (more properly, wage-price-money spiral) argument for reasons indicated in my paper, "Some Comments on the Significance of Labor Unions for Economic Policy," in *The Impact of the Union*, David McCord Wright (Ed.), New York: Harcourt, Brace and Co. (1951), pp. 217–21.

IV. MONETARY FACTORS

We have as yet found no answer to the question why the price rise was much the same in the three wars despite substantial differences in the magnitude of the war effort. The three reasons commonly adduced to explain the better performance in World War II than in World War I—larger tax effort, larger increase in real output, and direct controls—seem inadequate even for these two wars and, more significant yet, if anything they increase the difficulty of explaining the better performance in the Civil War than in World War I.

The one set of factors so far left largely out of account are those connected with changes in the quantity of money. Figures on these changes (lines 23 and 24), unlike the figures we have so far been grappling with, tell a simple, coherent, and consistent story and give at least a proximate explanation of price behavior during the three wars. Consider first the two world wars. The stock of money doubled in the first and nearly tripled in the second (line 23). But this difference is more than accounted for by the differential change in total output. The stock of money per unit of output, which is of course the figure that is relevant for price movements, rose somewhat more in World War I than in World War II; and so did prices and in almost exactly the same proportion. During the Civil War, the stock of money rose more than in World War I and less than in World War II.[7] Unfortunately, we cannot reliably translate this figure into the change in the quantity of money per unit of output; we do know enough, however, to demonstrate that if we could, the result might be perfectly in line with those for the other wars and can hardly be drastically out of line with them. The total rise in wholesale prices was the same in the Civil War and in World War I but at a higher rate per year; the higher rate of price rise might be expected to lead to a larger increase in velocity, so the stock of money per unit of output might be expected to have increased somewhat less than in World War I. An increase in output of about 20 per cent would be required for this result;[8] this is not unreasonable in the light of general considerations which suggest that output was relatively stable or rose moderately during the Civil War; even the extreme assumption of no change in output yields results that are not drastically out of line with those for the later wars.

Our conclusions about the three wars do not rest on or require any narrowly restrictive assumption about the constancy of the income velocity of circulation. Income velocity would be expected to rise during a period of rising prices

7. It should be noted that the estimates of the stock of money for the Civil War are entirely new estimates constructed by rather roundabout means from a considerable body of fragmentary evidence; so are subject to considerable error.

8. The 20 per cent is obtained by supposing the rise in income velocity in the Civil War to exceed that in World War I by the same amount as the latter exceeds the rise in World War II (see line 25).

because of the incentive not to hold cash; and it did rise in the two wars for which we have data (line 25). The significant thing is that it rose by roughly the same amount, and that the small difference in the magnitude of the rise is in the expected direction: the rise is somewhat greater in the war in which prices rose at a higher rate. Indeed, I would have expected the higher rate of price rise in World War I to have produced an even larger difference in the behavior of velocity.

V. REASONS FOR CHANGES IN STOCK OF MONEY

The finding that price rises of the same percentage in the three wars can be "explained" by rises in the quantity of money per unit of output of roughly the same percentage is, of course, no final answer to our basic question. What factors account for the common rise in the quantity of money per unit of output despite such wide differences in the magnitude of the war effort, the size of the deficit, the banking structure, and so on? More particularly, why was the rise as large as it was in World War I, given a smaller war effort than in either of the other wars and a larger tax effort than in the Civil War?

Lines 26 through 32 in the appended table are designed to push the analysis one stage farther by giving a particular breakdown of the factors determining changes in the stock of money and the effect of such changes on income. Lines 26 through 29 summarize the factors determining the amount of money created by government; lines 30 through 32, the factors determining its inflationary potency.

World War I involved a substantially smaller issue of money by government than either of the other wars (line 29), and in this sense a smaller inflationary stimulus; smaller than the Civil War despite total expenditures of roughly the same magnitude (line 26) because of both a smaller deficit relative to expenditures (line 27) and the financing of a smaller fraction of the deficit by money creation rather than bond issues (line 28); smaller than World War II, despite a larger deficit relative to expenditures and the financing of the same fraction of the deficit by currency creation, because of a drastically smaller level of total expenditures. Had the inflationary potency of government-created money been the same in the two world wars as in the Civil War, wholesale prices would have risen only about 50 per cent in World War I instead of 132 per cent; and only about 60 per cent in World War II instead of 113 per cent. These computations assume that the changes in output would have been as estimated in line 9 of the table and that velocity would have risen by about as much as it did.

But the inflationary potency of government-created money was not the same. And it is this factor, summarized in line 32 of the table, that is the key to our basic question. The smaller initial inflationary stimulus in World War I than in either of the other wars was offset by a higher sensitivity to government money creation. Each dollar of money printed by the government meant an increase of $7 per year in national income in the Civil War and of nearly $7.50 in the second World War; it meant an increase of about twice as much, or nearly $15, in the first World War.

The greater sensitivity of the economy to government money creation in World War I than in the Civil War is even more remarkable in view of the sharp decline in the income velocity of circulation, which worked in the opposite direction. The villain is the expansion ratio of the banking system, which was more than five times as large.[9] The lower sensitivity in World War II than in World War I is a resultant of a reduction both on the demand side—a decline of more than a quarter in the income velocity of circulation—and on the supply side—a decline of more than a quarter in the expansion ratio of the banking system. Compared to the Civil War, however, World War II shows essentially the same changes as World War I—a drastic decrease in the income velocity of circulation counterbalanced by an even more drastic increase in the expansion ratio of the banking system.

These differences in the expansion ratio in turn reflect changes in our banking structure: the much greater importance of currency relative to deposits in the Civil War than in the two later wars, the abandonment of the gold standard in the Civil War and its retention in the other wars, changes in the reserve ratio of the banking system from war to war, and so on. From this point of view—as, also, if I may add a parenthetical minority view, from almost every other—the establishment of the Federal Reserve System at the outbreak of World War I, far from being the unmitigated boon to war finance that it is generally considered, was a serious handicap. It had the effect of reducing the reserve ratio of the banking system and so increasing the expansion ratio. In addition, it doubtless meant an increase in the amount of money created by the government in both world wars because of the System's rediscount operations (particularly after World War I) and government bond purchases (particularly after World

9. In calculating the expansion ratios, I have treated as government-issued money only net noninterest-bearing obligations issued directly by the government and held outside government agencies. However, the Federal Reserve System has been regarded as part of the government and its accounts consolidated with those of the Treasury. Thus, the total stock of government created money is equal to currency outside the Treasury and Federal Reserve plus domestic deposits other than Treasury deposits in the Federal Reserve less gold stock (because regarded as privately created) less state and national bank notes (except for World War II when national bank notes were in the process of retirement) less deposits of U.S. Government and government agencies in commercial and savings banks less Federal Reserve float. The total stock of money used in calculating the numerator of the ratios is currency outside banks and the Treasury plus adjusted demand deposits plus time deposits.

This treatment implicitly makes a distinction between government securities sold to the Federal Reserve banks and other government securities but not between securities sold to commercial banks and securities sold to nonbank purchasers. The sale of securities to the Federal Reserve is not a "real" security sale; it is simply a bookkeeping operation involved in our system in the creation of money by the government. For the rest, little economic importance attaches to the distinction between sales to commercial banks and to others.

War II). These involved creation of money, not to meet government expenditures, but to enable private banks to expand.

The secular trend in the income velocity is less readily and satisfactorily explained. Numerous explanations have been offered, but so far as I know, no satisfactory test of their validity has yet been made. In any event, it presumably reflected factors largely outside of government control.

VI. CONCLUSION

This examination of changes in prices, income, and monetary magnitudes during three wartime periods has led to conclusions which, if accepted, clearly have important implications for both economic theory and economic policy. The explicit statement of a number of these implications will provide a convenient means of summarizing the analysis.

A crucial issue in economic theory in recent years has been the relative value of two competing theories of income determination: the quantity theory of money and the Keynesian income-expenditure theory. These two theories can, of course, be looked on as merely frameworks of analysis—as different languages or assemblies of truisms. In this sense, any statements expressed in the language of one theory can be translated into the language of the other. But I take it that the major issue has been about the theories, not as alternative languages, but as empirical hypotheses. In this sense they are different and competitive: the quantity theory asserts in essence that the velocity of circulation of money is the empirical variable that behaves in a stable or consistent fashion; the income-expenditure theory, that the propensity to consume, or the consumption function, is the empirical variable that behaves in a stable or consistent fashion.

Price and income changes during the three wartime periods seem more readily explicable by the quantity theory than by the income-expenditure theory. The quantity theory instructs us to look for a proximate explanation of the divergent magnitudes of the rise in money income in a similarly divergent rise in the stock of money and for a proximate explanation of the common magnitude of the price rise in a common behavior of the stock of money relative to real output. And it turns out that the percentage rise in the stock of money was larger in the first than in the second war period and larger in the third than in either of the others in roughly the same proportion as the corresponding increases in output; in consequence, the stock of money per unit of output increased by about the same percentage in all three periods. Indeed, even the minor difference between the two world wars in the percentage increase in the stock of money per unit of output is in the same direction and of the same magnitude as the minor difference in the percentage increase in prices. The quantity theory is thus clearly consistent with this empirical test.

The income-expenditure theory instructs us to pay little or no attention to the quantity of money or its behavior but to look for an explanation of the divergent behavior of money income in a correspondingly divergent behavior of "autonomous" or "income-creating" expenditures. But the facts appear inconsistent with this explanation. In all three wars government expenditures are the dominant autonomous expenditures to which the income rise must be attributed by the income-expenditure theory and taxes the chief "leakage" other than savings. The magnitude of government expenditures, measured throughout in units of an appropriate year's national income, was about the same in aggregate during the four years of the Civil War price rise as during the six years of the World War I price rise, hence about one and a half times as large per year; taxes were a smaller fraction of both expenditures and national income; so the per-year deficit was almost twice as large a fraction of the national income during the Civil War price rise. Yet despite not much difference in the behavior of output, prices rose by the same percentage in the two wars. In the second World War, incomes rose more than in either of the other wars though prices did not, thanks to the increase in real output, and total expenditures are larger both in aggregate and on a per-year basis than in either of the other wars. But the per-year deficit, though considerably larger than in the first World War, is no larger than in the Civil War, and the magnitudes of the differences seem to bear no consistent relationship to the magnitude of the changes in income. From an examination of the income or fiscal magnitudes alone, one would expect the rise in income in the second World War to have been much larger relative to the rise in the first than it was, and the rise in prices to have been much smaller relative to the rise in the Civil War than it was. The income-expenditure theory explains part of the difference between the two world wars and, with considerably more difficulty, may perhaps be interpreted as consistent with the whole difference. I have been unable to explain the difference between the Civil War and World War I in its terms. Indeed, the factors it stresses increase the problem of explanation.

This conclusion that the quantity theory is and the income-expenditure theory is not consistent with price and income behavior in the three wars would, I think, be strengthened by examination of the year-to-year changes in prices, incomes, and monetary and fiscal magnitudes, in addition to the changes from the outbreak of the war to the end of the price movement on which I have put major emphasis. The sharp drop in the government deficit and emergence of a surplus shortly after both world wars was not accompanied by a correspondingly sharp drop in income or in prices; at most, they were accompanied by a temporary halt and then a resumption of the rise in prices; and in both cases the stock of money continued rising after surpluses had appeared in the government budget and reached a peak in the general neighborhood of the price peak.

Such an examination would also, I think, provide a plausible explanation for the successively later timing of the price peak. In the Civil War, there was no central bank automatically creating "high-powered" currency at the initiative of commercial banks; so the price rise ended when the government no longer had to print money to meet its expenditures. In the first World War, there was

Selected Data on Price, Income, and Monetary Changes in the Civil War,
World War I, and World War II

GENERAL NOTES:

1. With minor exceptions, all figures refer to period from outbreak of war to subsequent price peak.
2. Ratios of a quantity at price peak to its value at outbreak of war are based on averages for a twelve-month period surrounding the price peak and a twelve-month period surrounding the outbreak of war, except for Civil War stock of money ratios.
3. Missing figures for Civil War reflect absence of independent evidence on change in real output.
4. All figures for Civil War are, so far as possible, for the North ("loyal states") only.

	CIVIL WAR	WORLD WAR I	WORLD WAR II
Timing Data			
1. Date of outbreak of war	April, 1861	July-Aug., 1914	Sept., 1939
2. Date of end of war	April, 1865	Nov., 1918	Aug., 1945
3. Date of price peak	Jan., 1865	May, 1920	Aug., 1948
4. Months from outbreak of war to price peak	45	69	107
Wholesale Prices			
5. Ratio (price peak/outbreak of war)	2.32	2.32	2.13
6. Rate of rise per year	25%	16%	9%
Money National Income			
7. Ratio (price peak/outbreak of war)	—	2.29	3.14
8. Rate of rise per year	—	16%	14%
Real National Income *(Deflated by Wholesale Prices)*			
9. Ratio (price peak/outbreak of war)	—	.99	1.48
10. Rate of rise per year	—	0	4.4%
Magnitude of War Effort Federal expenditures as fraction of national income in excess of base year fraction:			
11. Sum for all full fiscal years, outbreak of war to price peak	.54	.56	1.65
12. Per year	.14	.093	.18
Fiscal Performance			
13. Taxes as fraction of expenditures	.21	.43	.61
Deficit as fraction of national income:			
14. Sum all full fiscal years, outbreak of of war to price peak	.49	.39	1.13
15. Per year	.12	.065	.13
Deficit as fraction of national income in excess of base year fraction:			
16. Sum, outbreak of war to price peak	.46	.39	.76
17. Per year	.12	.065	.085

	CIVIL WAR	WORLD WAR I	WORLD WAR II
Money and Government Security Holdings of Nonbanking Public			
Money as fraction of national income:			
18. Ratio (price peak/outbreak of war)	—	.86	.88
Money plus securities as fraction of national income:			
19. Ratio (price peak/outbreak of war)	—	1.26	1.14
Stock of Money; Velocity			
Ratios (price peak/outbreak of war):			
20. Currency outside banks	2.49*	2.48	4.19
21. Demand deposits adjusted	2.54*	1.98	3.02
22. Time deposits	1.63*	1.83	2.13
23. Total stock of money	2.32*	1.96	2.75
24. Stock of money per unit of output	—	1.98	1.86
25. Income velocity of circulation	—	1.17	1.15
Factors Determining Changes in Stock of Money and Their Effect on Income			
26. Ratio of accumulated government expenditures to national income	.62	.69	2.88
27. Deficit as fraction of government expenditures	.79	.57	.39
28. Fraction of accumulated deficit financed by money creation	.23	.11	.11
29. (26) × (27) × (28) = Money created by government as a fraction of a year's national income	.11	.043	.12
30. Expansion ratio of banking system (total money created per dollar of money created by government)	1.49	7.78	5.53
31. Income velocity of circulation	4.70	1.90	1.35
32. (30) × (31) = Dollars of income per year per dollar of money created government	7.00	14.78	7.47

* Ratios of average for year ending June 30, 1865, to value on June 30, 1861. Data are not available on demand deposits adjusted and time deposits for Civil War. Ratios given are for all deposits other than deposits in mutual savings banks, and deposits in mutual savings banks, respectively.

---

such a central bank and it provided the sinews for continued expansion of the total stock of money after the close of the war through its rediscount operations, but at least there was no bond-support policy to prevent the central bank from calling a halt at long last; so the inflation continued only eighteen months after the end of the war. In the second World War, the bond-support policy had the same effect as the earlier rediscounting operations in providing a base for a larger money supply and in addition served as an excuse for letting the process continue; so the primary post-war inflation lasted thirty-six months after the end of the war.

The implications of our results for policy are, I think, no less clear than for economic theory. The debate between proponents and opponents of monetary policy has in truth been little more than a manifestation of the debate on alternative theories. Our conclusions favor the proponents of monetary policy. If you want to control prices and incomes, they say, in about as clear tones as empirical evidence ever speaks, control the stock of money per unit of output. The level of expenditures and of taxation, the extent of increases in real output, are all important for the problem of inflation primarily because of their effects on the stock of money per unit of output, and they are only important insofar as they have such effects. And at least as important as any of these is the expansion ratio of the banking system—the total number of dollars of money created per dollar of direct government money creation. For we found that the major factor that explained the relative income increases in the three wars was not the extent of money creation by the government, for this was less than half as large in the first World War as in either of the others, but the expansion ratio of the banking system. In the Civil War the total supply of money—currency plus deposits—increased about $1.50 for each $1 of money created directly by the government; in the first World War, it increased nearly $8; in the second World War, $5.50. If direct government money creation had been the same in both world wars as it was but had been combined with a 100 per cent reserve deposit banking system, a nongold money, and no private creation of money, prices would probably have risen vastly less than they actually did. The Civil War money creation took place in a system that by accident rather than design in effect closely approximated the one just described, which appears to be the main reason why prices rose no more in that war than in the others despite a larger war effort than in the first World War and a less effective tax effort and a substantially smaller demand for money than in either of the other wars.

Chapter 9

The Supply of Money and

Changes in Prices and Output

THIS PAPER DEALS WITH two broad issues that have arisen again and again in connection with movements in the general level of prices. One issue is the connection between such price movements and changes in the supply of money. The other is the relation between price changes and changes in output.

The course of economic history is replete with substantial price disturbances. Whenever such disturbances have occurred, two different explanations have been offered. One, common to all disturbances, is that the price movements reflect changes in the quantity of money, though the source of the monetary changes has varied widely—from clipping of currency to gold discoveries to changes in the monetary standard to the printing of paper money to the creation or destruction of deposit money by central banks and commercial banks. The other explanation has been in terms of some special circumstances of the particular occasion: good or bad harvests; disruptions in international trade; lack of confidence; the activities of "profiteers" or "monopolists" selling goods or of employers seeking to hold down wages; the activities of workers or unions pushing wages up; and so on in great variety. Perhaps the one common core of such explanations is that they generally attribute the price movements to the (socially)

Reprinted from *The Relationship of Prices to Economic Stability and Growth*, 85th Congress, 2nd Session, Joint Economic Committee Print, Washington, D.C.: U.S. Government Printing Office (1958).

misguided behavior of particular individuals or groups. My own view is that these alternative explanations play little or no role in either long run or large movements in prices, though they may in short and minor movements, except indirectly as they affect the supply of money. It is clearly impossible to argue this view in detail within the compass of this paper. My reason for stating it is to make clear that I am putting such explanations to one side and concentrating instead on the monetary forces at work.

The relation between the supply of money and prices has been explored so frequently and thoroughly that I can hardly hope to add much that is new on an analytical level. My reason for dealing with it nonetheless is twofold: on the one hand, though it is the essence of the problem of long run and large price movements, it tends to be pushed to one side and neglected—partly, perhaps, because of the desire to be novel; on the other hand, extensive empirical work that is currently underway puts flesh on the analytical skeleton to an extent that has not heretofore been possible. One of the major aims and justifications of this paper is to summarize some of the broad findings of this work.[1] I shall do so in section 1 for the longer term changes in money and prices, in section 2, for the shorter term changes.

Discussion of public policy with respect to prices necessarily involves the issue what kind of movements are socially desirable. One major problem is the relation of price movements to economic growth. Is a rising price level favorable or unfavorable to rapid growth in output? No conclusive answer can be given to this question in the present state of our knowledge. Some analysis and evidence to justify this assertion are given in section 3.

The final section of this paper presents some implications for policy that are suggested by the relation between monetary and price change and between price change and output change.

I. RELATION OF STOCK OF
MONEY TO PRICES OVER LONGER PERIODS

There is perhaps no empirical regularity among economic phenomena that is based on so much evidence for so wide a range of circumstances as the connection between substantial changes in the stock of money and in the level of prices.[2] To the best of my knowledge there is no instance in which a substantial

1. These are based partly on the preliminary results of an extensive study by Anna J. Schwartz and myself under the auspices of the National Bureau of Economic Research on the secular and cyclical behavior of the stock of money in the United States, partly on a series of studies done in the workshop in money and banking at the University of Chicago. The views expressed in this paper are of course my own and are not necessarily those of the organizations sponsoring these studies or of the other participants in them.

2. "The stock of money" is not of course an unambiguous concept. There is a wide range of assets possessing to a greater or lesser degree the qualities of general acceptability and fixity in nominal value that are the main characteristics of "money." It is somewhat

change in the stock of money per unit of output has occurred without a substantial change in the level of prices in the same direction.[3] Conversely, I know
of no instance in which there has been a substantial change in the level of prices
without a substantial change in the stock of money per unit of output in the
same direction. And instances in which prices and the stock of money have
moved together are recorded for many centuries of history, for countries in
every part of the globe, and for a wide diversity of monetary arrangements.

There can be little doubt about this statistical connection. The statistical
connection itself, however, tells nothing about direction of influence, and it is
on this question that there has been the most controversy. It could be that a rise
or fall in prices, occurring for whatever reasons, produces a corresponding rise
or fall in the stock of money, so that the monetary changes are a passive consequence. Alternatively, it could be that changes in the stock of money produce
changes in prices in the same direction, so that control of the stock of money
would imply control of prices. The variety of monetary arrangements for
which a connection between monetary and price movements has been observed
supports strongly the second interpretation, namely, that substantial changes in
the stock of money are both a necessary and a sufficient condition for substantial
changes in the general level of prices. But of course this does not exclude a reflex
influence of changes in prices on the stock of money. This reflex influence is
often important, almost always complex, and, depending on the monetary
arrangements, may be in either direction.[4]

This general evidence is reinforced by much historical evidence of a more
specific character demonstrating that changes in the stock of money, at least
when they are fairly large, can exert an independent influence on prices. One
dramatic example is from the experience of the Confederacy during the Civil
War. In 1864, "after 3 years of war, after widespread destruction and military

---

arbitrary just where the line is drawn which separates "money" from "near-money" or
"securities" or "other financial claims." For most of what follows, the precise line drawn
will not affect the analysis. For the United States at present, I shall treat as "money in the
hands of the public" the sum of "currency outside banks," "demand deposits adjusted," and
"adjusted time deposits in commercial banks," as these terms are defined in Federal Reserve
monetary statistics. I shall note explicitly any point at which the precise definition adopted
affects the statements made.

3. The nearest thing to an exception I know of is German experience from the midthirties
to 1944. See John J. Klein, "German Money and Prices, 1932–44", in Milton Friedman (Ed.),
Studies in the Quantity Theory of Money, Chicago: University of Chicago Press (1956), pp.
121–59.

The qualification, "per unit of output" is needed only to cover movements spanning long
periods of time, like the long-term decline in prices in the late 19th century. For moderately
short periods, even this qualification is unnecessary.

4. For example, under a gold standard, a rising level of prices discourages gold production
and so, after a lag tends to produce a decline in the stock of money. On the other hand,
under a fractional reserve banking system, if rising prices lead banks to reduce the ratio of
cash to liabilities, rising prices may tend to produce a rise in the stock of money.

reverses, in the face of impending defeat, a monetary reform that succeeded in reducing the stock of money halted and reversed for some months a rise in prices that had been going on at the rate of 10 per cent a month most of the war. It would be hard to construct a better controlled experiment to demonstrate the critical importance of the supply of money."[5] The effect of discoveries of precious metals in the New World in the 16th century and of gold in California and Australia in the 1840's, of the development of the cyanide process for extracting ore plus gold discoveries in South Africa in the 1890's, and of the printing of money in various hyperinflations, including our own Revolutionary War experience and the experience of many countries after World War I and World War II, are other striking examples of increases in the stock of money producing increases in prices. The long price decline in the second half of the 19th century in many parts of the world is a less dramatic example of a decline in the stock of money per unit of output producing a decline in prices.[6]

The relationship between changes in the stock of money and changes in prices, while close, is not of course precise or mechanically rigid. Two major factors produce discrepancies: changes in output, and changes in the amount of money that the public desires to hold relative to its income.

For the moment, we shall treat output as if it were determined independently of monetary and price changes, postponing to section 3 the relation between them. This is clearly a simplification that is to some extent contrary to fact, but certainly for the longer periods and larger changes that are discussed in this section, the simplification neither does serious violence to the facts nor leads to any significant errors in conclusions.

Suppose the stock of money were to remain unchanged for a period of years but total output over the same period were to double. Clearly, one would expect prices to fall—other things remaining the same—to something like half their initial level. The total amount of "work" for the money stock to do, as it were, is doubled, and the same nominal quantity of money could perform the "work" only at lower levels of prices. Roughly speaking, this is what happened in the United States in the period from the end of the Civil War in 1865 to the resumption of specie payments in 1879: The stock of money was roughly the same in 1879 as in 1865—if anything, some 10 per cent higher; output grew very rapidly over the period, probably more than doubling; and wholesale prices were half their initial level.[7] Thus, for price movements, the relevant variable is

5. Milton Friedman, "The Quantity Theory of Money—a Restatement," in *Studies in the Quantity Theory of Money*, p. 17, Chapter 2 in this volume. The quotation summarizes one item from a study by Eugene M. Lerner, summarized in his article, "Inflation in the Confederacy, 1861–65," in the same volume, pp. 163–75.

6. The decline in the stock of money per unit of output occurred as a result of (1) exhaustion of then-known gold mines; (2) the shift of many countries from a silver to a gold standard; (3) the rapid increase in output.

7. The basic data underlying this statement are from the National Bureau study mentioned in footnote 1 above. They will appear in a monograph by Anna J. Schwartz and myself that is now in preparation.

the stock of money per unit of output, not simply the global stock of money.

The second major factor that can introduce a discrepancy between movements in money and in prices is a change in the ratio that the public desires to maintain between its cash balances and its income[8]—the public including individuals, business enterprises other than banks, nonprofit institutions, and the like. The number of dollars an individual wants to keep in cash depends of course on the price level—at twice the price level he will want to hold something like twice the number of dollars—and on his income—the higher his income presumably the larger cash balances he will want to hold. But the price level is what we are trying to explain, and we have already taken account of the effect of changes in output. This is why we express this factor in terms of the ratio that the public desires to maintain between its cash balances and its income, rather than in terms of the number of dollars it desires to hold.

Broadly speaking, the public as a whole cannot by itself affect the total number of dollars available to be held—this is determined primarily by the monetary institutions. To each individual separately, it appears that he can do so; in fact an individual can reduce or increase his cash balance in general only through another individual's increasing or reducing his. If individuals as a whole, for example, try to reduce the number of dollars they hold, they cannot as an aggregate do so. In trying to do so, however, they will raise the flow of expenditures and hence of money income and in this way will reduce the ratio of their cash balances to their income; since prices will tend to rise in the process, they will thereby reduce the real value of their cash balances, that is, the quantity of goods and services that the cash balances will command; and the process will continue until this ratio or this real value is in accord with their desires.

A wide range of empirical evidence suggests that the ratio which people desire to maintain between their cash balances and their income is relatively stable over fairly long periods of time aside from the effect of two major factors: (1) The level of real income per capita, or perhaps of real wealth per capita; (2) the cost of holding money.[9]

(1) Apparently, the holding of cash balances is regarded as a "luxury," like education and recreation. The amount of money the public desires to hold not only goes up as its real income rises but goes up more than in proportion. Judged by evidence for the past 75 years in the United States, a 1 percent rise in real income per capita tends to be accompanied by nearly a 2 percent increase in the real amount of money held and thus by nearly a 1 per cent increase in the

---

8. The reciprocal of this ratio is termed "the income velocity of circulation."

9. On this subject, see Phillip Cagan, "The Monetary Dynamics of Hyperinflation," and Richard T. Selden, "Monetary Velocity in the United States," in *Studies in the Quantity Theory of Money*. The statements that follow are based also on additional work done in connection with the National Bureau study referred to in footnote 1.

For shorter periods, an additional factor enters. Cash balances are apparently adjusted to longer term income expectations ("permanent income") rather than to current income as measured on a monthly or annual basis. This introduces additional changes in the ratio of cash balances to current measured income. (See sec. 2 below.)

ratio of cash balances to income. This tendency is highly regular over the long sweep of time from 1875 to World War II; it has not been operative since the end of World War II but it is yet too soon to judge whether this is a fundamental change or simply a reaction to the abnormally high ratio of cash balances that was reached during the war.

(2) The cost of holding cash balances depends mainly on the rate of interest that can be earned on alternative assets—thus if a bond yields 4 per cent while cash yields no return, this means that an individual gives up $4 a year if he holds $100 of cash instead of a bond—and on the rate of change of prices—if prices rise at 5 per cent per year, for example, $100 in cash will buy at the end of the year only as much as $95 at the beginning so that it has cost the individual $5 to hold $100 of cash instead of goods. The empirical evidence suggests that while the first factor—the interest rate—has a systematic effect on the amount of money held, the effect is rather small. The second factor, the rate of change of prices, has no discernible effect in ordinary times when price changes are small—on the order of a few per cent a year. On the other hand, it has a clearly discernible and major effect when price change is rapid and long continued, as during extreme inflations or deflations.[10] A rapid inflation produces a sizable decline in the desired ratio of cash balances to income; a rapid deflation, a sizable rise.

Of course even after allowance is made for changes in real income per capita and in the cost of holding money, the ratio of cash balances to income is not perfectly steady. But the remaining fluctuations in it are minor, certainly far smaller than those that occur in the stock of money itself.

Some idea of the quantitative magnitude of the changes in the United States over long periods of time can be obtained by comparing average values of various items over the most recent complete business cycle—that running from a trough in 1949 to a peak in 1953 to a trough in 1954—with those over the earliest for which we have the relevant data—that running from a trough in 1878 to a peak in 1882 to a trough in 1885. The money stock multiplied 67-fold over these seven decades, and real income ninefold, so the money stock per unit of output rose about 7.5-fold. Prices something less than tripled, so the ratio of the money stock to money income roughly tripled. In the initial cycle, the stock of money averaged about 24 per cent of 1 year's money income—that is, cash balances were equal to the income of about 3 months; in the terminal cycle, the stock of money averaged about 67 per cent of 1 year's income—that is, cash balances were equal to the income of about 8 months. Over the period as a whole, the money stock rose at an average rate of 6 per cent per year, money income at nearly 5 per cent per year, prices at nearly $1\frac{1}{4}$ per cent per year, total output at about 3 per cent per year, and population at about $1\frac{1}{2}$ per cent per year.

Of course, these changes did not occur smoothly. Figure 1 shows the more detailed behavior based on average values for each of the 19 business cycles that

---

10. Evidence for this is presented in Cagan, *op. cit.*, and is available also from work by John Deaver on monetary changes in Chile.

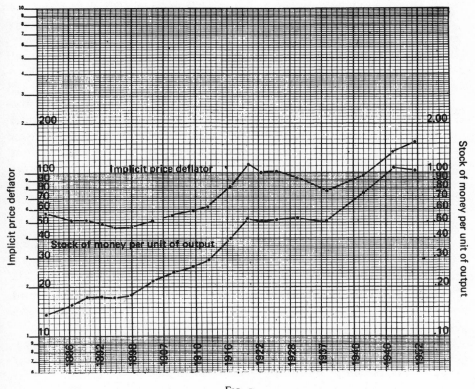

FIG. 1

we have experienced since 1879. It is clear that there is an exceedingly close connection between movements in the stock of money per unit of output and in prices. The only major difference is the more rapid long-term growth in the stock of money which in turn reflects the effect of the long-term growth in per capita real income and the associated rise in the desired ratio of money stock to money income.

II. RELATION OF STOCK OF MONEY TO PRICES OVER SHORTER PERIODS

Over the longer periods considered in the preceding section, changes in the stock of money per unit of output tend to dominate price changes, allowance being made for the effect of the growth of real income per head. This is less so over the shorter periods involved in the fluctuations we term business cycles, though the general and average relationship is very similar. The reason for the looser connection in such periods presumably is that movements in both the stock of money and in prices are smaller. Over longer periods, these movements cumulate and tend to swamp any disturbance in the relation between desired cash balances, real income, and the cost of holding money; in the ordinary business cycle, the disturbances, though perhaps no more important in an absolute sense, are much more important relative to the movements in money and prices.

On the average, prices rise during an expansion phase of a business cycle, and fall during the contraction phase. In the usual fairly mild cycle of peacetime since 1879, wholesale prices have on the average risen about 10 per cent from trough to peak, and have fallen by somewhat less than half that amount from peak to trough. The general pattern has not changed much except for the relation of the rise to the fall. During the period of generally declining prices from the 1880's to the mid-1890's, prices tended to fall more during the contraction than they rose during expansion; during the subsequent period of generally rising prices, the reverse was the case and in some instances prices continued to rise during part of the contraction; in the 1920's, the rise and fall were roughly the same; in the two post-war cycles the rise was decidedly larger than the fall, as in the pre-1914 period.

Taken as a whole, these mild cycles would have imparted a generally upward drift to prices. The failure of such a drift to develop during peacetime was a consequence of the more severe depressions that occurred from time to time. In the five business cycles for which the contractions were most serious and can be designated deep depressions (1891–94, 1904–08, 1919–21, 1927–33, and 1933–38), wholesale prices on the average rose about 10 per cent during expansions, about the same as in the mild cycles, but then fell during the contractions over twice as much, ending up on the average some 12 per cent below their level at the start of the cycle. It was the price declines during these deep depressions that, as a matter of experience, offset the upward tendency during mild cycles—"creeping inflation" in this sense is by no means a unique post-World War II phenomenon.

The stock of money shows the same relation to these cyclical price movements as that depicted in figure 1 for longer periods. During the mild cycles, the stock of money almost invariably rose during both expansion and contraction, but at a faster rate during expansions than during contractions. On the other hand, during the deep depression cycles listed above, the stock of money invariably fell during the course of the contraction, and there is only one other cycle during which there is an appreciable absolute decline during any part of the contraction (1894–97). This resemblance between the cyclical movement in the stock of money and in prices holds not only on the average but also from cycle to cycle, though of course with more variability for the individual cycles.[11]

11. One difference between the comparison made here and in the preceding section is that the money series used is the stock of money, not the stock of money per unit of output. The reason for this is the problem referred to in footnote 9 above. Over the longer periods, the stock of money rises more rapidly than money income; an increase in real income per

There can be little doubt on the basis of this evidence that there is a close link between monetary changes and price changes over the shorter periods within which business cycles run their course as well as over longer periods and during major wartime episodes. But three important considerations must be borne in mind if this fact is not to be a misleading guide to policy.

The first is that the direction of influence between the money stock and income and prices is less clear-cut and more complex for the business cycle than for the longer movements. The character of our monetary and banking system means that an expansion of income contributes to expansion in the money stock, partly through inducing banks to trim more closely their cash reserve position, partly through a tendency for currency in public hands to decline relative to deposits; similarly, a contraction of income contributes to a reduction or a slower rate of rise in the money stock by having the opposite effects on bank reserve ratios and the public's currency ratio. Thus changes in the money stock are a consequence as well as an independent cause of changes in income and prices, though once they occur they will in their turn produce still further effects on income and prices. This consideration blurs the relation between money and prices but does not reverse it. For there is much evidence—one important piece on timing will be presented in the next paragraph—that even during business cycles the money stock plays a largely independent role. This evidence is particularly direct and clear for the deep depression periods. There can be little doubt, for example, that Federal Reserve action in sharply raising discount rates in January 1920 and again in June 1920 (5 months after the onset of the contraction in January 1920) played an important role in the subsequent decline in the money supply and unprecedentedly rapid fall in prices or that Federal Reserve policy in the early 1930's played an important role in producing a decline of a third in the stock of money from 1929 to 1933—by far the largest decline in the whole period covered by our data.[12]

---

capita leads to a more than proportional increase in real money balances—income velocity falls with a rise in real income. Over the cycle, the reverse relation holds, if money income is measured by a figure like the regularly published national income or net national product estimates. Money stock falls relative to measured money income during expansion and rises during contraction—income velocity rises during expansion and falls during contraction. It turns out that this apparent contradiction can be accounted for, both qualitatively and quantitatively, by distinguishing between measured income and a longer term concept that I have called permanent income and also between measured prices and permanent prices. One implication of this interpretation of the behavior of velocity is that division of the money stock by measured national income in constant prices would yield estimates of the stock of money per unit of output that were formally comparable to those plotted in figure 1 but did not have the same significance and meaning; the latter use an average output figure that is closer to permanent output or income than to annual measured income. Unfortunately, full analysis of this issue is impossible within the confines of the present paper. The forthcoming annual report for 1957 of the National Bureau of Economic Research will contain a somewhat fuller summary; and the monograph referred to in footnote 7 above, a full analysis (See Chapter 6 above).

12. The other deep depression episodes are a bit more complex. The decline in the stock

A second, and perhaps more important consideration, has to do with the timing of the changes in the money supply and in income and prices. The generally upward trend in the money supply which accounts for its continuing to rise, though at a slower rate, during most contractions in economic activity as well as during expansions makes it difficult to judge timing relations from ups and downs in the money supply itself. For this and other reasons, we have found it most useful to examine instead the ups and downs in the rate at which the money supply is changing. The rate of change of the money supply shows well-marked cycles that match closely those in economic activity in general and precede the latter by a long interval. On the average, the rate of change of the money supply has reached its peak nearly 16 months before the peak in general business and has reached its trough over 12 months before the trough in general business.[13]

This is strong though not conclusive evidence for the independent influence of monetary change. But it also has a very different significance. It means that it must take a long time for the influence of monetary changes to make themselves felt—apparently what happens now to the rate of change of the money supply may not be reflected in prices or economic activity for 12 to 16 months, on the average. Moreover, the timing varies considerably from cycle to cycle—since 1907, the shortest time span by which the money peak preceded the business cycle peak was 13 months, the longest, 24 months; the corresponding range at troughs is 5 months to 21 months.[14] From the point of view of scientific analysis directed at establishing economic regularities on the basis of the historical record —the purpose for which the measures were computed—this is highly consistent behavior; it justifies considerable confidence in the reliability of the averages cited and means that they cannot easily be attributed simply to the accident of chance variation. But from the point of view of policy directed at controlling a particular movement such as the current recession, the timing differences are disturbingly large—they mean that monetary action taken today may, on the basis of past experience, affect economic activity within 6 months or again perhaps not for over a year and 6 months; and of course past experience is not exhaustive; the particular episode may establish a new limit in either direction.

---

of money from 1893 to 1894 seems connected with the uncertainty about silver; in 1907, quite clearly with the banking panic which was of course in part a consequence of a prior decline in economic activity but not through the particular channels described above and which once begun very likely served as an important factor in making the contraction as deep as it was; in 1937–38, with the doubling of reserve requirements by the Federal Reserve System in two steps in 1936 and in 1937—the first step coincides with a sharp reduction in the rate of growth of the money stock, the second with the beginning of decline.

13. The average at peaks is based on 18 observations, at troughs on 19. Of course, instead of interpreting the cycles in the rate of change as conforming positively with a lead, they could be interpreted as conforming inversely with a lag. A number of pieces of statistical evidence, however, argue strongly for the former interpretation.

14. These are for the period since 1907 because our money data prior to that date are annual or semi-annual. While the annual and semi-annual observations give the same average timing as the monthly, individual observations are not comparable.

The long time lag has another important effect. It leads to misinterpretation and misconception about the effects of monetary policy, as well as to consequent mistakes in monetary policy. Because the effects of monetary change do not occur instantaneously, monetary policy is regarded as ineffective. The most recent example is the tight money policy of 1956 and 1957 which coexisted with rising prices but whose delayed effects are with us in the current recession. A similar and even more dramatic example is the tight money policy from early 1928 on and the associated lack of growth in the money supply which coexisted with economic expansion but contributed to both the occurrence and the severity of the 1929 downturn. The fact that these policies had a delayed effect in turn misled the monetary authorities; on these occasions, and even more clearly in 1920, they were induced to believe that still stronger measures were required and so tended to overdo a repressive policy. On other occasions, notably in 1932 as well as earlier in that major catastrophe, the failure of tentative movements toward easy money to have an immediate effect led them to regard their actions as ineffective and to permit and contribute to the sharp decline in the stock of money which occurred and which played so crucial a role in that episode.

The third consideration is in some ways a different aspect of the one just discussed. The variation in timing means that there is considerable leeway in the precise relation between changes in the stock of money and in prices over short periods of time—there are other factors at work that lead to these variations and mean that even if the stock of money were to change in a highly regular and consistent fashion, economic activity and prices would nonetheless fluctuate. When the money changes are large, they tend to dominate these other factors—or perhaps one might better say, they will force these factors to work in a particular direction. Thus there seems little doubt that a large change in the money supply within a relatively short period will force a change in the same direction in income and prices and, conversely, that a large change in income and prices in short periods—a substantial short-period inflation or deflation—is most unlikely to occur without a large change in money supply. This is certainly the conclusion suggested by the evidence for the deep depression cycles and for sizable inflations. But when the money changes are moderate, the other factors come into their own. If we knew enough about them and about the detailed effects of monetary changes, we might be able to counter these other effects by monetary measures. But this is utopian given our present level of knowledge. There are thus definite limits to the possibility of any fine control of the general level of prices by a fine adjustment of monetary change.

III. CHANGES IN PRICES AND CHANGES IN OUTPUT OVER LONGER PERIODS

Over the cycle, prices and output tend to move together—both tend to rise during expansions and to fall during contractions. Both are part of the cyclical process and anything, including a monetary change, that promotes a vigorous expansion is likely to promote a vigorous rise in both and conversely. The preceding section implicitly assumes this connection.

Over the longer period, the relation between price changes and output changes is much less clear and in the first section we took the behavior of output for granted. Now this seems clearly valid, not only as an expository device but also as a first approximation to reality. What happens to a nation's output over long periods of time depends in the first instance on such basic factors as resources available, the industrial organization of the society, the growth of knowledge and technical skills, the growth of population, the accumulation of capital and so on. This is the stage on which money and price changes play their parts as the supporting cast.

One proposition about the effect of changes in the stock of money and in prices that is widely accepted and hardly controversial is that large and unexpected changes in prices are adverse to the growth of output—whether these changes are up or down. At one extreme, the kind of price rise that occurs during hyperinflation seriously distorts the effective use of resources.[15] At the other extreme, sharp price declines such as occurred from 1920 to 1921 and again from 1929 to 1933 certainly produce a widespread and tragic waste of resources.

So much is agreed. The more controversial issue is the effect of moderate change in prices. One view that is widely held is that slowly rising prices stimulate economic output and produce a more rapid rate of growth than would otherwise occur. A number of reasons have been offered in support of this view. (1) Prices, and particularly wages, are, it is said, sticky. In a market economy, the reallocation of resources necessitated by economic growth and development requires changes in relative prices and relative wages. It is much easier, it is argued, for these to come about without friction and resistance if they can occur through rises in some prices and wages without declines in others. If prices were stable, some changes in relative wages could still come about in this way, since economic growth means that wages tend to rise relative to prices, but changes in relative prices could not, and, of course, there would not be as much scope even for relative wage changes. (2) Costs, and in particular, wages, are, it is argued, stickier than selling prices. Hence generally rising prices will tend to raise profit margins, giving enterprises both a bigger incentive to raise output and to add to capital and the means to finance the capital needed. (3) The most recently popular variant of the preceding point is that costs are not only sticky against declines but in addition have a tendency to be pushed up with little

15. However, even open hyperinflations are less damaging to output than suppressed inflations in which a wide range of prices are held well below the levels that would clear the market. The German hyperinflation after World War I never caused anything like the reduction of production that was produced in Germany from 1945 to the monetary reform of 1948 by the suppression of inflation. And the inflationary pressure suppressed in the second case was a small fraction of that manifested in the first.

reference to the state of demand as a result of strong trade unions. If the money stock is kept from rising, the result, it is claimed, will be unemployment as profit margins are cut, and also a higher level of prices, though not necessarily a rising level of prices. Gently rising prices, it is argued, will tend to offset this upward pressure by permitting money wages to rise without real wages doing so. (4) Interest rates are particularly slow to adapt to price rises. If prices are rising at, say, 3 per cent a year, a 6 per cent interest rate on a money loan is equivalent to a 3 per cent rate when prices are stable. If lenders adjusted fully to the price rise, this would simply mean that interest rates would be 3 percentage points higher in the first case than in the second. But in fact this does not happen, so that productive enterprises find the cost of borrowing to be relatively low, and again have a greater incentive than otherwise to invest, and the associated transfer from creditors to debtors gives them greater means to do so.

In opposition to this view, it has been argued that generally rising prices reduce the pressure on enterprises to be efficient, stimulate speculative relative to industrial activity, reduce the incentives for individuals to save, and make it more difficult to maintain the appropriate structure of relative prices, since individual prices have to change in order to stay the same relative to others. Furthermore, it is argued that once it becomes widely recognized that prices are rising, the advantages cited in the preceding paragraph will disappear: escalator clauses or their economic equivalent will eliminate the stickiness of prices and wages and the greater stickiness of wages than of prices; strong unions will increase still further their wage demands to allow for price increases; and interest rates will rise to allow for the price rise. If the advantages are to be obtained, the rate of price rise will have to be accelerated and there is no stopping place short of runaway inflation. From this point of view, there may clearly be a major difference between the effects of a superficially similar price rise, according as it is an undesigned and largely unforeseen effect of such impersonal events as the discovery of gold, or a designed result of deliberative policy action by a public body.

Some who believe that slowly rising prices are adverse to economic growth regard stable product prices with slowly rising wage rates as most favorable, combining the advantages of stable price expectations with some easing of frictions involved in relative wage adjustments. Others view gently falling prices and stable wages as most favorable, arguing that additional problems in wage adjustments would be balanced by the stimulus to thrift and accumulation.

Historical evidence on the relation between price changes and output changes is mixed and gives no clear support to any one of these positions. (1) In the United States, the period from 1865 to 1879 was a period of exceedingly rapid progress; and during the same period, prices were cut in half. True, neither price changes nor output changes proceeded regularly within the period. Output apparently grew most rapidly during the cyclical expansions in the period when prices rose mildly or were roughly stable; most of the price declines occurred during cyclical contractions. Yet the problem at issue is less the cyclical relation than the longer period relation and there can be no doubt that during the period as a whole prices fell sharply and output rose sharply. (2) The period from 1880 to 1897 was a period of generally declining prices, from 1897 to 1913, of generally rising prices; taken as a whole, the second period has generally been regarded as displaying more rapid growth than the first. But it is not clear that this is a satisfactory interpretation. The period of great monetary uncertainty in the early 1890's was associated with generally depressed conditions and was followed by a rapid rebound. If both are excluded, the remaining periods show about the same rates of growth in real output per head, although prices were generally falling during the 1880's and rising after the turn of the century. Moreover, the period from 1908–14 is one of relatively slow growth despite rising prices. (3) The decade of the 1920's, after the recovery from the deep depression of 1920–21, was a decade of rapid growth and prices were relatively stable. (4) In Great Britain, output per head apparently grew at a definitely higher rate during the period of generally falling prices before the mid-1890's than during the subsequent period of rising prices up to World War I.[16] (5) On the other hand, the attempt to achieve mildly falling prices in Britain in the 1920's was associated with considerable economic difficulties and something close to stagnation.

All in all, perhaps the only conclusion that is justified is that either rising prices or falling prices are consistent with rapid economic growth, provided that the price changes are fairly steady, moderate in size, and reasonably predictable. The mainsprings of growth are presumably to be sought elsewhere. But unpredictable and erratic changes of direction in prices are apparently as disturbing to economic growth as to economic stability.

IV. POLICY IMPLICATIONS

The preceding account of the relation of money to prices over long and short periods and of price changes to output changes has some fairly direct and immediate implications for public policy with respect both to growth and stability.

(1) In order for the price level to be reasonably stable over the decades ahead, the total stock of money will have to grow to accommodate itself to the growth in output and in population. In addition, if past patterns continue, it will have to grow to satisfy the desire of the public to increase the ratio of cash balances to income as their real income rises. Past experience suggests that something like a 3 to 5 per cent per year increase in the stock of money is required for long-term price stability.[17]

16. See James B. Jefferys and Dorothy Walters, "National Income and Expenditure of the United Kingdom, 1870–1952," *Income and Wealth*, Series V, table III.

17. This range is for the stock of money as defined in footnote 2, namely, currency outside banks plus adjusted deposits, demand and time, of commercial banks. For a narrower definition, currency outside banks plus adjusted demand deposits, the required rate of growth is less; for a broader definition, the preceding plus all time deposits, in mutual savings

(2) An essential requirement for the avoidance of either substantial inflation or substantial deflation over the coming decades is the avoidance of a substantially more rapid or a substantially less rapid increase in the stock of money than the 3 to 5 per cent per year required for price stability. A substantially more rapid rate of growth in the money supply will inevitably mean inflation; conversely, continued inflation of substantial magnitude cannot occur without such a large rate of growth in the money supply. A substantially slower rate of growth in the money supply, let alone an absolute decline, will inevitably mean deflation; conversely, continued deflation of substantial magnitude cannot occur without such a small or negative rate of growth in the money supply.

(3) A highly fluctuating price level is as disturbing to economic growth as to economic stability. Given that this is avoided, it is not clear what pattern of long-term price behavior is optimum for economic stability—whether a roughly stable price level, a gently rising price level, or a gently falling price level. It does seem clear that any of these is consistent with rapid economic growth. If it is necessary to state objectives in terms of a price level goal, then a stable price level has the very great advantages of (a) ease of public understanding, (b) definiteness rendering successive alterations in the precise goal less likely, and (c) probably the closest approach to equitable treatment of the various members of the community. However, the difficulty of assuring the close attainment of any price level goal suggests that it might be better to express the immediate policy goal in terms of some variable other than the price level, for example the attainment of a steady 4 per cent per year rise in the stock of money, and then to let the price level be whatever would be consistent with this money goal. The resulting price level behavior could hardly depart much from relative stability and would certainly not be violently unstable.

(4) For cyclical movements, a major problem is to prevent monetary changes from being a source of disturbance. If the stock of money can be kept growing at a relatively steady rate, without erratic fluctuations in short periods, it is highly unlikely if not impossible that we would experience either a sharp price rise—like that during World Wars I and II and after World War I—or a substantial price or output decline—like those experienced from 1920–21, 1929–33, 1937–38.

(5) A steady rate of growth in the money supply will not mean perfect stability even though it would prevent the kind of wide fluctuations that we have experienced from time to time in the past. It is tempting to try to go farther and to use monetary changes to offset other factors making for expansion and contraction. Though the available evidence demonstrates a close connection between monetary change and price and income change in the course of business cycles as over larger periods, it also casts grave doubts on the possibility of

---

banks and the postal savings system as well as commercial banks, the required rate of growth is greater. The reason is that time deposits have been growing relative to demand deposits and currency, and, until 1957, mutual savings deposits relative to other time deposits.

producing any fine adjustments in economic activity by fine adjustments in monetary policy—at least in the present state of knowledge. The evidence suggests that monetary changes take a fairly long time to exert their influence and that the time taken varies considerably. In terms of past experience, for example, action taken now to offset the current recession may affect economic activity in 6 months or not for over a year and 6 months. The tight-money policy of late 1956 and most of 1957, which was taken to offset the then existing inflationary pressure, almost surely had little effect on that situation and is only now exerting its influence and contributing to the current recessionary tendencies; the inflationary pressures in 1956 may well themselves have been in part a delayed consequence of the expansionary monetary policy taken to offset the 1953–54 recession. There are thus serious limitations to the possibility of a discretionary monetary policy and much danger that such a policy may make matters worse rather than better. Federal Reserve policy since 1951 has been distinctly superior to that followed during any earlier period since the establishment of the System, mainly because it has avoided wide fluctuations in the rate or growth of the money supply. At the same time, I am myself inclined to believe that in our present state of knowledge and with our present institutions, even this policy has been decidedly inferior to the much simpler policy of keeping the money supply growing at a predesignated rate month in and month out with allowance only for seasonal influences and with no attempt to adjust the rate of growth to monetary conditions.[18]

(6) To avoid misunderstanding, it should be emphasized that the problems just discussed are in no way peculiar to monetary policy. Fiscal action also involves lags. Indeed the lag between the recognition of need for action and the taking of action is undoubtedly longer for discretionary fiscal than for discretionary monetary action: the monetary authorities can act promptly, fiscal action inevitably involves serious delays for congressional consideration. It has been argued that this defect of fiscal action is counterbalanced by a shorter lag between the action and its effects. This may well be, though there is little concrete empirical evidence that I know of; the belief is based on general considera-

---

18. This is not intended to be a full statement of the optimum monetary structure. I would prefer automatic arrangements that would reduce the area of discretion. One particular set of such arrangements is suggested in my "A Monetary and Fiscal Framework for Economic Stability," reprinted in my *Essays in Positive Economics*, Chicago: University of Chicago Press (1953), pp. 133–56.

The extensive empirical work that I have done since that article was written has given me no reason to doubt that the arrangements there suggested would produce a high degree of stability; it has, however, led me to believe that much simpler arrangements would do so also; that something like the simple policy suggested above would produce a very tolerable amount of stability. This evidence has persuaded me that the major problem is to prevent monetary changes from themselves contributing to instability rather than to use monetary changes to offset other forces.

On the issues in question, see also my "The Effects of a Full Employment Policy on Economic Stability: A Formal Analysis," reprinted in the same book, pp. 117–32.

tions of plausibility, which can be a misleading guide. And there are certainly no reasons for believing and no empirical evidence to show that the lag, whatever its average length, is any less variable for fiscal than for monetary action. Hence the basic difficulties and limitations of monetary policy apply with equal force to fiscal policy.

(7) Political pressures to "do something" in the face of either relatively mild price rises or relatively mild price and employment declines are clearly very strong indeed in the existing state of public attitudes. The main moral to be drawn from the two preceding points is that yielding to these pressures may frequently do more harm than good. There is a saying that the best is often the enemy of the good, which seems highly relevant. The goal of an extremely high degree of economic stability is certainly a splendid one; our ability to attain it, however, is limited; we can surely avoid extreme fluctuations; we do not know enough to avoid minor fluctuations; the attempt to do more than we can will itself be a disturbance that may increase rather than reduce instability. But like all such injunctions, this one too must be taken in moderation. It is a plea for a sense of perspective and balance, not for irresponsibility in the face of major problems or for failure to correct past mistakes.

Chapter 10

Money and Business Cycles

THE SUBJECT ASSIGNED for this session covers too broad an area to be given even a fairly cursory treatment in a single paper. Accordingly, we have chosen to concentrate on the part of it that relates to monetary factors in economic fluctuations. We shall still further narrow the scope of the paper by interpreting "monetary factors" to mean the role of the stock of money and of changes in that stock—thereby casting the "credit" market as one of the supporting players rather than a star performer—and by interpreting "economic fluctuations" to mean business cycles, or even more exactly, the reference cycles studied and chronicled by the National Bureau.

The topic so interpreted has been rather out of fashion for the past few decades. Before the Great Depression, it was widely accepted that the business cycle was a monetary phenomenon, "a dance of the dollar," as Irving Fisher graphically described it in the title of a famous article.[1] Different versions of monetary theories of the business cycle abounded, though some of these were really "credit" theories misnamed, since they gave little role to changes in the money stock except as an incident in the alteration of credit conditions; and there was

Written jointly with Anna J. Schwartz. Reprinted from *Review of Economics and Statistics*, vol. 45, no. 1, part 2: supplement (February, 1963).

1. "The Business Cycle Largely a 'Dance of the Dollar,' " *Journal of the American Statistical Association*, December 1923, pp. 1024–28.

nothing like agreement on the details of any one theory. Yet it is probably true that most economists gave the money stock and changes in it an important, if not a central, role in whatever particular theory of the cycle they were inclined to accept. That emphasis was greatly strengthened by the course of economic events in the twenties. The high degree of economic stability then achieved was widely regarded as a consequence of the effectiveness of the monetary policies followed by the only recently created Federal Reserve System and hence as evidence that monetary factors were indeed a central factor in the cycle.

The Great Depression radically changed economic attitudes. The failure of the Federal Reserve System to stem the depression was widely interpreted—wrongly as we have elsewhere argued[2] and elaborate below—to mean that monetary factors were not critical, that "real" factors were the key to economic fluctuations. Investment—which had always had a prominent place in business cycle theories—received new emphasis as a result of the Keynesian revolution, so much so that Paul Samuelson, in the best selling textbook in the country, could assert confidently, "All modern economists are agreed that the important factor in causing income and employment to fluctuate is investment."[3] Investment was the motive force, its effects spread through time and amplified by the "multiplier," and itself partly or largely a result of the "accelerator." Money, if it entered at all, played a purely passive role.

Recently, a revival of interest in money has been sparked less by concern with business cycles than with concern about inflation. Easy money policies were accompanied by inflation; and inflation was nowhere stemmed without a more or less deliberate limitation of growth of the money stock. But once interest was aroused, it naturally extended to the cycle as well as to inflation. In the United States, indeed, there has been something of a repetition of the 1920's. A high degree of economic stability has been accompanied by a large measure of talk about an active monetary policy, and the monetary authorities have often been given credit for playing an important role in promoting stability. As the experience of the twenties suggests, this fair-weather source of support for the importance of money is a weak reed.

Examining the present state of our understanding about the role of money in the business cycle, we shall first present some facts that seem reasonably well established about the cyclical behavior of money and related magnitudes and then speculate about some plausible interpretations of these facts. The facts we present are drawn largely from our own unpublished work done under the auspices of the National Bureau of Economic Research and associated unpublished work by Phillip Cagan.

---

2. See Milton Friedman and Anna J. Schwartz, *A Monetary History of the United States*, Princeton, N.J.: Princeton University Press for the National Bureau of Economic Research (1963), Chapter 7.

3. *Economics*, 3rd ed., New York: McGraw-Hill (1955), p. 224.

I. SOME FACTS ABOUT THE CYCLICAL BEHAVIOR OF MONEY

A. Cyclical Pattern of the Money Stock

The outstanding cyclical fact about the stock of money is that it has tended to rise during both cyclical expansions and cyclical contractions. This is clear from Chart 1, which plots (1) the stock of money from 1867 to 1960, with money

CHART 1. MONEY STOCK, INCLUDING COMMERCIAL BANK TIME DEPOSITS, 1867–1960, AND CURRENCY PLUS DEMAND DEPOSITS ADJUSTED, 1914–1960

———— Currency held by the public, plus demand deposits adjusted, plus commercial bank time deposits

— — — Currency held by the public, plus demand deposits adjusted

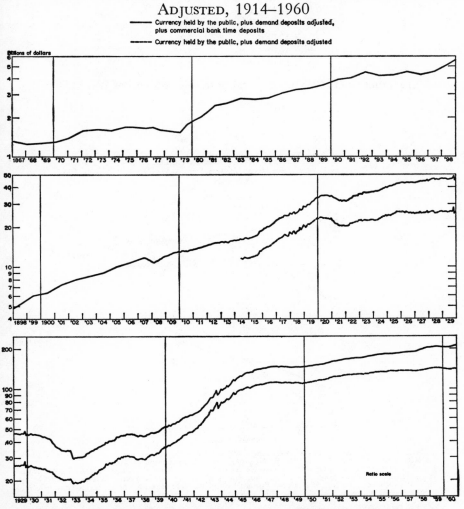

SOURCE: Friedman and Schwartz, *A Monetary History of the United States*, 1867–1960, Table A-1, cols. 7 and 8. These are seasonally adjusted figures, dated as of end of month, 1867–1946; for 1947–60, currency plus demand deposits adjusted is an average of daily figures, and commercial bank time deposits, a 2-month moving average of last-Wednesday-of-month figures, for a month centered at midmonth.

defined as including currency plus adjusted deposits in commercial banks (both demand and time) held by the nonbanking public (i.e., excluding both balances of the federal government and of banks); and (2) from 1914 on, a narrower total which excludes time deposits. From 1867 to 1907, our data are at annual or semi-annual dates; from 1907 on, monthly. The only major exceptions since 1867 to the tendency of the money stock to rise during both cyclical expansions and cyclical contractions occurred in the years listed in the following tabulation, which gives also the percentage decline during each exception.

Years of Exception	Percentage Decline
1873–79	4.9
1892–94	5.8
1907–08	3.7
1920–21	5.1
1929–33	35.2
1937–38	2.4

In addition, there were two minor exceptions since the end of World War II,

1948–49	1.4
1959–60	1.1

CHART 2.   MONEY STOCK: AVERAGE REFERENCE-CY-
CLE PATTERNS FOR MILD AND DEEP DEPRESSION CYCLES,
1867–1961

———— 1867–1908
— — — 1908–1961

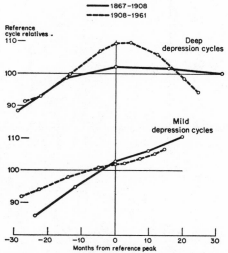

NOTE: War cycles, not shown, are 1914–19 and 1938–45. Deep depression cycles are 1870–79, 1891–94, 1904–08, 1919–21, 1927–33 and 1933–38. All others are mild depression cycles.
SOURCE: For method of deriving reference cycles relatives for the 9-point pattern, see A. F. Burns and W. C. Mitchell, *Measuring Business Cycles*, National Bureau of Economic Research (1946), pp. 160–170; we used a variant of National Bureau's standard technique for annual series (pp. 197–202) for the 5-point pattern.

Paul P. Tung
P. O. Box 839
Vacaville, Calif.   95688

ALDINE Publishing Company 529 South Wabash Avenue Chicago 60605

Dear Customer:

We are very sorry, but the book you requested, INFLATION AND THE THEORY OF MONEY, is going permanently out of print.

We are sorry for any inconvenience we have caused you.

Cordially,

Ellen M. Moore-College Dept.

Area Code: 312 Telephone: 939-5190 Cable: ALDINE

The major exceptions clearly did not fall in a random subset of years. Each corresponds to an economic contraction that was major as judged by other indicators; in the period covered, there was no other economic contraction more severe than any in the list; and there appears to be a considerable gap between the severity of those contractions and of the remainder, with the possible exception of the contraction of 1882–85, which might be regarded as a somewhat borderline case.

For mild depression cycles, therefore, the cycle does not show up as a rise and a fall. Chart 2 gives the average reference-cycle patterns for mild and deep depression cycles since 1867, excluding only war cycles. (Patterns are given separately for the period before and after 1907, because the availability of monthly data after 1907 permits the construction of a more detailed pattern—a nine-point instead of a five-point pattern.) The patterns for mild depression cycles rise almost in a straight line, though there is some indication of a slower rate of growth from mid-expansion to mid-contraction than during the rest of the cycle (especially in the nine-point pattern for monthly data). In its cyclical behavior, the money stock is like other series with a sharp upward trend—such as population, the total stock of houses, the number of miles of railroad track in operation in the pre-1914 period, the amount of electrical energy produced. In all of these, the cycle shows up not in an absolute rise and fall but in different rates of rise.

For deep depression cycles, the cyclical pattern is nearer the stereotype of a rise during expansion and a fall during contraction. From these patterns, it would be easy to conclude that the two groups of cycles distinguished are members of different species with respect to the behavior of the stock of money.

B. Cyclical Pattern of the Rate of Change in the Money Stock

Because the strong upward trend of the stock of money tends to dominate its cyclical behavior, it is desirable to eliminate the effect of the trend in order to reveal the cyclical behavior more clearly. There are various ways of doing this.[4] The method we have used is to take logarithmic first differences of the money stock, which is equivalent to using the percentage rate of change from one time unit to the next. Chart 3 plots the resulting series. It is clear that this device effectively eliminates trend. It is clear also that, as first differencing usually does, it produces a highly jagged series with a sawtooth appearance. The reason is that independent errors of measurement in the original stock series introduce negative serial correlation into first differences. But despite these short-term irregularities, the series shows clearly marked cyclical fluctuations corresponding to reference cycles.

4. See the discussion of this problem in "The Lag in Effect of Monetary Policy," Chapter 11 below.

CHART 3.   MONTH-TO-MONTH RATE OF CHANGE IN U.S. MONEY STOCK, 1867–1960

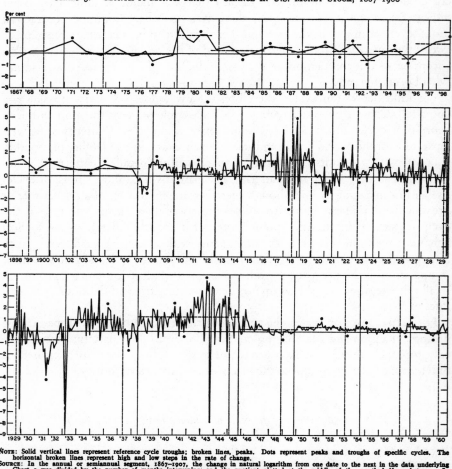

NOTE: Solid vertical lines represent reference cycle troughs; broken lines, peaks. Dots represent peaks and troughs of specific cycles. The horizontal broken lines represent high and low steps in the rate of change.
SOURCE: In the annual or semiannual segment, 1867–1907, the change in natural logarithm from one date to the next in the data underlying Chart 1 was divided by the number of months intervening, and the quotient plotted at the middle of the month halfway between. In the monthly segment, 1907–60, the month-to-month change in natural logarithm was plotted in the middle of the second month. Reference dates are from the National Bureau (see Table 1).

Chart 4 gives the reference cycle patterns for this series. They show a clear cyclical pattern with the mild and deep depression cycles distinguished, this time, primarily by their amplitude, so that they now look more like different members of the same species. The peak rate of change occurs early in expansion and the trough early in recession. Indeed these occur so early as to suggest the possibility of interpreting the rate of change series as inverted, i.e., as generally declining during reference expansion and rising during reference contraction. We have examined this possibility elsewhere.[5] A full presentation of our tests is

5. See "Monetary Studies of the National Bureau of Economic Research," Chapter 12 below. The patterns in Chart 4 differ in construction from the reference patterns for the stock of

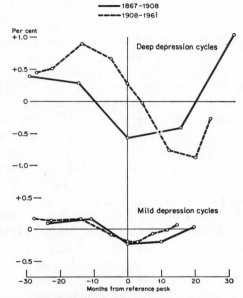

CHART 4.   RATE OF CHANGE IN MONEY STOCK: AVER-
AGE REFERENCE-CYCLE PATTERNS FOR MILD AND DEEP
DEPRESSION CYCLES, 1867–1961

——— 1867–1908
– – – 1908–1961

NOTE: War cycles, not shown, are 1914–19 and 1938–45. Deep depression cycles are 1870–79, 1891–94, 1904–08, 1919–21, 1927–33,
and 1933–38. All others are mild depression cycles.
SOURCE: See footnote 5.

not feasible in this paper; it will suffice to note that they rather decisively support treating the rate of change series as conforming to the reference cycle
positively with a long lead, rather than inversely with a somewhat shorter lag.
Though we have not analyzed in as much detail the narrower total of currency

money in Chart 2. The rate of change series, being the percentage change from month to
month, is already in a form that is independent of units of measure. In addition, the rate of
change in the money stock can be zero or negative as well as positive, and hence its average
value for a given cycle can hardly serve as a base for computing reference cycle relatives. For
these reasons, the basic data, instead of being expressed as relatives to the average for a cycle,
are expressed as deviations from the average for a cycle (as in A. F. Burns and W. C. Mitchell,
Measuring Business Cycles, New York: NBER (1946), pp. 137–38). This is why the base lines
in Chart 4 are labeled 0 instead of 100 as in Chart 2, and the scale is in terms of deviations
rather than of relatives.

Because of a discontinuity in the underlying money figures in early 1933, we have
estimated stage IX for the 1927–33 cycle and stage I for the 1933–38 cycle from the average
value for January, April, and May, 1933, instead of for February, March, and April. Restricted deposits before the banking holiday are counted in full in the recorded money stock.
However, after the holiday both restricted and unrestricted deposits in unlicensed banks are
excluded completely from the recorded money stock. That shift in treatment is the major
factor behind the sharp decline in the recorded figures in March 1933 (see our *A Monetary
History of the United States, 1867–1960*, Chapter 8, section 1).

plus adjusted demand deposits, its cyclical pattern since 1914 is very similar in general form to the pattern of the broader total.

C. Cyclical Timing of the Rate of Change in the Money Stock

Evidence on cyclical timing derived from a comparison of turning points is clearly not available from the stock of money series, because it has so few turning points. For the rate-of-change series, we have dated turning points in two ways: (1) We have sought to approximate the series by a step function, with successively high and low steps, because at times the series gives the impression of dropping suddenly from one level to a decidedly lower level, or of rising from one level to a decidedly higher level. The horizontal broken lines in Chart 3 indicate the steps we have used. We call the date at which a high step ends, the date of a step peak, the date at which a low step ends, the date of a step trough. (2) We have applied the usual National Bureau specific cycle dating procedure to the rate-of-change series, and have designated specific cycle peaks and troughs. They are marked by black dots in Chart 3.

Table 1 gives the step and specific cycle peaks and troughs we have selected, the dates of the reference cycle turns with which we have matched them, and the indicated lead (−) or lag (+) at the corresponding turn.[6] Clearly, leads predominate, and clearly also, there is much variability.

Table 2 gives the average lead and the standard deviations of the leads for mild depression cycles, deep depression cycles, all nonwar cycles and all cycles, for both step dates and specific cycle dates. For step dates, the average lead for all cycles is 7 months at the peak and 4 months at the trough; for specific cycle dates, the average lead is 18 months at the peak and 12 months at the trough; for step dates, the standard deviation of the lead is 6 months at troughs and 8 months at peaks; for specific cycle dates, the standard deviation of the lead is 6 months at troughs and 7 months at peaks.

Estimation of timing relations by a comparison of turning points seems inefficient, because it uses so little of the information contained in the series. Therefore, we have experimented extensively with other devices, in particular, cross-correlograms and cross-spectral analysis. While these devices, particularly

6. Though our money series starts in 1867, the first reference turn with which we have matched a specific cycle turn is the peak in October 1873. Hence we do not match the reference trough of December 1867, peak of June 1869, and trough of December 1870. The absence of a specific cycle turn to match with the December 1867 trough may simply result from the fact that our series does not go far enough back in time—a possibility suggested by the long average lead at troughs. For the other two reference turns, we conjecture that the annual data for successive Januarys—all we have for that period—may conceal by their crudeness turns that monthly data would reveal. This conjecture seems especially plausible because of the unusual brevity of the expansion phase, only 18 months, followed by a contraction of equal length.

Table 1. Timing of Specific Cycles and of Step Troughs and Peaks in the Rate of Change in the Money Stock Compared with Timing of Business Cycles

TROUGHS			LEAD(−) OR LAG(+) IN MONTHS AT REFERENCE TROUGH OF:		PEAKS			LEAD(−) OR LAG(+) IN MONTHS AT REFERENCE PEAK OF:	
DATE OF:					DATE OF:				
Step Trough	Specific Cycle Trough	Matched Reference Trough	Step Trough	Specific Cycle Trough	Step Peak	Specific Cycle Peak	Matched Reference Peak	Step Peak	Specific Cycle Peak
SEMI-ANNUAL AND ANNUAL DATA									
					2/72	7/71	10/73	−20	−27
2/79	5/77	3/79	−1	−22	8/81	5/81	3/82	−7	−10
6/85	12/83	5/85	+1	−17	6/87	12/85	3/87	+3	−15
6/88	12/87	4/88	+2	−4	6/90	12/89	7/90	−1	−7
6/91	12/90	5/91	+1	−5	6/92	12/91	1/93	−7	−13
6/93	12/92	6/94	−12	−18	6/95	12/94	12/95	−6	−12
6/96	12/95	6/97	−12	−18	6/99	12/98	6/99	0	−6
6/00	12/99	12/00	−6	−12	6/01	12/00	9/02	−15	−21
6/04	12/03	8/04	−2	−8	6/07	12/04	5/07	+1	−29
MONTHLY DATA									
2/08	1/08	6/08	−4	−5	6/09	10/08	1/10	−7	−15
8/10	4/10	1/12	−17	−21	6/12	10/11	1/13	−7	−15
7/13					5/14				
12/14	6/13	12/14	0	−18	7/17	12/16	8/18	−13	−20
5/18	5/18	3/19	−10	−10	3/20	12/18	1/20	+2	−13
7/21	1/21	7/21	0	−6	5/23	4/22	5/23	0	−13
3/24	6/23	7/24	−4	−13	9/25	7/24	10/26	−13	−27
12/26	12/26	11/27	−11	−11	4/28	11/27	8/29	−16	−21
4/33	10/31	3/33	+1	−17	7/36	4/36	5/37	−10	−13
5/38	10/37	6/38	−1	−8		2/41			
	10/41				10/45	6/43	2/45	+8	−20
		10/45				11/48			
1/50	1/49	10/49	+3	−9	12/52	11/51	7/53	−7	−20
4/54	9/53	8/54	−4	−11	9/55	2/55	7/57	−22	−29
1/58	12/57	4/58	−3	−4	5/59	6/58	5/60	−12	−23
6/60	12/59	2/61	−8	−14					

SOURCE: Chart 3. Step peaks and step troughs are last months of alternate steps shown there.

Reference dates through April 1958 are shown in *Business Cycle Indicators*, Geoffrey H. Moore (Ed.), Princeton, N.J.: Princeton University Press for NBER (1961), vol. 1, p. 670; subsequent dates are from an unpublished National Bureau table. For timing comparisons, both the rate of change series and the steps made from it are treated as well conforming, because of the nearly 1-to-1 correspondence between their turning points and reference cycle turning points, and because the money stock series from which both were derived has moderately high conformity indexes (100 for expansions, −43 for contractions, +71 for trough-to-trough full cycles, +50 for peak-to-peak full cycles, +61 for full cycles both ways). Matching of step and specific cycle turns with reference turns follows Burns and Mitchell, *Measuring Business Cycles*, pp. 115–28 Earlier versions of this table were based on data now superseded.

cross-spectral analysis, offer great promise for the future, as yet we have no substantive results worth reporting.

We have tested to determine whether there is any secular trend in the leads or lags; whether the pre-1914 timing, before the establishment of the Federal Reserve System, differs from the post-1914 timing; whether timing during mild depression cycles differs from timing during deep depression cycles; and whether there is any relation between the length of the lead and the amplitude of the subsequent or prior cyclical phase. Our results so far are negative: none of these criteria appears to be associated with a statistically significant difference in timing.

D. *Amplitude of Movements in the Rate of Change in the Money Stock*

1. The subdivision between mild and severe depression cycles in Chart 4 corresponds to a sharp difference in the amplitude of reference cycles in the rate of change. This result suggests that the amplitude of the change in the rate of change in the money stock is related to the severity of the cyclical movement in general business, even though the timing of the change in the rate of change in the money stock is not.

2. One way in which we have investigated this relation further is to correlate the ranking of the amplitudes of cyclical movements in the rate of change with the ranking of the amplitudes of the corresponding cyclical movements in general business, as measured by two different indicators: one, bank clearings to 1919 and bank debits thereafter; the other, an index computed by Geoffrey H. Moore. The correlations, summarized in Table 3, are throughout positive—for expansion alone, for contractions alone, and for full cycles, for the period before 1908 and for the period since, as well as for the whole period.

The correlations between the rate of change measure and the Moore index are sufficiently high so that, even with the small number of observations on which they are based, they could hardly have arisen from chance. There is a less close connection between the clearings-debits figures and the rate of change, especially in expansions. The Moore index is adjusted for trend and reflects primarily changes in physical units. Likewise, the shift from the total stock of money to the rate of change is, as noted earlier, equivalent to adjusting for trend; in addition, it involves a change from a measure expressed in nominal units—dollars—to a measure expressed in relative units—per cent—and as a flow—per month. The amplitude of clearings-debits, however, is not adjusted for intracycle trend, and clearings-debits are, in their original form, in dollars. It would be interesting to know whether the adjustment for trend, or the different weight given to financial and physical transactions, is primarily responsible for the closer connection of the Moore index than of clearings-debits to the rate of change.

The table as a whole leaves little doubt that there is a fairly close connection between the magnitude of monetary changes during the course of cycles, and

Table 2. *Average Timing of Specific Cycles and of Step Peaks and Troughs in the Rate of Change in the Money Stock and Standard Deviation of Lead or Lag, by Period and Type of Cycle*

| | NUMBER OF OBSERVATIONS | | | | MEAN LEAD (−) OR LAG (+) IN MONTHS | | | | STANDARD DEVIATION OF LEAD OR LAG IN MONTHS | | | |
| | STEP ANALYSIS | | SPECIFIC CYCLE ANALYSIS | | STEP ANALYSIS | | SPECIFIC CYCLE ANALYSIS | | STEP ANALYSIS | | SPECIFIC CYCLE ANALYSIS | |
Period	Trough	Peak	Trough	Peak	Trough	Peak	Trough	Peak	Trough	Peak	Trough	Peak
					ALL CYCLES							
1870–1908	8	9	8	9	− 3.6	− 5.8	− 13.0	− 15.6	5.7	7.7	6.7	8.3
1908–1960	13	12	13	12	− 4.5	− 8.1	− 11.3	− 19.1	5.7	8.3	5.2	5.5
1870–1960	21	21	21	21	− 4.1	− 7.1	− 12.0	− 17.6	5.6	7.9	5.7	6.9
					WAR CYCLES							
1908–1960	1	2	1	2	− 10.0	− 2.5	− 10.0	− 20.0	—	14.8	—	0
					DEEP DEPRESSION CYCLES							
1870–1908	2	3	2	3	− 6.5	− 8.7	− 20.0	− 23.0	7.8	10.6	2.8	8.7
1908–1960	4	3	4	3	− 1.0	− 8.0	− 9.0	− 15.7	2.2	9.2	5.5	4.6
1870–1960	6	6	6	6	− 2.8	− 8.3	− 12.7	− 19.3	4.8	8.9	7.2	7.4
					MILD DEPRESSION CYCLES							
1870–1908	6	6	6	6	− 2.7	− 4.3	− 10.7	− 11.8	5.4	6.4	6.0	5.6
1908–1960	8	7	8	7	− 5.5	− 9.7	− 12.6	− 20.3	6.3	6.9	5.3	6.3
1870–1960	14	13	14	13	− 4.3	− 7.2	− 11.8	− 16.4	5.9	7.0	5.5	7.2

SOURCE: Table 1. To avoid duplication, each cycle is represented only by its peak and terminal trough. War, deep depression, and mild depression cycles are grouped as in Chart 2.

the magnitude of the associated cyclical movement in business. The relation is by no means perfect for the measures we use. But we have no way of knowing from this evidence alone to what extent the discrepancies reflect the inadequacies of our indexes of economic change, the statistical errors in our money series, or a basic lack of connection between monetary and economic changes.

3. To get further evidence, we have investigated this relation in a different way using annual data. For the period from 1869 to 1960, we have annual estimates of net national product, and also, of course, annual estimates of the stock of money. For this period, we have computed logarithmic first differences (i.e., year-to-year percentage changes) of both series. We have then computed moving standard deviations (comparable to moving averages) from these rates

Table 3. Rank Difference Correlation Between Change in Rate of Change in Money Stock and Change in Two Indicators of General Business, 1879–1961, Excluding War Cycles and 1945–49

	RANK DIFFERENCE CORRELATION OF AMPLITUDES			
	NBER REFERENCE		NBER REFERENCE FULL CYCLE	
Specific Cycles in Rate of Change in Money Stock Correlated with:	*Expansion*	*Contraction*	*Trough-to-Trough*	*Peak-to-Peak*
Annual and semi-annual data, 1879–1907				
Number of pairs	8	8	8	7
Reference cycles in clearings–debits	.36	.64	.43	.68
Specific cycles in Moore index	.76	.85	.76	.79
Monthly data, 1907–1961				
Number of pairs	10	10	10	10
Reference cycles in clearings–debits	.30	.54	.37	.57
Specific cycles in Moore index	.82	.58	.75	.81
Whole-period data, 1879–1961				
Number of pairs	18	18	18	17
Reference cycles in clearings–debits	.27	.64	.41	.62
Specific cycles in Moore index	.77	.70	.78	.77

NOTE: In our full study we have used three measures of the amplitude of the change in money, each both in total and as a rate per month, measuring the change in cycle relatives between reference dates, between step dates, and between specific cycle peaks and troughs in the rate of change. To simplify our presentation here, we restrict the comparison to the total change in amplitude between peaks and troughs in the rate of change.

War cycles 1914–19 and 1938–45 are omitted because of their special characteristics. The 1945–49 cycle is omitted because the expansion is skipped by the rate of change series (see Table 1). No tied ranks correction is used in getting correlation coefficients. "Amplitude" of rate of change in money stock is expressed in units of the data as plotted in Chart 3, above. For expansions, it is the change in stages I–V of the specific cycle; for contractions, the change in stages V–IX of the specific cycle. For clearings–debits the reference cycle amplitude (stages I–V–IX), expressed in reference-cycle relatives, was used. For the Moore index, specific cycle amplitudes only are available, but they have a one-to-one correspondence with reference cycles. For full cycles, trough-to-trough, the change from V to IX was subtracted from the change from I to V to obtain the total rise and fall used in the correlations; for full cycles, peak-to-peak, the change from I to V was subtracted from the change from V to IX.

SOURCE: Rate of change in money stock: Figures underlying Chart 3 were analyzed for specific cycles, as in Burns and Mitchell, *Measuring Business Cycles*, pp. 115–41; matching of peaks and troughs with reference turns follows Table 1.

Clearings–debits: Bank clearings outside New York City, monthly, 1879–1919; bank debits outside New York City, monthly, 1919–61. 1879–1942: Seasonally adjusted from *Historical Statistics of the United States, 1789–1945*, Bureau of the Census, 1949, pp. 324–25, 337–88. 1943–61: Board of Governors of the Federal Reserve System, Division of Bank Operations, mimeographed table, "Bank Debits and Rates of Turnover" (C. 5, Revised Series, 1943–52), December 23, 1953; thereafter *Federal Reserve Bulletin*, adjusted for seasonal variation by NBER. Reference cycle analysis follows Burns and Mitchell, *op. cit.*, pp. 160–70.

Moore index: Unpublished memorandum by Geoffrey H. Moore, extending table in *ibid.*, p. 403, and revising and updating table in *Business Cycle Indicators*, G. H. Moore (Ed.), vol. I, p. 104. An average of three trend adjusted indexes of business activity—A. T. & T., Persons-Barrons, and Ayres—each of which was analyzed for specific cycles, suppressing specific cycle turns not corresponding to reference cycle turns.

of change involving 3, 4, 5, and 6 terms. To illustrate: for the 3-term moving standard deviation, we took the initial three rates of change (1869–70, 1870–71, 1871–72), computed their standard deviation by the usual statistical formula,[7] and dated the result as of 1870–71; then dropped the initial year and added a year, computed the standard deviation for the resulting triplet of rates of change (1870–71, 1871–72, 1872–73), and dated the results as of 1871–72; and so on.

These moving standard deviations are a measure of the variability of the rates of change—in the one case, of money; in the other case, of income. If such a computation were made for a strictly periodic series, say, a sine wave of fixed period and fixed amplitude, and if the length of the moving standard deviation were the same as the period of the sine wave (or an integral multiple of it), then the computed moving standard deviation would be constant over time, and its value would be equal to $\sqrt{\frac{1}{2}}$ times the amplitude of the sine wave.[8] If the length of the moving standard deviation were shorter than the period of the sine wave, the computed moving standard deviation would fluctuate over time, its value never exceeding the value just cited. The same proposition holds if the length of the moving standard deviation is longer than the period of the sine wave but not an integral multiple of it, though it is perhaps obvious that, as the moving standard deviation is lengthened, the standard deviation will approach the constant value noted above, since the fractional cycle becomes less and less important compared to the whole cycles included in the computation of the standard deviation.

It follows from these considerations that, for our purpose, which is to see how the amplitude of the cycles in the rate of change in the money stock is related to the amplitude of business cycles, we want to use a number of terms equal to the length of the cycle in which we are interested. This explains why we have used 3, 4, 5, and 6 terms; the reference cycle since 1867 has averaged four years in length but has occasionally been shorter or longer. As it happens, the results are not very different for different numbers of terms, so we present a chart for only the 4-term results, though we give some numerical data for all.

One more point before turning to the results. Net national product, which we are using as an index of general business and whose fluctuations we are interpreting as a measure of the amplitude of business cycles, has a sharp upward

7. That is, estimate of $\quad$ s. d. $= \sqrt{\dfrac{\Sigma(x-\bar{x})^2}{n-1}}$,

where x is the observation, $\bar{x}$, the mean, and n the number of items in the group, in this example, 3.

8. Let the sine wave be $A \sin (2\pi/m)t$, where t is time. Then m is the period of the wave and A the amplitude, the wave fluctuating from $+A$ to $-A$.

trend, though a less steep one than the money stock has, so that it typically declines absolutely during contractions. If we were to take a moving standard deviation of its absolute values, or their logarithms, the result would overestimate cyclical variability because of the intracycle trend, and the overestimate would vary over time as the intracycle trend did. Accordingly, to eliminate the effect of the intracycle trend from our measure of variability, we have used logarithmic first differences for net national product as well. This procedure is of the same class and for the same purpose as the National Bureau's standard technique of estimating full cycle amplitudes by subtracting the change during contraction from the change during expansion. However, the use of first differences can also be taken to mean that what we are calling the amplitude of business cycles refers to a construct rather different from the National Bureau's standard reference cycle; it refers to a cycle in the rate of change in aggregates rather than in the level of aggregates. As is well known, for a sine wave, the rate of change series has the same amplitude and pattern as the original series but differs in phase, its peaks and troughs coming one-quarter of a cycle earlier or three-quarters of a cycle later than the peaks and troughs of the original series.

Aside from removing the effect of intracycle trend, another advantage of using the first differences of net national product is that the results would be almost identical for total net national product and net national product per capita. Since population has grown at a steady rate over periods of 3 to 6 years, the use of per capita data would affect only the moving average of the rates of change but not the moving standard deviation.

Chart 5 plots the 4-term moving standard deviations for money and net national product. It should be noted that since we have used natural logarithms, the vertical scale can be interpreted directly in terms of percentage points. For example, a value of .100 means that the standard deviation is equal to an annual rate of growth of 10 percentage points.[9] The scale on the chart is logarithmic. The reason is that, since the standard error of the estimated standard deviation is proportional to the (true) standard deviation, the standard error of the logarithm of the standard deviation is roughly a constant, regardless of the size of the (true) standard deviation. Hence the logarithmic scale makes sampling fluctuations appear the same size throughout.

It is clear from the chart that there is a close relation between the variability

9. Let $\rho(t)$ be the continuous rate of growth from year t to year $t+1$, so that
$$X_{t+1} = X_t \, e^{\rho(t)},$$
where X_t and X_{t+1} are successive annual observations. Then $\log_e X_{t+1} - \log_e X_t = \rho(t)$. Note also that
$$\log_e X_{t+1} - \log_e X_t = \log_e \left(1 + \frac{X_{t+1} - X_t}{X_t}\right).$$
But $\log_e(1+k)$ is approximately equal to k for small k. Hence the first difference is approximately equal to
$$\frac{X_{t+1} - X_t}{X_t}.$$

CHART 5.   MOVING STANDARD DEVIATION OF ANNUAL RATES OF CHANGE IN MONEY, 1869–1958, AND IN INCOME, 1871–1958, 4-TERM SERIES

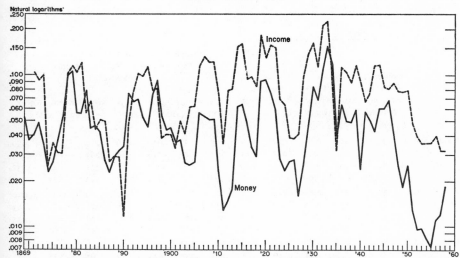

SOURCE: Money figures, described in source for Chart 1, are annual averages centered on June 30. Income figures are annual estimates of net national product, beginning 1869, from worksheets underlying Simon Kuznets, *Capital in the American Economy: Its Formation and Financing*, Princeton, N. J.: Princeton University Press for NBER (1961). For computation of moving standard derivation, see subsection 3 of this section, and footnote 7.

of money and of net national product: the two curves parallel one another with a high degree of fidelity, especially when it is borne in mind that standard deviations based on only four observations (three degrees of freedom) are subject to a good deal of sampling variation,[10] that the net national product and money series are, so far as we know, wholly independent in their statistical construction, and that both are subject to an appreciable margin of error.

At first glance, it appears from Chart 5 that income has become more variable relative to money over the period covered. Unless we are mistaken this is a statistical artifact. A closer look at the chart will show that the change comes shortly after the turn of the century. Before 1900, the standard deviations for money and for net national product are roughly equal in magnitude; subsequent to that date, the standard deviations for net national product are noticeably higher than for money. The reason, we conjecture, is the changing statistical character of the net national product estimates, in particular, the role played in them by interpolation between decennial census years. The effect of interpolation is to smooth greatly the year-to-year changes and so to reduce the estimated standard deviations. For the estimates before 1889, interpolation played a major role; for those from 1919 on, a much smaller role.[11] For the intermediate

10. A more precise statement for these data is hard to arrive at, since successive first differences are not statistically independent.

11. See Simon Kuznets, *National Product Since 1869*, New York: NBER (1946), pp. 90 ff. These considerations have the obvious implication that net national product estimates are untrustworthy as a source of evidence on secular changes in the amplitude of business cycles.

Table 4. *Moving Standard Deviations of Annual Rates of Change in Money and Net National Product: Means, Standard Deviations, and Correlation Coefficients for Different Numbers of Terms*

Period	Number of Terms in Moving Standard Deviations	MEAN STANDARD DEVIATION (NATURAL LOGARITHMS)		STANDARD DEVIATION OF STANDARD DEVIATION		CORRELATION COEFFICIENT BETWEEN STANDARD DEVIATIONS OF MONEY AND NNP						
						MONEY LEADING NNP BY: (YEARS)			SYN-CHRO-NOUS	NNP LEADING MONEY BY: (YEARS)		
		M	NNP	M	NNP	3	2	1		1	2	3
1869–1898	3	.049	.065	.022	.039	.293	.535	.616	.476	.114	−.011	−.099
	4	.052	.067	.023	.033	.364	.648	.718	.540	.263	−.049	−.163
	5	.054	.068	.022	.029	.378	.672	.717	.657	.431	.044	−.252
	6	.057	.069	.021	.027	.398	.583	.755	.759	.543	.144	−.069
1899–1960	3	.039	.081	.028	.048	.003	.113	.345	.670	.589	.248	.036
	4	.044	.089	.029	.046	.135	.243	.456	.814	.721	.472	.263
	5	.048	.095	.029	.046	.216	.385	.608	.840	.821	.637	.435
	6	.051	.100	.029	.044	.272	.481	.672	.870	.841	.707	.518
1869–1960	3	.042	.076	.027	.046	.001	.141	.349	.591	.429	.149	−.026
	4	.047	.081	.027	.044	.111	.242	.425	.687	.561	.311	.133
	5	.050	.085	.027	.043	.172	.348	.534	.721	.665	.465	.266
	6	.053	.089	.027	.042	.220	.404	.581	.748	.690	.536	.360

SOURCE: Same as for Chart 5.

decades, the role of interpolation relative to independent data for individual years became successively smaller. We cannot find any clear indication in the description of the statistical series that there was a sharp break around 1900 in the role of interpolation. However, the data behave as if there were such a break. For the period before 1900, we conjecture that the standard deviations appreciably understate the variability of income. For the subsequent period, it is much harder to make a comparable judgment. The statistical errors of estimation tend to raise the computed standard deviation; interpolation tends to lower it.

For money, the degree of interpolation in the annual estimates is small throughout (interpolation plays a much larger role in our monthly estimates). Hence the standard deviations for money are probably overestimates of the "true" standard deviations, thanks to the errors of estimation. However, because of the character of the basic data, such errors are probably appreciably smaller than for net national product.

Aside from the shift in the level of the standard deviations for net national product, the most striking feature of the chart is what appear to be fairly regular cyclical fluctuations, of about 8 to 15 years in length, in the standard deviations of both money and net national product; these are the counterparts of the long swings that have received much attention. However, a warning is in order about any such interpretation of these results. The moving standard deviations for successive years are highly correlated because they have three out of four items in common. As is well known, a moving average applied to a series of random terms will produce a series that seems to move systematically; and the moving standard deviation is a moving average and so has the same effect. For our purposes, what is important is the parallelism of the two series plotted in Chart 5, not the character of their common fluctuations.

Table 4 presents numerical evidence for all four lengths of moving standard deviations we have computed. Because of the break in the net national product data, the results are given separately for the period before and after 1899. We used 1899 as the dividing point because it is a census year. The results for the separate periods are more meaningful than the results for the period as a whole.

This table reinforces the visual evidence of Chart 5 and adds to it a number of important points. One is that the correlation is generally highest when the standard deviations are compared synchronously; it is generally lowered if standard deviations for money are compared with either later or earlier standard deviations for NNP though, for the earlier period, the correlation is highest when money leads one year for three of the four lengths of moving standard deviations. If there be any lead or lag for the later period, it is presumably less than a year in length. The slightly higher correlations for the later period for NNP leading by a year than for money leading by a year may reflect a lead of NNP by a fraction of a year. A second point added by the table is that the standard deviation for net national product for the period after 1899 is roughly double the standard deviation for money.[12] As a first approximation, therefore, the amplitude of cyclical fluctuations in income is twice that in money.

The correlations rise steadily as the number of terms in the moving standard deviations is increased. The rise presumably reflects the smoothing of the standard deviations introduced by the larger number of degrees of freedom and hence the reduction in the role of chance fluctuations. Calculations not summarized in the table indicate that the peak synchronous correlation is reached for seven terms. The fact that the mean standard deviations rise is less easily explained, since these should average the largest for a period equal to the average length of a cycle. The explanation is presumably the existence of the longer waves. We conjecture that the mean standard deviation would continue to rise as terms are added and reach a maximum at something like 10 to 15 terms.

To summarize these results: They strongly reinforce the evidence from the earlier comparison of reference cycle amplitudes. There is unquestionably a

---

12. The same reason that recommends a logarithmic scale for Chart 5 also suggests an advantage in making computations like those in Table 4 from the logarithms of the moving standard deviations. We have done so for the period from 1899 through 1960. The correlation results are quite similar. The synchronous results are .600, .797, .837, and .880 for 3, 4, 5, and 6 periods respectively.

The ratio of the geometric mean of the standard deviation of NNP to the geometric mean of the standard deviation of money is 2.31, 2.25, 2.19, 2.13, for 3, 4, 5, and 6 periods respectively. This method of estimation therefore suggests that income is roughly $2\frac{1}{4}$ times as variable as money.

CHART 6. INCOME VELOCITY: AVERAGE REFERENCE
CYCLE PATTERNS FOR MILD AND DEEP DEPRESSION
CYCLES, 1870–1958

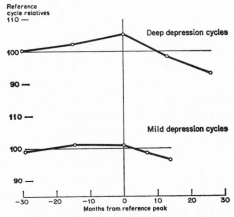

NOTE: War cycles, not shown, are 1914–19 and 1938–46. Deep depression cycles are: 1870–78, 1891–1904, 1904–08, 1919–21, 1927–32, and 1932–38. All others are mild depression cycles. These dates differ from those shown in Charts 2 and 4, because they are annual instead of monthly.

close relation between the variability of the stock of money and the variability of income. This relation has persisted over some nine decades and appears no different at the end of that period than at the beginning, if allowance is made for the changing characteristics of the statistical raw materials.

E. Cyclical Behavior of Velocity

1. The ratio of income to the stock of money, which is to say, the income velocity of money, has been rising in the post-World War II period. However, over the whole of the more than nine decades our data cover, it has declined sharply, from 4.6 at the outset of the period to 1.7 at the end. As a result, velocity has frequently declined during both expansions and contractions in general business. When this has not been the case, velocity has conformed positively to the cycle, rising during expansions and falling during contractions. When it has been, the cyclical effect has shown up in a slower rate of decline in expansions than in contractions. The average cyclical patterns of velocity, for mild depression and deep depression cycles (excluding war cycles), are given in Chart 6.

2. In an earlier article,[13] it was demonstrated that this cyclical pattern of velocity could be largely though not wholly accounted for by supposing that the amount of money demanded in real terms is linked, not to current measured

13. Friedman, "The Demand for Money: Some Theoretical and Empirical Results," Chapter 6 above.

income and current measured prices, but to longer-term concepts of permanent income and permanent prices. By this interpretation, the amount of money demanded rises during the expansion phase of a cycle in greater proportion than permanent income, as suggested by the secular results. However, measured income rises in still greater proportion, so that measured income rises relative to the stock of money, and conversely during a contraction. While this interpretation does not rule out the possibility that changing interest rates over the cycle play a role in the cyclical behavior of velocity, it assigns them a less important role than it assigns to the discrepancy between measured and permanent concepts.

3. This interpretation has been criticized as assigning much too small a role to interest rates. Henry A. Latané, in particular, has argued that the whole of the movement of velocity, both over longer periods and over the cycle, can be accounted for by changes in interest rates, higher interest rates leading to economy in the use of money and so to higher velocities, and conversely.[14] His analysis covers a shorter period than ours does (1909–58).

4. There is no necessary contradiction between these two interpretations, the appearance of contradiction arising primarily from our definition of money as the sum of currency plus all adjusted deposits in commercial banks, and Latané's definition of money as the sum of currency plus adjusted demand deposits alone.

(a). Time deposits in commercial banks appear to have a substantially higher income elasticity of demand than currency or demand deposits have, so that the income elasticity of money by our use of the term is doubtless higher than it is by Latané's use of the term. This can explain why we find it necessary to introduce an income effect to explain the secular decline in velocity, while he does not. To put this point differently, we find that the elasticity of demand for (real) money balances with respect to permanent income is about 1.8 when money is defined as we define it. This is consistent with a corresponding elasticity not much different from unity for Latané's narrower definition, provided the elasticity for time deposits is between 2.5 and 3.5.[15] Furthermore, since there is a considerable trend element in the movement of interest rates over the period Latané's analysis covers—as, of course, there is in income for a much longer period—any excess of the "correct" elasticity over unity could readily be confounded in the statistical analysis with the effects of interest rates. Our

---

14. "Cash Balances and the Interest Rate—A Pragmatic Approach," *Review of Economics and Statistics*, November 1954, pp. 456–60; also *idem*, "Income Velocity and Interest Rates—A Pragmatic Approach," *Employment, Growth, and Price Levels*, Joint Economic Committee, Hearings, part 10, 86th Cong., 1st sess., pp. 3435–43 (reprinted with minor changes in *Review of Economics and Statistics*, November 1960, pp. 445–49); and see Allan H. Meltzer, "The Demand for Money: The Evidence from the Time Series," presented at the Dec. 1961 meeting of the Econometric Society.

15. The elasticity of a total is a weighted average of the elasticities of the components, the weights being the ratio of each component to the total. Over the period from 1914 to 1960, commercial bank time deposits have varied from 19 to 44 per cent of money as we define it.

own readiness to attribute the decline in velocity to income, despite the strong trend in income, derives primarily from the consistency of such an interpretation with a wide range of other evidence, in particular, cross-section evidence for different states in the United States and for different countries.

(b). It is plausible that the division of currency plus deposits between currency plus demand deposits, on the one hand, and time deposits, on the other, is sensitive to rates of interest, since the differential between interest paid on time deposits and interest paid on demand deposits (which can be and for long periods has been negative) and on currency (typically zero) can be expected to widen as interest rates rise—and conversely. Hence a rise in interest rates might be expected to lead to an increase in commercial bank time deposits relative to commercial bank demand deposits plus currency—and conversely. It follows that the interest elasticity of demand can be expected to be greater in absolute value for currency plus demand deposits, than for currency plus demand deposits plus time deposits in commercial banks.

(c) The two preceding points have especial importance for the longer-term movements in velocity. For the cyclical behavior of velocity, the distinction between measured and permanent income can be combined with either demand function, and will help to explain the cyclical behavior of velocity.

Needless to say, neither definition of money can be said to be "the" correct definition. Just where the line is drawn between those temporary abodes of purchasing power we choose to term money and those we term "near-monies," or "liquid assets," or what not, is largely arbitrary. We have found it convenient to draw the line where we do largely because it enables us to use a single concept for the whole of our period, since the distinction between commercial bank demand and time deposits did not acquire its current significance—or indeed have much significance at all—until after 1914. In the course of using it, we have found it to have some other advantages.[16] In addition, even for the period since 1914, it is by no means clear that demand deposits as recorded correspond fully with the economic construct Latané wishes to measure, namely, deposits

16. Still another bit of evidence on which of the two definitions of money is to be preferred is available. We computed correlations like those in Table 4 for the period 1915–60 between the variability of the narrower definition and the variability of net national product, and also between the variability of our broader definition and the variability of net national product. The broader definition has almost always a somewhat higher correlation coefficient. The synchronous results for standard deviations of varying terms are shown in the following tabulation, giving correlation coefficients between synchronous standard deviations of annual rates of change in money—defined narrowly and broadly—and in net national product, for different number of terms.

Definition of Money	3-Term	4-Term	5-Term	6-Term	7-Term	8-Term	9-Term
M_1	.592	.833	.865	.909	.937	.931	.912
M_2	.596	.785	.842	.883	.907	.899	.874

M_1 = Currency held by the public, plus demand deposits adjusted, plus commercial bank time deposits.

M_2 = Currency held by the public, plus demand deposits adjusted.

subject to check. The lower reserves required against time deposits have given banks an incentive to classify as large a fraction of deposits as time deposits as possible. There is some evidence that, particularly during the 1920's, banks managed so to classify some deposits that were in effect demand deposits. A full understanding of the behavior of money in business cycles requires an analysis of the components of the money stock, however defined, and of near-monies as well, so, despite our reservations about the meaning of some of his data, we welcome Latané's analysis as a valuable complement to ours.

5. A basically more important question is the extent to which velocity can be regarded as passively reflecting independent changes in its numerator and denominator. This is the presumption implicit in the cycle theories, popular these past few decades, that have regarded investment as the dominant cycle-producing factor. These theories implicitly take for granted that an expansion of investment will produce an expansion in income regardless of what happens to the money stock. In their most extreme form, these theories imply that the magnitude of the expansion in income is independent of the size of any concurrent change in the money stock. If the money stock does not rise, then velocity will simply rise to fill the gap; if the money stock does rise, velocity will not rise as much or may even fall. The most rigorous explicit theoretical formulation of this position is in terms of either a "liquidity trap"—an infinitely elastic liquidity preference function at a finite interest rate—or a completely inelastic demand schedule for investment—a zero response of spending to a change in the rate of interest. Few economists would explicitly maintain that either the one or the other prevails currently, or has prevailed during most of our past history. But many would accept the logically equivalent assertions that the rate of cyclical expansion or contraction can be regarded as fairly rigidly determined by the rise or fall in investment or autonomous expenditure, that the link is far more crucial than any link with the contemporary behavior of the money stock, and can be reversed, if at all, only by a very atypical behavior of the money stock. Some relevant empirical evidence on this issue is summarized in the subsection below on the relative roles of money and investment.

F. Cyclical Behavior of Proximate Determinants of the Money stock

1. Changes in the stock of money can, arithmetically, be attributed to changes in three proximate determinants, each under the immediate control of a different class of economic actors:

(a) High-powered money, consisting of currency held by the public, plus currency held in bank vaults, plus deposits of banks at Federal Reserve Banks. This total is either a consequence of international payment flows and associated gold movements, or of Treasury or Federal Reserve policy.

(b) The division of the public's money holdings between currency and deposits, which can be summarized by any one of a number of ratios—of currency to the money stock; of currency to deposits; or of deposits to currency. This division is in the first instance determined by the public, the holders of money, though, of course, the public's decision is affected by the terms offered by banks for deposits.

(c) The relation between deposits and the amount of high-powered money held by banks, which can be termed their reserves. This relation can be summarized by either the ratio of reserves to deposits or its reciprocal, the ratio of deposits to reserves. This ratio is in the first instance determined by banks, though, of course, their decision is affected by legal requirements imposed by the government, by the terms they must offer to obtain deposits, and by the returns they can receive on the alternative assets they acquire.

Given the two ratios, a rise in high-powered money implies a proportional rise in the stock of money. Given the amount of high-powered money and the deposit-reserve ratio, a rise in the deposit-currency ratio implies a rise in the stock of money, because it means that less high-powered money is required to meet the currency demands of the public and more is available for bank reserves to be multiplied by the deposit-reserve ratio. Similarly, given the amount of high-powered money and the deposit-currency ratio, a rise in the deposit-reserve ratio implies a rise in the stock of money, because it means that each dollar of high-powered money held by banks gives rise to a larger number of dollars of deposits.

2. Phillip Cagan has analyzed in detail the contribution of changes in each of these three proximate determinants to the cyclical fluctuations in the rate of change in the money stock.[17] He finds that the deposit-currency ratio was the most important single contributor. Throughout the period from 1877 to 1954, it accounted on the average for roughly half the cyclical fluctuations in the rate of change in the money stock. Though this fraction varied from cycle to cycle, it did not change in any consistent secular fashion and was not markedly different for severe and mild movements. The main deviation in its contribution occurred at times of money panics in which it often played a dominant role.

Changes in high-powered money were as large in amplitude as changes in the deposit-reserve ratio but much less regular in timing. Changes in the deposit-reserve ratio were regular in timing but relatively small in amplitude.

3. Cagan finds that the main impact of the Federal Reserve System has been on the relative importance of changes in high-powered money and in the deposit-reserve ratio. By providing banks with an alternative source of liquidity, the Reserve System intensified a tendency for banks to trim any excess of reserves over legal requirements—a tendency fostered in earlier decades by the Treasury's assumption of enlarged money market responsibilities. The result was a reduction in the amplitude of cyclical movements in the reserve ratio after 1914. However, this was more than offset by an increase in the amplitude of cyclical movements in high-powered money.

17. See his monograph, *Determinants and Effects of Changes in the U.S. Money Stock, 1875–1960*, New York: National Bureau of Economic Research, 1965.

4. The deposit-currency ratio had a rising long-term trend to 1929, declined substantially thereafter until the end of World War II, and has since been rising. Relative to these longer-term movements, the deposit-currency ratio tended to rise during the early part of expansions, at first at an increasing rate; to reach a peak near mid-expansion; then to decline to mid-contraction; and then to start rising. Cagan shows that these movements played an important part in accounting for the tendency of the rate of change in the money stock to reach its peak around mid-expansion and its trough around mid-contraction. He attributes the timing of movements in the deposit-currency ratio to divergent cyclical patterns in the velocity of currency and deposits.

5. The deposit-reserve ratio rose during most of the period covered, except for its sharp decline during the later 1930's. Relative to trend, it tended to rise during expansions, reaching its peak before the reference peak, and tended to decline during contractions, reaching its trough before the reference trough.

6. These patterns bespeak a rather complex feedback mechanism whereby changes in business activity react on the stock of money. This feedback mechanism has not yet been worked out in the detail that would be desirable.

G. Relative Roles of Money and Investment in the Cycle

In an extensive statistical study using standard correlation techniques rather than the National Bureau's cycle analysis, one of us in collaboration with David Meiselman investigated the relative stability of monetary velocity and the investment multiplier.[18] Both the stock of money and the level of autonomous expenditures are positively related to consumption and to income over both short and long spans of years. However, it turns out that the correlation is generally much higher for money than for autonomous expenditures. Moreover, the partial correlation between money and consumption, holding autonomous expenditures constant, is roughly the same as the simple correlation, whereas the partial correlation between autonomous expenditures and consumption, holding the stock of money constant, is on the average roughly zero, being sometimes positive, sometimes negative. Similar results were obtained for year-to-year and quarter-to-quarter changes in the stock of money, autonomous expenditures, and consumption.

Additional evidence is provided by correlations between the variability of annual changes in money and in consumption, on the one hand, and between the variability of annual changes in investment and in consumption, on the other. Because there are occasional negative figures for net capital formation, we used gross capital formation as the measure of investment and computed first differ-

18. Milton Friedman and David Meiselman, "The Relative Stability of Monetary Velocity and the Investment Multiplier in the United States, 1897–1958," in *Stabilization Policies*, Englewood Cliffs, N.J.: Prentice-Hall for the Commission on Money and Credit (1963), pp. 165–268.

ences of logarithms and moving standard deviations of the first differences, as in Table 4, for money, consumption, and investment. The synchronous correlation coefficients we obtained are consistently higher, both for the period as a whole and for the period since 1899, for money-consumption variability than they are for investment-consumption variability. These are exactly the same results as in the Friedman-Meiselman study, although derived by a wholly different procedure. For the full period, the correlation coefficient for money-investment variability is slightly lower than for investment-consumption variability; for the period since 1899, slightly higher. In addition, the partial correlation between money-consumption variability, holding investment variability constant, is significantly higher than the partial correlation between investment-consumption variability, holding money variability constant; for the period since 1899, the partial correlation between money-investment variability, holding consumption constant, is significantly higher than the partial correlation between investment-consumption variability, holding money constant, although for the whole period, the former is lower. Essentially the same results were obtained for the simple and partial correlations with leads and lags.[19]

These results are striking because they contradict so sharply the widespread presumption among economists that investment (or, more generally, autonomous expenditure) is the prime mover in cyclical fluctuations, transmitting its influence to the rest of income via a multiplier effect on consumption. So far as these results go, they suggest that, *for a given stock of money*, there is no systematic relation at all between autonomous expenditures and consumption—in experience, the multiplier effect on consumption is as likely to be negative as positive.[20] These results may of course be misleading, because some crucial variables have been

19. The synchronous simple and partial correlation coefficients for the moving 4-term standard deviations of the first differences of logarithms are shown in the following tabulation for the full period and the period since 1899.

Period	SIMPLE CORRELATIONS			PARTIAL CORRELATIONS		
	r_{CM}	r_{CI}	r_{IM}	$r_{CM \cdot I}$	$r_{CM \cdot I}$	$r_{IM \cdot C}$
1871–1958	.749	.404	.330	.713	.252	.044
1899–1958	.811	.600	.677	.687	.120	.406

$C =$ Consumption
$M =$ Money stock
$I =$ Gross capital formation

If net capital formation is used as the measure of investment, first differences of absolute values must be obtained. We calculated the standard deviation of those first differences, and the logarithm of the standard deviation, and then correlated the logarithms as above. There is a trend element in these calculations that it would be desirable to eliminate but, even so, the correlation coefficients are similar to those described for the standard deviation of first differences of logarithms.

20. The investment multiplier is generally defined as the ratio of a change in *income* rather than in consumption to the change in autonomous expenditures to which the change in income is attributed. In these terms, the conclusion is that the multiplier is as likely in practice to be less than unity as greater than unity.

neglected, or because the definition used for autonomous expenditures is inappropriate, or for some other reason. But they tend to be supported by preliminary results for other countries, and we know of no contrary evidence for the United States. The widespread presumption to the contrary that unquestionably does exist, whether it be right or wrong, does not rest, so far as we can see, on any coherent, organized body of empirical evidence. [21]

II. SOME PLAUSIBLE INTERPRETATIONS
OF THE FACTUAL EVIDENCE

The stock of money displays a consistent cyclical behavior which is closely related to the cyclical behavior of the economy at large. This much the factual evidence summarized above puts beyond reasonable doubt.

That evidence alone is much less decisive about the direction of influence. Is the cyclical behavior of money primarily a reflection of the cyclical behavior of the economy at large, or does it play an important independent part in accounting for the cyclical behavior of the economy? It might be, so far as we know, that one could marshal a similar body of evidence demonstrating that the production of dressmakers' pins has displayed over the past nine decades a regular cyclical pattern; that the pin pattern reaches a peak well before the reference peak and a trough well before the reference trough; that its amplitude is highly correlated with the amplitude of the movements in general business. It might even be demonstrated that the simple correlation between the production of pins and consumption is higher than the simple correlation between autonomous expenditures and consumption; that the partial correlation between pins and consumption—holding autonomous expenditures constant—is

---

21. It is well established that (1) investment expenditures have a wider cyclical amplitude than consumption expenditures have relative to their mean value; (2) orders and other series reflecting investment decisions, as contrasted with expenditures, display a consistent tendency to lead cyclical turns; (3) there is a high correlation between consumption and income.

None of these is very strong evidence for the multiplier effect of investment on consumption, which is the point at issue. Item 1 simply means that investment is a more variable component of income than consumption is; it says nothing about whether both fluctuate in response to common influences, investment influences consumption, or consumption influences investment. Note that a strict multiplier model has no implications about whether autonomous or induced expenditures should show wider absolute fluctuations. Absolute fluctuations in induced expenditures would presumably be wider or narrower as the usual multiplier is greater or less than 2.

Item 2 has more significance and has some suggestive value. However, it may simply mean that decisions are affected early by whatever also affects spending later on (see page 231, below). Item 3 is entirely irrelevant. Consumption is a major component of income, as both are measured. For multiplier effects, what is important is the effect of investment on consumption. See M. Friedman and G. S. Becker, "A Statistical Illusion in Judging Keynesian Models," *Journal of Political Economy*, February 1957, pp. 64–75.

as high as the simple correlation; and that the correlation between consumption and autonomous expenditures—holding the production of pins constant—is on the average zero. We do not, of course, know that these statements are valid for pins and, indeed, rather doubt that they are, but, even if they were demonstrated beyond a shadow of doubt, they would persuade neither us nor our readers to adopt a pin theory of business cycles.

If the only decisive statistical evidence for money were comparable to the items just cited for pins, it would correspondingly not justify the acceptance of a monetary theory of business cycles. At the same time, it is worth noting that, even then, the monetary theory and the pin theory would by no means be on all fours. Most economists would be willing to dismiss out of hand the pin theory even on such evidence; most economists would take seriously the monetary theory even on much less evidence, which is not by any means the same as saying that they would be persuaded by the evidence. Whence the difference? Primarily, the difference is that we have other kinds of evidence. We know that while pins are widely used and occasionally of critical importance, taken as a whole, they are a minor, if not trifling, item in the economy. We expect the effect to be in rough proportion to the cause, though this is by no means always the case—a rock can start a landslide. We can readily conceive of an economy operating without pins yet experiencing cycles like those of history; we can readily conceive of large autonomous changes occurring in the production of pins, but we cannot readily conceive of any channels through which such autonomous changes could have wide-reaching effects on the rest of the economy. Men who have thought about and studied these matters have never been led to suggest the pin industry as a prime mover in the cyclical process. In all these respects, the monetary theory is on a wholly different footing. We know that money is a pervasive element in the economy; that the stock of money is sizable compared with other aggregate economic magnitudes; that fluctuations of the kind we call business cycles have apparently occurred only in an economy in which "economic activities are . . . carried on mainly by making and spending money."[22] We not only can conceive of the money stock's being subject to large autonomous changes, but we can also readily conceive of channels through which such changes could have far-reaching effects on the rest of the economy. Men who have thought about and studied these matters have been led to give money a critical role in their theories.

One more preliminary observation. The key question at issue is not whether the direction of influence is wholly from money to business or wholly from business to money; it is whether the influence running from money to business is significant, in the sense that it can account for a substantial fraction of the fluctuations in economic activity. If the answer is affirmative, then one can speak of a monetary theory of business cycles or—more precisely—of the need to assign money an important role in a full theory of business cycles. The reflex

22. Wesley C. Mitchell, *Business Cycles: the Problem and Its Setting*, New York: NBER (1927), Chapter II, and p. 62.

influence of business on money, the existence of which is not in doubt in light of the factual evidence summarized above, would then become part of the partly self-generating mechanism whereby monetary disturbances are transmitted. On the other hand, if the influence from money to business is minor, one could speak of a cyclical theory of monetary fluctuations but not of a monetary theory of business cycles. To illustrate again with pins: Changes in business conditions doubtless affect the production of pins, and no doubt there is some feedback effect of changes in the production of pins on general business. But, whereas the first effect may well be large relative to the total fluctuations in pin production, the feed-back effect is almost certainly trivial relative to the fluctuations in business. Hence we are ready to accept a business cycle theory of pin production but not a pin theory of business cycles.

The factual evidence summarized above goes beyond the list of items we conjectured for pins and contains some bits that are relevant to the key question at issue. The most important is the fact that the relation between money and business has remained largely unchanged over a period that has seen substantial changes in the arrangements determining the quantity of money. During part of the period, the United States was on an effective gold standard; during part, on an inconvertible paper standard with floating exchange rates, during part, on a managed paper standard with fixed exchange rates. The commercial banking system changed its role and scope greatly. The government arrangements for monetary control altered, the Federal Reserve System replacing the Treasury as the formal center of control. And the criteria of control adopted by the monetary authorities altered. If the predominant direction of influence had been from business to money, these changes might have been expected to alter the relation between business changes and monetary changes, but the relation has apparently remained much the same in both timing and amplitude.[23] Yet this evidence is by no means decisive. As noted above, Cagan shows that the public's decisions about the proportion in which it divides its money balances between currency and deposits is an important link in the feedback mechanism whereby changes in business affect the stock of money. The changes in monetary arrangements have affected greatly the trends in the deposit-currency ratio but appear not to have affected its cyclical behavior. Hence this part of the supply mechanism has been roughly constant and has played a roughly constant role over the whole period.

In our view, the most convincing evidence supporting the idea that money plays an important independent part is not the evidence summarized in the first part of this paper but evidence of a rather different kind—that garnered from study of the historical circumstances underlying the changes that occurred in the stock of money.[24] This evidence is much more clear cut for major movements than for minor.

23. See also comments in Friedman, "The Lag in Effect of Monetary Policy," Chapter 11 below.

24. For the United States, since the end of the Civil War, see our *A Monetary History of the United States, 1867–1960*.

A. Major Economic Fluctuations

Major movements in U.S. history include the deep depressions used here to distinguish deep from mild depression cycles in our classification of historical reference cycles (see Chart 2 for the classification); the substantial inflations which have occurred primarily during wartime; and a few long-continued movements in one direction, such as the generally rising level of money income and prices from 1896 to 1913. With respect to these events, the historical record justifies two important generalizations.

1. There is a one-to-one relation between monetary changes and changes in money income and prices. Changes in money income and prices have, in every case, been accompanied by a change in the rate of growth of the money stock, in the same direction and of appreciable magnitude, and there are no comparable disturbances in the rate of growth of the money stock unaccompanied by changes in money income and prices.

2. The changes in the stock of money cannot consistently be explained by the contemporary changes in money income and prices. The changes in the stock of money can generally be attributed to specific historical circumstances that are not in turn attributable to contemporary changes in money income and prices. Hence, if the consistent relation between money and income is not pure coincidence, it must reflect an influence running from money to business.

(1). *Inflationary Episodes.* The second generalization requires little more than its statement to be recognized as true for the inflationary episodes. During periods of U.S. engagement in wars, the increased rate of growth of the money stock stemmed from use of the printing press, in more or less subtle ways, to help finance government military expenditures. During our neutrality in World War I from 1914 to early 1917, it had its origin in use by the Allies of their gold reserves to finance war purchases here. During those war years, the reflex influence of the rising tide of business on the stock of money was in the opposite direction to the actual movement in the money stock, since business expansion of itself tended to produce a worsening in the balance of payments and hence an outflow of gold or a decreased inflow.

The situation is equally clear from 1896 to 1913. The rise in the stock of money reflected predominantly an increase in the U.S. gold stock, which was part of a worldwide growth of the gold stock emanating from the discovery of new mines and improvements in techniques of extracting gold from low-grade ore. The domestic expansion alone would have made for gold outflows. The feedback was therefore counter to the main current.[25]

For the wartime episodes, the evidence is equally consistent with a different theory, that the independent force was a major shift in government spending

---

25. This point is discussed in more detail in Cagan, *Determinants and Effects of Changes in the U.S. Money Stock, 1875–1960.*

propensities; that the shift in spending propensities would have had the same effect on income and prices if it had been financed wholly by borrowing from the public at large with an unchanged money stock, rather than being financed in part by the use of monetary reserves (as it was in the early years of World War I) or by government creation of money (as in the other war years); that it was not financed wholly by borrowing because resort in part to use of monetary reserves and the printing press was politically easier and perhaps financially cheaper.

Evidence from the study by Friedman and Meiselman (discussed in the subsection on the relative roles of money and investment above) rather decisively contradicts this alternative explanation. In any event, the alternative explanation will not hold for the 1896–1913 inflation, since there was no obvious independent shift of major magnitude in spending propensities. The only immediate factor producing such a shift that comes to mind is the income earned from gold production. However, although the increase in the stock of gold over that period was large compared to the gold stock at the start and was capable of producing large increases in the stock of money via a multiplicative effect on other kinds of money, the gold stock itself was a small fraction of the total money stock, and the increase in the money stock only a fraction of the increase in money income. Hence, the value of gold production was a small fraction indeed of the increase in income.[26] The increased gold production could hardly have produced the observed increase of money income through any spending multiplier effect. Any effect it might have had must have been through its effect on the stock of money.

(2). *Deep Depressions.* For deep depressions, the historical evidence justifying our second generalization is as clear as for the inflationary episodes, though less well known and hence less self-evident. A summary statement of the proximate source of the change in the money stock will in most instances enable the reader to judge for himself the extent to which the decline in the stock of money can be explained by the contemporary change in money, income, and prices.

1875–78: Political pressure for resumption led to a decline in high-powered money, and the banking crisis in 1873 and subsequent bank failures to a shift by the public from deposits to currency and to a fall in the deposit-reserve ratio.

1892–94: Agitation for silver and destabilizing movements in Treasury cash produced fears of imminent abandonment of the gold standard by the United States and thereby an outflow of capital which trenched on gold stocks. Those effects were intensified by the banking panic of 1893, which produced a sharp decline, first in the deposit-currency ratio and then in the deposit-reserve ratio.

26. For the United States from 1896 to 1913, the value of the gold stock increased by roughly $1.4 billion or by about $80 million a year; net national product increased from about $11 billion in 1896 to $34 billion in 1913 or at the rate of about $1,300 million a year.

1907–08: The banking panic of 1907 led to a sharp decline in the deposit-currency ratio and a protective attempt by banks to raise their own reserve balances, and so to a subsequent fall in the deposit-reserve ratio.

1920–21: Sharp rises in Federal Reserve discount rates in January 1920 and again in June 1920 produced, with some lag, a sharp contraction in Federal Reserve credit outstanding, and thereby in high-powered money and the money stock.

1929–33: An initial mild decline in the money stock from 1929 to 1930, accompanying a decline in Federal Reserve credit outstanding, was converted into a sharp decline by a wave of bank failures beginning in late 1930. Those failures produced (1) widespread attempts by the public to convert deposits into currency and hence a decline in the deposit-currency ratio, and (2) a scramble for liquidity by the banks and hence a decline in the deposit-reserve ratio. The decline in the money stock was intensified after September 1931 by deflationary actions on the part of the Federal Reserve System, in response to England's departure from gold, which led to still further bank failures and even sharper declines in the deposit ratios. Yet the Federal Reserve at all times had power to prevent the decline in the money stock or to increase it to any desired degree, by providing enough high-powered money to satisfy the banks' desire for liquidity, and almost surely without any serious threat to the gold standard.

1937–38: The doubling of legal reserve requirements in a series of steps, effective in 1936 and early 1937, accompanied by Treasury sterilization of gold purchases, led to a halt in the growth of high-powered money and attempts by banks to restore their reserves in excess of requirements. The decline in the money stock reflected largely the resultant decline in the deposit-reserve ratio.

A shift in the deposit-currency ratio and the accompanying bank crises played an important role in four of these six episodes. This ratio, as we have seen, has a systematic cyclical pattern which can be regarded as a feedback effect of business on money. However, in each of those episodes, the shift in the deposit-currency ratio represented a sharp departure from the typical cyclical response and, in at least two (1875–78 and 1892–94), represented a subsequent reaction to an initial monetary disturbance that had no such close link with contemporary changes in money income and prices. Moreover, in two episodes (1920–21 and 1937–38), neither a shift in the deposit-currency ratio nor bank failures played any role. And such a shift has played no important role in any of the large expansions in the stock of money. A fractional reserve banking structure susceptible to runs is an institutional feature that renders the stock of money sensitive to autonomous deflationary changes; hence runs may frequently play an important role in sharp declines. This feature, however, is clearly not essential for a large economic change to be accompanied by a large monetary change in the same direction.

The 1907–08 episode is a particularly nice example of the intermixture of autonomous monetary disturbances and a feedback. The failure of the Knickerbocker Trust Company in the fall of 1907 converted what had been a mild decline in the money stock as a result of gold exports and a consequent decline in high-powered money into a severe decline as a result of bank runs and a consequent decline in the deposit-currency ratio. The accompanying sharp rise in short-term interest rates and a premium on currency produced a large gold inflow. The accompanying sharp intensification in the business decline worked in the same direction by its effect on the balance of international payments. Since the runs were prevented from producing widespread bank failures through the concerted suspension by banks of convertibility of deposits into currency, these feedback effects fairly promptly reversed the money decline and, along with the reversal, the business decline came to an end.

(3). *Conclusions for Major Movements.* The factors that produced the changes in the stock of money are autonomous only in the sense of not being directly attributable to the contemporary cyclical changes in money income and prices. In a broader context, each of course has its origins and its explanation, and some are connected fairly clearly with longer-term economic developments. There can be no doubt, for example, that the silver agitation was intensified by prior declining agricultural prices, or that the financial boom in the early 1900's encouraged financial activities which laid the basis for Knickerbocker Trust's failure, or that the worldwide declining price trend of the 1870's and 1880's encouraged exploration for gold and improvement of refining techniques.

The narrower sense is, however, important for our purpose. The question at issue is whether the one-to-one relation between monetary change and major economic change can be explained by a relation running from economic change to money, as a one-to-one relation between changes in pin production and in economic activity could be explained if it existed. Such an explanation would require that the changes in money be connected rather rigidly with either the contemporary changes in economic conditions or more basic factors that could account alike for the course of economic events and for the changes in the stock of money. The demonstration that the major changes in the stock of money have been attributable to a variety of sources, many of which are connected directly neither with contemporary business developments nor with earlier business developments—which themselves can be regarded as determining the contemporary course of business—therefore contradicts any such explanation of the one-to-one relation between economic change and monetary change.

There seems to us, accordingly, to be an extraordinarily strong case for the propositions that (1) appreciable changes in the rate of growth of the stock of money are a necessary and sufficient condition for appreciable changes in the rate of growth of money income; and that (2) this is true both for long secular changes and also for changes over periods roughly the length of business cycles. To go beyond the evidence and discussion thus far presented: our survey of experience leads us to conjecture that a longer-period change in money income produced by a changed secular rate of growth of the money stock is reflected mainly in different price behavior rather than in a different rate of growth of output; whereas a shorter-period change in the rate of growth of the money stock is capable of exerting a sizable influence on the rate of growth of output as well.

These propositions offer a single, straightforward interpretation of all the historical episodes involving appreciable changes in the rate of monetary growth that we know about in any detail.[27] We know of no other single suggested interpretation that is at all satisfactory and have been able to construct none for ourselves. The character of the U.S. banking system—in particular, for most of its history, the vulnerability of the system to runs on banks—can come close to explaining why sizable declines in money income, however produced, should generally be accompanied by sizable declines in the stock of money; but this explanation does not hold even for all declines, and it is largely irrelevant for the rises. Autonomous increases in government spending propensities plus the irresistible political attraction of the printing press could come close to providing a single explanation for wartime inflations, accounting for the coincidence of rising incomes and rising stock of money without any necessary influence running from money to income; but this explanation cannot account for peacetime inflations, in which the growth of the money stock has reflected a rise in specie rather than in government-issued money; and it is not even a satisfactory explanation for the wartime episodes, since price rises in different wartime episodes seem more closely related to the concurrent changes in the stock of money than to the changes in government expenditure.[28]

It is perhaps worth emphasizing and repeating that any alternative interpretation must meet two tests: it must explain why the major movements in income occurred when they did, and also it must explain why such major movements

27. Though we have summarized here and have, ourselves, investigated in detail only the U.S. experience since 1867, this statement is deliberately worded so as to cover a wider range of experience. For example, it is consistent with the hyperinflations studied by Cagan ("The Monetary Dynamics of Hyperinflation," *Studies in the Quantity Theory of Money*, M. Friedman (Ed.), Chicago: University of Chicago Press (1956, pp. 25–117); with U.S. experience during the 1830's and 1840's, studied by George Macesich ("Monetary Disturbances in the United States, 1834–45," unpublished Ph.D. thesis, University of Chicago, June 1958); with U.S. experience during the Revolutionary War, the War of 1812, and the Civil War; with Chilean experience, as studied by John Deaver ("The Chilean Inflation and the Demand for Money," unpublished Ph.D. thesis, University of Chicago, 1961); with the price revolution in the sixteenth century, as studied by Earl J. Hamilton (*American Treasure and the Price Revolution in Spain, 1501–1650*, Cambridge, Mass.: Harvard University Press, 1934).

28. See Friedman, "Price, Income, and Monetary Changes in Three Wartime Periods," Chapter 8 above.

should have been uniformly accompanied by corresponding movements in the rate of growth of the money stock. The monetary interpretation explains both at the same time. It leaves open the reasons for the change in the rate of growth of the money stock and, indeed, at this point is highly eclectic, taking account of the fact that historically there have been many different reasons.

We have emphasized the difficulty of meeting the second test. But even the first alone is hard to meet except by an explanation which asserts that different factors may from time to time produce large movements in income, and that these factors may operate through diverse channels—which is essentially to plead utter ignorance. We have cited several times the apparently widespread belief in investment as the prime mover. The alternative explanation for times of war, suggested above, is a special application of this theory, with investment broadened to mean "autonomous expenditures" and government spending included in the same category. But even for the first test alone, we find it hard to accept this theory as a valid general explanation: can a drastic collapse in autonomous investment explain equally 1873–79, 1892–94, 1920–21, 1929–33, 1937–38? Capital formation at the end of the seventies was apparently one and one-half times its level at the beginning and seems not to have slumped seriously at any time during the decade, judging by the rough indications given by Kuznets' figures.[29] The 1890's saw some decline, but the following decade was marked by a vigorous and sustained rise. The 1920–21 episode was destined to be followed by a construction and investment boom. If the experience of 1920–21 is to be interpreted as a result of an investment collapse, that decline must have been a consequence of the decline in government expenditures and the subsequent collapse of inventory speculation before fixed capital expenditures had developed to take their place. But why, then, did the sharp decline in government expenditures after World War II not produce a subsequent economic collapse? Emphasis on inventory speculation involves a highly episodic interpretation, since it characterizes few of the other episodes. Surely, one cannot argue that in World War I, slow using up of investment opportunities—often implicitly or explicitly called on to explain why, from time to time, there is allegedly a collapse of investment or a position of stagnation—was responsible for the 1920–21 recession. This is an equally implausible explanation for 1937–38 and, as already implied, for earlier episodes as well.

Of course, in most or all of these contractions, the incentive to invest and the actual amount spent on investment declined. The question at issue, however, is whether the decline was a consequence of the contemporary economic collapse —triggered, we would say, by monetary changes—or the ultimate working out of autonomous elements of weakness in the demand for investment that themselves triggered the contraction.

Even if all these episodes of contraction can somehow be interpreted as reflecting an autonomous decline in investment, is a sharp increase in investment

29. Kuznets, *Capital in the American Economy: Its Formation and Financing*, Princeton, N.J.: Princeton University Press for NBER (1961), p. 572.

opportunities a satisfactory explanation for the worldwide 1897–1913 rise in money income? If money is not a critical link but only a passive accompaniment of change, how is it that China escaped the early years of the Great Depression? We would say thanks to being on a silver standard and hence having a floating exchange rate vis-à-vis gold currencies, ˜˜hereas all countries linked to gold were enmeshed in the depression. And how is it that China had the most severe contraction of all in the years from 1933 to 1936, when our silver purchase program drained silver from China and caused a sharp decline in its money stock, whereas the rest of the world was in a period of business expansion? And we could extend this list of embarrassing questions without difficulty.

We feel as if we are belaboring the obvious and we apologize to any reader who shares that feeling. Yet repeated experience has led us to believe that it is necessary to do so in order to make clear how strong is the case for the monetary explanation of major movements in money income.

Of course, it is one thing to assert that monetary changes are the key to major movements in money income; it is quite a different thing to know in any detail what is the mechanism that links monetary change to economic change; how the influence of the one is transmitted to the other; what sectors of the economy will be affected first; what the time pattern of the impacts will be, and so on. We have great confidence in the first assertion. We have little confidence in our knowledge of the transmission mechanism, except in such broad and vague terms as to constitute little more than an impressionistic representation rather than an engineering blueprint. Indeed, this is the challenge our evidence poses: to pin down the transmission mechanism in specific enough detail that we can hope to make reasonably accurate predictions of the course of a wide variety of economic variables on the basis of information about monetary disturbances. In the section below on the relation between variations in income and money, we outline one part of the transmission mechanism which can account for the greater amplitude of variation in income than in money and on which we have some empirical evidence; in the last section, we sketch in a much more tentative way the major channels through which monetary fluctuations might be able to account for economic fluctuations, both the major movements we have so far been considering, and the minor movements to which we now turn.

B. Minor Economic Fluctuations

The case for a monetary explanation is not nearly so strong for the minor U.S. economic fluctuations that we have classified as mild depression cycles as the case is for the major economic fluctuations. Clearly, the view that monetary change is important does not preclude the existence of other factors that affect the course of business or that account for the quasi-rhythmical character of business fluctuations. We have no doubt that other factors play a role. Indeed, if the evidence we had were solely for the minor movements, it seems to us most unlikely that we could rule out—or even assign a probability much lower than 50 per cent to—the possibility that the close relation between money and business reflected primarily the influence of business on money.

If we are inclined to assign a probability much lower than 50 per cent, it is primarily because the evidence for minor movements does not stand alone. If money plays an independent role in major movements, is it likely to be almost passive in minor movements? The minor movements can be interpreted as less virulent members of the same species as the major movements. Is not a common explanation for both more appealing than separate explanations, especially when there is no well-tested alternative separate explanation?

A fully satisfactory explanation of the minor movements would require an explicit and rigorously stated theory, which could take the form of a series of simultaneous differential equations describing the reaction mechanism of the economy, together with a specification of the joint distribution function of the random disturbances impinging on it, and a specification of the systematic disturbances that could be introduced into it. Our belief that money plays an important role in minor movements is equivalent to asserting that some of these differential equations would contain the stock of money as a variable; that disturbances in the stock of money are among the random or systematic disturbances impinging on the system; and that these disturbances alone would be capable of generating a path for such major economic variables as money income, prices, output, and the like, comparable to the path they actually follow during mild depression cycles.

One factor that has doubtless contributed to skepticism about a monetary theory is the fact, documented above, that fluctuations in income are wider in relative amplitude than fluctuations in the stock of money. We have seen that income velocity varies positively over the cycle, which means that income varies more widely than money. We have seen also that the standard deviation of year-to-year percentage changes in income tends to be roughly double the standard deviation of year-to-year changes in the stock of money. How is it that such small changes in money can produce so much larger changes in income? Why should marginal velocity be systematically higher than average velocity?

While we are far from having a rigorous and comprehensive theory to answer this and related questions, in the next section we outline one element of such a theory which can, in our view, explain the difference in amplitude; and later we outline even more broadly a tentative transmission mechanism.

C. Relation between Amplitude of Cyclical Variations in Income and Money

One of us has elsewhere suggested that holders of money can be regarded as adjusting the nominal amount they demand to their views of their long-run income status—itself a measure of their wealth—of the long-run level of prices, and of the returns on alternative assets.[30] Let us neglect for the time being the effect of returns on other assets, as well as still other possible variables, so that we can write the relationship for the community as

$$M_d = P_p f(y_p),\tag{1}$$

where M_d is nominal amount of money per capita, P_p is permanent prices, and y_p is permanent aggregate real income per capita.[31] The capital letters here and later refer to magnitudes in nominal terms or current prices, the lower-case letters, to magnitudes in real terms or constant prices.

Let us suppose further that estimates of per capita permanent income and permanent prices are compounded of two elements: (1) an expected average annual rate of change to allow for secular trend at a rate of, say, α_y for income and α_P for prices; (2) a weighted arithmetic or geometric average of past per capita incomes and prices adjusted for such a trend.

For the present, we shall assume that α_y and α_P are both zero, or alternatively that the actual past record is replaced by the past record adjusted for trends of α_y and α_P in magnitude. At the present level of discussion, this assumption involves no loss of generality, since the only effect of nonzero values of α_y and α_P is to add secular trends without affecting cyclical fluctuations. On a more sophisticated level, it would make a difference, since both α_y and α_P might be variables in the demand function for money, the former since future prospects might modify present demand for money, the latter since it would affect the returns on some alternative assets.

We can then write:

$$P_p(T) = F[P(t); t < T]\tag{2}$$

$$y_p(T) = G[y(t); t < T],\tag{3}$$

where $P(t)$ and $y(t)$ are measured prices and measured real income per capita at time t, and the functions are to be interpreted as saying that permanent prices and income are functions of the past history of measured income or prices. If we consider discrete data, say, annual data, we can approximate equations (2) and (3) by either

$$P_p(T) = \sum_{i=0}^{\infty} w_i' P(T-i) = w_0' P(T) + (1 - w_0') P_p(T-1),\tag{2a}$$

$$y_p(T) = \sum_{i=0}^{\infty} w_i' y(T-i) = w_0' y(t) + (1 - w_0') y_p(T-1),\tag{3a}$$

30. Friedman, *The Demand for Money*, Chapter 6 above.

31. We call to the reader's attention the difference in this notation from that in *The Demand for Money*. M_d and y_p here refer to per capita money and income, whereas in the earlier paper they were used to refer to aggregate money and income. The shift was prompted by the desire to simplify the expressions that follow. The same shift is made for all variables referring to money and income. The remaining symbols all have the same meaning here as in *ibid*.

where
$$\sum w_i' = 1;$$
or by
$$\log P_p(T) = \sum_{i=0}^{\infty} w_i \log P(T-i) = w_0 \log P(T) + (1-w_0) \log P_p(T-1), \quad (2b)$$

$$\log y_p(T) = \sum_{i=0}^{\infty} w_i \log y(T-i) = w_0 \log y(T) + (1-w_0) \log y_p(T-1), \quad (3b)$$

where
$$\sum w_i = 1.$$

Note that, in both cases, we have assumed that the same weights are used for income and prices.

Suppose the community is regarded as always being on its demand curve for money. Then an increase in the stock of money will require an increase in permanent income or prices or both sufficient to make the community satisfied with the new stock of money, and these increases can be brought about only by increases in measured income or prices or both. To illustrate: Suppose, for simplicity, real measured income and real permanent income remain unchanged. Then from equation (1), a one per cent change in M will require a one per cent change in P_p. But from equation (2a) or (2b), a one per cent change in P_p will require that $P(T)$ rise by more than one per cent, or by $1/w_0'$ per cent for equation (2a) and $1/w_0$ per cent for equation (2b). But w_0' and w_0 are less than unity. Hence, the percentage rise in measured prices and income will be larger than the percentage rise in money.

To be more specific and to allow for changes in both prices and income, let us replace equation (1) by a special form we have found to work rather well empirically:

$$\frac{M}{P_p} = \gamma (y_p)^\delta, \quad (4)$$

where γ and δ are numerical constants (or, more generally, functions of omitted variables, such as returns on other assets), all the variables are at time T, and we have dropped the subscript d from M because of our assumption that the amount demanded is always equal to the amount supplied. In logarithmic form, (4) is

$$\log M(T) = \log \gamma + \log P_p(T) + \delta \log y_p(T). \quad (4a)$$

Substitute (2b) and (3b) into (4a), giving

$$\log M(T) = \log \gamma + w_0(1-\delta) \log P(T) + \delta w_0 \log Y(T)$$
$$+ (1-w_0)[\log P_p(T-1) + \delta \log y_p(T-1)], \quad (5)$$

where
$$\log Y(T) = \log y(T) + \log P(T),$$

i.e., $Y(T) =$ measured income per capita. Replace the final bracket in (5) by its equivalent from (4a) for $T-1$, namely, $[\log M(T-1) - \log \gamma]$, and then solve (5) for $\log Y(T)$. This gives

$$\log Y(T) = \frac{1}{\delta w_0} \{\log M(T) - \log \gamma - w_0(1 - \delta) \log P(T)$$

$$- (1 - w_0)[\log M(T-1) - \log \gamma]\}. \quad (6)$$

Differentiate equation 6 with respect to $\log M(T)$, allowing for the fact that $P(T)$ will change along with $Y(T)$. This gives

$$\frac{d \log Y(T)}{d \log M(T)} = \frac{1}{\delta w_0} \left[1 - w_0(1 - \delta) \frac{d \log P(T)}{d \log Y(T)} \times \frac{d \log Y(T)}{d \log M(T)} \right] \quad (7)$$

Solve for $d \log Y(T)/d \log M(T)$ to get

$$\frac{d \log Y(T)}{d \log M(T)} = \frac{1}{w_0[\delta + (1 - \delta)\eta]}, \quad (8)$$

where η is the elasticity of the measured price level with respect to measured income, and can be expected to be between zero and unity for cyclical fluctuations (i.e., both prices and output can be expected to move in the same direction as money income). We may designate $d \log Y(T)/d \log M(T)$ the money multiplier, analogous to the investment multiplier, though it should be noted that the analogy is somewhat incomplete. The money multiplier gives the ratio of the *percentage* change in income to the *percentage* change in the money stock.[32] To get the number of dollars of income change per dollar change in the stock of money, it is necessary to multiply the money multiplier by the income velocity of money.

It so happens that our earlier work furnishes empirical estimates for the United States of all the quantities entering into the right-hand side of equation (8). Hence, we can construct an estimate of the elasticity of money income with respect to the money stock. These estimates are as follows:[33]

32. Because of the assumption that α_y and α_P are zero, or alternatively that the actual past record is replaced by the past record adjusted for trend, what is here called a change in the money stock is logically equivalent to a change in the money stock relative to its trend, or to a change in the rate of change.

33. From Friedman, *The Demand for Money*, Chapter 6 above. (1) A value of $\beta = .4$ implies a weight for the first year of .33; (2) the value of δ is from equation (9) of *ibid.*; (3) the value of η is derived from Table 1 of *ibid.* by dividing the entry for "implicit price deflator" in column (3) by the entry for "money income" in the same column.

With respect to (1), it should be noted that permanent income and prices were computed in *ibid.* by equations (2a) and (3a) rather than (2b) and (3b). We have nonetheless taken the resulting value of w'_0 in our present notation as an estimate of w_0. This is correct as a first approximation, but in further work it would probably be better to work directly with equations (2b) and (3b).

With respect to (3), the number used is for aggregate money income, not per capita. However, since the number is the difference between the per month rates of rise during expansion and contraction, and since population shows little response to cycles, the per capita figures would be lower by roughly the same amount for expansion and for contraction, and hence the difference would be unaffected.

$$w_0 = .33$$

$$\delta = 1.81$$

$$\eta = .20.$$

Inserting these figures in equation (8) gives

$$\text{Estimate } \frac{d \log Y(T)}{d \log M(T)} = 1.84. \tag{9}$$

This estimate is certainly remarkably close to the estimate, based on Table 4, of the ratio of the variability of income to the variability of money. It will be recalled that we there found this ratio to be almost exactly 2.0. So far as we can see, these two numbers are estimates of the same theoretical construct.[34] Yet, statistically, they are almost completely independent. The estimate in equation (9) comes from the following sources: w_0 is based on a study of the consumption function which used no data on money whatsoever; δ is based on a correlation between average cycle bases of money and estimated permanent income; and η is based on the ratio of per month cyclical amplitudes computed from average cycle patterns of money income and prices. Hence, so far as we can see, no one of these items uses in any way the intracyclical movements of money. Yet the

---

34. One way to see this is to consider the problem of estimating directly the magnitude of the money multiplier from data on actual year-to-year changes in the logarithms of income and money. The first step would be to express the first differences as deviations from some mean values, designed to be the empirical counterparts of our theoretical constructs: $\alpha_y + \alpha_P =$ the expected rate of change in money (permanent) income; and $\alpha_P + \delta\alpha_y =$ the rate of change in the stock of money that would be consistent with a rate of change of α_y in real income and α_P in prices. That is, if money income, prices, and the stock of money all changed at exactly these rates, all expectations would be realized and there would be no disturbances to set the money multiplier, as we have defined it, to work. This first step is accomplished in our moving standard deviation analysis by computing, first, moving averages, and then expressing the observed first differences as deviations from the relevant average. Call these deviations from means, $\Delta' \log Y$ and $\Delta' \log M$.

The second step would be to estimate the mean ratio of $\Delta' \log Y$ to $\Delta' \log M$. But it would be undesirable to do this by averaging the ratio of the one to the other, since either might on occasion be close to zero (i.e., the variance of the ratio is in principle infinite). It would be better to estimate a value of, say, K in

$$\Delta' \log Y = K \Delta' \log M.$$

But as a statistical matter, there is no particular reason to prefer the estimate obtained by regressing $\Delta' \log Y$ on $\Delta' \log M$ to the estimate obtained by regressing $\Delta' \log M$ on $\Delta' \log Y$. In its rigid form the money multiplier analysis would imply perfect correlation, so the two regressions would be the same except for statistical errors of estimate. The "correct" regression then depends on the magnitude of errors in $\Delta' \log Y$ and $\Delta' \log M$. As is well known, the two simple regression coefficients give upper and lower bounds to any estimates obtained by treating both variables as subject to error. The geometric mean of these two bounding estimates is precisely the ratio of the standard deviation of $\Delta' \log Y$ to the standard deviation of $\Delta' \log M$.

estimate of 2.0 based on Table 4 has in its denominator the average standard deviation of sets, containing 3, 4, 5, or 6 years, of year-to-year percentage changes in the stock of money. The close agreement of two estimates, statistically so independent, certainly strongly suggests that the theoretical structure which produced them deserves further exploration.[35]

In such further exploration it would be desirable to generalize this analysis in a number of respects. (1) η should not be treated as a numerical constant. One would expect it to be different at different stages of the cycle and under different circumstances. Under conditions of full employment and inflation, it would be unity or close to it, which—given that δ is greater than unity—would make the money multiplier a maximum of $1/w_0$, or with our estimate of w_0, 3. At the other extreme, if there were extensive unemployment, η might be close to zero (though it is by no means clear that this has been true in experience), which would make the money multiplier a minimum of $1/w_0\delta$, or with our estimates 1.67. More generally, η plays an important role not only in any theory along the general lines we have been sketching but also in income-expenditure theories.[36] It deserves much more systematic study than it has received. (2) The demand equation (4) should be expanded to include interest rates and perhaps the rate of change in prices. Though our studies suggest that these are far less important than income in affecting the demand for money, interest rates do have a statistically significant effect and, since they have a fairly regular cyclical pattern, should be included in a cyclical analysis. (3) The effect of expected trends in prices and income should be allowed for explicitly and not simply neglected, as we have done. (4) For cycle analysis, the demand equations should be estimated on a quarterly rather than annual basis. (5) In generalizing to a quarterly basis, it will no longer be satisfactory to suppose that actual and desired money balances are always equal. It will be desirable to allow instead for a discrepancy between these two totals, which the holders of balances seek to eliminate at a rate depending on the size of the discrepancy. This will introduce past money balances into the estimated demand equation not only as a proxy for prior permanent incomes but also as a determinant of the discrepancies in the process of being corrected. In addition, it will permit lag patterns other than the simple exponential kind we have used.

---

35. We have used the estimates of w_0, δ, and η above because they are available in published form. We have been experimenting further with estimating demand equations using annual data instead of cycle bases, and estimating w_0 internally from the money correlations themselves, rather than externally. This work is still tentative but one set of results may be cited, because they are at the moment the most divergent from those given above.

For the years 1885–1960, one estimate of w_0 is .22 and of δ is 2.27. Inserting these along with $\eta = .20$ into equation 8 gives an estimate of the money multiplier of 2.25, or on the other side of the estimate of 2.0 from Table 4. Interestingly enough, this estimate is very close to the ratio, formed from the geometric means of the computed standard deviations, which ranges from 2.13 to 2.31 for different numbers of terms (see footnote 12).

36. See Friedman and Meiselman, "The Relative Stability of Monetary Velocity."

III. A TENTATIVE SKETCH OF THE MECHANISM
TRANSMITTING MONETARY CHANGES

However consistent may be the relation between monetary change and economic change, and however strong the evidence for the autonomy of the monetary changes, we shall not be persuaded that the monetary changes are the source of the economic changes unless we can specify in some detail the mechanism that connects the one with the other. Though our knowledge is at the moment too meager to enable us to do this at all precisely, it may be worth sketching very broadly some of the possible lines of connection, first, in order to provide a plausible rationalization of our empirical findings; second, to show that a monetary theory of cyclical fluctuations can accommodate a wide variety of other empirical findings about cyclical regularities; and third, to stimulate others to elaborate the theory and render it more specific.

Let us start by defining an Elysian state of moving equilibrium in which real income per capita, the stock of money, and the price level are all changing at constant annual rates. The relation between these rates depends on whether real income is rising or falling, whether wealth is remaining constant as a ratio to income or is rising or falling relative to income, on the behavior of relative rates of return on different forms of wealth, and on the wealth elasticity of demand for money. To simplify, let us suppose that all interest rates in real terms (i.e., adjusted for the rate of change in prices) and also the ratio of wealth to income are constant, so that the wealth elasticity of demand for money can be approximated by the elasticity of demand for money with respect to permanent income. If real income is rising at the rate of α_y per year, the stock of money demanded will then be rising at the rate of $\delta\alpha_y$ per year, where δ is the income elasticity of demand for money, and prices will be rising at the rate of $\alpha_P = \alpha_M - \delta\alpha_y$, where α_M is the rate of rise in the nominal stock of money per capita. For example, if income per capita is rising at 2 per cent per year, the stock of money at 4 per cent a year, and δ is $3/2$ then prices would be rising at 1 per cent a year.[37] If δ and α_y were to be the same, and the stock of money were to rise at, say, 10 per cent a year, prices would be rising at the rate of 7 per cent a year; if the stock of money were to be declining at 10 per cent a year, prices would be falling at the rate of 13 per cent a year.[38]

37. These are roughly the actual values of α_y, α_P, and α_M over the 90 years 1870–1960 in the U.S. They yield a rather smaller value of δ (1.5) than we estimate by multiple regression techniques (roughly 1.8).

38. It may seem strange that a 1 percentage point difference in the rate of change of the stock of money produces precisely a 1 percentage point difference in the rate of change of prices regardless of the magnitude of the rate of change of money. Will there not, it is tempting to say, be a flight from money as the rate of change in prices and hence the cost of holding money rises? The answer is that we are comparing states of equilibrium, not the transition from one state to another. In a world in which prices are rising at 7 per cent a year, the stock of money will be smaller relative to income (i.e., velocity will be higher) than it

Let us now suppose that an unexpected rise to a new level occurs in the rate of change in the money stock, and it remains there indefinitely—a single shock, as it were, displacing the time path of the money stock. In tracing the hypothetical effects of the higher rate of growth of the money stock, there will be some difference in detail depending on the source of the increase—whether from gold discoveries, or central bank open-market purchases, or government expenditures financed by fiat money, or a rise in the deposit-currency ratio, or a rise in the deposit-reserve ratio. To be definite, therefore, let us suppose it comes from an increased rate of open-market purchases by a central bank.

Although the initial sellers of the securities purchased by the central bank were willing sellers, this does not mean that they want to hold the proceeds in money indefinitely. The bank offered them a good price, so they sold; they added to their money balances as a temporary step in rearranging their port-folios. If the seller was a commercial bank, it now has larger reserves than it has regarded before as sufficient and will seek to expand its investments and its loans at a greater rate than before. If the seller was not a commercial bank, he is not likely even temporarily to want to hold the proceeds in currency but will deposit them in a commercial bank, thereby, in our fractional reserve system, adding to the bank's reserves relative to its deposits. In either case, therefore, in our system, commercial banks become more liquid. In the second case, in addition, the nonbank seller has a higher ratio of money in his portfolio than he has had hitherto.

Both the nonbank seller and commercial banks will therefore seek to readjust their portfolios, the only difference being that the commercial banks will in the process create more money, thereby transmitting the increase in high-powered money to the total money stock. The interposition of the commercial bank in the process means that the increase in the rate of growth of the money stock, which initially was less than in high-powered money, will for a time be greater. So we have here already a mechanism working for some overshooting.

It seems plausible that both nonbank and bank holders of redundant balances will turn first to securities comparable to those they have sold, say, fixed-interest coupon, low-risk obligations. But as they seek to purchase these they will tend to bid up the prices of those issues. Hence they, and also other holders not involv-ed in the initial central bank open-market transactions, will look farther afield: the banks, to their loans; the nonbank holders, to other categories of securities —higher-risk fixed-coupon obligations, equities, real property, and so forth.

As the process continues, the initial impacts are diffused in several respects: first, the range of assets affected widens; second, potential creators of assets now more in demand are induced to react to the better terms on which they can be sold, including business enterprises wishing to engage in capital expansion, house

---

would be in a world in which prices are falling at 13 per cent a year. But, in both, velocity will be *changing* only in response to the change in real income, which is by assumption the same in the two worlds. Of course, it is possible that δ is different at different levels of cost of holding money; but that would be an effect of a rather subtler kind.

builders or prospective homeowners, consumers – who are potential purchasers of durable consumer goods—and so on and on; third, the initially redundant money balances concentrated in the hands of those first affected by the open-market purchases become spread throughout the economy.

As the prices of financial assets are bid up, they become expensive relative to nonfinancial assets, so there is an incentive for individuals and enterprises to seek to bring their actual portfolios into accord with desired portfolios by acquiring nonfinancial assets. This, in turn, tends to make existing nonfinancial assets expensive relative to newly constructed nonfinancial assets. At the same time, the general rise in the price level of nonfinancial assets tends to raise wealth relative to income, and to make the direct acquisition of current services cheaper relative to the purchase of sources of services. These effects raise demand curves for current productive services, both for producing new capital goods and for purchasing current services. The monetary stimulus is, in this way, spread from the financial markets to the markets for goods and services.

Two points need emphasis at this stage. The first is that the terms "financial markets," "assets," "investment," "rates of interest" and "portfolio" must, in order to be consistent with the existing empirical evidence, be interpreted much more broadly than they often are. It has been common to restrict attention to a small class of marketable financial securities and the real capital it finances, to regard "the" rate of interest as the market yield on such securities, and the "investment" which is affected by changes in the rate of interest as solely or mainly the items classified as "capital formation" in national income accounts. Some of the empirical results summarized earlier are inconsistent with this view.[39] To rationalize the results, it is necessary to take a much broader view, to regard the relevant portfolios as containing a much wider range of assets, including not only government and private fixed-interest and equity securities traded on major financial markets, but also a host of other assets, even going so far as to include consumer durable goods, consumer inventories of clothing and the like and, maybe also, such human capital as skills acquired through training, and the like. Similarly, it is necessary to make "rate of interest" an equally broad construct, covering explicit or implicit rates on the whole spectrum of assets.[40]

The second point is to note how readily these tentative lines on our sketch accommodate some of the documented regularities of business cycles. The cyclical counterpart to our assumed initial shock is the rise in the rate of growth of the money stock that generally occurs early in contraction. On the basis of the sketch so far, we should expect it to have its first impact on the financial markets, and there, first on bonds, and only later on equities, and only still later on actual flows of payments for real resources. This is of course the actual pattern. The financial markets tend to revive well before the trough. Historically, railroad bond prices have risen very early in the process. Equity markets start to recover

39. In particular, those in Friedman and Meiselman, "The Relative Stability of Monetary Velocity."

40. See *ibid.* for a fuller discussion of these points.

later but still generally before the business trough. Actual expenditures on purchases of goods and services rise still later. The consistent tendency for orders to lead actual purchases would of course be expected on this theory, but it would follow simply from the mechanics of the production process. Hence it gives no definite support to this or any other theory. It is simply a stage in the way any impulse, however generated, will be transmitted. The tendency for the prices of financial assets to rise early in the pattern is quite a different matter. If the initial impulse were generated by an autonomous increase in spending on final goods and services, it would be plausible to expect the timing to be the reverse of what it actually is. Of course, on the theory being sketched, the precise timing will depend on the source of the initial monetary impulse. However, under the banking structure of the United States and other financially developed countries, whatever the initial impulse, commercial banks will play a key role in transforming it into an increased rate of growth in the money stock, and this will impose a large measure of uniformity on the outcome.

One other feature of cyclical experience that our sketch may be able to rationalize and that is worthy of special note is the behavior of the deposit-currency ratio. The initial monetary impulse is concentrated among holders of financial assets and is then diffused to the rest of the community. But this means, as we have noted, that the redundant balances are initially in the hands of asset holders with a high ratio of deposits to currency. As the redundant balances are diffused, they spread to a more nearly representative group in the population. Consistently with this sequence, the ratio of deposits to currency starts to rise early in contraction, not very far removed in time from the trough in the rate of rise in the money stock; the deposit-currency ratio continues to rise during the rest of contraction and early expansion but then reaches a peak around mid-expansion, and falls. The turning point, on this sketch, reflects the point at which the net tide of redundant balances has shifted from the financial community to the rest of the community.

To return to our sketch, we had reached the stage at which the demand for the services of factors of production was rising, which means, of course, a rise in money incomes. This will tend to be partly reflected in a rise of the prices of resources and of final goods; at the same time, the prices of nonfinancial assets will already have been rising as demand shifted to them from financial assets. These price rises themselves tend to correct portfolios by making the real value of monetary assets less than they otherwise would be. The result is to reduce the relative redundancy of monetary assets, which sets the stage for a rise in the structure of interest rates in place of the prior decline. The exact sequence of rises in prices, whether it affects first prices of final products, and only later prices of factors and so shifts profit margins—and so on—depends on the structure of the product and factor markets. Like the relation between new orders and production, this is part of the transmission mechanism common to all theories and tells little or nothing about the generating impulse. This does not mean it is unimportant. On the contrary, it may well determine the sequence of events once the stage is reached at which income is rising, as well as the time duration of subsequent reactions.

However, the important point for our purposes is very different. It is that the process we have described will tend to overshoot the mark; it will not simply produce a smooth movement to the new path consistent with the new rate of growth of the money stock assumed to prevail. There are two classes of reasons embodied in our analysis that explain why the process will overshoot. One, and in our view the more basic theoretically, has to do with the demand for money. At the higher rate of price rise that is the new ultimate equilibrium, the amount of money demanded will be less in real terms than it was initially, relative to wealth and hence income. But this means that, in the process of going from the initial to the new equilibrium, prices must rise at a faster rate than their ultimate rate. Hence the rate of price rise must overshoot. This effect is reinforced by that embodied in the model of subsection II C. above. In the initial stages of the process, money holders overestimate the extent of monetary redundancy, since they evaluate money stocks at unduly low levels of prices; they are slow, that is, to revise their estimates of permanent prices upward, hence they initially seek more radical readjustments in their portfolios than will ultimately turn out to be required. (If this analysis is applied to a cyclical process rather than to our special case of a shift from one moving equilibrium to another, a second element from that model would also enter to produce overshooting—a slow revision of estimates of permanent real income.) The second class of reasons for overshooting has to do with feedback effects through the monetary mechanism. Two of these have already been mentioned. First, the effect of the initial assumed shock is to cause a greater rate of rise in high-powered money than in the money stock as a whole. But since there is nothing about the shock that will permanently alter the ratio of money to high-powered money, it follows that the money stock must for a time grow faster than ultimately in order to catch up. Second, there is reason for the deposit-currency ratio to rise in the initial stages of the process above its long-run equilibrium level. In addition to these two classes of reasons for overshooting, which derive from the specifically monetary elements in our sketch, there may of course be those arising from the other elements of the transmission mechanism common to almost any theory.

The tendency to overshoot means that the dynamic process of transition from one equilibrium path to another involves a cyclical adjustment process. Presumably, these cyclical adjustments will be damped, though no merely verbal exposition can suffice to assure that the particular mechanism described will have that property. Presumably also, the extent of over-shooting will not be negligible relative to the disturbance, though again no merely verbal exposition can suffice to assure that the mechanism described will have that property.

The passage from this analysis of a single displacement of the rate of growth of money to a monetary theory of partly self-generating cyclical fluctuations is direct and has in large part been embodied in the preceding statement. It may be worth noting, however, that it would be rather more plausible to suppose a shock to take the form of an unusually high or low rate of growth of the stock of money for some time, with a reversion to a previous level rather than a shift to a permanently new level. Such a shock is equivalent to two shocks of the kind we have been considering—but shocks in opposite directions. Hence the shock itself gives rise to a cyclical movement in addition to the cyclical adjustment to each shock separately. The fact that in the cycle there is never that complete adjustment to the existing state of affairs that is present in the assumed initial Elysian state of moving equilibrium is of no decisive importance. It merely means that one state of incomplete adjustment succeeds another and that successive widenings and narrowings of discrepancies between actual and desired portfolios replace the introduction of a discrepancy and the correction of it. As noted parenthetically earlier, of somewhat more moment are the fluctuations in real income and employment over the cycle, which introduce an important reason for overshooting.

The central element in the transmission mechanism, as we have outlined it, is the concept of cyclical fluctuations as the outcome of balance sheet adjustments, as the effects on flows of adjustments between desired and actual stocks. It is this interconnection of stocks and flows that stretches the effect of shocks out in time, produces a diffusion over different economic categories, and gives rise to cyclical reaction mechanisms. The stocks serve as buffers or shock absorbers of initial changes in rates of flow, by expanding or contracting from their "normal" or "natural" or "desired" state, and then slowly alter other flows as holders try to regain that state.

In this stock-flow view, money is a stock in a portfolio of assets, like the stocks of financial assets, or houses, or buildings, or inventories, or people, or skills. It yields a flow of services as these other assets do; it is also subject to increase or decrease through inflows and outflows, as the other assets are. It is because our thinking has increasingly moved in this direction that it has become natural to us to regard the rate of change in the stock of money as comparable to income flows and to regard changes in the rate of change as a generating force in producing cyclical fluctuations in economic activity.

IV. SUMMARY

The statistical evidence on the role of money in business cycles assembled in Section I demonstrates beyond any reasonable doubt that the stock of money displays a systematic cyclical behavior. The rate of change in the money stock regularly reaches a peak before the reference peak and a trough before the reference trough, though the lead is rather variable. The amplitude of the cyclical movement in money is closely correlated with the amplitude of the cyclical movement in general business and is about half as large as the amplitude of cyclical movements in money income. The most important single determinant, from the supply side, of the cyclical pattern of money is the cyclical pattern in the division of the public's money holdings between currency and deposits. The stock of money is much more closely and systematically related to income over business cycles than is investment or autonomous expenditures.

In Section II we suggested plausible interpretations of these facts, pointing out that the close relation tells nothing directly about whether the cyclical changes in money are simply a consequence of the changes in income or are in large measure the source of those changes. For major movements in income, we concluded that there is an extremely strong case for the position that sizable changes in the rate of change in the money stock are a necessary and sufficient condition for sizable changes in the rate of change in money income. For minor movements, we concluded that, while the evidence was far less strong, it is plausible to suppose that changes in the stock of money played an important independent role, though certainly the evidence for these minor movements does not rule out other interpretations. In Section II C, we formalized one element of a theory designed to account for the observed tendency of cyclical fluctuations in income to be wider in amplitude than cyclical fluctuations in money. The theory, plus earlier empirical work, yielded an independent statistical estimate of what we call the money multiplier, or the ratio of the percentage change in income to the associated percentage change in the stock of money. The independent estimate was 1.84; the directly observed ratio 2.0. This agreement does not reflect any common statistical origin of the two estimates. It therefore suggests that further elaboration of the theory might be well worthwhile.

Finally, in Section III, we sketched in broad strokes the kind of transmission mechanism that could explain how monetary changes can produce cyclical fluctuations in income, and that is consistent with our knowledge of economic interrelationships. The final picture that might ultimately develop out of this sketch could be of a partly self-generating cyclical mechanism. Disturbances in the rate of change in the money stock set in train a cyclical adjustment mechanism.including a feedback to the rate of change in money itself. Additional disturbances from time to time would prevent the fluctuations from dying out. The mechanism emphasizes the reciprocal adjustment of stocks to flows, with money playing a key role as a component of the stock of assets. We emphasize that this sketch is exceedingly tentative and, of course, not preclusive. The mechanism outlined can be combined with other adjustment mechanisms.

Chapter 11

The Lag in Effect of

Monetary Policy

FOR SOME YEARS NOW, I have been engaged in extensive empirical studies of the relation between the stock of money and economic activity. Though a full report on this work is not yet in print, and will not be for some time, I have had occasion to summarize some of the results in a paper submitted to the Joint Economic Committee, in subsequent testimony before that committee, and in a series of lectures on monetary policy.[1] These necessarily condensed and pre-liminary statements of results without the full evidence underlying them have apparently given some readers a misleading impression of the exact content of the findings and of the kind and strength of the empirical evidence underlying

Reprinted from *The Journal of Political Economy*, vol. 69, no. 5, October 1961, I am indebted to J. M. Clark, Harry G. Johnson, David Meiselman, Harry V. Roberts, Anna J. Schwartz, and members of the Money and Banking Workshop of the University of Chicago for helpful criticisms of an earlier draft of this note.

1. The earliest and most complete summary of results is contained in "The Supply of Money and Changes in Prices and Output," in U.S. Congress, Joint Economic Committee, *The Relationship of Prices to Economic Stability and Growth: Compendium* (Doc. No. 23734 [Washington: Government Printing Office, March 31, 1958]), pp. 241–56, hereinafter referred to as "*Compendium*" (Chapter 9 above).

Other items are: Statements before the Joint Economic Committee and the transcript of subsequent discussion in U.S. Congress, Joint Economic Committee, *Hearings on Employment, Growth, and Price Levels* (86th Cong., 1st sess. [Washington: Government Printing Office, 1959]), Part IV, pp. 605–69, and Part IXA, pp. 3019–53; and *A Program for*

238 THE OPTIMUM QUANTITY OF MONEY AND OTHER ESSAYS

them. I therefore welcome the opportunity offered by J. M. Culbertson's recent thoughtful criticism of my views to clarify some of these issues.[2]

The central empirical finding in dispute is my conclusion that monetary actions affect economic conditions only after a lag that is both long and variable. Culbertson infers that the major evidence leading me to this conclusion is the timing of peaks and troughs in the rate of change of the stock of money relative to peaks and troughs in general business. He regards this evidence as faulty on three grounds:

1. It refers to the rate of change in the stock of money and not its level.
2. It relates turning points in one series to turning points in business rather than to "the point at which things begin to go differently than they would have in the absence of the action."
3. It "implies that monetary change has been an exogenous variable and that causation runs only from monetary change to economic developments. In fact . . . causation also has run in the other direction."

As counterevidence, Culbertson argues that:

4. "The suprising moderateness of the economic fluctuations that we have suffered in the past decade" is direct testimony against a long and variable lag, since such a lag in the effects of policy actions would imply a similar lag in the "natural stabilizing forces."

Monetary Stability, New York: Fordham University Press (1959), esp. pp. 9–22 and 87–88.

Two monographs by Anna J. Schwartz and me report in full on our joint study for the National Bureau of Economic Research. The first presents an analytical narrative of the historical background of the stock of money. It has appeared since this article was first published under the title, A Monetary History of the United States, 1867–1960, Princeton, N.J.: Princeton University Press for the National Bureau of Economic Research (1963). The second, tentatively entitled The Secular and Cyclical Behavior of the Stock of Money in the United States, 1867–1960, has been subdivided into three monographs, none of which has yet appeared. They will present a statistical analysis.

A monograph by Phillip Cagan reports on another phase of the National Bureau study. This monograph has appeared under the title Determinants and Effects of Changes in the Money Stock, 1875–1960, New York: National Bureau of Economic Research, 1965.

A preliminary report to the Commission on Money and Credit by David Meiselman and myself entitled The Relative Stability of the Investment Multiplier and Monetary Velocity in the United States, 1897–1958, reports on part of a separate study under the auspices of the Workshop in Money and Banking at the University of Chicago. This study is intended to cover a considerable number of other countries as well as the United States. The report dealing with the United States has been published by the Commission in Stabilization Policies, Englewood Cliffs, N.J.: Prentice-Hall (1963), pp. 165–268.

2. "Friedman on the Lag in Effect of Monetary Policy," Journal of Political Economy, LXVIII (December, 1960), 617–21. The other main items that have come to my attention and that reflect the same or related misconceptions are J. M. Clark, The Wage-Price Problem, New York: American Bankers Association (1960), p. 5, n.; James R. Schlesinger, "The Friedman Proposal of a Fixed Monetary Rule," Rivista di diritto finanze, 1960, n. 8; Albert Ando, E. Cary Brown, R. M. Solow, and John Karaken, "Lags in Fiscal and Monetary Policy," a paper prepared for the Commission on Money and Credit, and published in Stabilization Policies, pp. 1–163.

His own conclusion is that:

5. "The broad record of experience . . . support[s] the view that anticyclical monetary, debt-management, and fiscal adjustments can be counted on to have their predominant direct effects within three to six months, soon enough that if they are undertaken moderately early in a cyclical phase they will not be destabilizing."

On policy issues, Culbertson makes two main points:

6. Even if the lag were long and variable, this fact would not by itself determine appropriate stabilization policy. It would imply that "policies should not attempt to be actively anticyclical but should behave in a manner that is cyclically neutral. However . . . there would be considerable disagreement as to what constitutes 'neutrality' in this connection."
7. He finds me "guilty of an inconsistency in reaffirming in connection with . . . the lag doctrine the automatic system [I] prescribed earlier for stabilization policy."[3]

I shall consider first the questions of fact and then, more briefly, the policy issues.

The empirical conclusion that Culbertson questions consists of three separable parts, each important in its own right. The conclusion is that changes in the behavior of the stock of money (A) exert an important independent influence on the subsequent course of events with a lag that is (B) on the average sizable and (C) highly variable, relative to the usual length of cyclical movements.[4]

It is important to distinguish these three parts for two reasons. First, the evidence for them is very different. For example, the items in Culbertson's critique I have numbered 1 and 2 refer primarily to Part B and have little or no relevance to either A or C; item 4 refers primarily to C. Second, their relevance to policy is also very different. Part A is a precondition for any effective monetary policy, and Culbertson clearly accepts it despite item 3. Given A, either B or C alone would suffice to cast serious doubt on the effectiveness of discretionary monetary policy. Suppose the mean lag were zero or the 4.5 months implied in Culbertson's item 5. If the lag were highly variable, this would still mean that monetary actions in large measure introduce a random disturbing element into economic affairs. On the other hand, suppose the standard deviation of the lag were the 0.9 months or less implied in Culbertson's item 5,[5] but the mean lag were, say, 12 months. This would mean that effective monetary action requires an ability to forecast a year ahead, not an easy requirement in the present state of our knowledge.

I shall, therefore, consider each part of the empirical conclusion separately.

3. In "A Monetary and Fiscal Framework for Economic Stability," *American Economic Review*, vol. 38, June, 1948, pp. 245–64 (reprinted in my *Essays in Positive Economics*, Chicago: University of Chicago Press [1953], pp. 133–56).

4. Of course, "lag" in this context is a shorthand expression for a complex and ill-defined concept (see Section II, B below).

5. This assumes a rectangular distribution between 3 and 6 months. A unimodal distribution would, of course, imply a smaller standard deviation.

I. AUTONOMOUS INFLUENCE OF MONETARY CHANGE

There is no basic difference between Culbertson and me on this point, though there may well be between both of us and other critics. The appearance to the contrary arises only because Culbertson attributes to me a view that I do not hold and that is not implied by the factual assertions I have made, namely, the view that "causation runs *only* from monetary change to economic developments" (italics mine). Let me quote from an article of mine to which Culbertson does not refer and which he apparently has not read—most unfortunately, since it contains the fullest summary I have so far published of my views on the point at issue:

The direction of influence between the money stock and income and prices is less clear-cut and more complex for the business cycle than for the longer movements. . . . Thus changes in the money stock are a consequence as well as an independent cause of changes in income and prices, though once they occur they will in their turn produce still further effects on income and prices. This consideration blurs the relation between money and prices but does not reverse it. For there is much evidence . . . that even during business cycles the money stock plays a largely independent role.[6]

A two-way relation between monetary change and business conditions is, indeed, one reason why the lag in the effect of monetary action might be expected to be long and variable. For example, suppose we tentatively accept as correct Culbertson's expression of faith that anticyclical adjustments "have their predominant direct effects within three to six months." This would be decisive for policy only if "predominent direct effects"—whatever this phrase be taken to mean—approximated total effects. However, a feedback from business conditions to money means further indirect effects as the induced changes in money exert their influence in turn, and so on ad infinitum, though presumably with diminishing amplitude. The more important the feedback, the larger will be these indirect effects and the longer, and presumably also the more variable, will be the average lag between a monetary adjustment and the whole of its effects.

What evidence is there for the "largely independent" cyclical role of the money stock? One piece is the empirically observed tendency for monetary changes to precede changes in general business, to which Culbertson's items 1 and 2 refer. While this is a suggestive bit of evidence, on which I shall have more to say in Section II, I agree with Culbertson that it is by no means decisive. One series may precede another in time not because the first influences the second but because both are the common result of still other forces and these common forces have a quicker impact on the first than on the second. For example, movements in stock market prices on the average precede movements in business. My own conjecture is that the explanation is neither that the stock market exerts any significant influence on business nor that traders in the market are

6. *Compendium*, p. 249 (Chapter 9 above).

good forecasters but that both the stock market and business reflect the influence of monetary changes, which precede both but operate more quickly on prices of equities than on flows of money expenditures. And, of course, there are still other possible explanations of an apparently consistent lead of one series over another.

As Culbertson suspects, there is other and much stronger evidence for the largely independent role of money. The most important is from an examination of the historical circumstances accompanying changes in the stock of money. There are numerous episodes for which it is crystal clear that the factors producing the changes in the stock of money were predominantly independent of the contemporaneous or prior course of business, except as these may have affected the actions of monetary authorities; for example, during wars, or in 1873–79, in 1890–96, in 1920–21, or in 1937–38. In this note, I can clearly only refer to this evidence, not give it.[7]

A third kind of evidence is from examination of the effect of substantial differences in monetary arrangements on the relation between cyclical movements in money and in general business. Suppose the main channel of influence is from money to business. Then the monetary arrangements matter but only because they affect directly the movements in money itself; there is no reason for the relation between the movements in money and in general business to be different under different monetary arrangements; the relation will be determined primarily by the channels through which money affects business. Suppose, alternatively, that the main channel of influence is from business to money. A change in business then affects the money stock only through the monetary institutions and may have very different effects under different monetary arrangements. Under one set of arrangements, for example, business expansion may produce a contraction in the stock of money; under another, an expansion; or if the effects are in the same direction, the effects may differ in amplitude or in timing.[8] For the United States for a century, we have found that cyclical

7. See brief references in the *Compendium* article (Chapter 9 above) and chap. i of *A Program for Monetary Stability*. The first of the two monographs by Anna J. Schwartz and myself referred to in n. 1 examines the whole period from 1867 to date in considerable detail.

The desire to accumulate historical evidence for specific episodes as a check on the direction of influence stimulated a number of studies done as doctoral theses under the auspices of the Workshop in Money and Banking at the University of Chicago, notably by Eugene Lerner, "Inflation in the Confederacy, 1861–65," in Milton Friedman (ed.), *Studies in the Quantity Theory of Money* (Chicago: University of Chicago Press, 1956), pp. 163–75; James Kindahl, "The Economics of Resumption: The United States 1865–1879," and George Macesich, "Monetary Disturbances in the United States 1834–45," both unpublished Ph.D. theses at the University of Chicago.

8. For example, before World War I, a business expansion in the United States tended to generate a deficit in the balance of payments, an outflow of gold, and downward pressure on the stock of money. This particular influence, and it was an important one in those days, therefore made for an inverted relation between cyclical movements in business and in money. After World War I, the changed character of the gold standard and the establish-

movements in money have apparently had much the same relation in both timing and amplitude to cyclical movements in business under very different monetary arrangements, though of course the movements in money or in business alone have been very different.[9]

Taken together, these three kinds of evidence establish a strong presumption that changes in the stock of money play a largely independent role in cyclical fluctuations, though of course they give only indirect testimony on the importance of that role in determining the timing and character of the cyclical fluctuations in general business.

II. THE LENGTH OF THE LAG

Culbertson apparently takes it as self-evident that timing comparisons between peaks and troughs in the rate of change of the money stock and in general business are "misleading," and that the relevant comparison is between the rate of change of the money stock and the rate of change of general business or between the level of the money stock and general business. It has become a commonplace of economics as a result of discussion of the acceleration principle that the rate of change of a smooth cyclical series will tend to move in the same direction as the series itself roughly one-quarter of a cycle earlier (of course, it will also do so three-quarters of a cycle later, and move in the opposite direction three-quarters of a cycle earlier and one-quarter of a cycle later; on arithmetic considerations alone each of these has as much claim to consideration as the particular relation Culbertson singles out). Hence, says Culbertson, "on a more [sic] proper basis of comparison the 'lag' might largely disappear."

Since Culbertson is in distinguished company in regarding these considerations alone as constituting a devastating criticism of some of the timing comparisons

---

ment of the Federal Reserve System rendered this influence mostly absent or minor and introduced another working in the opposite direction. Business expansion raised interest rates and thereby stimulated banks to increase their borrowings from the Federal Reserve System, tending to make for positive conformity between cyclical movements in business and in money. Needless to say, this is not intended to be a full analysis of the connection between business and money either before or after World War I.

9. Evidence for this assertion will be presented in the second of the two monographs by Anna J. Schwartz and me referred to in n. 1.

Additional evidence somewhat more detailed in character is contained in the related monograph by Phillip Cagan. Cagan isolates the statistical determinants of changes in the stock of money and examines the relation of each to changes in business conditions, thereby developing an ingenious technique for getting additional information on whether the direction of influence is from business to money or money to business.

More recently, George Macesich has been examining for Canada the timing of changes in the stock of money relative to movements in general business. This is another good test case, since the Canadian and United States financial structures differ substantially. Macesich finds roughly the same timing for Canada as Mrs. Schwartz and I have found for the United States.

I have published, a rather full examination of the appropriate way to measure lags is perhaps in order.[10] The mathematical relation between a series and its derivative can hardly by itself dictate what series it is economically relevant to compare with what other series.

Four main points require attention: (a) The general considerations bearing on the comparisons that are likely to be the most meaningful are of three kinds: dimensional, statistical, and economic. These can at most be suggestive. For what they are worth, however, they suggest that comparison of the rate of change in the stock of money with the level of business is likely to be more meaningful for cyclical analysis than either of the comparisons Culbertson and others prefer. (b) Any single comparison by itself may not be sufficient for either scientific description or policy guidance. "The" lag is a sophisticated and complex concept. (c) We have in fact made a number of different comparisons, and recent experience has provided a particularly striking quasi-experiment, all of which are consistent with a long lag in the effect of monetary actions. (d) Consideration of the channels through which monetary policy may be expected to operate renders a long lag highly plausible.

A. Dimensional, Statistical, and Economic Considerations

We must beware of semantic traps. Because we speak of the "level" of business and also the "level" of the stock of money, it does not follow that these are necessarily comparable magnitudes. By the "level of business" we generally refer to a flow: the number of dollars of expenditures per year; man-hours of employment or unemployment per year; cars produced per year—all magnitudes having the dimensions of dollars or physical units *per unit of time*. The "level" of the stock of money refers to an amount at a point in time, to a stock not a flow. Its dimensions are simply dollars, not dollars per unit of time. The rate of change of the stock of money on the other hand, does have the dimensions of dollars per unit of time and therefore has the same dimensions as the so-called level of business.

It may help to make the same point in terms of economic categories. Investment in inventories, which is a component of national income, is the derivative (or rate of change) of the stock of inventories; net investment in residential construction is the derivative of the stock of houses; and so on. Indeed, every item in the flow of income can be regarded as the derivative of a corresponding stock, though no doubt it is forcing matters to treat in this way such items as the rental value to the owner-occupant of the services of the land he occupies.[11] From this

10. Clark dismisses the comparison I have made as "fallacious," like Culbertson, entirely on the grounds that the derivative of a cyclical curve will lead the curve by a quarter-cycle and Schlesinger quotes Clark with apparent assent. Ando, Brown, Solow, and Karaken are less succinct but hardly any more sophisticated (see references in n. 2).

11. Moreover, it should be noted that the income flow need not be the only source of

point of view, the stock of money is comparable to the stock of housing or to the stock of durable goods, in short, to wealth rather than to income. The imputed value of the services rendered by the stock of money is comparable to such income items as the rental value of land; the rate of change of the stock of money is comparable to such items as residential construction, production of durable consumer goods, net investment in inventories, and so on. Similarly, the rate of change of business is a second derivative of a stock comparable dimensionally not to the rate of change of money stock but to the second derivative of the money stock.

These dimensional considerations are suggestive, but they are not the primary grounds on which one should determine what comparisons are most meaningful. The crucial question is not arithmetic but substantive: What relations are empirically stable and dependable? What form of expressing variables yields the simplest and most easily handled relations? For example, the quantity equation in its income form relates money as a stock to income as a flow, the dimensional difference being allowed for by velocity, which has the units of the reciprocal of time. If velocity were a numerical constant over the cycle, either for contemporaneous money and income or for the variables separated by a fairly fixed time difference, or even if velocity were a highly regular function of a few variables, the quantity equation might be the most useful relation over the cycle —as indeed we have found it to be for longer secular movements. But even then, of course, *if* the rate of change of the stock of money were a good predictor of the movements in money, it would by that same token be a good predictor of movements in income. The consistency of the relation would offer a a challenge to theory and an opportunity to policy, but, to repeat a point already made, the timing relations would not by themselves be decisive about the direction of influence.

We have accordingly placed heavier reliance on statistical and economic considerations than on purely dimensional ones.

The chief statistical consideration is the problem of allowing for trend. The availablity of National Bureau of Economic Research reference cycle dates gives a general-purpose timing scale that obviates the necessity of choosing any single series as an index of that elusive concept "general business." The reference chronology can be used to explore the timing relation between another series and general business by estimating for that other series a set of dates to be regarded as comparable to reference cycle peaks and troughs.[12] This is a fairly

---

change in the stock. Capital consumption is not treated as a deduction from income for many items (for example, consumer durable goods, human capital) so the corresponding flows are gross or the derivatives of a gross stock; in addition, most income estimates do not treat so-called capital gains or losses as components of the income flow; that is, they regard some changes in wealth as taking place independently of the income flow.

12. We generally visualize the reference dates as corresponding to turning points in some index of general business, but it should be recognized that they are much more complex and less easily specifiable in principle than that. For example, in principle, the turning dates in a

crude technique for estimating timing relations—I take it that this is the gravamen of item 2 in Culbertson's critique[13]—and should preferably be supplemented by other techniques as we have in fact done to a limited extent (see below, Sec. C). But it is one of the few techniques currently available in anything like tested form;[14] it is the only technique for which there is a large stock of comparable results for other series; and, by rendering it unnecessary to choose a particular series to represent general business, it not only saves much labor, but more important, permits comparable observations over a much longer period.

The technique is reasonably straightforward for a series that shows clearly

---

measure of aggregate "real" output will be different than in aggregate value of output, or in aggregate employment, or in real output per capita, or value of output per capita, and so on; yet there is no clear reason to choose one rather than another. It is an empirical finding that the Bureau chronology is in fact reasonably reproducible and meaningful despite the failure to define precisely its meaning in terms of some single such measure (see A. F. Burns and W. C. Mitchell, *Measuring Business Cycles*, New York: National Bureau of Economic Research [1946], esp. pp. 71–76).

13. Unless this be his point, I must confess that I do not know what Culbertson is getting at in his point 2 on p. 620, which I have tried to summarize in item 2. A change in monetary policy need not, of course, show up immediately as a peak or trough in the rate of change of money, and generally will not. It will at first presumably affect the second or some higher derivative of the stock of money and only after some time reverse the direction of the first derivative. But similarly, insofar as changes in money affect business conditions, they will have a similarly drawn out and distributed effect on the course of business. For example, the initial tendency for "tight" monetary action simply to slow down, say, the rate at which the rate of change in the money supply is rising may, after a lag, only slow down the rate at which business is rising, that is, in Culbertson's words, at that point make "things begin to go differently than they would have in the absence of the action." It may well be some time before the cumulative effects of the monetary actions produce a decline in the rate of change in the stock of money, and also some time before the cumulative effects of the altered behavior of the monetary stock produces a peak in business (see also discussion in Sec. II, B below). A comparison of the peak in the rate of change of money with a peak in economic activity uses only a small part of the potential information on timing relations and hence is inefficient. But I do not see why it should be biased in one direction or the other.

In the rest of his point 2 on p. 620, if I interpret Culbertson rightly, he is saying that the time delay between monetary action and its effects may vary with circumsntaces, depending on "other forces"; for example, the length of time since a business-cycle trough. This is almost certainly so and is one of the reasons why the lag might be expected to be variable. Of course, if one knew the "other forces" that determined the length of the lag, they could be taken into account in policy determination and the associated variability in the lag might be no obstacle to policy. Culbertson concludes instead that "this difference in outcome could not properly be interpreted as a difference in the 'lag in the effect of monetary policy.'" This seems to me simply wrong.

14. Multiple correlation with lagged variables is about the only other. This is one reason why I have myself become very much interested in cross-spectral analysis since it offers a potentially more efficient way to extract information about timing relations from our recalcitrant time series. The experiments I have so far made under John Tukey's expert tuition are as yet inconclusive. Jon Cunnyngham is currently making a more thorough and extensive study of its potentialities for economic time series.

marked ups and downs roughly comparable in duration to reference cycle phases. Consider, however, series like the total stock of housing or the total stock of money, which generally rise during both expansions and contractions in general business. This fact does not mean that either series is unrelated to the cycle, whether as cause or effect. But it does mean that the cyclical behaviour of the series cannot be described in terms simply of ups and downs; and equally that the occasional turning points in either series are inadequate indicators of their cyclical timing.

The obvious statistical solution is to separate the cyclical behavior of such series from their secular behavior by allowing in one way or another for trend. The two most common ways of doing so are either to express the data in terms of deviations from a trend or to use first differences.[15] The use of first differences, where it is applicable, has great advantages over the fitting of trends. True, first differences have the disadvantage of often yielding a rather erratic, choppy series with serial correlation of successive items. But they require no decision about the kind of trend to fit or the period to cover, the observations for any one period do not depend on the far distant observations for other periods that affect fitted trends, and the series can be extended backward or forward without either recomputing or extrapolating trends. It so happens that first differences of the logarithms of the stock of money (that is, percentage rates of change) display no significant trend. Hence statistical considerations on the whole recommend this device for describing the cyclical behavior of the money series.[16]

Economic considerations reinforce the statistical, in respect both to the desirability of allowing for trend and of doing so by using percentage rates of change. A trend in the stock of money, almost whatever it might be, is unlikely to give rise to cyclical fluctuations if it is widely and correctly anticipated. Deviations from the expected longer period movement in the stock of money seem far more relevant for cyclical fluctuations than the stock of money itself. At the same time, there is no reason to expect a single long-time trend to prevail of the kind that one might approximate or extrapolate by curve-fitting. Throughout the period we have studied, the stock of money in the United States has been subject to control by political authorities, either by alteration of the monetary arrangements, or, more recently, by continuous discretionary control. Any trend is therefore a creation of the authorities. Nothing outside the political

15. It should be noted that there are many other devices for allowing for trend in part or whole without actually fitting trends. For example, expressing the series in real terms rather than money terms or as per capita rather than as an aggregate may reduce the secular element relative to the cyclical.

16. As I shall note later, we have also used an approximation to turning points in deviations from a trend.

Clark Warburton has used deviations from a fitted trend with considerable success (see Clark Warburton, "The Volume of Money and the Price Level between World Wars," *Journal of Political Economy*, vol. 54, June, 1945, pp. 153–54; "The Theory of Turning Points in Business Fluctuations," *Quarterly Journal of Economics*, vol. 64, November, 1950).

sphere prevents a shift from one trend to another or produces a return to an earlier trend after a departure, though, of course, both the effects of given monetary arrangements and the actions taken by discretionary authorities will be conditioned, if not determined, by contemporaneous and past economic developments. Hence, we must allow for a trend that can shift drastically from time to time. The use of first differences does so.

Still another set of economic considerations recommends the logarithmic first difference of the stock of money (percentage rate of change) as the relevant magnitude for cyclical analysis. Consider a hypothetical long-run moving equilibrium in which both output and the stock of money are rising at constant percentage rates, the rise being fully anticipated so that actual, expected, and desired stocks of money are equal. The result would tend to be a roughly constant percentage rate of change in prices, which might of course be zero or negative.[17] The percentage rate of change in prices itself is the opportunity cost of holding money rather than goods, so a constant percentage rate of change in the stock of money corresponds to a constant opportunity cost of holding money rather than goods. An unanticipated change in the rate of change of the stock of money would then produce a deviation of the actual from the desired stock of money for two reasons: initially, it would make the actual stock deviate from the expected stock and therefore from the desired stock; subsequently, by altering the cost of holding money, it would change the desired stock itself. These discrepancies will set up adjustments that may very well be cyclical, involving overshooting and reversal. It is therefore theoretically appealing to regard the "normal" or secular monetary base around which cyclical fluctuations occur as described by a constant percentage rate of change in the stock of money and to regard changes in the percentage rate of change as the feature of monetary behavior that contributes to the generation of cycles.

B. The Meaning of "The" Lag

The selection of one or another feature of monetary behavior as most important for cyclical change does not settle the question how best to describe the cyclical timing relation between money and business. Strictly speaking, there is no such thing as *the* lag in the effect of monetary action. Suppose the effect on, say, national income of a single instantaneous monetary change could be isolated in full from the surrounding matrix. The effect would no doubt be found to begin immediately, rise to a crescendo, then decline gradually, and not disappear fully

---

17. "Roughly" because changes in real income, interest rates, and the like may alter the desired "real" stock of money and need not do so at a constant percentage rate. Our studies of the secular demand for money indicate that over longer periods changes in the desired real stock of money are dominated by changes in real income and proceed fairly regularly (see Milton Friedman, "The Demand for Money: Some Theoretical and Empirical Results," Chapter 6 above).

for an indefinite time. There is a distributed lag. When we refer to *the* lag, we mean something like the weighted average interval between the action and its effects; and when we refer to an "average" lag, we mean the average of such weighted averages for several episodes. And even this description is over-simplified. The effects may change sign after a time, the original effects setting up forces that tend to produce not merely a reversal but an overshooting, as, for example, when the feedback effects of business on money are in the opposite direction from the initial effects of money on business. Fortunately, perhaps, this connection is likely to be submerged by another: monetary changes are never single and instantaneous. They consist rather of a time sequence of changes, the effects of which accumulate, and which are themselves in part the accumu-lated effect of other changes in the economy rather than in any sense strictly autonomous. The concept of "lag" therefore becomes still more complex, re-ferring to the timing relation between the resulting monetary series and a result-ing series of effects. In principle, identification of the effects would require the determination of what national income, say, would have been in the absence of whatever changes in money are regarded as autonomous. Even then, a full description of timing relations might require an indefinitely large number of dimensions.

In practice, we evade the explicit isolation of the effects of autonomous monetary changes by the usual device of relying on the averaging out of the effects of other changes, which is to say, we take the average relation between the actual changes in money and in income as an estimate of the relation to be expected between an autonomous change in money and the resultant change in income.[18] In practice, also, the problem of description is simplified because the observed time series on the money stock and on national income each has its own internal consistency and persistence, expressible statistically by its serial correlation function or its frequency spectrum. It is a fact that peaks in the rate of change of the stock of money tend to precede peaks in the deviation between the money stock and a smooth secular trend and these, in turn, tend to precede such peaks as occur in the money stock itself; it is a fact also that troughs in the rate of change of the money stock tend to precede troughs in the deviation from trend, and these, in turn, tend to follow such troughs in the money stock as occur. No one of these characteristics alone is a full description of the money series, any more than one feature in a face is a full portrait. But also the regu-larities in the series may mean that a few such characteristics suffice to give an adequate description, just as the few lines of a sketch may convey an unmis-takable likeness. Similar comments hold for national income or any other series intended to portray fluctuations in economic activity. Finally, while a full de-scription of the interrelations between two series would require showing the links among all their features, the regularities in each may render a much more

18. The point at issue is the so-called identification problem so much discussed in the literature on the estimation of multiple equation systems.

condensed description sufficient. It is simultaneously true that peaks in the rate of change of the money stock precede reference cycle peaks by sixteen months (on the average); that peaks in the deviation of the money stock from its trend do so by five months; that such absolute peaks as occur in the money stock precede reference cycle peaks by less than five months and may even lag; that peaks in the rate of change of income precede such peaks as occur in the stock of money; that they probably also precede peaks in the deviation of the money stock from its trend; that they probably follow peaks in the rate of change of money. I have not made detailed calculations for any but the first two items but those plus what we know about trends in money and income clearly imply the others. And note that there is no inconsistency between the view that changes in income are a consequence of monetary changes and the inclusion in this list of some comparisons in which the monetary feature follows rather than precedes the income feature.

What is true for description is true also for policy. If my conclusions about the independence and importance of money changes are valid—conclusions not themselves based primarily on observed timing relations—then monetary policy actions that produce a peak in the rate of change of the stock of money can be expected on the average to be followed by a peak in general business some sixteen months later partly because these same actions and their consequences will also produce a peak in the deviation of the money stock from its trend some eleven months later. The timing of the peak in the rate of change is not a full description of the behavior of the money stock; or of the effects of monetary policy on the money stock; it is rather one summary measure of that behavior and of those effects that has been found to have a consistent relation with the subsequent course of business. Presumably, one reason for this consistent relation is because this feature of monetary behavior is consistently linked with other features, and one reason for variability in the relation is because these links are not rigid.

C. The Empirical Evidence

We have, in fact, made two sets of timing comparisons. In addition, experience has recently provided a most interesting bit of evidence.

1. The basic set of timing comparisons were made in connection with the National Bureau of Economic Research study on which I am collaborating with Anna J. Schwartz. It consists of two different timing comparisons.

(a) One is the comparison to which Culbertson refers and the only one I have so far published, namely, between peaks and troughs in the percentage rate of change of the money stock and peaks and troughs in general business as dated by the National Bureau reference chronology. On the average of eighteen nonwar cycles since 1870, peaks in the rate of change of the stock of money precede reference peaks by sixteen months and troughs in the rate of change of the stock of money precede reference troughs by twelve months.[19] (see also Chapter 10 above.)

The problem of interpretation with respect to these results that has concerned us the most and the one to which we have devoted the most attention is not the problem that bothers Culbertson but a very different one. "Instead of interpreting the cycles in the rate of change as conforming (to the business cycle) positively with a lead, they could be interpreted as conforming inversely with a lag."[20] Since peaks in the rate of change precede the cyclical peaks by more than a quarter of a cycle, they follow cyclical troughs by less than a quarter of a cycle; a comparable statement holds for troughs in the rate of change. Interpreting the rate of change series as moving inversely to the cycle with a lag therefore has the statistical appeal that it yields a shorter time interval between the movements regarded as corresponding to one another. An inverse relation with money lagging would be much easier to rationalize in terms of business influencing money than of money influencing business, whereas the opposite is true of a positive relation with money leading. Hence, the interpretation of the statistical results that is accepted is of considerable importance. Accordingly, we have made a number of different empirical tests of the two interpretations. The results argue strongly for interpreting the rate of change as conforming positively with a lead rather than inversely with a lag.[21]

(b) Because of the difficulty of dating peaks and troughs in so choppy and erratic a series as the rate of change of the stock of money, we have also made timing comparisons on a different basis. The rate of change series often seems to shift abruptly from one level to another. This suggests approximating it by a step function consisting of alternating high and low steps. We call the date at which the high step ends, the "step" peak. and the date at which the low step

19. It may be worth noting that even if the rates of change were regarded as derivatives of a smooth cyclical (that is, sine curve) stock-of-money series, and even if the relevant comparison were regarded as being between the latter and general business, these results imply that turns in the stock-of-money series precede those in general business. For sine curves, the derivative moves in the same direction as the series one quarter-cycle earlier (or three quarters of a cycle later). The average length of the reference cycles is roughly forty months, hence a quarter-cycle is ten months. Subtracting ten months from the sixteen-month lead of the rate of change at the peak or the twelve-month lead at the trough gives six or two months, respectively, as the amount by which turns in the hypothetical sine curve stock-of-money series would precede those in general business. Of course, expansions are longer empirically than contractions on the average so that a more refined model would treat a quarter-cycle as longer for an expansion than for a contraction. This would shorten the apparent lead at peaks and lengthen it at troughs; in both cases, the lead of the rate of change of the stock of money is about 60 per cent of the relevant phase.

Perhaps this is where Culbertson gets the "three to six months" of item 5, since he gives no indication what the "broad record of experience" that supports his view is.

20. *Compendium*, p. 250 (Chapter 9 above).

21. The two most telling pieces of evidence are a comparison of (1) the stability of timing observations computed in the two ways, and (2) the serial correlations of the amplitudes of successive cyclical movements in money and general business. (see Chapter 12 below.)

ends, the "step" trough. This procedure is equivalent to approximating the stock-of-money series itself by a series of connected semilogarithmic straight line segments. The dates of the kinks where two straight line segments meet are the step dates. For a series which can be fitted reasonably well in this way, it is perhaps intuitively obvious that the step dates approximate the dates at which deviations from a trend fitted to the stock of money reach their peaks and troughs. The step method, however, has the great advantage of requiring no fitting of trends.

The step dates necessarily come later than the dates of the turning points in the rate of change, since the date that marks the shift from a "high" rate of change to a "low" rate of change necessarily comes later than the date that marks the shift from a "rising" rate of change to a "falling" rate of change. Yet even so, the step dates on the average precede the reference dates by five months at peaks and four months at troughs.[22]

We had hoped that the data would discriminate between these two methods of comparison by demonstrating that one or the other yielded a stabler and more consistent timing relation. As it happens, the two run nearly a dead heat in this respect, so we have had to rely on other considerations.

For reasons already noted, these other considerations lead me to regard the first comparison as economically the more meaningful and as probably giving a better estimate of the mean interval between a monetary policy action undertaken to counter the cycle and its effects. However, it is perhaps worth stating explicitly that it would not affect my conclusion about the likely ineffectiveness of discretionary monetary policy if major reliance were to be placed on the second comparison. Minor reasons are because the relevant lag for policy must include the time required to recognize the need for action and to translate this recognition into action, and because even a mean lag of four to five months is a significant fraction of the duration of a cycle phase and imposes a considerable strain on foresight in the present state of knowledge. Major reasons are because variability of the lag is alone a decisive obstacle to effective discretionary policy and because political and other pressures on the monetary authorities will confuse objectives and open the way to the possibility of major error (see Sec. IV below). With respect to variability, it would be cold comfort to know that on the average action taken today would have its mean effects four to five months later if in some instances the relevant time period is negligible, in others, ten to twelve months, and there is no way of telling which is likely to be the case in the particular instance.

2. Another set of timing comparisons are available as a by-product of a study by David Meiselman and me made for a different purpose, namely, to compare the relative stability of the investment multiplier and monetary velocity in the

---

22. For a sine curve superimposed on a linear trend, the peak and trough deviations from trend will tend to come one quarter-cycle later than the peak and trough rates of change. Hence these results confirm the rough calculations of n. 19 and are therefore entirely consistent with the results of the preceding comparison.

United States since 1896. For the period before World War II our data are mostly annual and hence not very useful for the analysis of timing. For the period since World War II, we have computed from quarterly data correlations between the stock of money and consumption and the stock of money and income and various transformations of these variables, for various leads and lags.[23] The results supplement the preceding findings because they are based on correlations of time series rather than on a comparison of turning points. They are less significant because they are for a much shorter period of time and, at that, one greatly affected in the earlier years by the heritage from the war, and because they do not sharply isolate cyclical movements from secular movements On the whole, as we shall see, the results tend to confirm the preceding findings, so questions of the relative weight to be attached to the two sets are of no great practical importance.

(a) The correlations that are most nearly comparable with the timing comparison 1(a) are between quarter-to-quarter percentage changes in the money stock and the percentage deviations of income and consumption from a trend.[24] For 1948 through 1958, the correlations are highest when the rate of change of money is correlated with consumption or income three or four quarters later and decline smoothly as the lead is either shortened or lengthened. The correlation coefficients, though moderate in size, are clearly larger than could be expected from chance.[25] The implied lead of nine to twelve months is somewhat shorter than the lead of twelve to sixteen months found in 1(a), but the difference is almost surely within the range to be expected from sampling fluctuations, so these results are highly consistent with those obtained from a comparison of turning points for a much longer period.

(b) There is more of a choice in obtaining correlations comparable to the timing comparison 1(b) and the results are less clear cut. (i) Correlation of the stock of money with consumption or income, all in their original form, gives little if any information relevant to cyclical timing, since all three series are dominated by a sharp upward trend. The correlations are very high and remain high for widely varying leads or lags, as is to be expected if the correlation is

23. The reason for using consumption as well as income in these correlations is because of the desire for our main purpose to have comparable correlations for money and for investment (more precisely, autonomous expenditures). Since income as measured equals consumption plus investment, the correlation between income and investment introduces a spurious element that can be eliminated by correlating consumption with investment (see Milton Friedman and Gary S. Becker, "A Statistical Illusion in Judging Keynesian Models," *Journal of Political Economy*, vol. 65, February (1957), 64–75).

24. Income and consumption in their original form are dominated in the postwar period by a sharp upward trend, cyclical fluctuations showing up only as minor interruptions Hence, correlating the rate of change of money with them without adjusting for trend would be equivalent to correlating it with a rising straight line and would give no information on cyclical timing. See also next paragraph of text.

25. The peak correlation is .52 for consumption, .58 for income. Both are significantly different from zero at less than the .001 level.

essentially between two trends.[26] (ii) An alternative is to correlate percentage deviations of money from a trend with corresponding percentage deviations for consumption and income. Partly because of the difficulty of fitting a single satisfactory trend to the money stock,[27] the correlations are extremely low for all timing relations. They are highest when money is correlated with consumption or income in the same quarter but even then are not higher than the value that would plausibly be attributed to chance alone.[28] (iii) Another alternative is to correlate first differences of the stock of money with first differences of income or consumption.[29] This is apparently the comparison Culbertson prefers. It is also the only variant that Ando, Brown, Solow, and Karaken use and on the basis of which they are prepared to conclude that there is no evidence that money leads business. These correlations too are not very satisfactory. For the postwar period as a whole (third quarter 1945 through 1958), they are rather low for money and consumption, but their highest value is statistically significant and is reached when money is correlated with consumption one quarter later;[30] however, for money and income, the correlations are negative for all leads and lags.[31] For the shorter period from 1948 through 1958, positive correlations are obtained for both consumption and income, though all are very low. The highest correlation is for money and consumption one quarter later and for money and income, two quarters later.[32] If we neglect the puzzling negative correlations, these results show a lead for money of three to six months,

26. Because of a lower rate of rise of money during the immediate postwar period than subsequently, the timing that gives the highest correlation is sensitive to choice of period. For the period from the third quarter of 1945 through 1958, the correlation is highest when money is correlated with income or consumption one or two quarters later; for the period from 1948 through 1958, when money is correlated with income or consumption one quarter earlier. For the longer period, the peak correlation for income is .981, for consumption, .989; for the shorter period, the peak correlation for income is .985, for consumption, .990. The extent to which the correlations are simply between trends is indicated by the high correlations for long differences in time in the series correlated. When money is correlated with income or consumption ten quarters later (the longest lead we tried), the correlations for the longer period are .944 for income, .957 for consumption; for the shorter period, .956 and .971, respectively.

27. The trends were fitted graphically.

28. The peak correlations for 1948 through 1958 are .26 for income, .20 for consumption. Neither is statistically significant at the .05 level, and the second is not at the .10 level.

29. The correlations to be cited are between first differences of the variables in absolute form. We happened to have these as a by-product of our other work, which is why I use them. For the present purpose, I would prefer logarithmic first differences.

30. The highest value is .34, which is significantly different from zero at the .02 level.

31. The negative correlation reflects the most puzzling result of the entire study, namely, a negative correlation between the quarter-to-quarter changes in consumption and in autonomous expenditures as we defined them, that is, a negative "multiplier."

32. The peak correlations are .26 for consumption, .21 for income; neither is significantly different from zero at the .05 level, the former but not the latter is at the .10 level.

which is highly consistent with the lead of four to five months found in 1(b).[33]

3. The timing of Culbertson's note is most unfortunate for his argument that the "lag" might largely disappear if emphasis were put on ups and downs in the stock of money itself rather than in its rate of change. He must have written it just as experience was providing an unusually striking counter-example. The cyclical expansion from April, 1958, to May, 1960, was the shortest since 1933. Its untimely end was foreseen by few business analysts. In retrospect, two factors stand out as possible explanations of the shortness of the expansion: an unusually early slowing down in the rate of rise of the money stock followed by an absolute decline; and an unusually sharp shift in the government account from a deficit to a surplus.[34] Needless to say, this is not the place to assess the relative importance of these two factors. It will suffice for our purpose simply to note that the historical relation between money and business described above would have led one to expect the behavior of the stock of money on this occasion to produce an early cyclical peak.[35] The rate of change of the stock of money reached a peak about April, 1958, or simultaneously with the cyclical trough and twenty-five months before the cyclical peak; and the stock of money reached an absolute peak in August or September, 1959, or sixteen or seventeen months after the trough and eight or nine months before the cyclical peak, whereas the stock of money generally rises throughout both cyclical expansion and contraction. Moreover, the decline in the stock of money, which lasted until May, 1960, while small in absolute magnitude, was large relative to earlier experience. It has been exceeded in the past ninety years only during severe depressions.[36] It is clearly plausible that the early monetary change—which almost surely was the result of a deliberate act of policy and not itself, at least in its early stages, a reflex effect of changes in business—contributed to, if it did not produce the early termination of the expansion. True, the lags were unusually long in this episode, though not outside the range of earlier experience, and I entirely agree with Culbertson that this may be—to apply to this particular episode a comment

33. Culbertson asserts that "the chart Friedman offers in evidence (*Hearings*, p. 639) suggests that . . . the maximum rates of increase in the money supply and in economic activity seem commonly to have coincided." This conclusion, whether right or wrong, cannot possibly be derived from my chart, since it contains only the rate of change of the stock of money and the reference chronology and no series whatsoever purporting to represent "economic activity." Hence, I am baffled as to where Culbertson got the evidence to which he says he is referring.

34. To point to inventory movements is to describe, not explain, the recession.

35. And, in fact, did lead some of us to expect this result.

36. These statements are for money defined as currency outside banks plus adjusted demand deposits plus time deposits in commercial banks, the concept used in the timing comparisons referred to earlier. Currency plus adjusted demand deposits experienced its maximum rate of rise in October, 1958, or 19 months before the cyclical peak and its absolute peak in July, 1959, or 10 months before the cyclical peak. The difference in behavior of the two different monetary totals was greater than usual, thanks to special factors affecting time deposits.

he made in a more general context—because the peak in the rate of change occurred "early in a cyclical expansion when the economy has a strong upward momentum." But does this not simply mean that the episode speaks for both a long and a variable lag?

D. Why Should "The" Lag be Long?

How can one rationalize a lag in the effects of monetary policy as long as the twelve to sixteen months by which turning points in the rate of change of money tend to precede turning points in business? Or even the four to five months by which the ends of the steps in the rate of change precede turning points in business? However persuasive the statistical evidence for such a lag, is it consistent with what we think we know about economic interrelationships?

Clearly this is not the place for anything like a full answer, but a few comments may at least suggest that so long a lag is not prima facie implausible.[37] Suppose the monetary authorities increase the stock of money by open-market purchases. The initial effect is to alter the structure of assets and liabilities of the non-banking community, which is to say, its balance sheet. The new balance sheet is in one sense still in equilibrium, if the former one was, since the open-market transaction was voluntary. But it is only in momentary equilibrium. An asset was sold for money because the terms were favorable; however, the seller did not necessarily intend to retain the money indefinitely. Indeed the prime function of money is to permit a barter transaction to be separated into two parts, a purchase and a sale.

From a longer-term view, the new balance sheet is out of equilibrium, with cash being temporarily high relative to other assets. Holders of cash will seek to purchase assets to achieve a desired structure. This will bid up the price of assets. If the extra demand is initially directed at a particular class of assets, say government securities, or commercial paper, or the like, the result will be to pull the prices of such assets out of line with other assets and thus to widen the area into which the extra cash spills. The increased demand will spread, sooner or later affecting equities, houses, durable producer goods, durable consumer goods, and so on, though not necessarily in this order. In the process, of course, the price rise will be reduced in magnitude as it is spread over a wider area. These effects can be described as operating on 'interest rates,' if a more cosmopolitan interpretation of "interest rates" is adopted than the usual one which refers to a small range of marketable securities.

The key feature of this process is that it tends to raise the prices of sources of both producer and consumer services relative to the prices of the services

37. The following comments draw on a longer discussion of the channels through which monetary policy operates in the report by Meiselman and me referred to above. That discussion was an attempt to explore some of the implications of our finding that monetary velocity is very much stabler than the investment multiplier.

themselves; for example, to raise the prices of houses relative to the rents of dwelling units, or the cost of purchasing a car relative to the cost of renting one. It therefore encourages the production of such sources (this is the stimulus to "investment" conceived broadly as including a much wider range of items than are ordinarily included in that term) and, at the same time, the direct acquisition of services rather than of the source (this is the stimulus to "consumption" relative to "savings"). But these reactions in their turn tend to raise the prices of services relative to the prices of sources, this is, to undo the initial effects on interest rates. The final result may be a rise in expenditures in all directions without any change in interest rates at all; interest rates and asset prices may simply be the conduit through which the effect of the monetary change is transmitted to expenditures without being altered at all, just as a greater inflow into a lake may, after an interval, simply increase the rate of outflow without altering the level of the lake itself.

Of course, all these forces operate simultaneously and there are ebbs and flows and not merely movement in one direction. Changes in balance sheets affect income flows and these in their turn react on balance sheets.

Two features about this grossly over-simplified sketch seem particularly relevant for judging the likely lags. In the first place, the process operates through the balance sheet, and it is plausible that balance-sheet adjustments are sluggish in the sense that individuals spread adjustments over a considerable period of time. The ripples produced by the initial monetary action may therefore take a rather long time to reach the whole range of assets. In the second place, the effects on expenditures will also be spread over time. And what is relevant for our purposes, it should be recalled, is not when the effects on expenditures start but the weighted average interval between the monetary change and the effects. It may be, for example, that monetary expansion induces someone within two or three months to contemplate building a factory; within four or five, to draw up plans; within six or seven, to get construction started. The actual construction may take another six months and much of the effect on the income stream may come still later, insofar as initial goods used in construction are withdrawn from inventories and only subsequently lead to increased expenditures by suppliers. Or again, trace the chain via the encouragement to a consumer to convert relatively low yielding securities, say, into the purchase of a new automobile or a new wardrobe somewhat sooner than otherwise, and the secondary effects of this purchase in turn via inventories ultimately on the income stream. The lag we are interested in is not between monetary change and its impact on the financial markets, which may indeed be short for some financial markets, but between monetary change and its impact on the flow of income, which might be expected to be very much longer.

The period of time over which the effect spreads is lengthened still further, as already noted, by the feedback effects of changes in the financial markets and in expenditures on the stock of money itself. These may, of course, be in either direction, depending on the monetary institutions.

II. THE VARIABILITY OF THE LAG

The main piece of quantitative evidence on the variability of the lag is the variation from cycle to cycle in the estimated time interval between specified characteristics of the money-stock series (either turning points in the rate of change or the step dates) and reference cycle turning points. The standard deviation of these time intervals is about six or seven months for both comparisons. However, this standard deviation is composed of two elements: the "true" variability in the lag and errors of measurement. Though errors of measurement largely cancel in estimating the average lag, they do not cancel at all in estimating the standard deviation of the lag. For this reason, the evidence on the variability of the lag is less satisfactory than the evidence on the average lag.

Anyone who has tried to date turning points in a series like the month-to-month percentage changes in the stock of money will recognize that the error in estimation is not negligible. The standard deviation of six or seven months may therefore overestimate considerably the "true" variability of the lag. It seems to me hardly credible, however, that the standard deviation of the lag in the total effects of monetary policy can be as small as the less than .9 month implicitly asserted by Culbertson for the "predominant direct effects," a result which would require that statistical error account for over 97 per cent of the variance in the estimated timing measures.

What, however, about item 4 in Culbertson's critique, namely, that the "surprising moderateness of the economic fluctuations that we have suffered in the past decade" is direct testimony against a long and variable lag? The amplitude of economic fluctuations depends, first, on the amplitude, time pattern, number, and independence of the disturbances impinging on the economic system; and, second, on the reaction mechanism of the economic system to the disturbances. Contrary to the theorem implicit in Culbertson's comment, neither the length nor the variability of the average time interval between a disturbance and its effects is connected in any simple way with the amplitude of the economic fluctuations produced by a given set of disturbances. The lag may be long because the effects are distributed over an extended period rather than being concentrated in time; if so, a long lag may mean a larger damping of disturbances than a short lag and hence a smaller amplitude of resulting fluctuations. For a given length of lag, large variability in the lag may simply mean greater irregularity in length and timing of the resulting fluctuations. But it may also mean a smaller amplitude. At any one time, numerous disturbances impinge on the economic system, and they affect it through a variety of reaction mechanisms. If each mechanism separately has a variable reaction time, the several mechanisms actuated at any one time may well differ in reaction time more than they otherwise would, which would contribute to spreading the ultimate effects from accidentally bunched disturbances. I do not mean to assert that these results are necessary. My remarks are intended only to illustrate the subtlety of the theoretical issues, and to make it clear why no far-reaching conclusions about the length or variability of lags can be derived from a casual observation about "the surprising moderateness of the economic fluctuations."

Culbertson's mistake in this respect probably accounts for another: his mis-understanding of the reason why I believe that long and variable lags in the effect of monetary or fiscal policy may well render attempted countercyclical actions destabilizing.[38] The reason is not at all that such lags imply that the reaction structure is destabilizing or explosive. We have just seen that they need not do so. The reason is rather that long and especially variable lags mean that policy actions are likely to be poorly adapted to countercyclical needs. I have never argued that policy actions are either necessarily or on the average perverse, though, in fact, monetary actions have been perverse on many occasions, but only that they are largely random relative to the actions that in retrospect would have been appropriate. The result is to convert actions taken for countercyclical purposes into additional and unnecessary random disturbances. Moreover, they are disturbances with a peculiarly high potential for mischief. The monetary and fiscal authorities can and do act on a scale that is extremely large relative to the actions of other independent economic groups. They can continue an action that is inappropriate for longer than any other group, and they are likely to do so both because of the sheer inertia of the government decision-making process and because of the political costs of implicitly or explicitly admitting error by reversing course rapidly. Hence the actions of the monetary and fiscal authorities are likely to constitute large disturbances with very high serial correlations, just the kind that contribute most to the temporal variance of time series.

Needless to say, the conclusions I have reached about the effects of discretionary monetary policy are not based solely on the empirical evidence that monetary forces have played an independent cyclical role with a long and variable lag plus the abstract argument of the preceding paragraph. They have been tested by examining how monetary policy has in fact operated in the United States. I have studied individual episodes and have also compared United States experience before and after the Federal Reserve System.[39] The relatively mild cyclical fluctuations of the postwar period, far from contradicting the conclusions suggested by earlier periods, tend to confirm them. The postwar period has been notable for the absence of any active countercyclical monetary measures on a large scale and testifies to the desirability of such self-restraint.

38. See "The Effects of a Full-Employment Policy on Economic Stability: A Formal Analysis," in my *Essays in Positive Economics*, Chicago: University of Chicago Press (1953), pp. 117–32, for the theoretical analysis underlying my conclusion.

39. See *A Program for Monetary Stability*, chaps. i and iv.

IV. POLICY ISSUES

I agree completely with Culbertson that the confirmed existence of a long and variable lag would not by itself determine appropriate stabilization policy (item 6 in my summary of Culbertson's critique). Of course, "neutrality" is a complicated concept. Indeed, I had thought that this was one of my main themes, which I had been repeating *ad nauseam*.[40] I do not, however, understand the relevance of Culbertson's point. He seems to imply that the failure of an asserted statement of fact to have clear and unambiguous policy implications somehow throws doubt on the fact. Surely this is to stand the proper relation on its head.[41]

Parents are naturally fond of their progeny and loath to disinherit them, so I cannot fail to recognize that I have a bias in favor of the automatic stabilization framework I proposed in 1946. Yet allowing as much as I can for this bias, I cannot see that my judgment that discretionary countercyclical action is more likely than not to be destabilizing is necessarily inconsistent with my judgment that the automatic framework is more likely than not to be stabilizing (item 7 in Culbertson's critique). True, the latter judgment may be mistaken. As I wrote in my original article, "These lags make impossible any definite statement about the actual degree of stability likely to result from the operation of the monetary and fiscal framework described above. . . . The proposed framework could intensify rather than mitigate cyclical fluctuations." But, as I then went on to say, "There is a strong presumption . . . discretionary actions will in general be subject to longer lags than the automatic reactions and hence will be destabilizing even more frequently."[42]

If anything, I now regard the automatic framework as having an even greater advantage over discretionary action than I attributed to it in my earlier article, and this for two main reasons not considered in that earlier analysis at all. First, discretionary policy at times tends to be dominated by goals other than, and even contradictory to, stabilization (for example, pegging bond yields, halting gold outflows), whereas the automatic framework cannot be so readily exploited for other purposes. Second, the inertia and the political considerations referred to above that inhibit the ready reversal of discretionary policies when they turn out to be in the wrong direction make for a longer lag than would otherwise exist between the recognition of the need for action and the taking of action and introduce much higher serial correlation into perverse discretionary actions than into perverse automatic reactions.

40. For examples, see *ibid.*, pp. 40–44, 85–99.

41. I am reminded of a reviewer who listed as a criticism of a book of mine that some of its empirical conclusions seemed to him adverse to policy statements I had made elsewhere.

42. *Essays in Positive Economics*, pp. 144–45. The basis for this conclusion is outlined on pp. 145–48.

In discussing my earlier proposal, Culbertson cites the large change in the federal cash deficit during and following the 1957–58 recession as demonstrating that it is "an extravagantly anticyclical monetary proposal." This is hardly cricket. Much of the change in the deficit was produced by changes in expenditures explicitly designed to counter the recession. My proposal called for "no attempt . . . to vary [government] expenditures [on goods and services] in response to cyclical fluctuations" or to change the transfer program.[43] The strictly automatic changes in the government deficit that would have been called for under my proposal would have reached their maximum much sooner than the actual changes and would have been much smaller. Is there any doubt in retrospect that such changes would have been preferable to the course actually followed?[44]

V. CONCLUSION

It is a commonplace in economics that one can seldom get something for nothing. Casual theorizing like Culbertson's assertion that long and variable lags in response of the economy to monetary changes imply wide cyclical fluctuations in economic activity; casual empiricism like Culbertson's assertion that "the broad record of experience" gives reason to expect that the "predominant direct effects" of monetary and other changes will occur "within three to six months" —these are superficially attractive but exceedingly unreliable routes to building a cumulative economic science resting on firm foundations. As yet, no substitute has been found for the explicit examination of a wide range of evidence, the rigorous excogitation of the links between premises and conclusions, and the thorough testing and amending of tentative findings.

A reasonably full presentation should be available in print within the next year or two of the evidence that has led me to the tentative conclusion that changes in the stock of money exert an independent influence on cyclical fluctuations in economic activity with a lag that is both long and variable relative to the average length of such fluctuations. The reader will then be able to judge the adequacy of the evidence for himself. In the meantime, I hope that this article has clarified the meaning of the conclusion and has at least suggested the kind and breadth of evidence on which it rests.

43. *Ibid.*, pp. 136–37.

44. Using the irrelevant actual changes as measures of the changes that would have been produced by my proposal, Culbertson asks the rhetorical question: "Who else proposes an anticyclical variation in money supply at the rate of $10 billion a year or more?" The facts do not support the implied answer, at least if we judge by actions. From July 1957, to January 1958, the seasonally adjusted money supply, defined as currency plus adjusted demand deposits fell at the annual rate of $3.8 billion; from January 1958, to July 1958, it rose at the annual rate of $6.0 billion; a cyclical variation of $9.8 billion. For money defined as currency plus all adjusted deposits in commercial banks, the definition I have generally used in my work, the corresponding figures are a rise at the annual rate of $1.2 billion and a rise at the annual rate of $16.8 billion, or a cyclical variation of $15.6 billion.

Chapter 12

The Monetary Studies
of the National Bureau

TO THE THEOLOGIAN, the love of money is the "root of all evil." To the economist, money had hardly less importance up to the early 1930's. It was then widely accepted that long-period changes in the quantity of money were the primary source of trends in the level of prices and that short-period fluctuations in the quantity of money played an important role in business cycles and might be the major explanation of them. For example, in his monumental book on business cycles published in 1913, Wesley C. Mitchell, while by no means promulgating or accepting an exclusively monetary theory of the cycle, gave much attention to monetary factors, constructing new estimates of various monetary components which are still part of the statistical underpinning of our present series on the stock of money.

The Keynesian revolution in economic thought in the mid-1930's produced a radical change in the attention paid by economists to money. The fact that the Federal Reserve System did not stem the Great Depression was interpreted as meaning that money was of secondary importance, at most a reflection of changes occurring elsewhere. Though this conclusion was a *non sequitur*, it was nonetheless potent. And it was all the more readily accepted because Keynes provided an intellectually appealing alternative explanation of the Great Depres-

Reprinted from *The National Bureau Enters its 45th Year*, 44th Annual Report, pp. 7–25, with the permission of the National Bureau of Economic Research, © 1964.

sion. For nearly two decades thereafter, money became a minor matter in most academic economic writing and research, to be mentioned almost as an afterthought. And economic research on money was notable by its absence.

Recently there has been a revival of interest in money and a great increase in the amount of economic research on money. Several causes combined to produce this revival of interest. One was dissatisfaction with the predictions yielded by the Keynesian analysis—the most dramatic being the failure of the much-predicted postwar depression to occur. A second was the emergence of inflation as a major problem in all countries that adopted the easy-money policy widely regarded as called for by the Keynesian analysis. No country succeeded in stemming inflation until it replaced the easy-money policy by more "orthodox" monetary measures. A third was scholarly criticism and analysis of Keynes' theoretical structure, and the resulting attribution of an important theoretical role to the so-called "real-balance" effect. A fourth was the accumulation of empirical evidence bearing on the behavior of money and its relation to other economic magnitudes. The combined effect has been striking. Ten years ago, we at the National Bureau and an associated group at the University of Chicago were almost the only academic economists working intensively on money. Today, I am glad to say, we have a host of competitors.

I. THE STUDIES COVERED BY THIS REPORT

The National Bureau's monetary research has throughout been closely connected with its studies of business cycles. Wesley Mitchell's preliminary manuscript on business cycles contained a long chapter on the role of money and credit in the cycle. For that chapter, he had collected many series bearing on money and credit, which remain the backbone of the Bureau's collection of series in this area. The chapter was the starting point of the studies covered by this report, as other chapters were of so many of the major National Bureau studies.

This report covers only those monetary studies of the Bureau for which Anna J. Schwartz, Phillip Cagan, and I have had responsibility. The group of studies, begun well over a decade ago, is now, I am glad to report, nearly completed. Hence, this report deals mostly with work already done or nearly done. Needless to say, just as our studies built on the earlier work of the Bureau and other investigators, so, I trust, they will in their turn open up new avenues of future research for the Bureau and for others. The test of success in any scientific research is dual: the questions it answers and, even more, the new questions it raises. Though I shall refer incidentally to some of the questions our work raises and on which further research is needed, I shall not attempt a comprehensive survey. Research must lead its own life. I am all too aware how much our own work departed from the lines we initially expected it to follow to want to peer too deeply into that clouded (and crowded) crystal ball.

As our work proceeded, we came to plan three monographs. One, *A Monetary*

History of the United States, 1867–1960, by Anna J. Schwartz and myself, was published in 1963. A second, "Determinants and Effects of Changes in the Money Stock, 1875–1955," by Phillip Cagan, will soon go to press. The third, "Trends and Cycles in the Stock of Money in the United States," by Anna Schwartz and myself, is in first draft form. The major unfinished work is the substantial revision and expansion of the present draft, which was completed years ago and then put aside while we finished the *Monetary History.* We hope that by the next annual meeting we can report that this monograph too is ready or nearly ready for review by the Board of Directors.

In addition, four other Bureau publications have come from our studies. "Money and Business Cycles," by Friedman and Schwartz (Conference on the State of Monetary Economics, *Review of Economics and Statistics,* Feb. 1963 suppl., Chapter 10 above), is something of a preview and advance summary of one part of our projected volume, "Trends and Cycles." Friedman, *The Demand for Money* (Occasional Paper 68, 1959, Chapter 6 above), is a preliminary version of another chapter of that work, and Friedman, *The Interpolation of Time Series by Related Series* (Technical Paper 16, 1962), is a by-product of our monetary estimates. Phillip Cagan's *The Demand for Currency Relative to Total Money Supply* (Occasional Paper 62, 1958) is a preliminary version of part of his monograph.

II. THE MEANING OF "MONEY" AND OUR ESTIMATES OF THE QUANTITY OF MONEY

It will help put our work in proper perspective to distinguish at the outset between different senses in which the word "money" is used. In popular parlance, there are three main senses—as in pocket money, money market, and making money. In the first sense, money refers to a class of assets of wealthholders; in the second, to credit; in the third, to income. Our work has been concerned with money in the first sense. We have of course had to consider both credit conditions and income: credit conditions as affecting the quantity of money, as being in turn affected by changes in the quantity of money, and as one of the channels through which changes in the quantity of money may affect income; similarly, income as perhaps the central total whose fluctuations constitute business cycles, as a source of changes in the quantity of money, and as itself affected by changes in the quantity of money. We have repeatedly been impressed in the course of our work with the importance of clearly distinguishing between money as an asset—as a stock at a point in time—and these other phenomena for which the word money is frequently used. Indeed, a key finding in our *Monetary History* is that the confusion of money and credit has been a primary source of difficulty in monetary policy. And recent experience indicates this is still so.

Credit conditions are affected by a much broader range of factors than those linked to the quantity of money and they require study in their own right. This is being done in the National Bureau studies of consumer credit, interest rates, and the quality of credit.

Our emphasis on money as an asset led us to take as our first major project the construction of a consistent and continuous set of estimates on the quantity of money for as long a period as possible. This turned out to be a more arduous task than anticipated, involving as it did piecing together numerous bits of data from a wide variety of sources. The final series starts in 1867, is for semi-annual or annual dates to 1907, and monthly thereafter. Though the series is now available (in an appendix to *A Monetary History*), a full description of sources and methods, and supplementary tables giving various components of the series and related series, are yet to be published. They will be included in our planned volume, "Trends and Cycles."

These estimates, as well as our subsequent work, brought to the fore the more specific question of precisely how to define money. Should it include only literal pocket money—that is, paper currency and coin? Or also demand deposits subject to transfer by check? Commercial bank time deposits? Mutual savings bank deposits? Savings and loan shares? Cash surrender values of life insurance policies? Series E bonds? And so on toward the outer bound defined by some of the broad concepts of liquidity; or, in a different and more appealing direction, toward weighted aggregates of the several elements.

Our statistical estimates, so far as feasible, give the components separately, so that each user can make his own choice within the limits of what we could estimate. In our work, we have generally found that the most useful single total is an intermediate one—currency held by the public, plus demand deposits adjusted of commercial banks, plus time deposits of commercial banks. Hence, we have termed this total "money" for our purposes and have used other expressions for other totals. The forthcoming volume on trends and cycles will discuss the question of definition in some detail and present the empirical evidence which led us to adopt this particular definition. So far as I can see, no issue of principle is involved in the choice of definition, only a question of the empirical usefulness of one or another admittedly imperfect approximation to a theoretical construct. So far as I can see, no important substantive issues are involved either. Judged by the criteria we used, alternative definitions are not much inferior to the one we adopted, so that a strong case against them cannot be made. Whenever possible, we have tried systematically to see whether any substantive conclusion is affected by substituting an alternative concept. Typically, none is, though some of the numerical relations may be different for one concept than for another. The occasional impression in the scientific literature that important substantive issues are involved generally turns out to be a result of the use of the word money to refer to different things.

All of our studies have been heavily dependent on the new estimates of the quantity of money we constructed. Our *Monetary History* "traces the changes in the stock of money . . . examines the factors that accounted for the changes, and analyzes the reflex influence that the stock of money exerted on the course of events."[1] In his monograph Cagan examines intensively the sources of changes in the stock of money and gives a detailed statistical analysis of the cyclical and secular behavior of each of the proximate determinants of the quantity of money, as we term them: high-powered money, the ratio of deposits at banks to their reserves, and the ratio of the public's holdings of deposits to its holdings of currency. The "Trends and Cycles" volume will, besides giving the basis for our new estimates, present a full statistical analysis of the secular and cyclical behavior of the stock of money and of monetary velocity in relation to other economic magnitudes. We shall rely heavily on the standard Bureau techniques to determine characteristic cyclical amplitude and timing. We plan also to supplement these techniques with both correlation techniques and—hopefully—spectral analysis, to see whether different techniques give consistent results.

The major scientific contribution of the studies probably will prove to be their quantitative findings about a host of specific magnitudes and relations. Most of our findings to date are summarized in the final chapter of *A Monetary History*, in the final chapter of Cagan's monograph, and in "Money and Business Cycles." They constitute building blocks to be incorporated in that general theory of the cycle which is the ultimate aim of scholars in the field.

Rather than try to summarize those findings here again, I should like instead to give something of the flavor of our work by considering an important specific issue, outlining the kind of evidence that is available from our published work on it, and giving some additional evidence from our unpublished work. I shall then summarize the general qualitative conclusions we have reached, with special stress on their limitations, and, finally, illustrate the applicability of some of our results to the interpretation of recent economic changes.

III. THE DIRECTION OF INFLUENCE
BETWEEN MONEY AND BUSINESS

The specific issue I propose to consider is in some ways the central issue in dispute about the role of money in business cycles, namely, whether the cyclical behavior of money is to be regarded as a major factor explaining business fluctuations or as simply a reflection of business fluctuations produced by other forces. In Irving Fisher's words, the issue is whether the cycle is largely a "dance of the dollar" or, conversely, the dollar is largely a dance of the cycle. Stated still differently, the issue is whether the major direction of influence is from money to business or from business to money.

In each of these statements of the issue, I have used an adjective like "major" or "largely." One reason is that the alternatives contrasted are not mutually

1. Milton Friedman and Anna Schwartz, *A Monetary History of the United States, 1867–1960*, Princeton, N.J.: Princeton University Press for the National Bureau of Economic Research (1963), p. 3.

exclusive. Undoubtedly there can be and are influences running both ways. Indeed, insofar as the cycle is in any measure self-generating and not simply a response to external shocks, and insofar as money plays any systematic role in producing the cycle, the influences must run both ways, the changes in the stock of money producing changes in business that produce changes in the stock of money that continue the cycle.

A second reason for the qualifying words is that there can be and almost certainly are factors other than money that contribute to the cycle, whatever may be the role of money. The question at issue is, therefore, whether money exerts an important independent influence, not whether it is the only source of business fluctuations and itself wholly independent of them.

What kind of evidence can be cited on this issue?

A. Qualitative Historical Circumstances

Perhaps the most directly relevant kind of evidence emerges from an examination of the historical circumstances surrounding changes in the quantity of money. They often have decisive bearing on whether the changes could have been an immediate or necessary consequence of contemporary changes in business conditions. This is particularly true about policy changes deliberately instituted by monetary authorities, which is why, as we say in *A Monetary History*, "the establishment of the Federal Reserve System provides the student of money a closer substitute for the controlled experiment to determine the direction of influence than the social scientist can generally obtain."[2]

From such evidence, it is possible to identify a number of occasions on which monetary changes have clearly been independent of contemporaneous changes in business conditions. On those occasions, the monetary changes have been accompanied by economic changes in the same direction, monetary contractions (or more precisely, reductions in the rate of change in the stock of money) being accompanied by contractions in money income, prices, and output; and monetary expansions, by the opposite. The relation between monetary and economic change at those times also has been very much the same as on other occasions when historical circumstances were less decisive about the source of the monetary change. We ended our summary of this evidence in the final chapter of *A Monetary History* as follows: "Mutual interaction, but with money rather clearly the senior partner in longer-run movements and in major cyclical movements, and more nearly an equal partner with money income and prices in shorter-run and milder movements—this is the generalization suggested by our evidence."

2. *A Monetary History*, p. 687.

B. *The Behavior of the Determinants of the Money Stock*

In his monograph, Cagan provides a rather different kind of evidence. Any change in the money stock can be attributed to changes in the three proximate determinants mentioned earlier: high-powered money, the deposit-reserve ratio, and the deposit-currency ratio. Any influence of business conditions on money must operate through one or more of these determinants. If this is the major direction of influence, the determinants separately should be more closely related to business conditions than the money stock as a whole is; moreover, the observed relation should be consistent with what we know about the character of the monetary institutions regarded as producing it. Hence, examination of the relation of money and each determinant separately to business conditions provides evidence on the direction of influence.

For secular movements, Cagan finds that high-powered money is the major source of changes in the stock of money. During most of the period studied, increases in prices would be expected to have reduced the quantity of high-powered money by discouraging gold output and encouraging gold exports. Conversely, decreases in prices would have encouraged gold output and stimulated gold inflows. Yet the actual relation is the other way: price increases are associated with a higher than average rate of rise in high-powered money; price decreases, with a lower than average rate of rise. Moreover, there is a closer relation between income and changes in the total money stock than between income and the separate determinants. Cagan concludes that, for secular movements, the predominant direction of influence must run from money to income. "To explain secular movements in prices," he writes, "we should look primarily to the supply of money and then secondarily to nonmonetary factors that may also have been important."

For cyclical fluctuations, Cagan finds the evidence more mixed. It is clearest for the severe business contractions. For these, he does not find it possible to attribute the changes in the stock of money to the effect of business on the determinants of the stock of money. Hence, the uniform coincidence of severe monetary contraction and severe economic contraction seems persuasive evidence for an influence running from money to business. As Cagan writes, "a monetary explanation of why some business contractions become severe, whatever may have started them, is hardly novel, but the supporting evidence is much stronger than is generally recognized." Incidentally, this explanation of severe business contractions is not necessarily inconsistent with an alternative explanation suggested by Moses Abramovitz in his work on long cycles. The relation between the two explanations will be examined in our "Trends and Cycles" volume.

For business cycles not containing severe contractions, Cagan finds clear evidence of the influence of business on money operating through the determinants. The deposit–currency ratio was the most important single source of cyclical fluctuations in the rate of change in the money stock. Cagan attributes most of the fluctuations in the deposit–currency ratio to the effect of the contemporaneous cyclical movements in economic activity. Similarly, he regards the fluctuations in the reserve ratio as reflecting cyclical movements in credit demands. For mild cycles, there is therefore clear evidence of a feedback effect of business on money. But Cagan also finds evidence of the same kind of effect of money on business which is so clearly present in secular movements and severe contractions. That evidence is the fact that the relation between money and business during mild cycles remains the same over a long period despite substantial changes in the institutional structure connecting business and the separate determinants.

C. Consistency of Timing on Positive and Inverted Basis

A third type of evidence is provided by the cyclical timing of monetary changes. However, to explain the relevance of this evidence. I shall have to digress briefly to describe our measures of the cyclical timing of money.

In studying the cyclical timing of money, we have found it more useful to examine the rate of change in the money stock than its absolute level. The reason is that the upward secular trend in the quantity of money has been so strong that the quantity of money has frequently tended to rise during both cyclical expansions and cyclical contractions. Cyclical forces show up much more clearly in the rate at which the stock of money rises than in whether it rises; or, alternatively, cyclical forces show up more clearly in the deviations of the stock of money from a secular trend.

We have used two alternative methods to describe the timing of the cyclical fluctuations in the rate of change in money. One is the standard Bureau specific cycle analysis: we date the months in which the series reaches peaks and troughs, and designate the resulting dates, the peaks and troughs in the rate of change. However, we have been hesitant to rely on this method alone. The major reason is purely statistical. Rate-of-change series are very erratic and jagged, having a characteristic saw-tooth appearance. This often makes it difficult to choose a particular month as the peak or trough. Several months, sometimes separated by a long interval, often seem about equally plausible. A subsidiary reason that we have been hesitant to rely on the rate-of-change peak and trough dates alone is analytical. What feature of the money series is most relevant to the cycle is by no means clear; whether the rate of change alone, or some cumulative total such as the deviation from a trend.[3]

Accordingly we have used a second method of dating suggested by the

---

3. For a fuller discussion of this point and also some of the other points considered in this subsection see Milton Friedman, "The Lag in Effect of Monetary Policy" (Chapter 11 above).

empirical observation that the rate-of-change series often seemed to move around the same level for a time and then shift abruptly to a new level. This suggested approximating the rate-of-change series by a set of horizontal steps, which turn out typically to alternate between high and low steps. We designate as a "step peak" the month in which a high step ends and is succeeded by a low step, and as a "step trough" the month in which a low step ends and is succeeded by a high step. It turns out that these dates approximate the dates at which the deviation from a trend would reach a peak or trough. Their use obviates the necessity of actually fitting a trend.

We had hoped that one of these methods would yield dates bearing a more consistent relation to the timing of reference cycles than the other, giving us a basis for choosing between the two methods. So far, this hope has not been realized (see Table 1); the two yield about equally consistent timing measures. Hence, we have continued to use both, regarding this as a way both to average out errors and to take account of different characteristics of the money series.

Both the rate-of-change peak and the step peak in the money series tend regularly to come earlier than the peak in general business (the reference peak) to which we match them, and both the rate-of-change trough and the step trough to come earlier than the matched reference trough. The interval is somewhat longer at peaks than at troughs, and decidedly longer for the rate-of-change turning points than for the step turning points. On the average of twenty-one matched cycles (from 1870 to 1961) the rate-of-change peak comes 17 months earlier than the reference peak, and the step peak, 6 months earlier; the rate-of-change trough comes 13 months earlier than the reference trough, the step trough, 4 months earlier. As to consistency, the rate-of-change turning point comes earlier than the reference turning point at every one of the 42 turning points included in the above averages; the step turning point does so in 29 out of the 42.

These regular and sizable leads of the money series are themselves suggestive of an influence running from money to business but they are by no means decisive. One reason is that both the monetary changes and the business changes might be the common consequence of some other influences which have their effect on money more promptly than on business. A second is that the characteristics of business change affecting money may not be those that are dated by the Bureau reference dates.

The most important reason, however, why the consistent leads of the money series are not decisive is that, given a recurrent cyclical process, these leads may be simply the reflection of an earlier influence of business on money; they may be a statistical artifact resulting from our matching the turning points in money with the wrong turning points in business. Instead of matching a peak in the money series with the subsequent reference peak, we could match it with the prior reference trough; similarly, we could match the rate of change trough with the prior reference peak. This procedure yields shorter average timing differences for the rate-of-change dates—an average lag of 6 months at reference peaks and 13 months at reference troughs—and longer average timing differences for the step dates—an average lag of 16 months at reference peaks and 19 months at reference troughs.[4]

The question whether it is preferable to interpret the money series as mainly conforming positively to the cycle with a lead or inversely with a lag is therefore relevant to the more general question whether the predominant direction of influence is from money to business. All theoretical analysis I know of which would explain how money can play an independent role in the cyclical process also implies that the connection is positive, that is, that unusually high rates of rise in money promote business expansion, unusually low rates, business contraction. Hence, inverted conformity, whether with a lag or a lead, would sharply contradict the existence of a strong influence from money to business, and positive conformity, especially with a lead, would be consistent with such an influence. On the other hand, many of the links between business and money, as Cagan has shown, may be expected to produce an inverted response; the clearest example is the tendency of business expansion to produce gold outflows and hence downward pressure on high-powered money. Inverted conformity with a lag would therefore be entirely consistent with an influence running from business to money. Positive conformity could be, too, since some of the effects of business on money are in a positive direction, for example, the effect of business expansion on bank reserve ratios. However, it is not easy to rationalize positive conformity with a lead as reflecting supply response.

The nub of these considerations is that inverted conformity would clearly contradict a predominant influence of money on business; positive conformity would be consistent with such an influence and, especially with a lead, would constitute evidence in favor of it but would not rule out an influence of business on money. And, of course, as with the more general question, positive and inverted conformity are not mutually exclusive, both exist; and both are plausible. The question is, which is dominant.

How can our timing measures help us choose between positive and inverted conformity? One obvious answer is by seeing which interpretation yields more consistent timing measures. Are the leads or lags more nearly the same from cycle to cycle on one interpretation than on the other?

Table 1, which comes from our unfinished manuscript, "Trends and Cycles," contains the relevant evidence. It gives, for all cycles from 1870 to 1961, the dispersion (as measured by the standard deviation) of the leads and lags as computed under the two interpretations and as determined both from rate-of-change and step dates. The dispersion is uniformly lower when the money

---

4. Of course, given a recurrent cycle, a money peak could be matched with a prior reference peak as well, and similarly for the trough, implying a long-delayed positive effect of business on money; or a money peak and trough, with a succeeding reference trough and peak, implying a long-delayed inverted effect of money on business, and so on. We have restricted the discussion to the simplest alternative interpretations.

series is treated as conforming positively, and the difference is substantial.[5] So far as this evidence goes, it clearly supports positive conformity.

Table 1. *Comparison of Timing Measurements of Rate of Change in Money Stock on Positive and Inverted Basis, 1870–1961*

	KIND OF SPECIFIC CYCLE TURN IN RATE OF CHANGE IN MONEY STOCK			
	LAST MONTH OF STEP AT		TROUGH OR PEAK IN RATE OF CHANGE AT	
	Reference Troughs	*Reference Peaks*	*Reference Troughs*	*Reference Peaks*
Mean lead (−) or lag (+), in months				
Positive basis	− 4.0	− 6.1	− 13.2	− 16.9
Inverted basis	19.5	15.6	12.8	6.4
Standard deviation of lead or lag, in months				
Positive basis	5.6	7.1	6.0	7.6
Inverted basis	11.7	15.8	15.1	12.3
Number of observations	21	21	21	21

NOTES: Matching with reference turns follows Arthur F. Burns and Wesley C. Mitchell, *Measuring Business Cycles*, pp. 115–28, with a few exceptions. Strict adherence to the Burns and Mitchell procedure would not reverse the finding that the standard deviations are larger on the inverted basis than on the positive basis.

SOURCE: Money stock: 1870–1946, from *A Monetary History*, Table A-1, col. 8; 1947–61, *Supplement to Banking and Monetary Statistics*, sect. 1, Board of Governors of the Federal Reserve System, Oct. 1962, pp. 20–22.

D. Serial Correlation of Amplitudes of Cycle Phases

A very different kind of evidence on positive versus inverted conformity is provided by the size of cyclical movements in money. In order to explain what this evidence is, I shall again have to digress, this time to describe a most interesting feature of business cycle behavior which has implications for many problems besides the one under discussion.

The feature in question is the relation between successive phases of business cycles. Is the magnitude of an expansion related systematically to the magnitude of the succeeding contraction? Does a boom tend on the average to be followed by a large contraction? A mild expansion, by a mild contraction? To find out,

5. If the standard deviations on the two interpretations could be regarded as statistically independent of one another and each based on independent observations, the ratio of the larger to the smaller that would be exceeded by chance less than one time in twenty would be 1.46, and less than one time in 100, 1.73. For three of the four comparisons in Table 1, the ratio considerably exceeds the latter level, and for the fourth, the former. The specified conditions are not satisfied by these data but it is not clear in which direction the comparison is biased.

we have used two different measures of the amplitude of cyclical phases: one, the Moore index,[6] as an indicator of the change in the physical volume of activity; the other, the volume of bank clearings or debits, as an indicator of the change in money values. Lines 2 and 3 of Table 2 (which, like Table 1, is taken from the present draft of "Trends and Cycles") show that, when the amplitude of an expansion is correlated with the amplitude of the succeeding contraction, the resulting correlation is negligible for both measures. Surprisingly, perhaps, there appears to be no systematic connection between the size of an expansion

Table 2. *Rank Difference Correlation between Change in One Cycle Phase and Change in Next Succeeding Cycle Phase, Rate of Change in Money and Two Indicators of General Business, 1879–1961, Excluding War Cycles and 1945–49*

	Annual and Semiannual Data 1879–1908	Monthly Data 1908–61	Whole Period 1879–1961
Series Correlated with Itself			
Expansion in Indicated Series and Succeeding Contraction in Same Series			
1. Rate of change in money stock, per cent per month in specific cycles	−.02	.33	.24
2. Moore index, in specific cycle relatives (indicator of physical change in general business)	−.07	.10	.10
3. Clearing–debits, in reference cycle relatives (indicator of dollar-value change in general business)	−.05	−.39	.15
Number of pairs	8	10	18
Contraction in Indicated Series and Succeeding Expansion in Same Series			
4. Rate of change in money stock, per cent per month in specific cycles	.83	.68	.74
5. Moore index, in specific cycle relatives	.71	.85	.86
6. Clearing–debits, in reference cycle relatives	−.17	.46	.26
Number of pairs	8	7	15

NOTE: War cycles 1914–19 and 1938–45 are omitted because of their special characteristics. The 1945–49 cycle is omitted because the expansion is skipped by the rate-of-change in money series. Specific cycles are those matched with reference cycles in the column headings. There was a one-to-one correspondence between specific and reference cycles.

SOURCE: Money stock: see Table 1. Specific cycle analysis follows Burns and Mitchell, *Measuring Business Cycles*, pp. 115–41.

Moore index: Unpublished memorandum by Geoffrey H. Moore, extending table in

6. The Moore index is our designation of an average of three trend-adjusted indexes of general business used by Arthur F. Burns and Wesley C. Mitchell (*Measuring Business Cycles*, New York: National Bureau of Economic Research (1946), p. 403) as a broad indicator of the amplitude of cycles, and revised and extended by Geoffrey H. Moore (*Business Cycle Indicators*, G. H. Moore (Ed.), Princeton, N.J.: for NBER (1961), vol. I, p. 104; and an unpublished memorandum).

Measuring Business Cycles, p. 403, and revising and updating table in *Business Cycle Indicators*, Vol. I, p. 104. An average of three trend-adjusted indexes of business activity—A. T. & T., Persons-Barrons, and Ayres—each of which was analyzed for specific cycles, suppressing specific cycle turns not corresponding to reference cycle turns.

Clearing-debits: Bank clearings outside New York City, monthly, 1879–1919: bank debits outside New York City, monthly, 1919–61: 1879–1942: Seasonally adjusted from *Historical Statistics of the United States, 1789–1945* Bureau of the Census, 1949, pp. 324–25, 337–38. 1943–61: Board of Governors of the Federal Reserve System, Division of Bank Operations, mimeographed table, "Bank Debits and Rates of Turnover" (C. 5, Revised Series, 1943–52), Dec. 23, 1953; thereafter *Federal Reserve Bulletin*, adjusted for seasonal variation by NBER. Reference cycle analysis follows Burns and Mitchell, *Measuring Business Cycles*, pp. 160–70.

Values of the rank-difference correlation coefficient that would be exceeded in absolute value by chance in the indicated proportion *P* of independent samples are:

Value of *P*	NUMBER OF OBSERVATIONS				
	7	8	10	15	18
.10	.71	.64	.56	.44	.40
.05	.79	.74	.65	.52	.48
.01	.93	.88	.79	.69	.63

and of the succeeding contraction, whether size is measured by physical volume or by dollar value.

Let us now ask the same question, except that we start with a contraction and ask how its amplitude is related to that of the succeeding expansion. As lines 5 and 6 of Table 2 show, the results are very different for the physical-volume measure though much the same for the dollar-value measure. A large contraction in output tends to be followed on the average by a large business expansion; a mild contraction, by a mild expansion.

This phenomenon, if it should be confirmed by a fuller analysis of data for the United States and other countries, would have important implications for the analysis of business cycles in general, not solely for our monetary studies. For one thing, it would cast grave doubt on those theories that see as the source of a deep depression the excesses of the prior expansion.[7] For another, it would raise serious questions about both the analytical models, in terms of which most of us have come to approach the analysis of cycles, and the statistical methods we use to analyze them.

Our analytical models generally involve a conception of a self-generating cycle, in which each phase gives rise to the next, and which may be kept going by a sequence of random shocks, each giving rise to a series of damped perturbations. The corresponding physical analogy is of an electrical network in which responses are described by sine waves. The asymmetric serial correlation pattern suggests that this analogy may be misleading, that a better one is what can be

7. The major qualification that must be attached to our result for this purpose is the definitions of the cycle and of expansion and contraction phases on which it rests. Proponents of the view cited might well argue that what matters is the cumulative effect of several expansions, as we define them, and that the relevant concept of expansion is of a "major" expansion or a phase of a long cycle.

termed a plucking model. Consider an elastic string stretched taut between two points on the underside of a rigid horizontal board and glued lightly to the board. Let the string be plucked at a number of points chosen more or less at random with a force that varies at random, and then held down at the lowest point reached. The result will be to produce a succession of apparent cycles in the string whose amplitudes depend on the force used in plucking the string. The cycles are symmetrical about their troughs; each contraction is of the same amplitude as the succeeding expansion. But there is no necessary connection between the amplitude of an expansion and the amplitude of the succeeding contraction. Correlations between the amplitudes of successive phases would be asymmetric in the same way the correlations in lines 2 and 5 of Table 2 are. Expansions would be uncorrelated with succeeding contractions, but contractions would be correlated with succeeding expansions. Up to this point, the peaks in the series would all be at the same level. To complete the analogy, we can suppose the board to be tilted to allow for trend and the underside of the board to be irregular to generate variability in the peaks, which would also introduce something less than perfect correlation between the size of contractions and subsequent expansions.

In this analogy, the irregular underside of the rigid board corresponds to the upper limit to output set by the available resources and methods of organizing them. Output is viewed as bumping along the ceiling of maximum feasible output except that every now and then it is plucked down by a cyclical contraction. Given institutional rigidities in prices, the contraction takes in considerable measure the form of a decline in output. Since there is no physical limit to the decline short of zero output, the size of the decline in output can vary widely. When subsequent recovery sets in, it tends to return output to the ceiling; it cannot go beyond, so there is an upper limit to output and the amplitude of the expansion tends to be correlated with the amplitude of the contraction.

For series on prices and money values, the situation is different. The very rigidity in prices invoked to explain the decline in output may mean that the declines in prices vary less in size than the declines in output. More important, there is no physical ceiling, so that there is nothing on this level of analysis to prevent the string from being plucked up as well as down. These differences make it plausible that the asymmetric correlation would be much less marked in money-value series than in output and perhaps entirely absent in price series. This is so for the correlations in Table 2. which are small for clearing-debits. The same conclusion is suggested also by graphic inspection of a wide variety of physical-volume and price series. A symmetric pattern of downward pluckings can be clearly seen in many of the physical-volume series; such a pattern is much less clear in the price series; and, in some price series, symmetric upward pluckings seem about as numerous.

The contrast between the physical-volume and dollar-value or price series can be put somewhat differently. The indicated pattern in physical-volume series is readily understandable regardless of the reason for the cyclical fluctuations in the series—of the source of the pluckings, as it were. A similar pattern in value or price series would have to be explained by some similar pattern or asymmetry in the source of the cyclical fluctuations, some factor that prevents upward plucking from being as important as downward plucking.

Let us now return to our major theme and see how we can use this feature of business cycles to get additional evidence on the appropriate interpretation of the money series. If positive conformity is dominant, and if the monetary changes are linked with physical-volume changes, then the serial correlations for money should be the same as for the Moore index. On the other hand, if inverted conformity is dominant, and changes in business produce later changes in the opposite direction in money, then the correlations for money should be the opposite of those for the Moore index, that is, the amplitude of an expansion should be correlated with that of the succeeding contraction; and the amplitude of a contraction should be uncorrelated with that of the succeeding expansion.

The relevant correlations for the specific cycle amplitudes of the rate of change in money are given in lines 1 and 4 of Table 2. We have as yet no parallel analysis for step amplitudes, though we plan one. The correlations we have for money are roughly the same as for the Moore index. The simplest interpretation of this result is that the pattern for business is a reflection of the pattern for money. In terms of our analogy, every now and then the money string is plucked downward. That produces, after some lag, a downward movement in economic activity related in magnitude to the downward movement in money. The money string then rebounds, and that in turn produces, after some lag, an upward movement in economic activity, again related in magnitude to the upward movement in money. Since the downward and subsequent upward movements in money are correlated in amplitude with one another, so are downward and subsequent upward movements in economic activity. Since the upward and subsequent downward movements in money are not correlated in amplitude, neither are the upward and subsequent downward movements in economic activity.

Personally, I find this bit of evidence in favor of dominant positive conformity particularly persuasive for two reasons. The first is that I have been unable to construct an explanation of how the observed asymmetric correlation pattern for money could be produced by an inverted response of money to business cycles. The second is that our historical studies have uncovered a number of episodes that correspond precisely to the notion of downward pluckings of the money string.

E. Evidence from Foreign Countries

All the evidence so far cited is for the United States. In addition, there is much evidence of a similar kind for other countries.[8] Cagan's earlier work on hyper-

8. I exclude the well-known studies which deal chiefly with long-period secular rather than short-period cyclical relations, such as Earl J. Hamilton's classic work on the price revolution in the sixteenth century as a result of the inflow of specie from the New World,

inflations provides some striking results of a positive relationship for rather extreme monetary episodes.[9] Several studies on Chile, done by students or faculty members of the University of Chicago, provide similar evidence for a more moderate though still substantial inflation.[10] Some unpublished work on Canada by George Macesich demonstrates that the timing relations between monetary and economic change there are very similar to the relations in the United States.

In order to expand the range of evidence on this and related issues, I went on something of a fishing expedition last year (on leave from both the University of Chicago and the National Bureau) to explore the data available for foreign countries differing as widely as possible from the United States, and to learn something about their monetary arrangements. The countries I studied in some detail were Yugoslavia, Greece, Israel, India, and Japan. For each, I collected data on the quantity of money, income, prices, indexes of industrial production, interest rates, and the like. There is no doubt that sufficient data are available to make comparative studies feasible.

So far, I have been able to do little analysis of the data I gathered. But even that superficial analysis has uncovered some interesting bits of additional evidence on the direction of influence. For Yugoslavia, for example, there happens to be an episode for which the direction of relation is hardly doubtful: the stock of currency (which seems the appropriate measure of "money" for such a country) and income in current prices both have been rising rather rapidly in the past decade, with one marked exception in both. There is one year in each series in which the upward trend is replaced by a horizontal movement. That year comes one year earlier in the currency series than in the money income series! For Israel, the data, which are carefully compiled, show roughly the same relation between rates of change as for the United States, with rates of change in currency leading rates of change in income by about a year. For Japan, cyclical fluctuations of the past ten years or so seem readily interpreted as a strictly self-generating monetary cycle in response to changes in the rate of change in the money stock. The contractionary monetary changes are produced by the reactions of the monetary authorities to recurrent balance of payments difficulties, which are a response to prior expansionary monetary changes that

---

or J. E. Cairnes' "Essays Toward A Solution of the Gold Question" (*Essays in Political Economy*, London: Macmillan (1873), pp. 1–165), in which he analyzed in advance the effects to be expected from the gold discoveries in Australia and California and then after the event added postscripts checking his predictions with the actual outcome—one of the earliest and still one of the best applications of the scientific method in economics.

9. Phillip Cagan, "The Monetary Dynamics of Hyperinflation," in *Studies in the Quantity Theory of Money*, Milton Friedman (Ed.), Chicago: University of Chicago Press (1956).

10. John Deaver, "The Chilean Inflation and the Demand for Money," unpublished Ph.D. dissertation, University of Chicago, 1960; Arnold C. Harberger, "The Dynamics of Inflation in Chile," in Carl Christ *et al.*, *Measurement in Economics*, Stanford, Cal.: Stanford University Press (1963), pp. 219–50.

occur when the balance of payments eases. The Japanese data show about a three to six-months' lead of the rate of change in the money supply over the rate of change in production and prices. We have as yet no conceptually similar timing comparisons for the United States, though we are in the process of making them. Perhaps the closest are the timing comparisons between the step dates and reference turns. Those show a roughly similar lead.

F. The Combined Weight of the Evidence

In a scientific problem, the final verdict is never in. Any conclusion must always be subject to revision in the light of new evidence. Yet I believe that the available evidence of the five kinds listed justifies considerable confidence in the conclusion that the money series is dominated by positive conformity, which reflects in some measure an independent influence of money on business. The feedback effect of business on money, which undoubtedly also exists, may contribute to the positive conformity and may also introduce a measure of inverted conformity.

In the "Trends and Cycles" volume, we hope to carry farther our analysis of the evidence based on the timing and amplitude of fluctuations in the money series (subsections C and D above). We have no present plans for doing any further work on the qualitative historical evidence or on that provided by the determinants of the money stock (subsections A and B). Data for foreign countries (subsection E) merit much fuller analysis, and I have interested a number of students in research for doctoral dissertations which will make a start in that direction. However, this is not part of the Bureau's program, though it is obviously relevant to our common intellectual interests.

IV. OUR CENTRAL QUALITATIVE CONCLUSIONS
AND THEIR LIMITATIONS

The central conclusion we have reached in our studies is of a piece with that reached on the specific issue considered in the preceding section, and like that, though still tentative, in our opinion justifies much confidence. Stated simply, it is that money does matter and matters very much. Changes in the quantity of money have important, and broadly predictable, economic effects. Long-period changes in the quantity of money relative to output determine the secular behavior of prices. Substantial expansions in the quantity of money over short periods have been a major proximate source of the accompanying inflation in prices. Substantial contractions in the quantity of money over short periods have been a major factor in producing severe economic contractions. And cyclical variations in the quantity of money may well be an important element in the ordinary mild business cycle.

These qualitative conclusions, and even more, specific quantitative findings, are important. But they are also limited. Because they go sharply counter to what has been so widely believed for nearly two decades, there has been some tendency to interpret our claims as being far more sweeping than they are. For example, one newspaper story referring to similar views interpreted them as asserting that "the growth of the money supply is the single most important factor affecting the nation's economy"—which is very far indeed from what we are saying. To avoid misunderstanding, let me state explicitly some of the limitations of our conclusions.

One limitation is linked to the distinction between "real" magnitudes—relative prices, quantities of output, levels of employment, efficiency of production, accumulation of capital, and the like—and "nominal" magnitudes—absolute prices, quantity of money, nominal money income, and so on. The quantity of money in general appears not to be an important factor affecting secular changes in the real magnitudes. They are determined primarily by such basic phenomena as the kind of economic system, the qualities of the people, the state of technology, the availablity of natural resources, and so on. These, not monetary institutions or policy, are the critical factors that ultimately determine the "wealth of nations" and of their citizens. In general, the major long-run impact of the quantity of money is on nominal magnitudes, and especially on the absolute level of prices. Our conclusions are in no way inconsistent with that celebrated—and much misunderstood—statement of John Stuart Mill, "There cannot, in short, be intrinsically a more insignificant thing, in the economy of society, than money; except in the character of a contrivance for sparing time and labor. It is a machine for doing quickly and commodiously, what could be done, though less quickly and commodiously, without it; and like many other kinds of machinery, it only exerts a distinct and independent influence of its own when it gets out of order."[11]

What we can now add to this is a much more explicit specification of what it means for the machinery of money to "get out of order." It gets out of order, we have tentatively concluded, when the quantity of money behaves erratically, when either its rate of increase is sharply stepped up—which will mean price inflation—or sharply contracted—which will mean economic depression—and especially when such erratic movements succeed one another. One of our major findings is that, over periods spanning several cycles, the average rate of growth of the stock of money—so long as it is relatively stable and within moderate limits—has no discernible effect on the rate of growth of real output. Differences in monetary growth are reflected instead in prices. Our findings give no support to the view, now widely popular, that long-run inflation is favorable to economic growth. Deviations from the average rate of growth of the stock of money, if sharp, account for the inflations or severe contractions already referred to. If mild, the deviations are linked to the usual business cycle, and appear

11. *Principles of Political Economy* (1848), Ashley ed., London: Longmans, Green (1929), p. 488.

to be reflected partly in prices and partly in quantity, though we know little as yet about what determines how much of the effect is on prices and how much on quantity. The general subject of the division of changes in money income between prices and quantity badly needs more investigation. None of our leading economic theories has much to say about it. Yet knowledge about it is needed for better understanding of the impact not only of monetary changes but also of other factors significant in the business cycle.

A second limitation is linked to the distinction between average behavior and behavior in a particular episode. The fact that we can predict within fairly narrow limits the number of heads that will come up in a thousand tosses of a fair coin does not enable us to predict what will come up the next time. As students of business cycles, we are concerned largely with average behavior. The data for any particular episode are bound to be subject to considerable errors of measurement and to be affected by casual events peculiar to that episode. We can largely compensate for both bad data and erratic behavior by constructing averages for a number of episodes. The results may be well established, on the average, yet not reliable for predicting an individual case. Our earlier discussion of cyclical timing is an excellent example. As noted above, data on the month-to-month changes in the quantity of money are highly erratic and irregular, and there is often much uncertainty for an individual cycle about which month shows the highest rate of change (rate-of-change peak), or which month is followed by a shift in the rate of change to a lower level (step peak). Hence there is also much uncertainty about the difference in time between the rate-of-change peak and the reference peak or between the step peak and the reference peak—a date which is itself subject to error. But such errors may be expected to cancel out, so the average timing may be well determined. For example, in the course of 21 matched cycles from 1870 to 1961, the estimated difference in timing between the step peak and the reference peak varied from a lag of 4 months to a lead of 17 months with a standard deviation of 7 months. These estimated differences average out to a lead of 6 months, and this average is rather accurately determined. The standard error of the *average* is only 1.6 months, which means that the odds are 2 to 1 that the error in the average time is less than 1.6 months and 20 to 1 that it is less than 3.2 months.

Looked at another way, the fact that, on the average, the step peak comes 6 months before the estimated reference peak does not enable us to say very much about any particular occasion. Even if we could know that an observed shift to a lower rate of growth of the money stock is one that we would later regard as a step peak—much easier to know by hindsight than at the time—about the most we could say would be that there was roughly a 50-50 chance that a turn in business that we could later regard as a reference peak would occur between 1 and 11 months later. Our inability to be more precise may reflect our inability to measure the various magnitudes very accurately, or it may reflect inherent variability in the economic response to monetary stimuli. At the present stage of our knowledge, we do not know which.

Our assertion that money matters is therefore very far indeed from an assertion that we know enough about the role it plays and can measure sufficiently accurately the relevant magnitudes to predict precisely what effect an observed change in the quantity of money will have in a particular case. Needless to say, the aim of further research is to improve the precision of such predictions.

A third limitation, and the last one I shall mention, is that we are still a long way from having a detailed and tested theory of the mechanism that links money with other economic magnitudes. For long-period secular changes, for short-period rapid inflations, and for severe contractions, there exist reasonably well-formulated theories and a good deal of empirical evidence on transmission mechanisms. But for the ordinary business cycle, we are in a much less satisfactory position. In "Money and Business Cycles," we sketched very broadly some of the possible lines of connection between monetary changes and economic changes "in order," as we wrote, "to provide a plausible rationalization of our empirical findings . . . to show that a monetary theory of cyclical fluctuations can accommodate a wide variety of other empirical findings about cyclical regularities, and . . . to stimulate others to elaborate the theory and render it more specific."[12] We shall try to improve and elaborate this sketch in our 'Trends and Cycles' volume, but I am not sure just how far we can get within the limits we have imposed for ourselves. Identification of the channels through which short-run monetary changes work their effects, and specification in quantitative terms of the characteristics of the channels and of the effects exerted through them, remain major tasks for future research.

V. THE STOCK OF MONEY
AND RECENT ECONOMIC CHANGES

A look at recent history will enable us to illustrate many of the points made in the preceding sections and to show the relevance of some of our findings to current problems.

The upper panel of Chart I shows for the past seven years three series: (1) the money stock, as we define it, which is to say currency plus all commercial bank deposits adjusted; (2) currency plus demand deposits adjusted only, an alternative concept which is often referred to as the money supply; (3) the Federal Reserve index of industrial production, as a single index of the physical volume of general economic activity. The vertical scale is logarithmic, to show relative not absolute changes.

The two money series illustrate why the total stock of money is not by itself a very useful magnitude for studying cyclical movements. The series are smooth and dominated by their trends. Cyclical fluctuations show up in the form of waves about the trend and only occasionally in the form of absolute ups and

---

12. Friedman and Schwartz, "Money and Business Cycles," p. 59.

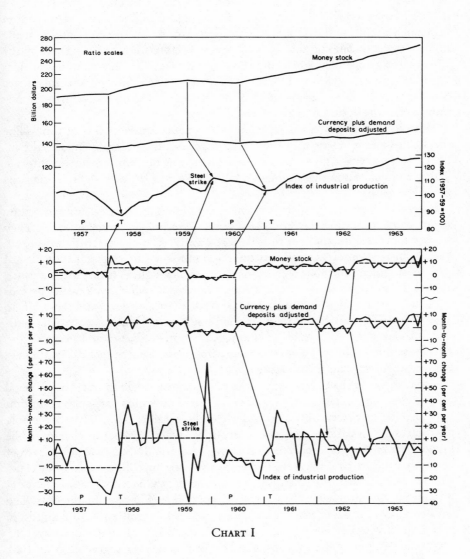

CHART I

downs. For this period, there is only one absolute decline in the money stock series (from 1959 to 1960). The trends of the two series differ much more for that period than for most, reflecting the recent rapid rise in the time deposits of commercial banks, apparently largely in response to the successive rises in the rates of interest banks have been permitted, and have been willing, to pay on them. But aside from the trend, it is perhaps obvious even from these series that the two show very much the same movements.

The series on industrial production is much less smooth. It shows three decided declines: the first, a reflection of the 1957–58 recession; the second, of the steel strike—this one, we would be inclined to smooth out as a random movement; and the third, of the 1960–61 recession. The letters T and P at the bottom of each panel on the chart correspond to the months designated by the Bureau as reference troughs and peaks, respectively. The first trough coincides with the upturn in the production index; the succeeding peak comes three months after the downturn in the production index; and the second trough, one month after the upturn in the production index.

Whereas the money series represent stocks at successive points of time—like the stock of housing or the level of inventories—the index of industrial production represents a flow—like new construction or additions to inventories. This is a major reason the production index is so much more variable than the money series are.

In the lower panel of Chart I, we have converted the money series into flow series, also, by plotting the month-to-month percentage changes in them. They show the cyclical fluctuations much more clearly. The characteristic saw-tooth pattern in first-difference series is obvious, and so is the frequent difficulty of picking single months to represent the peaks and troughs. This segment of time, 1957–63, also shows clearly the tendency—noted above for much earlier periods —of the rate of change to move around a rather constant level and then shift to a new level. The horizontal lines are the "steps" with which we have approximated the series, and the ends of the steps are our step peaks and step troughs. For this segment, the step dates seem less ambiguous than the specific cycle dates, but for other segments the opposite is true.

Comparison of the two money series in the lower panel illustrates our general finding that the substantive results do not depend on which particular definition is used. The two series are obviously closely parallel. The only appreciable differences are in early 1958 and in early 1962, when the rate of change of the broader series is higher relative to its level before and after than is the rate of change of the narrower series. The reason for the first difference is not clear. The second comes immediately after the Board of Governors raised the rates of interest that commercial banks were permitted to pay on time deposits. The dates we have chosen for the ends of our steps are identical for both definitions, except the low step in early 1962. We date that step as beginning February 1962 and ending August 1962, for the narrower concept, and as beginning May 1962 and ending September 1962, for the broader. Because of the disturbances introduced by the change in the rates of interest on time deposits, we are inclined to prefer the date derived from the narrower concept—but clearly no great error will be introduced, whichever is used.

Comparison of the money series with the production index illustrates the positive conformity and the lead that we have found so characteristic, as well as the variability of the lead. To bring this out arrows have been drawn from the ends of the steps in the rate-of-change money series in the lower panel and from the corresponding dates on the stock series in the upper panel to the turning points of the production index. For the step dates, the leads at the two troughs are 3 months and 7 months (8 months to the terminal reference trough) and at the intervening peak 6 months (10 months to the reference peak). These are certainly very much in line with the average timing over the past 90 years, which is 4 months at the trough and 6 months at the peak (see Table I). So this segment illustrates very well the stability we have found in monetary relations.

The reason for drawing the arrows from the stock series as well as from the rate-of-change series is to show how the movements which show up so clearly in the rate-of-change series can be seen also in the stock series, once one looks for them.

The money series show a low step in 1962 that we have so far not matched with any corresponding movement in the upper panel for the production index. However, though the production index has risen since early 1961 except for an occasional month, it is clear that there was a distinct retardation in late 1962. The retardation was the source of much concern at the time and was associated with the lower level of national income attained than had been forecast early in the year. To bring that movement into sharper relief, we have used the same technique for the production index as for the money series, namely, plotted month-to-month percentage changes. This series is even more erratic than the money series, but there is clearly a low step in 1962 to correspond with the low step in the money series. Its onset, as we have dated it, comes 2 months after the beginning of the low step in currency and demand deposits, and 1 month before that in the broader money total. The shift to a new higher level comes 5 months after the shift to a higher level in the rate of change in money.

This minor perturbation in industrial production will not and should not be classified by the National Bureau as a reference cycle; hence, neither its occurrence, its correspondence to the shift in money, nor the timing of the two movements would be revealed in a standard Bureau cyclical analysis. This is one of that species of subcycles that Ruth Mack has brought to our attention. The existence of such episodes is one of the reasons we plan to supplement the standard cycle analysis in our "Trends and Cycles" volume with correlation analysis of at least quarterly series.

The chart shows very much wider fluctuations in industrial production than in the rate of change in money series. If instead of industrial production a measure of aggregate output had been used, the contrast would have been narrower but still present. The contrast is even greater for aggregate money income than for output. We reported in "Money and Business Cycles" that, on the average, the percentage fluctuations in income were twice as large as those in the rate of change in money and offered a hypothesis to explain why this should be so.

So far, I have used the recent period to illustrate some of our technical problems and some of our descriptive findings. But it can also serve to illustrate the problems of interpretation. I have described Chart I entirely in terms of a positive conformity of the money series; trying to describe it in terms of inverted conformity will perhaps suggest some of the difficulties we have found with such an interpretation and some of the reasons we have rejected it. The still more important question is whether we should interpret the positive conformity as reflecting the influence of money on business, or of business on money. If these were the only alternatives, I would find the former much more appealing for this segment of time in particular. There have been in this period five rather clear-cut shifts in monetary action—as judged by the rate of change in the stock of money. Each has been followed after some months (with one possible exception, early 1962, if the link is made with the broader money series) by a shift in the same direction in the rate of growth of economic activity, as judged by the production index. Perhaps this pattern reflects the common effect of some third force; it is hard to explain it by any direct influence of business on money.

Chapter 13

In Defense of
Destabilizing Speculation

TWO PROPOSITIONS ABOUT private speculation are widely held: first, that speculation is in fact often destabilizing, in the sense that it makes fluctuations in prices wider than they would "otherwise" be; second, that destabilizing speculation necessarily involves economic loss. This pair of propositions underlies much current opinion about commodity policy—where they lead to support for "buffer stocks" and similar plans, and about balance of payments policy—where they constitute a chief criticism of floating exchange rates.

This note is not intended to be an exhaustive analysis of this pair of propositions, or of speculation in general. Its purpose is much more limited: to point out that the second proposition is invalid, that destabilizing speculation, though it may in some cases lead to economic loss, may in others confer economic benefit. The empirical generalization about the prevalence of destabilizing speculation, which is what gives the theoretical proposition its interest seems to be one of those propositions that has gained currency the way a rumor does— each man believes it because the next man does, and despite the absence of any substantial body of well documented evidence for it. It is a proposition that

Reprinted from Ralph W. Pfouts (Ed.), *Essays in Economics and Econometrics*, Chapel Hill, N.C.: University of North Carolina Press (1960). I am indebted for comments on an earlier draft to Martin Bailey, Harry Johnson, James Meade, Joan Robinson, and Dennis Robertson.

badly needs intensive empirical investigation. My own conjecture is that such an investigation would show it to be unfounded. But this is simply a conjecture and plays no part in what follows.

The ready acceptance of the proposition that destabilizing speculation is economically harmful reflects, I believe, a natural bias of the academic student against gambling and in favor of insurance. It is natural for him to regard a futures market, for example, as a market in which a "legitimate" producer hedges his risks by transferring them to a "speculator"; the producer is viewed as buying "insurance" from the speculator. But granted that this is a possible and indeed likely interpretation of an actual futures market, it is not the only possible one. May such a market not be one in which the "legitimate" producer engages as a side-line in selling "gambles" to speculators willing to pay a price for gambling and knowingly doing so? And if so, moral scruples about gambling aside, is any economic loss involved?

In arguing that destabilizing speculation need not involve economic loss I do not mean in any way to deny the usual view that stabilizing speculation confers benefit. In this usual view, the economic function of speculation is taken to be the reduction of inter-temporal differences in price. In a commodity market, for example, a speculator is viewed as performing this function by buying when the crop is plentiful and prices "abnormally" low, holding stocks of the commodity until prices have risen, and then selling when the crop is short and prices "abnormally" high. In this way, speculators transfer resources from less to more urgent uses. The difference between the prices at which they sell and buy is their margin, which must cover costs of storage and furnish their remuneration. The excess over storage costs is a payment for specialized skill in knowing when to buy and when to sell and perhaps also for bearing risk.

This model takes for granted that there is a meaningful distinction between speculative and other transactions, that one can speak of what the price would have been in the absence of speculation. This is a point that raises many difficulties and requires careful examination in any full analysis of speculation.[1] We can, however, evade it for our purposes by narrowing the question under discussion. Consider any market in operation. Suppose that an additional set of transactions are made in that market by an additional group of people whom we shall call "speculators" or "new speculators". We shall then deal only with the question whether this additional set of transactions increases the fluctuations in price and, if it increases them, whether it involves an economic loss or confers a gain. By dealing in this way with a change in the amount of speculation, we can avoid the troublesome intellectual problem of defining zero speculation without any essential loss in generality. We shall make one further assumption to evade a troublesome problem: namely, that the activities of speculators do not affect the quantities demanded and supplied by other participants in the

---

1. See, for example, the comments by W. J. Baumol, "Speculation, Profitability, and Stability," *Review of Economics and Statistics*, vol. 39, no. 3, August, 1957, pp. 263–71.

market at each current price. This implies that there is a well-defined price that will clear the market at each point in the absence of speculation and that this price is not affected by speculation.

With these assumptions, it is clear that, if carrying costs are neglected, our model implies that speculators gain if they reduce inter-temporal differences in price, and lose if they widen such differences.Speculators can fill in the troughs of price movements only by buying net when prices would otherwise be low; they can flatten out the peaks only by selling net when prices would otherwise be high; unless they carry this so far as to reverse peaks and troughs, they gain by the difference. Conversely, speculators can make fluctuations wider (in the same direction) only by selling net when prices would otherwise be low and buying net when prices would otherwise be high. But this means that they sell at a lower price than they buy and so make losses. Our model therefore implicitly defines stabilizing speculation as speculation yielding gains (carrying costs aside) and destabilizing speculation as speculation yielding losses. The circumstances, if any, under which this will not be true deserve extensive examination in a full analysis of speculation but can be neglected for our limited purposes, which is simply to show that destabilizing speculation need not involve economic loss, not that it cannot do so.[2]

One reason why actual speculation might not conform to the model described in the preceding three paragraphs is *avoidable* ignorance. By no means all actions that are mistakes when viewed *ex post* fall into this category. If I wager even money that a coin will come up tails and it comes up heads, I clearly have made a mistake *ex post*, in the sense that I shall wish that I had chosen heads. If, in addition I discover by an examination of the coin that it has heads on both sides or in some other way is biased toward heads, and if I could have made this examination before the wager, then I have also made a mistake *ex ante*. On the other hand, if such additional examination gives me no more reason than I had before to question my belief that the coin is fair, then my initial choice of tails may be bad luck but cannot be described as a mistake. The distinction between the two cases is, in principle, whether I would have acted differently in advance of the actual toss if I had had the knowledge I gained after the toss except for the actual outcome itself, i.e., if I had had the knowledge that it would have been possible for me to have had before the toss. In the same way, the mere fact that speculators make losses over a particular period and in fact destabilize prices for that period is no evidence either that the losses could have been avoided given the general state of knowledge when the speculation

2. See *ibid.* for one such fuller examination. It will be clear that our assumptions rule out the main case there considered.

Baumol also considers a special case corresponding to our assumptions (pp. 269–70). His own conclusion is ambiguous but only because in judging the profitability of the speculation he does not require it to be carried through to completion, in the sense that the speculators end up in their initial position with respect to the holdings of the speculative commodity.

was entered into or that speculation is on balance destabilizing in any more fundamental sense.

If destabilizing speculation does arise from avoidable ignorance, it must be granted immediately that there is an economic loss. The loss is borne primarily by the speculators, though, if the operation is sufficiently large, second order effects on others may not be negligible in the aggregate. It may be noted in passing that insofar as this case justifies any action by government, it justifies solely the distribution of knowledge. Suppose private speculation is destabilizing because ignorant speculators behave against their own interests, but speculation by government officials trying to achieve the same end as private speculators would be stabilizing because of greater knowledge. The appropriate solution is then for the government officials to make their knowledge available either by providing the information on which their price forecasts rest or by making and publishing the price forecasts themselves. If these are more accurate, on the whole, than the forecasts private speculators would otherwise use, private speculators have a strong incentive to act in accordance with them and in the process will produce the same results as government speculation in accordance with the same forecasts. If the forecasts are not more accurate, they will tend to be disregarded and no great harm will be done.[3]

To see how destabilizing speculation can arise without avoidable ignorance, let us start with a commodity market which is in operation. Suppose that there exist independent gambling establishments in which all gambling takes the form of betting on the future price of the commodity in question—say, rubber. The people who bet on the price of rubber in the hypothetical gambling establishment do not buy or sell rubber, and neither do the people who run the establishment. Their operations therefore have no direct effect on the price of rubber; the rubber market simply takes the place of the roulette wheel at Monte Carlo.[4] We may suppose the proprietors of an establishment to operate solely as brokers, engaging in no gambling themselves but being paid a fee for providing facilities and bringing together people willing to take opposite sides of a common wager. And we suppose throughout that the people engaging in the gambling do so deliberately and are reasonably well informed: they like to gamble and are willing to pay a price to do so. Let us put to one side any moral objections to gambling, and suppose that the gambling services are provided under competitive conditions. The proprietors of the gambling house are then devoting economic resources to producing services to satisfy the wants of consumers, who are willingly buying the services and paying a price equal to the

3. One case in which publication of forecasts or the equivalent might be especially called for is if the authorities feel it necessary to suppress some relevant information for security reasons. They might be able to offset the effects of such suppression on the judgments of traders by issuing price forecasts.

4. There could be an indirect effect if, for example, information about the odds ruling in the gambling transactions altered the expectations about future prices of the people trading on the spot market and so changed amounts diverted to stocks.

cost of the alternative services that could have been obtained with the same resources. Clearly there is economic gain rather than loss through the operation of the gambling house.[5]

Of course, there may in fact be no demand for this service at a price sufficient to call it forth. Whether there is depends on the preferences of the public for gambling of various types, the kind of gambling provided by the rubber market—that is, the probability distribution of the price of rubber—the alternative sources of gambling services, their cost and character, and so on. The willingness of people to buy lottery tickets at less than their actuarial value even though they know full well the probabilities of prizes of various size is sufficient evidence that people are willing to pay a price to bear at least certain kinds of risks, to be subjected to increased uncertainty. In any event, our concern is not with the likelihood that gambling establishments of the kind described would be profitable but only with the consequences if they were.

Consider an individual who wants to bet that the price of rubber will be higher a month from now than it is now. He can place such a bet in the gambling establishment at some odds and subject to paying a commission to the proprietors. An alternative way in which he can subject himself to the same uncertainty is to buy rubber in the market, store it for a month, and then sell it: he can accumulate positive stocks. The cost in this case is the cost of storage over the month. Similarly an individual who wants to bet that the price will fall can accomplish the same objective by selling rubber now, borrowing the physical commodity in order to make delivery currently: he can accumulate negative stocks. He may be paid for doing so, because he saves someone storage costs. Presumably, however, the amount he is paid will be less than the storage costs, the difference being the fee for lending the commodity. And if the loan requires dipping into stocks needed, say, to facilitate production, storage costs may be, as it were, negative and he may have to pay to borrow the goods. (Remember that we are considering the effect of the actions of an additional group of people. Their holding negative stocks simply means that total stocks are less than they would otherwise be). Suppose individuals find this alternative way of gambling cheaper. The gambling establishments will then disappear and the gambling services be provided by the rubber market.

If purchases and sales just offset, there is no effect on current price and the net costs are the various commissions paid to transact the business. The market dealers have taken the business of providing gambling services away from the gambling institutions proper. But purchases and sales need not just offset one another—indeed, the lack of necessity for them to do so may be one of the advantages of operating through the market, though a similar possibility could

5. It will be noted that a pure futures market is very close to such a gambling establishment. A transaction on a futures market does not by itself have any effect on the spot market. It affects current price only to the extent that the price established leads to operations on the spot market and thereby to a change in the size of stocks carried over. This is analogous to the indirect effect described in the preceding footnote.

be provided by the gambling establishments if their proprietors "made book" rather than simply acted as brokers. If purchases and sales do not offset one another, the price of the commodity is affected.

We have now combined the two activities: gambling on the price of rubber, and the rubber market proper. Given competitive conditions, this combination will occur only if it is a cheaper way to provide gambling services and so in this respect represents increased efficiency in the use of resources. If the total expenditures of the gamblers on gambling services exceeds the commissions involved, this is equivalent to saying that, viewed as a body of speculators, they engage in destabilizing speculation. But their losses are someone's gain. In the first instance, they will be the gain of the initial participants in the rubber market. Operating on the rubber market has now become a more attractive business since one can now engage in joint production, producing gambling services as well as trading services. The result will be to attract more people into the activity. Temporary gains will be competed away and the trading margin proper reduced, so raising the average net price of rubber to the producer. But this in turn will stimulate output and so reduce the average net price of rubber to the consumer. The provision of gambling service is now being rendered jointly by the producers of rubber, the middle men, and the consumers of rubber. In return for wider fluctuations in price—which are required to provide the gamblers or speculators with the uncertainty they want to bear—the producer gets a higher average price and the consumer pays a lower average price.

Any individual producer or consumer who disliked the wider fluctuation of prices could insure himself against it. But, given our assumptions, it cannot be that producers and consumers would be willing to pay more on the average than the difference between old and new average prices to insure themselves against the wider fluctuations. For this would contradict the initial assumption that there was a demand for the services of the gambling establishments at a positive price. The people who were willing to make bets on the price of rubber —willing to assume risks—would then have found that they were paid, instead of having to pay, for doing so. Instead of the market being supplemented by gambling institutions, it would have been supplemented by insurance companies, insuring people against the fluctuations in prices.

I grant readily that this picture of a world in which increasing fluctuations in the prices of commodities is a service that commands a positive price is hard to accept as a valid description of the actual world; not so much because people are not willing to pay for gambling—they clearly are—but because there seem to be so many cheaper ways of producing the gambles that people want to buy, though it must be noted that some of these are illegal in many countries. However, this is the picture that is implicit in the acceptance of the empirical generalization that destabilizing speculation often occurs in practice, except for such destabilizing speculation as is attributable to avoidable ignorance, or as may be consistent with deviations from our initial assumptions.

Whether particular services command a positive or negative price—are consumption services or productive services—is not determined by physical or technical considerations alone; it depends also on the tastes and preferences and the capacities and opportunities, of the community at large. Painting a fence is generally regarded as a productive service that must be paid for, as an activity yielding disutility, and so the price of painting a fence is generally negative; Tom Sawyer was able to reverse this attitude and to make it an activity yielding utility; he was able to charge a positive price for the privilege of painting a fence. This is the essential issue involved in judging speculation. Is bearing uncertainty a service that must be paid for? Or a privilege for which people are willing to pay? Is speculation the rendering of a productive service that commands a reward? Or is it a means of gaining utility on which people spend part of their income? If it turns out to be the second rather than the first, is this any reason for regarding it as involving economic loss? Does not the tendency to do so simply reflect the preconceptions of the academic?

Index